THE
STATUS OF WOMEN IN THE EPICS

Dr. (Miss) Shakambari Jayal M.A., PH.D.
Assistant Professor,
D. S. B. Government College, Nainital

MOTILAL BANARSIDASS
DELHI :: VARANASI :: PATNA

First Edition 1966

ISBN: 978-81-2084-008-9

Also available at:

MOTILAL BANARSIDASS
41 U.A. Bungalow Road, Jawahar Nagar, Delhi 110 007
8 Mahalaxmi Chamber, Warden Road, Mumbai 400 026
120 Royapettah High Road, Mylapore, Chennai 600 004
Sanas Plaza, Subhash Nagar, Pune 411 002
16 St. Mark's Road, Bangalore 560 001
8 Camac Street, Calcutta 700 017
Ashok Rajpath, Patna 800 004
Chowk, Varanasi 221 0011

PRINTED IN INDIA
BY JAINENDRA PRAKASH JAIN AT SHRI JAINENDRA PRESS,
A-45 NARAINA, PHASE I, NEW DELHI 110 028
AND PUBLISHED BY NARENDRA PRAKASH JAIN FOR
MOTILAL BANARSIDASS PUBLISHERS PRIVATE LIMITED,
BUNGALOW ROAD, DELHI 110 007

PREFACE

Title, the importance of the subject and need for its study

The present book is an attempt to delineate "The Status of Women in the Epics". Many scholars have thrown light on the position of women in the Vedic, Buddhist and later periods of ancient Indian History, and have also made a study of their status in the legal literature of the times.[1] So far the only notable attempt in the Epic field, however, has been that of Meyer but it is restricted in its scope as it mainly deals with sexual life in the Epics.[2] There have been other minor attempts in the form of articles, which naturally cannot give and are not intended to give any comprehensive idea of this vast subject.[3] It is indeed strange that the study of women as depicted in the Epics has so long escaped separate treatment and has not been given the attention it deserves. It is all the more essential to pursue this subject as the two great Epics still exert a great influence on the life and mind of India in particular and the whole of South-East Asia in general. In fact post-Epic-literature mostly borrows from, or improves and reconstructs on, the themes taken from the Epics. Moreover, the women characters of the Epics have been held as ideals by Indian women. Deep-rooted-notions about such characters have stood in the way of a scientific and objective study of the various customs, manners and status of women as gleaned from the Epics. There is a need today for a dispassionate and impartial study of the background of the position of women in India since this is an age of reform, when the position and status of Indian women in society

1. Upādhyāya "Women in the Ṛg-Veda" ; B.C. Law "Women in Buddhism"; Horner "Women under Primitive Buddhism"; S. Rao Śāśtrī "Women in the Vedas" and "Women in the Sacred Laws".

2. Meyer "Sexual Life in Ancient India" in 2 volumes.

3. Dr. P.C. Dharmā "The Status of Women During the Epic Period"; J.I.H. Vol. XXVII, part I. ; J.O.A.S. Vol. XIII Hopkins, appendix on "The Status of Women" in the article "The Position of the Ruling Castes."; Dr. P.C. Dharmā "Women During Rāmāyṇa Period" JIH. XVII, pp. 1-28.

is undergoing a vast change. While the Rāmāyaṇa, on the one hand, mirrors ideal characters for people to look up to and follow, the Mahābhārata on the other, with its variety of situations and characters through generations gives a truer insight into the character and position of women in Ancient India.

Sources of the study

The original sources drawn upon are the two great Epics, the Mahābhārata (Poona Edition), ascribed to Vyāsa and the Rāmāyaṇa of Vālmīki (Nirṇaya Sāgar edition). The secondary sources are commentaries, translations and dissertations written on these works.

Method of study

In tracing the status of women in the Epics we have strictly endeavoured to draw conclusions from the evidences gathered from these two great Epics. The very nature of the Epic literature, which will be dealt with in detail in the "Introductory" Chapter makes it almost impossible to understand the growth and development, as well as the general trend of ideals, institutions and customs depicted in the Epics, without the aid of ancient literature. The Pre-Vedic and Vedic traditions provide the social background of the Epic society. The characters of the Epics, particularly those of the Mahābhārata, belong to the Brāhmaṇa and Upaniṣad period. The customs traced in the narrative parts of the Epics are those found in the Sūtras. The didactic portions prove that the age depicted therein is the age more or less corresponding to the age of the Dharmaśāstras particularly to the age of the Manusmṛti. Wherever possible attempts have been made to collect, collate and scrutinize parallel evidences of customs and conditions from the above mentioned literature on the one hand and the Epics on the other. This method has also helped in reconstructing the chronology and the sequence of many customs.

It is easier to understand the position of woman in the different stages of her life as related to man and society. But in order to estimate the position and character assigned to her as regards the sex, it is necessary to interpret the data with sociological and anthropological approach.

The scope of the thesis

The thesis contains twelve chapters. In the introduction is discussed the nature (or value) of the sources and other data available. Thereafter, the place assigned to woman in the different stages of her life has been dealt with, viz., as a maid, in marriage with its complex problems, as a wife, as a mother and as a widow. The seventh chapter concerns "Niyoga", a peculiar custom of that age. The ninth chapter deals with adultery and extra-marital relations. These relations are also significant developments in the historical evaluation of woman's status. The attitude of society towards her which affected her religious position as well as property rights is assigned a separate chapter. A brief account of some illustrious Epic heroines, which has been given in the chapter following may not seem to be relevant to this book yet it is very necessary to trace the story of their lives to indicate the actual place assigned to women in society. The concluding chapter sums up the status of women in various fields.

This work was originally submitted as a thesis and was approved by the Banaras Hindu University for the degree of Doctor of Philosophy in 1958.

It is my pleasant duty to acknowledge my deep sense of gratitude to Late Dr. R. S. Tripathi, Ex-Principal, Central Hindu College, and Head of the Department of History, Banaras Hindu University, under whom I worked as a research scholar, and whose able guidance and encouragement were available to me at all times. I am also indebted to Dr. Mangal Dev Śāstrī, Ex. Vice-Chancellor of Varānaseya Sanskrit University and Dr. Rājbalī Pāndey, Ex-Principal, Indology College, Banaras Hindu University, who aided me with valuable suggestions from time to time. My thanks are also due to Miss Jyoti Pande, M.A., who often helped me in proof reading. I am only too conscious of the faults and oversight sometimes typographical in this work for these I seek indulgence of the reader.

D. S. B. Government College, *S. Jayal*
Nainital.
Nov. 1966.

CONTENTS

CHAPTER — PAGE

I. Nature of the Sources 1
Ancient Indian conception of history ... 1
Tradition and History 2
Preservers of Traditions 3
Tradition gradually compiled in history ... 3
Importance of tradition and history (as realised in Ancient India) 4
The Rāmāyaṇa as an Itihāsa 5
The Mahābhārata as an Itihāsa 7
Date of the Rāmāyaṇa 8
Dates of events of the Mahābhārata ... 9
Date of the composition of the Great Epic ... 10
Assessment of the data 11

II. The Maid, her status and her education 15
The birth of a daughter—How far the ... source of anxiety 17
Her place : In the family 18
In the society 18
Rights and privileges 18
(i) Nature of protection given by the society and family 18
(ii) Freedom of movement and action ... 19
(iii) Legal Rights 20
Her duties 20
Her education 21
Intellectual and religious 22
Traditional 26
Military and physical 27
In arts, specially in fine arts 28
Agency of education (modes and methods) ... 29
Merits and demerits of the system ... 30 31
Gradual decay and disappearance of sound education 33

CHAPTER PAGE

III. Marriage (Part I) 35
Varying emphasis on obligation. What sort of obligation ? 37
Importance of marriage in the life of woman ... 39
Age of marriage 41
Connection of the age required with the question of chastity 47
Order of seniority in marriage ... 49
The question of consent—right of selection ... 50
Qualifications 57
Marriage ceremony 61
Dowries 65
Sacramental Character 66
IV. Marriage (Part II) 69
Freedom and Limitations in contracting marriage some peculiar features 69
Freedom 69
Forms of marriage 69
Limitations 84
Inter-Racial marriage 85
Anuloma and Pratiloma 86
(Inter-Caste marriages) ... ...
Varṇa endogamy 90
Gotra 91
Pravara 91
Sapiṇḍa 92
Fatherless and Brotherless girl 93
Polyandry and Polygamy 94
Conclusion 96
V. Married Life 97
Importance of married life 97
Wife's place in the family 99
Wife—from Sahdharmiṇī to Pativratā. The position of women under these two ideals ... 101
The duties and responsibilities of a house wife ... 103
Duties towards the elders 103
Duties towards the husband 105
Duties as a member of prosperous home ... 115

CHAPTER		PAGE
Responsibilities towards the servants	...	115
Duties of hospitality	... ...	116
Other social obligations	... ...	117
The household duties	... ...	117
Duties and responsibilities of child-bearing	...	118
Her rights and benefits (in the family)	...	120
In relation to mother-in-law	...	120
In relation to father-in-law	... ...	121
In relation to husband	... ...	122
In relation to others	... ...	126
Her conjugal rights	... ...	126
Conclusion	... ...	126
VI. Woman as mother	... ...	132
Introduction	... ...	132
Woman as mother occupies a great place of honour and prestige in the epics	... ...	132
The high status of motherhood...	...	132
Efforts to attain the status of motherhood	...	134
Mother—Responsibilities	... ...	135
Towards expectant mother	... ...	135
Towards mother in general	... ...	137
High status of mother reflected in the good results attending on one who served the mother	... ...	138
The same point illustrated by bad results of disregarding one's duties towards one's mother	... ...	138
Feelings and regard for mother	...	139
Breach of the rule	... ...	141
Feelings and conduct towards the step-mother		142
Duties of daughter towards the mother	...	142
The position of widowed-mother	...	143
Mother worship	... ...	144
Responsibilities of mother—Her high status in consequence of her onerous responsibilities		147
Maintenance—excellent rearing of her child		147
As protector	... ...	149
Mother's affection unparallel sentiment		150

CHAPTER PAGE

As an educator 153
As an integrating force 155
VII. Niyoga 156
Introduction—Niyoga explained ... 156
The Practice in the Epics 156
Motive and basis of Niyoga 157
Agents of Niyoga 159
Who could perform Niyoga ? 159
How was such a one found ? ... 160
Illustrative cases 160
Niyoga—Indirect cases 165
Niyoga—(a) Objections and opinions ... 167
(b) The same considered ... 168
(c) benefits 169
Its decline and collapse 170
VIII. Women as Widow 172
Introduction 172
Social attitude : Not inauspicious but an object of pity 172
Widows express their sorrow freely. No inhibitions but strong in mind 176
Sati (not common) in the Mahābhārata ... 179
(a) Sahamaraṇa (b) Anumaraṇa ... 180
(c) group suicide 181
Remarriage (rare) 183
Austerities (in forest) (b) in the matter of living and dress 188
Position in society 192
Conclusion 196
IX. Adultery and extra-marital relations ... 198
Adultery classified 199
Social stigma attached to adultery ... 204
Adultery in practice 206
Extra-marital relations 209
Concubinage, slave girls etc. 210
Apsarās 212
Prostitutes 213
Gaṇikā 215

CHAPTER			PAGE
References to free Society	...	...	216
Conclusion	...	...	217
X. The Attitude towards women		...	219
Man's different relations to women : factors in deciding the attitude	...	...	219
The factors that enhance woman's prestige ... (i) Motherhood (ii) Women as inspirers (iii) As nourishers	...	...	219
Respect reflected in manners	...	...	221
Women as a weak creature : Privileges accorded to woman due to her weakness	...	...	222
Injunction against woman murderer		...	222
Transgression of the rule	...	...	223
Women to be treated with compassion		...	224
The factors that really degraded the position of women	...	...	225
Impurity	...	...	225
Object of distraction and weakness		...	226
Ascetic attitude	...	...	227
Character assigned to women in general		...	228
Kings warned against women	...	...	230
Women in public administration		...	231
Women and religion		...	232
(a) Wife's actual part in sacrifices gradually disappearing	...	...	233
(b) Women given in charity—objects of pity	...	...	234
Liberty enjoyed by woman	...	...	235
(a) Ladies of the commoners		...	236
(b) Freedom enjoyed by royal ladies		...	236
(i) Seclusion; (ii) Inner apartment;		...	237-238
(iii) Guards; (iv) Strī-adhayakshas;		...	239
(v) Entrance allowed to a few;		...	240
(vi) Seclusion—a sign of respectability			240
(c) Some reasons for restrictions of movements and thereby the fall of women		...	241
Treatment in calamities	...	...	241
Women as property	...	...	243

CHAPTER			PAGE
Property rights of woman (a) of wife (b) Strīdhana : (i) Its classification (ii) Dominion over Strīdhana (iii) Devolution of Strīdhana (c) Rights of Putrikā (d) Rights of daughter's son (e) Inheritance of sons influenced by mother.			244-253
Conclusion	...	...	252
XI. An estimate of some Important women characters of the Epics	...	...	254
I. Of Mahābhārata :	...	...	
Draupadī	...	...	254
Kuntī	...	...	259
Gāndhārī	...	...	261
Śakuntalā	...	...	265
Vidulā	...	...	265
Gautami & others	...	...	265
Sulabhā	...	...	266
II. Of Rāmāyaṇa :	...	...	
Sītā	...	...	266
Kauśalyā; Sumitrā and Kaikeyī		...	275
Tārā, Maṇḍodarī, Saramā	...	...	284-285
Conclusion	...	...	285
XII. Epilogue	...	...	287
Introduction : the main trends and reasons for it			287
Continuity, Varieties and Contradictions		...	287
Social status (a) Place of honour in society		...	288-290
and family (b) Inferior status		...	290-295
in society : its reasons		...	
Freedom of thought movement and action: its loss			295
Religious status: its decline		...	297
Political status	...	...	299
Low economic status gradually improved		...	300
Variety	...	...	302
Survival	...	...	303
Conflict and adjustment	...	...	303
Appendixes	...	...	306-316
BIBLIOGRAPHY	...	...	317-325
INDEX	...	...	327

LIST OF ABBREVIATIONS

AIHT	:	Ancient Indian Historical Tradition: by Pargiter
Ap. Dh. S.	:	Āpastamba Dharma Sūtra
Ap. G. G.	:	Āpastamba Gṛhya Sūtra
Ai. Br.	:	Aitareya Brāhmaṇa
Asv or ASW. G.G	:	Āśwalāyana Gṛhya Sūtra
Baud. Dh.S. or B.D.S.	:	Baudhāyana Dharma Sūtra
B.O.R.I.	:	Bhandarkar Oriental Research Institute, Poona.
Bṛ or Bṛh	:	Bṛhaspati Smṛti
Chhan. Up.	:	Chhandogya Upanishad
G.	:	Bhagwadgītā
Gaut. Dh. S.	:	Gautama Dharma Sūtra
Gobh. G. S. or G. G. S.	:	Gobhila Gṛhya Sūtra
HCAI	:	History of Civilization in Ancient India : R. C. Dutt.
Hist. of Dh. or H. of Dh.	:	History of Dharma Śāstra by Kāṇe
HIL	:	History of Indian Literature by Winternitz
HSL	:	History of Sanskrit Literature : Macdonell
IHQ	:	Indian Historical Quarterly
JIH	:	Journal of Indian History
JAOS	:	Journal of American Oriental Society
JRAS	:	Journal of Royal Asiatic Society
Kh. G.S. or Khadira G.S.	:	Khādira Gṛhya Sūtra
Kau. Br.	:	Kaushītakī Brāhmaṇa
Mbh.	:	Mahābhārata
M. or Manu	:	Manusmṛti
Mait. Sam.	:	Maitrāyaṇī Samhitā
Mit.	:	Mitākshara's Commentary
Nārada	:	Nārada Smṛti
P. G. S. or Pārsakara	:	Pāraskara Gṛhya Sūtra
P. W. H. C.	:	Position of Women in Hindu Civilization : Altekar
QJMS	:	Quarterly Journal of Mythical Society, Bangalore
Rām.	:	Rāmāyaṇa
SHW or ASHW	:	A Short History of Women : J. L. Davies

Sat. Br.	: Śatapatha-Brāhmaṇa
SLAI	: Sexual Life in Ancient India : Meyer
SAESHI	: Some Aspects of Early Social History of India : Sarkar
San. G. S.	: Sankhāyana Gṛhya Sūtra
Ṛg V.; Ṛ. V.	: Ṛg Veda
Taitta. Up.	: Taittarīya Upanishad
Taitta. Sam.	: Taittarīya Saṁhitā
Vāt. "K. S." or Kām. S.	: Kāma Sūtra by Vātsyāyana
Vas. Dh. S.	: Vaśishṭha Dharma Sūtra
Vi. Dh. S. or Vi. S.	: Viṣṇu Dharma Sūtra
Y. S. or Yāj. S.	: Yāgvavalkya Smṛti
Art.	: Article
Acc.	: According
Cp.	: Compare

In the Mahābhārata, Parvas and in the Rāmāyaṇa Kāndas are indicated by Roman figures in the footnotes. Next figure after Roman one denotes Sarga in the Rāmāyaṇa and Adhyāya in the Mahābhārata while the third one stands for ślokas. Where Adhyāya or Sarga are quoted from the same Parva or Kānda Roman figures are not again repeated.

e. g. Mbh. I. 54. 3; 53. 8, 9, 10.

Here 53 Adhyāya is from the same Parva (I) and 8, 9, 10 ślokas from 53 Adhyāya.

Similarly in the Rāmāyaṇa

Rām. V. 2.8; 6.17, 8, 9. Here sixth Sarga is from the same Kānda (V) and Śloka 9, 8 from same sarga.

The Mahābhārata has been mentioned as the great Epic or the Great Epic and Rāmāyaṇa and Mahābhārata together has been referred to as the Epics or the epics.

The system of transliteration adopted is as follows:

अ or अ	=	a	स	=	Sa	च	=	cha
आ or आ	=	ā	श	=	Śa	छ	=	chha
इ	=	i	ष	=	Sha	क्ष	=	ksha
ई	=	ī	थ	=	tha	ण or ण	=	ṇa
उ	=	u	त	=	ta	ड	=	ḍa
ऊ	=	ū	ठ	=	tha	ट	=	ṭa
ऋ	=	Ṛ	द	=	da			

CHAPTER I

INTRODUCTORY

NATURE OF THE SOURCES

Ancient Indian Conception of History

In order to appreciate and estimate the historical value of the epics an understanding of the conception of ancient Indians is essential. The ancient Indian conception of history was quite different from the western conception, so much so that Macdonell was led to think that "History is the one weak spot in Indian literature. It is, in fact, non-existent. The total lack of the historical sense is so characteristic, that the whole course of Sanskrit literature is darkened by the shadow of this defect, suffering as it does from the entire absence of exact chronology."[1] There is, of course, no denying the fact that the ancient Indians were not in the habit of preserving the oral or written traditions of a king who had not achieved greatness or the record of an event which was not noteworthy. The need of such omissions must have been felt much more when the traditions were dealing with centuries and were preserved through the aid of memory. Therefore the Indian traditions as well as literature, which are the storehouse of ancient Indian history, certainly lack in the chronological sense. But chronology alone is not history. The cultural and social aspect of it which is a true mirror of a people and civilization have been well maintained in ancient Indian writings and traditions. An eminent scholar, R. C. Dutt remarks "………There is a difference between the records of the Hindus and the records of other nations………Ancient Hindu works are of a different character. If they are defective in some respects, as they undoubtedly are, they are defective as accounts of dynasties, of wars, and so-called historical incidents. On the other hand they give us a full, connected, and clear account of

1. Macdonell "HSL", p. 10.

the advancement of civilization, of the progress of the human mind, such as we shall seek in vain among the records of any other equally ancient nation. The literature of each period is a perfect picture—a photograph, if we may so call it—of the Hindu civilization of that period and the works of successive periods form a complete history of ancient Hindu civilization for three thousand years, so full, so clear, that he who runs may read it." He continues, "And those who have pursued Hindu literature through different periods of ancient Hindu history, are equally aware that they form a complete and comprehensive story of the progress and gradual modifications of Hindu civilization, thought and religion through three thousand years."[1] All these literary sources, particularly the epics, which acquaint us with the civilization of the Hindu people, are mainly based on tradition.[2]

Tradition and History

Ancient Indian history and the traditions of the times have been so well-knit that it is very difficult to separate the two. The wars and conquests and the foundation of new kingdoms, in fact all the exploits of the victorious kings were sung in many a ballad.[3] In a country permeated with a highly religious atmosphere, the patronage of kings to the Brāhmaṇas and Ṛshis was naturally regarded as an act of glory and was celebrated in songs. It is difficult to agree with Pargiter's assertion[4] that the Kshatriya and Brāhmaṇa traditions were different, for, in the epics, Purāṇas, and Vedas the story of Brāhmaṇas is intermingled with the tales of royal dynasties. The genealogies of the kings and Ṛshis really existed when the great Epic was written and were well-known to those well-

1. Dutt, R. C. "HCAI" Vol. I. 'Introduction' p. 1-3.
2. Pargiter "AIHT" p. 1.
3. Mbh. I. 1. 220-275.
4. Pargiter "AIHT" Chap. I and II, p. 1-33. He thinks that the Vedas enshrine the Brāhmaṇic traditions and the Mbh. and Purāṇas the Kshatriya ones. Others like Holtzmann think that the Mbh. was a Buddhist book revised by the Brāhmaṇas. Theories analogous to this inversion theory are propounded by L. Von Schröder and Grierson. All these three scholars suggest different and mutually contradictory motives for inversion of the Epic and this is a serious objection against soundness of these theories. For further reference see "Studies in Epics and Purāṇas of India" by A. D. Pusālker. Introduction XXVII-XXX.

versed in ancient lore.[1] The ancient traditions—tales known as Purāṇas and narration of facts,—which was Itihāsa (Iti-Ha-Āsa so it actually was) are often quoted in the epics as old history (Itihāsa Purātanam) Śrutam, Ākhyānam, Śuśruma.[2] Rightly does Pargiter observe, "Our knowledge of the most ancient times in India mainly rests on traditions... Almost all the information therefore comes from tradition."[3] and "Tradition is human testimony concerning the long past; hence it is not to be discarded simply because it contained discrepancies."[4]

Preservers of Traditions

These traditions were very well-preserved in the hoary past by the Sūta—the Paurāṇika, the Māgadha—a genealogist (Vamśa-Śamsaka), and the Vādin—an eulogist (Stāvaka).[5] The Rāmāyaṇa and the Mahābhārata mention all these.[6] The Purāṇavids (such is the epithet of Sumantra in the Rāmāyaṇa) or Purāṇikas, although never esteemed as much as the Veda-knowing Brāhmaṇas, were greatly respected in the court circles.[7]

Tradition gradually compiled in History

Now the ancient traditions and ballads variously known

1. Mbh. III. 201. 3

विदितास्तव धर्मज्ञ देवदानवराक्षसाः ।

राजवंशाश्च विविधा ऋषिवंशाश्च शाश्वताः ॥

Macdonell "HSL" p. 304 states that there is no reason for supposition that parts of Book I and VII are due to Brāhmaṇa revision of warrior poems.

2. Mbh. VII. 71. 1, 2, 4; VII. 56-69 (secs) All stories in Shoḍasarājānopākhyāna begin with "Susruma" i.e. "We have heard" quoting traditional history. Rām. I. 70. 30 बभूवतुरिति श्रुतिः II. 110. 28. नः श्रुतम् In the Mahābhārata Itihāsa means "Saying" or "proverb" also.

3. Pargiter "AIHT" Chap. I. p. 1.

4. Ibid. p. 13.

5. Pargiter "AIHT" p. 17.

6. Rām. II. 6. 6; 65. 1-4 Mbh. III. 236. 10; XV. 38. 5. mentions सूतमागधसंघैः Mbh. XIII. 48. 10, 12 (Cf. M. X. 11-17) but Harivamśa Chap. II p. 8, 25 says that Sūta and Māgadha were born for Pṛthu to sing his glory, who conferred Anūpa and Māgadha on them respectively. Pargiter AIHT Chp. II pp. 16-17 on the basis of Kauṭilya "Arthaśāstra" proves Paurāṇika Sūta and Māgadha were different from the Pratiloma ones.

7. Rām. II. 15. 18 Purāṇavit Sumantra could even enter inner apartment of Daśaratha. See next page also.

as Ākhyānas, Itihāsa, Purāṇa, Gāthā, Nārāśamsī,[1] contain glorious deeds of heroes sung by the Sūtas and Māgadhas and are thus the sources of epic poetry.[2] Gradually when the art of writing developed these heroic traditions were compiled. This task was done according to Indian tradition by Vyāsa, (which means a compiler) who after compiling the Purāṇas took up the composition of the great Epic, which he meant to be an Itihāsa.[3]

Importance of Tradition and History (as realised by ancient Indians)

Even when history was preserved through traditions, kings used to employ Sūtas, Māgadhas and Vādins for singing and preserving the old traditions.[4] The Sūtas, who had gained wisdom through tradition also acted as advisers, counsellors and consolers.[5] King Yudhishṭhira was advised by Bhīshma to listen to Purāṇas, Itihāsa and Ākhyānas daily.[6] The ancient Indians were very fond of listening to the traditions on certain occasions like those of sacrifices and the ceremony of Sīmantonnayana. Even today among the orthodox people, when a family has suffered some severe loss after the death of some dear one, the mourners listen to the stories of Itihāsa and Purāṇas for ensuring auspicious future.[7] Yudhishṭhira after

1. Gītā and Gāthā were also used in the sense of Itihāsa—a saying or proverb—Cf. Mbh. III. 29. 35; III. 135. 45, 54. "These Gāthās incorporated legal and philosophical literature also." Story of Nala Mbh. III. 79, 10, 11, 16, 13 is called "Kīrtanam", "Itihāsa","Purāṇas" Cf. M. Krishṇamāchārī "History of classical Sanskrit literature" Book 1, p. 2 "in the Vedic literature there is no essential difference between "Atīta" "Ākhyāna" "Purāṇa" "Itihāsa" and generally "Kathā". They meant ordinarily an old tale, story, legend or incident and they were often interchangeable. But the essential characteristic is narration of stories of the great kings or gods in the past."

2. Cf. Pargiter "AIHT" Chap. II. p. 16-22.

3. Ibid Chap. II. pp. 21-22. Although scholars believe Purāṇas in the present form were written much later than the epics. Winternitz "History of Indian Literature." Vol. I. Sec. II. "Epics and Purāṇas".

4. Mbh. III. 236. 10. See page 3 footnote 6.

5. Rām. II. 34. 4. ff; VII. 50. 9 ff. Rām. 11. 16. पुराणवित् is his epithet; 15. 18.

6. Mbh. XIII. 104. 149 cf. Vishṇu Dh. S. III. 70. Kings are advised to appoint Purohitas conversant in the Vedas and Epics. Here itihāsa has been translated as epics by Julius Jolly. S. B. E. Vol. VII. p. 20. Itihāsa was important subject to be studied by the princes cf. Mbh. I. 109. 20.

7. Rām. I. 9 p. 1-2; VII, 94. 5, 9. Śat. Br. XIII. 4. 3 Śānkhāyan G. S. I. 22. 11-12ff. Āśv. G. S. I. 14. 6ff. and IV. 6. 6. Pāraskara G. S. I. 15. 7ff. Āp. G. S. 6. 14. 4ff. Winternitz "A History of Indian Literature" Vol. I. Sec. II. p. 311-312.

the death of Abhimanyu was thus consoled by Nārada through such stories of sixteen kings, from the old history.[1] So was king Dyumatsena's grief assuaged by the tales of ancient kings.[2]

When the traditions were put down in writing in the form of Itihāsa and Purāṇa their study was recommended even to a Brāhmaṇa who was well-versed in the Vedas with Angas and Upanishads. He was not regarded as having attained the necessary proficiency if he was unacquainted with the Purāṇas or, as the author of the Mahābhārata puts it, with "this tale". This was because the study of the Vedas was thought to be reinforced by Itihāsa and Purāṇa. It was stated that the Veda is afraid of him who is deficient in ancient tradition, thinking such a man will harm its cause,[3] meaning thereby that it would be misinterpreted. In other words the knowledge of religion and religious rites could never help in gaining perfect wisdom unless it was supplemented by the study of biographies of great men (i.e. history). In the Upanishads Itihāsa has been considered as "Panchama Veda"[4] or the fifth Veda (Veda means knowledge). Mentioning it after Atharva Veda, Kauṭilya also classifies Itihāsa with the Vedas.[5] Itihāsa though referring to the Mahābhārata is used for the Rāmāyaṇa as well. Both put forward this claim.

The Rāmāyaṇa as an Itihāsa

The Rāmāyaṇa, the life history of the great king Rāma is a "fairly unified heroic poem".[6] It is Ākhyāna, Kāvya, an

1. Mbh. VII. 71. 4 राजर्षीणां पुराणानां० ।
2. Mbh. III. 298. 7; I. 140. 74.
3. Mbh. I. 2. 382; I. 1. 267.

यो विद्याच्चतुरो वेदान्साङ्गोपनिषदो द्विजः ।
न चाख्यानमिदं विद्यान्नैव स स्याद्विचक्षणः ॥
इतिहासपुराणाभ्यां वेदं समुपबृंहयेत् ।
बिभेत्यल्पश्रुताद्वेदो मामयं प्रहरिष्यति ॥

the same verse in Vāyu Purāṇa I. 200. 1. Padama. p. v. 2. 50. 2. the second line being न चेत्पुराणं संविद्यान्नैव स स्याद्विचक्षणः ।

4. Chhāndogya Upanishad VII. 4. 1-2 (page 197. Natesan Madras, 1899) इतिहासपुराणं पञ्चमं वेदानाम् ।

5. Kauṭilya "Arthaśāstra" Śyāmsāstry's Eng. Tr. Bk. I. Chap. III. lines 1-3.

6. Winternitz "History of Indian Literature" Vol. I. Chap. II, p. 475.

old history and Saṁhitā.[1] Its aim too is that of enforcing the Veda through its study[2] and as such puts forward the claims somewhat similar to those of the Mahābhārata.[3] Its study has been recommended for all irrespective of caste or sex.

The hold of Rāma's story on the Hindū mind persists to this day. Vālmīki's introduction that he was writing about the most renowned king of his time as well as the dynastic chart of Pargiter would show beyond doubt that Rāma's story has a historical background.[4]

Indian tradition refers to the Rāmāyaṇa as "Ādikāvya." Vālmīki was the originator of the ornate style of poetry (i.e. Kāvya) which is certainly not identical with the epic poetry[5] and which does not prevent one from thinking that certain portions of the great Epic may be older than the Rāmāyaṇa. As it was finished before the Mahābhārata, it was the first specimen of secular poetry[6] to be completed. According to Indian tradition the whole of Rāmāyaṇa was composed by Vālmīki. The main story of the Rāmāyaṇa consists of Book I to VI, though it is Book II to VI according to some scholars. Evidently the composition of these parts belongs to an earlier date than that of Book I and VII. The later books as well as some interpolations in the former books, according to Professor Jacobi, are so loosely attached that the junctures are easy to recognize. But the style of the legends as well as that of the main book is, however, the same.[7] It is quite possible that

1. Rām. I. 4. 1, 7 'Kāvyam'; 'Ākhyānam'.
Rām.. VI. 128. 115. 'Itihāsa' 'Purātanam'; VI. 128. 120 'Saṁhitā.'

2. Rām. I. 4. 6 वेदोपबृंहणार्थाय ।

3. Rām VI. 128. 110 ff VII. 111. 4 ff "Vedasamān". See p. 7-8 for claims put forward by Mbh.

4. Rām. I. 1. 1ff. Pargiter "AIHT" tables of royal genealogies p. 144, 149 (Rāma on 65th line). Macdonell "HSL" p. 311ff. Lessen and Weber think that it is an allegorical representation of the first attempt of the Āryans to conquer south and Jacobi opines that it is based on Indian mythology but none of the views are held at present.

5. Macdonell "HSL" p. 281. calls it only one class of epic poetry. Sanskrit epic poetry falls into two main classes. That which comprises old stories goes by the name of "Itihāsa",—"Legend", "Akhyāna" —"Narrative", or "Purāṇa"—ancient tale, while the other is called "Kāvya" or artificial epic. The Mahābhārata is the chief and oldest representative of the former group, the Rāmāyaṇa of the latter.

6. Ibid., p. 281 points to archaic style of the Mbh. but opines in p. 306 that Rāmāyaṇa was finished before the Mahābhārata kernel had assumed definite shape. (Two lines of Rāmāyaṇa in Book VI of the Mahābhārata Rāmopākhyāna).

7. Ibid., p. 304-305.

these additions tracing older traditions were added by the bards formerly (when Rāmāyaṇa was not reduced to writing) to satisfy the popular demand. This interpolated portion in the Rāmāyaṇa does not assume a great bulk and therefore the Rāmāyaṇa has maintained its character as 'Kāvya.' It is not a 'Saṁhitā' or encyclopedia like the great Epic.

The Mahābhārata as an Itihāsa

The Mahābhārata, primarily an Itihāsa[1], puts forward great claims. It is a Saṁhitā, Purāṇa, Ākhyāna, Kathā, Dharmaśāstra, Kāmaśāstra and Kāvya.[2] It is the chief of all the Śāstras,[3] greater than all the Vedas,[4] and enables man to attain heaven and emancipation.[5] Originally it was meant to be the history of victory—'Jaya', then it assumed more extended dimensions and came to be known as "Bhārata"—the history of the great Bhārata dynasty.[6] As the ancient Indians saw life as a whole with its various aspects, no Itihāsa was complete for them unless it dealt with the manifold aspects of human life,[7] so as to improve and help society. The later composers or redactors, therefore, could not resist the temptations of adding any subject of legal, religious and philosophic import to the

1. Mbh. I. 1. 166-67; I. 2. 85.
2. Mbh. I. 2. 382-86.
3. Mbh. XVIII. 5. 45-47.
4. Mbh. I. 124. 6 cp. I. 1. 62ff. XVIII 5. 45-47.
5. Mbh. I. 1. 62ff. XVIII. 5. 51-52.

M. Krishṇamāchāriar "History of Classical Sanskrit Literature" p. 3. In thus describing his work Vyāsa must have had in mind some special characteristic of each class and therefore added that his work possesses all these qualities so as to stand forth as an encyclopedia of all learning. In the extant literature, the term Itihāsa and Purāṇa have acquired a distinct use. Itihāsa may correspond to an epic and Purāṇa to a series of narrations without any main prop of a running tale, meant solely to explain cosmological and theological tenets. Broadly speaking, therefore, the epic literature in India consists of Itihāsa and Purāṇa; of the former we have the Ramāyaṇa and the Mahābhārata.

6. 'Jaya Itihāsa' (Mbh. XVIII. 5. 5) is the original name of Mahābhārata given at the beginning of each chapter. Asv. G. S. III. 4. 4. and 'Mahābhārata Śravaṇa Mahimā' 89. 92 mention "Bhārata" and "Mahābhārata" Mbh. XVIII. 5. 43 "Ākhyāna" old legend. Mbh. (Cr. Ed.) I. 56. 31 भारतानां महज्जन्म महाभारतमित्युत ।
निरुक्तमस्य यो वेद सर्वपापैः प्रमुच्यते ।
Mbh. (Cr. Ed.) I. 1. 209 महत्त्वाद् भारवत्त्वाच्च ।

7. Macdonell "HSL" p. 281-282 for the various strata in details.

Bhārata, which according to them was of great importance. Although it is difficult to follow the thread of the narrative[1] because-of vast additions yet the encyclopedic character of the Mahābhārata gives an insight into the character and soul of the Indian people. It provides ample material for the study of social and cultural aspects. As it was redacted many times, it depicts conditions of many societies. It is rather difficult to state the number of times the Mahābhārata was redacted, but from internal evidence one can be sure of its three composers Vyāsa, Vaiśampāyana and Sauti. The three beginnings are quite clear. The first from the invocation of Nara and Nārāyaṇa and conversation of Sauti and Ṛshis of Śaunaka's hermitage, the second from "Sarpa Satra" where commences the "Āstīka Parva" and the third from the commencement of the actual narration of the Bhārata race i.e. Amśāvataraṇa Parva.

Regarding the age of these histories and their composition, different dates have been assigned by different scholars, but as the celebrated American scholar Whitney remarks, "All dates given in Indian literary history are pins set up to be bowled down again." Although it is difficult to assign any definite date to these compositions, it will be interesting to mention some of the observations of scholars.

Date of the Rāmāyaṇa

Weber's assumption of Greek influence in the Rāmāyaṇa and thus placing the date of its composition in the 3rd or 4th century A. D., is not accepted generally.[2] Jacobi arguing that the references to Buddhism and Yavana (Greeks) in the Rāmāyaṇa are interpolations, fixes the probable date of its composition between the 6th century and the 8th century B.C.[3] Keith more or less agrees with this view.[4] Macdonell opines that the Rāmāyaṇa was composed before 500 B.C.[5] Winternitz holds that the Rāmāyaṇa was probably written in the 3rd century B. C. by Vālmīki, although in its present extent and

1. Ibid., p. 283 the main narrative barely consists of 20,000 ślokas.
2. Macdonell "HSL" p. 307 ff.
3. Dharmā P. C. "Rāmāyaṇa Polity" Chap. I. p. 5.
4. J. R. A. S. 1915, p. 318.
5. Macdonell "HSL" p. 306-309.

content it was finished about the close of 2nd century A. D.[1] M. Williams thinks[2] that the Rāmāyaṇa was composed about the beginning of the 3rd century B.C.

There is no mention of Sāketa, (described by the Buddhists, Jains, Greeks and Patañjali) and of Pāṭaliputra (founded by Kālāśoka who lived about 380 B. C.) in the Rāmāyaṇa. Śrāvastī, capital of Kosala during Buddha's time, has been described as founded by Lava, eldest son of Rāma, only once in the last book.[3] The Rāmāyaṇa also depicts a political condition when kings ruled small territories.[4] The idea of empire, which developed with the rise of Magadha in the 4th century B. C., is not reflected in the Rāmāyaṇa. It is likely that its main part was composed before the 4th century B. C. But the mention of Buddha once,[5] although made disparagingly, of Yavanas twice, and of the Śakas once[6] indicates that interpolations were freely added between the time of the Buddha and the first or second century A.D.

Dates of the Events of the Mahābhārata

The Mahābhārata in its present form is the production of later ages but it preserves the vigorous life of the sturdy and warlike Kurus and Pāñchālas as well as the Vedic and the pre-Vedic traditions. The characters of the great Epic belong to the Saṁhitā, Brāhmaṇas and Upanishadic periods. According to Macdonell the historical germ of the great Epic cannot be later than the tenth century B.C. and R. C. Dutt on the basis of genealogy assigns twelfth and thirteenth century B.C. for the date of events.[7] While Hopkins thinks 1700 to 700 B. C. as the date of the events as well as of some legends.[8] Jaiswal on the

1. Winternitz, "HIL" Vol. I. p. 516-517.
2. M. Williams "Indian Wisdom" p. 316. cf. M. Krishṇamāchāriar "History of Classical Sanskrit Literature" p. 17.
3. Macdonell "HSL" p. 308.
4. P. C. Dharmā "Rāmāyaṇa Polity" Chap. II. p. 13.
5. Rām. II. 109. 34
यथा हि चोरः स तथा हि बुद्धस्तथागतं नास्तिकमत्र विद्धि ।
6. Rām. I. 55. 3.
7. R. C. Dutt "History of Civilization in Ancient India" Vol. I. assigns 1400 B. C. to 1000 B. C. to the composition of these. Kaṇe "Hist. of Dh. S." Vol. II. Part I Chronological table assigns 4000 B. C. to 1000 B. C. Macdonell "HSL" p. 285.
8. Hopkins "The Great Epic" Chap. VI. p. 386.

similar basis fixes 1424 B. C. as the date of the Bhārata War.[1] While Pargiter after checking the genealogies of various dynasties from the Purāṇas and establishing synchronisms assigns less number of years to each reign and thus opines that the Bhārata battle was fought about 950 B.C.[2] Mr. Vaidya's date of this battle 3101 B. C. cannot be relied upon. The question[3] has been discussed at some length by Kaṇe who points out that no two authors agree on the exact date which ranges from 1193 B. C. to 3101 B. C. He further proves that even the astronomical data in the Mahābhārata is inconsistent.[4]

Date of the Composition of the Great Epic

According to Macdonell the date of the composition of the Mahābhārata is between the 5th century B. C. to the 1st century A. D. It must have acquired the Dharmaśāstra character positively by about 350 A.D.[5] Hopkins opines that the Mahābhārata was written between the 4th century B. C. and 4th century A.D.[6] and Winternitz after a long and sound discussion agreed with this view.[7] C. V. Vaidya fixes the date of the extant epic at 250 B. C. as the Illiad of one lac ślokas was well known in the south by 50 A. D. according to Dion Christrosom.[8] While Dikshita states on the basis of astronomical evidence that the Mahābhārata in its present extent was composed before 450 A.D.[9]

There cannot be any doubt about the growth of the great Epic as already mentioned. It assumed its original form by the 5th century B. C., for in Āśwālāyana Gṛhya Sūtra a Bhārata and Mahābhārata are mentioned.[10] The Mahābhārata of the Sūtra was not so well-known as the extant Mahābhārata.

1. Pargiter "AIHT" Chap. XV, p. 180. Footnote 2.
2. Pargiter "AIHT" Chap. XV, 179-183.
3. Vaidya "Mahābhārata—a criticism" 1904, p. 55-78 and appendix note V (pp. 180-190).
4. Kaṇe "Hist. of Dh." Vol. III. Chap. XXXIV, pp. 898-922.
5. Macdonell "HSL" p. 285-287.
6. Hopkins "The Great Epic." Chap. 4, pp. 386-402.
7. Winternitz "Hist. of Indian Literature" Vol. I. Sec. II 474-475.
8. "Mahābhārata Mīmānsā" C. V. Vaidya p. 43-44.
6. M. Krishṇamāchāriar "History of Classical Sans. Lit." Book I, p. 52.
10. Kaṇe assigns 800 to 400 B. C. to these Sūtras on his chronological table "History of Dh." Vol. II, Part I. p. XI.

The worship of Śiva and Vishṇu, the mention of the Yavanas, Śakas, Pahlavas and the Buddhist relic mounds indicate another redaction. As Megasthenes writes about these two prominent gods, Macdonell thinks that this redaction must have taken place after 300 B. C. and by the beginning of the Christian era.[1] Hopkins thinks that the didactic material and worship of Kṛshṇa as god was inserted between 400 to 200 B. C. The last books, the Śānti and Anuśāsana, an introduction to the first book, and later Dharmaśāstra material were added between 200 B. C. to 200 A. D. From 200 A. D. to 400 A. D. the Anuśāsana parva was separated from Śānti Parva.[2]

The complete Mahābhārata cannot be later than 4th or 5th Century A. D., which has been proved by Professor Bhandārkar and Bühler through inscriptional evidence.[3]

The above mentioned dates will provide a rough idea of time assigned to the events and compositions of the epics. It is hardly necessary to enter into a discussion about the validity of these dates. The subject is beyond the province of our dissertation and may form a separate topic for research. An eminent writer like Kaṇe observes that it is impossible to enter into any discussion as to the age of these two epics and also to the earlier and later strata in them.[4] For our present purpose we can safely assign 1400 B. C. to 1000 B. C. as the probable date of the events of the epics, the date of the composition of the Mahābhārata from the 4th century B. C. to 4th century A. D., and the date of the kernel of the Rāmāyaṇa before the 4th century B. C. although it was redacted till the 2nd century A. D.

Assessment of the Data

The dates assigned to these epics, as well as the genealogies of the kings given in them may not be completely trustworthy. The authenticity of many narrations may not be relied upon by one who is dealing with chronology and synchronism.[5] The historical value of the epics, however, is not

1. Macdonell "HSL" p. 286.
2. Hopkins "The Great Epic" Chap. VI. p. 397, 398 ff.
3. Hopkins ibid. p. 387. Macdonell "HSL" p. 287.
4. Kaṇe "Hist. of Dh. " Vol. I, page 159.
5. Pargiter "AIHT" Chap. X and XI.

diminished by these discussions. There can be no doubt about the main theme of the epics. The network of legend and stories interwoven around these is also important from the sociological point of view.[1] These stories enshrine old wisdom and history and were first handed down through memory by sages, bards and minstrels and were later put down in writing by the various composers of the epics who sometimes adapted them according to the condition prevailing in their times. These should be taken as depicting the condition of societies at different times. It is certain, therefore, that these stories provide us with opportunities for the study of various cultures and societies and speak for the various contradictions, specially in the great Epic, for it depicts the picture of the time when it was enacted as well as of the various times when it was put down in writing and was redacted. All these factors must be taken into account. Thus it must also be borne in mind that the old legends and themes contained much that is new while the new material traces many old customs and traditions. The Mahābhārata thus contains old and new ideals as well as different popular practices; it also propounds moral law of the Dharma Śāstras. Rightly does Macdonell remark that the Mahābhārata "is a conglomeration of epic and didactic matter divided into eighteen books called Parvas."

The Rāmāyaṇa being mainly composed by a single author presents more or less an ideal point of view to be followed by the Āryans. Many different customs of the non-Āryan tribes are described but they clearly show a tendency to adopt similar Āryan ideals.

Thus, in adjudging the position of women in the Rāmāyaṇa one is not confronted with contradictions. It is true that as it is a popular human poem—sometimes women as depicted, show human weaknesses. But either they are seen to return to the ideal at once, when advised by some one (as in case of Kauśalyā when she was reminded of her duty once by Rāma and at another time by Daśaratha) or (as in the case of Kaikeyī) the forces of goodness are too powerful for their evil tendencies which are defeated betimes. Women

1. R. C. Dutt, "A Hist. of Civilization in Ancient India" Vol. I, p. 122-123, 138 although doubts the mythical character of the story, still states that both the epics throw valuable side-light on the society of that time.

mostly follow the ideals and are respected, but the passages decrying women (although some of them may refer to interpolations due to ascetic influence) are few and can be justified with reference to the context. Still it must be said that social ideals were tending towards a condition where women were assigned a low position in the social set up.

In the Mahābhārata, however, one is confronted with numerous contradictions while approaching the subject of the status of women. These, as already stated, are due to the vast time factor as well as to the differences in ideals and practices followed by various races of India. From the immense data at our disposal it will not be an exaggeration to state that this epic specially deals with the condition of women in India from pre-historic times to the age when neo-Hinduism of the Purāṇas was finally being evolved i.e. the condition of women of the entire Hindū period.

The women as depicted in the narrative part of the great Epic preserve their independence in thought as well as in action. They mostly speak for themselves. These portions of the Mahābhārata present an account of women, who rose to great heights in every field, such as in the domestic, in the service of humanity and in the emancipation of soul. But the Mahābhārata also traces the story of the fall of the status of women in the Hindū society. By the time the didactic portions were written the social and religious status of women had declined. She was denied Vedic education and was married when she had no idea of matrimony. At home she entirely depended on menfolk. She was no more a real partner in her husband's mundane and spiritual efforts but a mere devotee and follower. So much so that A. C. Das remarks "womanhood was sacrificed at the altar of supposed social convenience and purity and out of its ashes arose a race of cribbed, cabined, confined and delicate creatures, too fragile for the propagation of vigorous life and too ethereal and womanly to be of any earthly use."[1] This enervation may have resulted from many factors. It may have been due to some inner change in the realm of thought as asceticism was definitely gaining ground. The climatic conditions of India, fusion of different cultures or their encounters might have also contributed to this change.

1. A. C. Das "Ṛg-Vedic Culture" p. 259.

An impartial effort to interpret the status of women in the epics will provide the opportunity to correct many erroneous ideas about the status of women in the past. For "history gives us the information about the evolution in the past and is necessary to understand the present"[1] and "History by exhibiting to us a great number of different societies, prepares us to understand and tolerate the variety of usages; by showing us that the societies have often been transformed, it familiarises us with the variation in social forms and cures us of a morbid dread of change."[2] The epics are historical works; particularly the Mahābhārata is a great history in this respect, as it deals with various types of societies, which show vicissitudes in the status of women. Here an humble attempt has been made to trace their conditions, as they actually were and not as they ought to have been or could have been. The race of spirited heroines and great scholars were later transformed into mere shadows of their masters. How this came to pass gradually is a long story which will be unfolded in the following chapters.

1. Longlois and Seignobos "Introduction to the study of History," p. 320. footnote 1.

2. Ibid., "Introduction to the study of History", p. 321.

Chapter II

THE MAID, HER STATUS AND HER EDUCATION

The status of women in a particular society may be judged by the manner in which the birth of a female infant is received. It has been established by the Indian and European scholars that the exposure ot the female child in the Saṁhitās as discussed by some foreign authors was never a fact.[1] If female infanticide was not prevalent in the age of the Saṁhitās it would have been utterly unthinkable in the times that followed it i.e. when the epic stories were being enacted or even in the subsequent ages. From the epics it is clear that the doctrine of non-violence was gaining ground.[2] Thus in the society in which foetus-murder was considered to be a crime, there could be no possibility of exposure of the female infant.[3]

Place in the family. Birth of the daughter

In one case the birth of several daughters is mentioned among the bad omens but there it may well be due to the unusual fact of their dancing, singing and laughing at the very time of their birth.[4] Excepting this solitary reference nowhere in the epics is the birth of a daughter considered an unhappy event.[5] Had it been so the custom of adopting daughters would not have existed at all, but the daughter-adoption was frequent enough. Sītā, Kuntī, Śakuntalā and Prmadvarā[6]

1. Altekar "PWHC" Chap. I. p. 8-9.
2. Mbh. XIII. 106. 35 ff ; XIV. 46. 18, 29 ; XIV, 90. Rām. III 9 (Sec.). Nakulopākhyāna supports Ahiṁsā as opposed to animal sacrifices.
3. Mbh. XII. 161. 6; V. 35-46-48 foetus-murder is equal to Brāhmaṇa murder. Vyāsa S.N. "Rāmāyaṇa Kalīna Samāj" chap. 10. pp. 150 ff. suspects exposure of girl infants just after their birth but the cases of Śakuntalā and Pramadvarā prove that the exposure, was due to their being born of extra-marital relations.
4. Mbh. VI. 3. 7. स्त्रियः काश्चित्प्रजायन्ते चतस्रः पञ्च कन्यकाः ।
जातमात्राश्च नृत्यन्ति गायन्ति च हसन्ति च ॥
5. Mbh. I. 167. 44. Rām. I. 67. 13-16.
6. Although Śāntā is an adopted daughter of Lomapīda according to N. India recension of the Rāmāyaṇa, this, however, is not upheld by Aśoka Chatterjee in art. "Śāntā's Parentage." I. H. Q. June 1957. Vol. XXXIII. No. 2. P. 145 ff.

were all adopted daughters.[1] It may be argued, that Sītā, Śakuntalā and Pramadvarā, had just fallen to the lot of their adoptive fathers but they could have been easily disposed off to others by them just as king Uparichara gave away Satyavatī although ṣhe was gifted with beauty and possessed every virtue.[2] The birth of a daughter was sometimes desired as the affection felt for her and the son-in-law was much greater than that felt for the son. The merits of 'kanyā-dāna' as well as the worlds attained on a son being born to one's daughter were factors that gave some importance to her birth.[3] Moreover, the son was not absolutely necessary for performing the death rites of the ancestors. The brotherless daughter was known as putrikādharmiṇī which meant that her son was to inherit his maternal grand-father's property and perform his funeral rites. Yayāti attained heaven through the grace of his daughter's son even though he had sons. Some passages do prove that daughters were considered as sons, and that they inherited wealth and kingdoms.[4] Thus from the religious point of view as well as that of inheritance the son was not utterly indispensable. On the contrary there are examples to prove that some people were eager to have daughters. For it was ordained that by performing Śrāddha on second day of the bright fortnight one got several daughters.[5] According to one passage the good results of visiting a certain holy place was getting a hundred daughters.[6] As rewards for penances performed, bright and famous daughters were born.[7]

1. Rām. I. 67. 13-16 ; Mbh. I. 71-72 (sec.); I. 8. 5-13. I. 111. 1-3 cf. S. Rao Shāstrī "Women in the Sacred Laws" Chap. VI, p. 183 Even later evidences prove adoption of daughters.

2. Mbh. I. 63. 67-68.

3. Mbh. I. 116. 10-13; 157. 36. Rām. 72. 15.

4. Mbh. XIII. 45. 14; I. 93. 28 (Yayāti attains heaven) XII. 33. 45.; I. 215. 23-25.

5. Mbh. XIII. 87. 10 स्त्रियो द्वितीयां जायन्ते; 104. 151; XIII. 83.51.

पुत्रार्थी लभते पुत्रं कन्यार्थी तामवाप्नुयात् ।
यदर्थमिष्यते भार्या प्राप्तः सोऽर्थस्त्वया मयि । Mbh. I. 158. 7.
कन्या चैका कुमारश्च कृताहमनृणा त्वया ॥

Thus wife was needed not only to have sons but daughters as well. I. 62. 22 cf. R. C. Dutt. "HCAI" Vol. I. Chap. VI. p. 167. Quotes "Bṛhadāraṇyaka Upanishad" VI. 4. 17-18. for the wish of the birth of the learned daughter.

6. Mbh. III. 83. 189-190. लभेत्कन्याशतं दिव्यं स्वर्गलोकं च गच्छति ।

7. Mbh. III 293. 8-18. Rām. I. 25. 5-6.

Daughter—how far the source of anxiety

Surely the daughter in those days, as even now, was a source of anxiety, inasmuch as she was to be given away in marriage. Her future welfare and happiness depended entirely on the character and ability of her future husband. It was a great worry for the parents to find a suitable husband, obviously a more difficult task in an age when the daughter too may have had a voice in the matter. Still when the story part of the great Epic was being written, various forms of marriages, which will be discussed later, were prevalent. Adherence to some of these forms e.g. Gāndharva and Asura might have made this task easy and sometimes a source of income for parents. Marriage of the daughters was, nevertheless, an important and sacred duty of the father,[1] more so in the didactic portions. Generally, a father only laments the birth of a daughter when he is unable to get an eligible match for her.[2] It was only in these circumstances that she has been declared a source of pity and distress.[3]

An object of affection

The life of daughters and even adopted daughters at their parental homes proves that they were brought up with great care and affection, and were never to be displeased.[4] Some fathers felt equal affection for the sons and daughters.[5] The example of Devayānī indicates that sometimes fathers were so fond of their daughters that they even spoilt them. Such was the power of Devayānī over her father and the tenderness felt by him for her that the Devas instruct Kacha to please her in order to gain the knowledge of Sanjīvinī from Śukrāchārya and he acts accordingly.[6]

1. Rām. I. 72. 15. परो धर्मः (कन्याप्रदानरूपः) कृतो मह्यम् ।
2. Rām. II. 118. 34-36 ; VII. 9. 10-11; Mbh. V. 97 14-16 ; I. 157. 35 states that the daughter is others' property.
3. Mbh. I. 159. 11 कृच्छ्रं तु दुहिता किल XII. 243. 20. Cf. Aitareya Brāhmaṇa 33. I. M. IV. 185.
4. Mbh. XII. 243. 16 दुहित्रा दासवर्गेण विवादं न समाचरेत् ।
5. Mbh. I. 157. 37.
6. Mbh. I. 76. 15-16.

Place in Society—maidens considered auspicious

It was the general belief of society that the Goddess of wealth resided in maidens.[1] Chastity was considered to be a perfect ornament of woman-kind. The maiden, as the personification of chastity was naturally thought to be propitious. Thus their presence was required in auspicious ceremonies like coronations.[2] They went out to welcome and to send off the distinguished guest.[3] When the heroes went to battle, they touched the maiden along with other lucky objects.[4]

Rights and Privileges (i) Nature of protection given by the society and the family.

It was natural that such a symbol of auspiciousness and an object of affection was to be given sufficient protection by the society and the family. It was also essential for guarding the chastity as well. Of such importance was the protection of a maiden that the kings were ordained, despite their multifarious duties, to protect them.[5] Perhaps this protection which was a social duty of the king was given to those maidens who were orphans. It was, however, the duty enjoined upon a father to protect his daughters.[6] But it appears that they had also great independence in their father's homes. It is really surprising how Kuntī could hide the fact of her pregnancy and if her parents knew about it perhaps they did not mind. The son of a maiden according to later didactic portions was considered a disgrace.[7] Even in Kuntī's case, it might have been so as she abandoned her child and has a sense of guilt throughout her life.[8] But there was in existence another social standard according to which one did not mind such incidents.

1. Mbh. XIII 11. 14.
2. Rām. VI. 128. 38, 63 ; II, 14. 36; II. 118. 38. Cf. Vishṇu Dh. S. LXIII 33. 39; XCIX. 14.
3. Mbh. IV. 68. 29 ; 37. 33 ; V 86. 16 ; VII, 112. 65.
4. Mbh. VII. 82. 21 ; VII 7. 9 in Poona edition it is सुभगानर्तितैस्तथा although in Cal. ed. it is सूतानां नर्तितैः ।
5. Mbh. XII. 90. 39.
6. Mbh. XIII. 46. 14 ; 20. 21.
7. Mbh. XIII 36. 17 गर्भेण दुष्यते कन्या ।
8. Mbh. XV. 30. 2 ff.

Kṛshṇa states that those conversant in scriptures recognised a Kānīna as the legitimate son of his mother's husband,[1] he was even ready to coronate Karṇa, in case he agreed.[2] Vyāsa, himself a Kānīna, does not deplore the circumstances of Karṇa's birth.[3] From the conversation between Śarmishthā and Devayānī we may well infer that Devayānī was only worried lest the father of Śarmishthā's children turned out to be Yayāti, otherwise there was no restriction on the maidens and they could have Kānīna sons through Brāhmaṇa ṛshis, without knowing their lineage.[4] The lists of sons in the great Epic approve such sons.[5] From the modern standard, however repugnant the custom may be, it shows that the then society was a free one. There was no downright or perpetual condemnation attached to any one for no fault of his own. The sins of parents were not visited upon the children and thus Vyāsa, a Kānīna was greatly revered. Nevertheless, it can not be assumed that fathers were always careless about the duty of protection of their daughter's virtue. In the great Epic, according to another story, Agni loved king Nīla's daughter and was accepted by her. One day in the guise of a Brāhmaṇā he was enjoying the pleasure of that maiden's company. The virtuous king on the discovery of the truth, punished the Brāhmaṇa according to the law.[6] This clearly indicates that such relations were forbidden by law.

(ii) *Freedom of movement and action*

The maiden's innocent activities were, however, not restricted.[7] They used to go to gardens for sports, and some-

1. Mbh. V. 140. 7-9 Kānīna is a maiden's son.
2. Mbh. V. 140. 15.
3. Mbh. XV. 30. 20 ff.
4. Mbh. I. 83. 6 ff It seems Kānīna was recognised.
5. Mbh. I. 120. 32-33 ; XIII. 49. 25-26.
6. Mbh. II. 31. 30-31

   ततः स भगवानग्निश्चकमे तां सुदर्शनाम् ।
   नीलस्य राज्ञः सर्वेषामुपनीतश्च सोमवत् ।।
   ततो ब्राह्मणरूपेण रममाणो यदृच्छया ।
   चकमे तां वरारोहां कन्यामुत्पल-लोचनाम् ।
   तं तु राजा यथाशास्त्रमशासद्धार्मिकस्तदा ।

7. Mbh. XIII. 23. 75 ब्राह्मणानां च गवां चैव कन्यानां च युधिष्ठिर।
   येऽन्तरं यान्ति कार्येषु, ते वै निरयगामिनः ।

times were courted by lovers when they were out for pleasure.[1] Mixed parties were arranged at Raivataka mountain and it was on her way back from such a party that Subhadrā was abducted.[2]

The great independence exercised by maidens in shaping their own future and the loss of such independence due to gradually increasing parental control over the decision of the question of marriage, will be dealt with in the next chapter. For this discussion properly comes under the purview of the marriage question.

(iii) *Legal rights*

The attitude of society towards women determines her property and legal rights. Therefore such rights of maidens will be discussed under that scheme. It will suffice here to state that generally after marriage, except in the case of Putrikā, the daughter had nothing to do with her parental home and property. An unmarried daughter, however, had the right to inherit her mother's dowry.[3]

Domestic duties—helping the parents

The duties of the maidens at home were mostly for preparing them for their future career i.e. the domestic life. The greatest duty of a house-holder was to entertain the guests. As a practical part of their education daughters performed this duty at their parental homes. Śakuntalā offered seat, water, and 'Arghya' to Dushyanta while her adoptive father was absent.[4] Kuntī entertained and pleased sage Durvāsā.[5] She not only saved her father from a difficult situation but also received a boon for herself. Sṛnjaya ordered his daughter Sukumārī to look after the guests,—Nārada and Parvata.[6] The daughters of poor people might have helped their fathers in their daily work for Satyavatī served her father by plying the

1. Mbh. III. 224. 1-3.
2. Mbh. I. 219. 7 ff ; I. 219, 18 ff.
3. Mbh. XIII. 45. 12.
4. Mbh. I. 71. 5.
5. Mbh. I. 111. 4-7 ; III. 305. 1. ff.
6. Mbh. XII. 30. 12-16 ; MBh. (k) I. 241. 8 ff Maidens to look after Yati Arjuna.

boat.[1] Their duties on the ceremonial occasions, of welcoming the guests, have already been referred.

Like Kuntī others also saved their fathers or their race from difficult situations. Śarmishṭhā, although a princess, readily became a slave, for the departure of Śukrāchārya would have been a great calamity for the Asura kingdom.[2] Although Lopāmudrā's father hesitated, she herself consented to marry the poor Agastya in order to save her father from that ṛshi's curse.[3] Sukanyā did not utter a word of opposition when she was given away to the old blind ṛshi Chyavana.[4] Jaratkāru toiled like a slave to save the race of the Nāgas.[5] This self-sacrificing spirit, an essential factor in harmonious family relations, was inculcated in maidens through the education they received at home. As will be shown presently their education was in keeping with their place as well as their secular and religious activities at home.

Education

From the accounts of the heroines it appears that the responsibility of educating the daughters was fully realised by the parents but there is little corroborative evidence. The epics being hero-lauds present no data of this kind. However the fact cannot be denied that the epic heroines were highly educated. Draupadī has been mentioned as Paṇḍitā and Brahmavādinī (and so are Oghāvatī and Arundhatī.)[6] Her advice to Yudhishṭhira is indicative of her practical wisdom.[7] Draupadī confesses that she had instructions from learned Brāhmaṇas who were appointed by her father to instruct her brother on the duties expounded by Bṛhaspati. When she

1. Mbh. I. 63. 69.
2. Mbh. I. 79. 19-20.
3. Mbh. III. 97 5-6.
4. Mbh. III. 122. 26 ff.
5. Mbh. I. 47. 11

तथैव सा च भर्तारं दुःखशीलमुपाचरत् ।
उपायैः श्वेतकाकीयैः प्रियकामा यशस्विनी ॥

6. Mbh. IV. 1. 3; XIII. 2. 83; 14. 95 Altekar "PWHC" p. 13 and "Education in Ancient India" p. 225—states on the basis of Harīta that Brahmavādinīs were never married. But Dr Mukerji in "Ancient Indian Education" p. 51 opines that they were married after their education. Draupadī was Brahmavādinī in the latter sense.

7. Mbh. XII. 14. 6-39; III 27. 3 ff; 32. 1 ff.

went out of the inner apartment and sat on her father's lap, the learned Brāhmaṇas, recited the sweet and consoling truths to her.[1] Kuntī's admonitions to the Pāṇḍavas show that she was well instructed in mind and heart, and was fit to be the mother of heroes. Like the parents of to-day she worried not so much about the safety of her sons, as for their duty and righteous fame.[2] To her their death was better than their parasitical existence. Kuntī's advice is fully worthy of a Kshatriya mother of heroic age.

Intellectual and religious education

Certain passages in the epics prove that the maidens were given Vedic education. Women were able to perform sacrifices alone, even without their husbands. In the Rāmāyaṇa, Kauśalyā on the eve of Rāma's installation offered oblation to fire, reciting 'mantras'.[3] Similarly when Vali was going to fight Sugrīva, Tārā performed 'swastyayana' with the chanting of 'mantras' and so also Kauśalyā when Rāma was going to the forest.[4] Women recited daily Vedic prayers (Sandhyā).[5] Tārā had knowledge of the Vedas.[6] Sulabhā discussed 'Yoga', 'samādhi', 'moksha' and qualities of speech with the philosopher Janaka, who was confuted by her,[7] for she was initiated in the philosophy of emancipation.[8] In the Mahābhārata there is mention of a learned Brāhmaṇī who wanted to be enlightened on the mysteries of religion, life and death.[9] Śivā another ascetic woman was well versed in the Vedas.[10] Even Ṛshis, deities and the manes went to Arundhatī to learn the secrets of religion and duty and were duly instructed by her.[11]

1. Mbh. III. 32. 60ff.
2. Mbh. V. 132-137 (Sections)
3. Rām. II. 20. 15.
4. Rām. IV. 16. 12 ; II. 25. 44 Cf. Kaṇe P. V. "H. Of Dh" Vol. II, part II, p. 1107 for 'Swastyayana'.
5. Rām. V 14. 49.
6. Rām. IV. 24. 37.
7. Mbh. XII. 320 (Section).
8. Mbh. XII. 320. 83 ff.
9. Mbh. XIV, 20-22 (Section)
10. Mbh. V. 109. 18. according to Bombay Ed. while Poona Ed. has different reading.
11. Mbh. XIII. 130. 2 ff.

As the great Epic records many strata of societies, perhaps this period, in which Vedic religious and philosophic education is mentioned to have been imparted to women, corresponds roughly with the Upanishad and the Sūtra period.[1] These works contain enough evidence of the intellectual activities and educational attainments of women. Draupadī's lively discussions remind one of Gārgī and Maitreyī of Bṛhadāranyaka Upanishad.[2] Āśwalāyana Gṛhya-sūtra records Samāvartana ceremony for the girls.[3] There were girls' schools and learned women when Pāṇinī wrote Ashṭādhyāyī.[4] Pārāskara Gṛhya-Sūtra narrates 'mantras' to be uttered by a mother.[5] True, the mere fact that these women could recite 'mantras' does not warrant the conclusion that they have a knowledge of the Vedas. The claim rests on ampler evidence. In the commentary on Gobhila Gṛhya-Sūtra we are told,[6] "the women folk should be taught, for without such study, they cannot perform Agnihotra." And Agnihotra was definitely performed by the ladies[7] in the epics, Kauśalyā could quote from a Dharma-sūtra.[8]

Women ascetics and performers of penances

It seems that when the epics were first being written the conservative attitude of the Dharmaśāstras had not gained ground. Those women who performed penances for the liberation of soul must have had some intellectual and philosophic education. At any rate the fact is undeniable that they had excellent mental training. The austerities performed by Ambā and Anusūyā were beyond the capacities of many Ṛshis.[9] A hermitage near Kurukshetra, seat of women ascetics,

1. R. C. Dutt "HCAI" Vol. I, p. 168 ff—assigns 1400 B. C. 1000 B. C. See pp. 12-17 of "Introductory."

2. Bṛ. Up. II. 4. 5. 5.

3. Asv. G. S. III. 8. 4. 14. S. B. E. Vol. XXIX, p. 228.

4. Agrawal, V. S. ('Pāṇini kālīna Bhārata' p. 281, 295) Pāṇinī's work has been assigned 4th century B. C. i. e. when the epics were still being written and to him Bhārata and Mahābhārata were known p. 322.

5. P. G. S. IX, 2. 1.

6. R. K. Mukerji "Ancient Indian Education" p. 208 ff and Cf. G. G. S. I. 3 15 ; II 3; I. 4. 13-19 P. G. S. III 2.

7. Rām. II. 20. 15; II 25. 44 ; II 24. 28.

8. Rām. II. 103. 30. Cf. Ap. Dh. S. II. 2. 3. 12.

9. Mbh. V. 186. 19 ff ; XIII. 14. 96 Rām. II. 117. 9-10.

deserves special mention. Here, observing the vow of Brahmacharya (celibacy) from her young age a Brāhmaṇī maiden rose to a high point in ascetic eminence. She acquired unusual yogic power and became Siddhā.[1] While another, not a child of poverty but of affluence, the daughter of king Śāṇḍilya, self-restrained, wedded to severe vows, performed austerities, usually too hard to be accomplished by women. On the basis of merits thus acquired she obtained a place in heaven, and was worshipped by the Gods and Brāhmaṇas.[2] Diśā and Swayamprabhā had taken the vow of celibacy i.e. Brahmacharya and were living as ascetics.[3] Śramaṇī, Śabarī used to put on barks and skin of antelope and has been described as "Jaṭilā Tāpasī" with her aśrama at Pampā and with Mātanga her late preceptor.[4] In the epics we come across such words as "Bhikshuṇīs", "Pravrajitā" and "Ṭapaswinī", which clearly point to the fact that the women too practised asceticism and performed penances.[5]

Penances were sometimes performed with some worldly object in view.[6] Nevertheless, these examples also indicate that women had considerable mental discipline and physical endurance which would compare well with similar attainments of their male counter-parts.

Conditions changed by the time the didactic portions of the Mahābhārata were being written, religious as well as the literary education was not imparted to girls. Women were considered incompetent to perform sacrifices.[7] The wife of a learned preceptor, Deva-Sharmā talks in prākṛt—a clear indication that women were not given literary education. Ruchī could only speak in Sanskrit when she was hypnotized

1. Mbh. IX. 54. 5-6.
2. Mbh. IX. 54. 7-8.
3. Mbh. XIII. 19-21 (Sections) Rām. IV. 51. 1 & 16.
4. Rām. III. 74. 5-33.
5. Rām. II. 29. 13. Mbh. XIII. 104. 132 ; 23. 64 cf. Vātsyāyana "Kāmsūtra" I. 5. 32 (12) p. 41.
6. Rām. VII 17. 18. Mbh. III. 173. 7-8.
7. Mbh. XII. 165. 21-22 unless we infer by Śloka 22

नैव कन्या न युवतिर्नामिन्त्रज्ञो न बालिशः ।

that old women were allowed to perform sacrifices, which will be rather a far-fetched conclusion. This was a transitionary period for Āśwalāyana G. S. allows it. See Nīlkaṇṭha's commentry of the śloka 22.

by Vipula.[1] Many reasons have been advanced by scholars for the fast disappearance of Vedic education from amongst women. One of the reasons was that sacrificial religion was becoming highly specialised, and naturally this as such took years to be completed. The marriageable age for girls, everywhere lower than that of the boys, was in the later recensions of the epics lowered further still.[2] Therefore they could not be imparted an education which took years to be completed. According to Dr. Altekar, "the spoken dialect of the age had begun to differ considerably from the language of the Vedic hymns, and the theory had found universal acceptance that to commit a single most minor mistake in the recitation of the Vedic mantras would produce most disastrous consequences to the reciter. As a natural consequence, society began to insist that those who wanted to undertake Vedic studies must be prepared to devote a fairly long period of about twelve to sixteen years to the task...as a consequence lady Vedic scholars began to be rarer and rarer."[3] Similar reasons may be put forward for the denial of the Vedic education for girls in the epic recensions. These grounds were still stronger in the case of non-Āryan women, who were denied Vedic education in case they entered Āryan homes. Temperamentally, however, they would not have had any appreciation for the Vedic sacrament. More devout by nature and more fond of ceremonies than men, these non-Āryan women could have little appreciation for the Vedic sacrament. This deficiency was sought to be remedied by the fusion of Āryan and non-Āryan cultures. Thus the non-Āryan woman, by bringing her own ritualistic religion might have contributed to the development of the Paurāṇika devotional cult which came later. This new religion was particularly suited to the disposition of women. As women dominated homes, the sacrificial Vedic religion, now confined to men, naturally gave place to the observances of new devotional religion. We can find a parallel to this in our own times, in the case of the girls educated in secular institutions or the European women married into orthodox

1. Mbh. XIII. 41. 15.
2. Mbh. XIII. 44. 14; Rām. III. 47. 4 and 10.
3. Altekar "PWHC" p. 238.

Indian homes. Their outlook and training make them averse to the Hindu sacraments which are being abandoned.

The woman who was once a Sahadharmiṇī in the Vedic rituals,[1] after the above mentioned circumstances remained a custodian of customs, superstitions and rites without mantras.[2] As the theological education was the only intellectual education available in those days; women, denied of the benefit of this education, had their intellect completely clogged and unorientated. This was a great calamity for liberal Hindū culture. This led not only to the extinction of the Brahma-Vādinīs but to a more pervasive damage to society by making room for the vitiating influence of ignorant mothers.

Traditional Education

In the traditional (ancient) view the aim of education was not limited to mere intellectual attainment. Character building was considered an indispensable function of education.[3] Listening to the story of Itihāsa and Purāṇa which were handed down from generation to generation was considered highly conducive to a sound character. Therefore this item had an important place in the scheme of education. In this way one gained considerable wisdom and sagacity.[4] The girls too had a right to listen to the Itihāsa and Purāṇas.[5] Mothers and mothers-in-law had a great part in educating daughters and daughters-in-law in the accepted precepts and practices about

1. Rām. I. 13. 41 ; Mbh. XIV. 89. 2.

2. Mbh. XIII. 40. 12 according to Āp. GṚ. S. II. 15
आवृत्ताश्च स्त्रीभ्यः प्रतीयेरन् ।

People should understand from the women customs of the country—Har Datta comments मन्त्ररहिता क्रिया आवृत्ता उच्यन्ते ।

3. Mbh. II. 5. 112 ; V. 39. 66 शीलवृत्तफलं श्रुतम् ।
III. 313. 108 ff. states that a Brāhmaṇa without character is a Śūdra.

4. The Mahābhārata narrates many such stories from the ancient history beginning with अत्राप्युदाहरन्तीममितिहासं पुरातनम् । अत्र ते वर्णयिष्यामि यथावृत्तं यथाश्रुतम् । e. g. Mbh. XIII. 5. 2 ; 6. 2 ; 11. 2 As wife of the crown prince Sītā was 'अभिज्ञा राजधर्माणाम्' । Rām. II. 26. 4.

5. Sītā gives evidence of such knowledge many times cf. Rām. II. 29. 8, 9, 18; II. 30. 6, III. 9. 13-23, V. 24. 8-14, VI. 48. 2, VI. 113. 41 ff.

character and conduct.[1] As "Śrūti" means tradition[2] a learned lady in traditional lore was known as Bahuśrūtā. In Vidulā's case such epithet indicated her proficiency in the Kshatriya lore.[3]

Military and Physical Education

Although later a Kshatriyā woman was given military education,[4] in the epics themselves there is no evidence that such education was imparted. A few cases that might be cited in favour of such a presumption would not bear close scrutiny. For instance there is a case of Kaikeyī helping Daśaratha. But Kaikeyī's help to Daśaratha in the war was in the form of tending his wounds.[5] Similarly, Subhadrā's being skilful chariot driver, which she was according to the Kumbhakoṇam edition of the Mahā-Bhārata does not necessarily imply military education.[6] If military education had been imparted in those days Sītā and Draupādī would have certainly offered some resistance to Rāvaṇa and Jayadratha respectively but they both appear quite helpless before abductors. The position, however, is different in respect of physical education. The Epic-women were definitely trained in physical exercises. The game of ball as one of the amusements of the girls has been often referred to. Kuntī and some other women played this game with fine coloured balls.[7] The Rāmāyaṇa represents girls going to the gardens in the evening with their friends for playing.[8] The slaughter of the sacrificial horse by Kauśalya is evidence of her excellent physical power.[9]

1. Rām. V. 27. 10. II. 39. 20-5, II. 118. 8 ; Mbh. II. 79. 3 ff ; I. 192. 4ff Kuntī to Draupadī. Mbh. XIII. 64. 3 also.
2. Pargiter "AIHT" 1922 London p. 19-22. Rām. II. 110. 15-18.

   भरतात्तु महाबाहोरसितो नाम जायत ।
   द्वे चास्य भार्ये गर्भिण्यौ बभूवतुरिति श्रुतिः ।

3. Mbh. V. 133. 3.

   विश्रुता राजसंसत्सु श्रुतवाक्या बहुश्रुता ।

4. Altekar "PWHC" p. 25 ff.
5. Rām. II 9. 16.
6. Mbh. (k) I. 243. 12 ff. Meyer "SLAI" p. 75, foot-note 2. Cf. P. G. S. III. 14. 9 'a woman shall not be a charioteer'. S. B. E. Vol. XXIX Part I.
7. Mbh. V. 90. 63 ; III 111. 16.
8. Rām. II. 60. 9-10, 67. 17; VII. 2. 10-11.
9. Rām. I. 14. 33.

Education in Arts (1) *The sixty-four Arts*

The sixty-four arts mentioned by various Sanskrit writers have been referred to in the Mahābhārata also.[1] The slave girls of the kings used to be well versed in these.[2] Vātsyāyana recommends these sixty-four arts as arts of women to be taught to the daughters of rich families, princesses and Gaṇikās.[3] These arts include a liberal scheme of education for women, which was suited to their aptitude.[4] Proficiency in these arts meant hard work, required ample leisure and immense expense. Such high standard of attainment was not possible for poor people, who had no time at their disposal. Even at present, with all modern equipments and facilities, it is not possible for any home-science college to aspire for such an ambitious curriculum. It is due to these facts that from the epics we find that these arts were patronised by the kings and practised in the inner apartments. The slave girls used to be well versed in them.[5] As the scheme of sixty-four arts includes physical, mental and aesthetic training the ladies well versed in these must have run artistic, comfortable and happy homes.

Education in fine Arts (2) *Dancing, music and playing on instruments*

It would have been rather difficult to excel in all these arts. Thus it seems that dancing, music and playing on instruments were most common of all these. These arts have been

1. Mbh. II. 61. 9

XIII. 104. 149 ; 18. 38 Vātsyāyana "Kāmasūtra" I. 3. 16. According to Vātsyāyana 'Kalās' nos. 28, 33, 45-47, 51-56 and 62 give literary accomplishments, 'Kalās', nos. 10-25 give knowledge of domestic arts, 'Kalās' nos. 23, 24 knowledge of culinary arts, 'Kalās' nos. 5, 6. 8, 14-19, 14-58 knowledge of arts relating to toilet, dress, comforts and luxury, 'Kalās' nos. 7, 22, 36, 37, knowledge of manual arts, 'kalās' nos. 12, 29, 26, 23, 24, 32-33, 42, 43, 45, 49, 52, 53, 57, 59-61 knowledge of recreative arts, 'kalās' nos. 9, 13, 17, 21, 34, 25, 38-41, 50, knowledge of scientific arts, 'Kalās' nos. 1, 2, 11, 27 knowledge of music, 'kalā' no. 32, knowledge of drama, 'kalā' no. 4 knowledge of painting, 'kalās' nos. 3, 63, 69, knowledge of physical exercises. These 'kalās' have also been mentioned in "Lalit-vistāra", "Śukranītisāra" and "Prabandh-kosha"

2. Mbh. II. 61. 9. चतुःषष्ठिविशारदाः
3. Vātsyāyana "Kāmasūtra" I. 3. 22-23, p. 26.
4. Same as notes Nos. 1 and 2.
5. Mbh. II. 61. 9 Rām. V. 10. 38 ff.

described as "unmanly" in the later Vedic texts,[1] and were forbidden for students in the Sūtras.[2] In the sacrifices and marriages, dancing and music were associated with women according to older traditions.[3] In the great Epic these arts were part and parcel of women. So much so that even their manner of talking and wailing was considered musical.[4] We find that the girls were trained and were well versed in these arts.[5] Kuśanābha's daughters, Hemā as well as the wives of Rāvaṇa were all adept in these arts.[6] The royal households resounded with the music of women. We come across the name of various instruments like Maṇḍuka, Paṭaha, Viṇā, Vipanchī, Muruja, Chhelikā, Mṛdanga, Dimḍima, Āḍamvara, in the description of Rāvaṇa's palace. All these were played by women.[7] The three octaves were well known to them.[8] Uttarā used to learn dancing along with other girls in the hall during the day time.[9]

Agency of Education—mode and methods

It is difficult to say how education was imparted as we have no data on this point. The two more or less clear cases that there are—those of Uttarā and Draupadī[10] would clearly not permit generalisation in this matter. In Uttarā's case the teacher Bṛhannalā, when appointed, was examined in dancing, music and other fine arts. This shows that great care was taken in the appointment of a teacher who was to be a person of proved competence. Sītā and Draupadī refer to the advice of Brāhmaṇas, mothers and mothers-in-law.[11] From

1. Tait. Sam. VI. 1. 6. 5. MAIT. Sam. III 7. 3. Śat. Br. III. 2. 4. 3-8.
2. P. G. S. II. 7. 3. Gaut. Dh. S. II. 13. Āp. Dh. S. I. 1. 3. 11.
3. Kaṇe, P. V. "Hist. of Dh." Vol. II, Part II, p. 1244-5. San. G. S. I. 11. 5. Tait. Sam. VII. 5. 10. 1.
4. Mbh. IV, 17. 14. वीणेव मधुरालापा गान्धारं साधु मूर्च्छती ।

   Mbh. XI. 25. 4-8 मनःश्रुतिहरो नादो मनो मोहयतीव मे ।
5. Rām. V. 10. 38 ff. Rām. IV. 51. 17.
6. Rām. I. 32. 12 ; IV. 51. 17.
7. Rām. V. 10. 39 ff.
8. Rām. V. 4. 10 त्रिस्थानस्वरभूषितम्
9. Mbh. IV. 22. 16.
10. Mbh. IV. 11. 11-12 ; III. 32. 60.
11. Rām. II. 29. 8, 9, 19. Rām. II. 118. 7-8, Mbh. III. 32. 60 ff; 232. 33.

neither of these can we infer with certainty how education was generally imparted—whether there was any general system or not. The slave girls of kings might have been educated in the manner laid down by Kauṭilya, i.e. they were taught by private tutors appointed by the State.[1] There is no mention of Gurukulas for the girls. As has been shown already some of them lived in the āśramas and might have been educated there. Education through private tutors would have been expensive for the commoners and so could not have been a general practice. They might have received their education through folk lore and traditions, through their parents and parents-in-law. It is, however, clear that there was no academic or institutional education for girls. At least such does not appear to be the case from the available evidence.[2]

Merits of the Home Education

The general education such as was there, was imparted at home. As the sphere of the future activity of the daughter was to be her home, this education was a sort of preparation for the duties of that life through lessons in practical wisdom. This home education made women more practical and gave them greater understanding of men and matter. Yudhishṭhira was no match for the practical wisdom of Draupadī.[3] Men were sometimes dogmatic due to one sided education, but women were never so. Thus while Bhīshma sticks to the vow of chastity even at the risk of the extinction of the family, after Vichitravīrya's death, Satayawatī for whose consideration the vow was taken thinks that either Bhīshma should marry or his brother's widows should practice Niyoga.[4] Home training also made women sympathetic, loving and giving. Whatever might have been the relations between the Kauravas and the Pāṇḍavas, the Kaurava ladies did lament Draupadī's fate after

1. Kauṭilya "Arthaśāstra" Eng. Tr. by Syām Śāstry Bk. II. Chap. 27th Sūtra 1-5.

2. Moreover, it was not an age of educational institutions. It would have been much more difficult to have separate educational institutions for women in those days. In polygamous society every girl was married. It would not have been possible for married women to run institutions. As foi the ascetic women it was rather difficult as they all were busy with penances.

3. Mbh. III. 27 ff. (Sec.)

4. Mbh. I. 103. 11.

the game of dice.[1] Gāndhārī, although it was too late to mend, wanted to show the right path to Duryodhana. Kuntī pointed out to the Pāṇḍavas what she considered to be the right path.[2] Gāndhārī did not wish for Duryodhana's victory as his cause was unrighteous.[3] Later, after the carnage she was equally sympathetic towards Draupadī and Uttarā as towards her own daughters-in-law.[4] Whatever the later didactic portions might have to say against women,[5] according to the actual story they possess deep understanding of men, events and society and had excellent qualities of heart—which was the result of an education relative to life. Some epic women like Gāndhārī, Lopāmudrā, Anusūyā, Sītā, Draupadī and Sāvitrī acted as great educative forces in those times and are still examples of ideal Indian womanhood. It may not be possible to state definitely the system of education then prevalent. Still the above account shows that some of the women were really spirited, had deep insight in matters, understanding of life and had also attained a high standard of ethics and morality.

Defects of Home Education

Home education had its defects also. It appears to have developed the virtues of heart but not so much the powers of intellect. Thus the social instinct did develop but at the cost of the individuality. In the family atmosphere of love and affection one thinks of giving only. This attitude has certainly great virtue but it was pushed to the extreme in the ideal of Pātivrata. As for the Pativratā there was no God other than her husband, the ideal of Sahdharmiṇī received a great set back and started losing ground as the ideal of Pātivrata advanced more and more.[6] Thus Gāndhārī, by bandaging her eyes, blinded herself. She could not help her husband in any way and also denied the care of a mother to the Kaurava

1. Mbh. II. 79. 32-33.
2. Mbh. V. 129. 18 ff. ; 90. 72 ff from Sec. 132 to 137.
3. Mbh. XI. 14. 9 ; IX. 63. 60-62.
4. Mbh. XI. 15. 40 ; 17. 25 ff ; II. 79. 32-33.
5. Mbh. XIII. 38-43 (Sec.).
6. See Chap. on "Married Life".

princes. It would have been difficult for those under whose charge the princes were committed, to chide and correct them when they went wrong. By virtue of their position as parents, Gāndhārī and Dhṛtarāshṭra could have guided the Kauravas in their impressionable years. But they were both unable to perform this duty on account of their artificial and natural blindness. The wives of the Kauravas weep for Draupadī's fate but not a single one of them could exert any influence and check her husband from performing inhuman atrocities. Gāndhārī and these princesses who were not Sahadharmiṇīs in the true sense of the term, were also responsible for tragedies that followed after the game of dice and the war. They were all weaklings and had no character to show the right path to their husbands. Not once in the great Epic do we come across the wife of a hero like Duryodhana, leading him to righteousness, as a true partner in life should have done.[1] She only appears weeping helplessly after the tragedy.[2] In the same way Rāvaṇa's mother and Maṇḍodarī failed to bring him to the right path.[3] But they were better in the sense that they at least made efforts. Sītā when exiled suffers quietly the unjust treatment meted out to her by Rāma. Fiery personalities like Sulabhā and Vidulā are cited as ancient examples.[4] There are some examples like those of Draupadī and Kuntī, who still wielded great influence but surely the race of heroines like these was dying. Most of the Kshatriyā ladies lacked self-confidence and assertive individuality, and were incapable of exercising their benevolent influence. In short, that development of personality, which true education promotes by bringing one in contact with outside world had not taken place in them. A sound academic education could have developed these qualities of personality but such a development could not be promoted by the home education which was necessarily limited in scope and therefore inadequate for the purpose. It was really a great tragedy in the life of a nation where its

1. It may be well argued that the epics deal with external action or as Vaidya in "Mahābhārata—Mīmānsā" page 341 contends that Duryodhana's personality may have been weakened by representing such scenes, nevertheless from our points of view it was a failing on his wife's part.

2. Mbh. XI. 17. 25 ff.

3. Rām. VI. 34. 20 ff; V. 58. 76 ff.

4. Mbh. XII. 320. 3; V. 133. 3-4 ff.

women folk could understand the right path but were helpless to pursue it.

Gradual decay and disappearance of sound education

The aim of integrated education is to develop mental, physical and emotional powers and to maintain a balance between these. A person thus equipped will possess the fully developed personality and will not only desire the good but will act according to such a desire. It would appear from the above-mentioned evidence that when the epic stories were being enacted or being written for the first time maidens were given opportunities to develop all these powers in them. However, the conditions were changing. The denial of religious education clogged intellectual advancement of women. Therefore, judged from the criterion of integrated personality, only a few who were intellectually equipped like Draupadī were intellectual equals and religious partners of their husbands, a position which women were losing gradually. The general education at home prepared the girls almost exclusively for their domestic duties and ignored the needs of an all round development of personality. As already shown there was no relation between the feelings and actions of women educated thus. The training in sixty-four arts did furnish a comprehensive scheme but it was not meant for the maidens of commoners. The physical fitness was maintained through various kinds of sports and dancing but in the didactic portions dancing as a profession is deprecated,[1] although it was still cultivated and appreciated as an art[2] which may lead to the conclusion that it was practised by a few. Aesthetic education through private tutors points to a similar inference. Free movement of women, however, does not seem to be checked[3] but early marriages may have retarded the intellectual and physical growth of maidens.[4] The perfection of personality was not thus attained.

To conclude, the daughter was an object of affection. The birth of a daughter might not always have been hailed

1. Mbh. XII. 36. 37.
2. Mbh. XIII. 18. 38 ; 104-149.
3. Mbh. XII. 68. 32.
4. Mbh. XIII. 44. 14. See in Chapter "Marriage"

with enthusiasm, but neither was it looked upon with horror as is often erroneously believed. It was only when the parents found there were meagre chances of giving away their daughter in a happy wedlock, that they despaired of them, and looked upon the birth of a daughter as something unhappy. On the contrary a maiden had a place of significance both in the family and in society. In the family maidens were charged with some of the most important duties, i.e., looking after the guests. They led a carefree and comfortable life at their parental homes. In society, too, they had a place of honour. Thus their presence was required in auspicious ceremonies and for welcoming honoured guests and heroes, which is indicative of their benign influence. The Vedic religious education of a girl was gradually being neglected and the general education imparted at home, while it developed excellent qualities of heart, it did not develop a strong individuality. It must not be however forgotten that besides these petted and pampered daughters there were slave girls who were treated as property and this was really a great blot on the social systems described in the epics. An account of these will be given elsewhere.

Chapter III

MARRIAGE—PART I

INTRODUCTORY

The institution of marriage though not older than family, must be as old as human civilization itself. While there cannot be any doubt about the fact that human beings once lived in premarital stage, the existence of promiscuity among mankind is controversial and highly improbable.[1] The change from the pre-marital to the marital state was almost inevitable. Love, social and economic integration, desire for progeny, above all security in self-continuation must have been the factors that contributed towards the formation of the marriage institution. This lasting relationship was later recognized by law and custom.

Pre-marital and promiscuous stages in the great Epic

It is due to its character as an Itihāsa,[2] that the great Epic refers to pre-marital promiscuous stages as well as to the origin of marriage,[3] although there is no mention of such primitive conditions in the Ṛg-Veda. As Uttara Kuru is believed to be a mythical land the reference to pre-marital stage there, may itself be incorrect.[4] It may well be that this single reference just relates to the laxity in morals and to polyandry

1. Westermarck "History of Human Marriage" p. 537-538—Westermarck, an eminent sociologist has proved that many of the assertions made in respect of promiscuity have been shown as erroneous and the accuracy of others is at least open to question. It is highly incredible that promiscuity was ever a natural practice among human beings when even animals like apes and birds have a tendency to stick to a mate. Cf. Essay on "Genesis of Marriage" by A. W. Nieuwenhuis in "The Book of Marriage" edited by Count H. Keyserling p. 53-76.

2. See 'Introduction' p. 10 ff Pargiter "AIHT" Chap. II. p. 21-22.

3. Mbh. XII. 207. 38-40. The origin is however mythical and sounds like the theory of origin of the state of 18th century political philosophers of Europe. For even before Kaliyuga, an age when the great Epic was written marriage was well established institution.

4. Mbh. XIII. 102 25-26 ; I. 122. 7.

prevalent in certain parts of the Himālayas.[1] The cases of promiscuity hinted in the great Epic appear to be conjectures. Such accusation of Karṇa against Madra and Vāhīka[2] may just have been disregarded as he was abusing Śalya[3] but for the fact that these people have been denounced elsewhere[4] also. While promiscuity among the Vāhīka-women is the fulfilment of a curse of a chaste women violated by the Ārāṭṭas[5] similar conditions in Māhishmatī prevailed as the fulfilment of a boon granted by the fire god.[6] The latter episode might have been just added to make the dull accounts of battles more interesting for the same story repeated in the Anuśāsana Parva has no such reference.[7] These, references to pre-sex-relations among the women of Vāhīka and Māhishmatī are dubious and unreliable. For the regression to a pre-marital and promiscuous stage of societies where marriage institution has been firmly established, is most unlikely. These accounts, most probably, based on hearsay, may again be referring to laxity in morals. The border land of the Punjab was being frequently invaded by foreign tribes who were naturally influencing the Āryans there. Thus the Āryans of the interior, where the Āryan culture was firmly established, wanted to keep aloof from the Punjab Āryans and looked upon them with some degree of contempt.[8] While in the Punjab the laxity of morals might have been due to foreign influence, in Māhishmatī it may have been due to luxury for it was a great trading centre of Ancient India.

1. In the Kulhu valley, Sipiti, Lahul are such areas. Laxity in morals is quite prevalent in Simla hills. Jaunsar Bāwar may be Uttar Kuru for it is in the north of Kuru land as unbelievable stories about its customs and manners are prevalent in adjacent areas. R. C. Dutt "HCAI" Vol. I, p. 120-121. Identifies it with Kashmir.

Cf. Saksena "Social Economy of a Polyandrous People" Agra University School of Social Sciences, 1955. Foreward by K. M. Munshi (p. i, ii).

2. Mbh. VIII. 40. 36 ff ; 44. 13.

3. हरिदत्त वेदालंकार "हिन्दू परिवारमीमांसा" पृष्ठ ४-६

4. Mbh. V. 39. 80. मलं पृथिव्यां वाह्लीकाः ।

Nīlkaṇṭha identifies it with the Punjab (p. 79 footnote Udyoga Parva) and so is Vāhika VIII. 44. 7.

5. Mbh. VIII. 45. 11-12.

6. Mbh. II. 31. 37-38.

7. Mbh. XIII. 2. 20 ff.

8. Mbh. VIII. 44. 7.

The account that promiscuous conditions were abolished by Śvetaketu's reforms, can also be dismissed as fiction. For this Śvetaketu, son of Uddālaka is described as a living personality in different Upanishads,[1] and conjugal fidelity was firmly established even in the Ṛg Vedic times not to speak of the later period to which Upanishads belong. It was a common practice among the composers of the Itihāsa and the Purāṇas to attach to certain things or events the name of a famous historical person so as to make the narration more vivid and lively and also to lend it an air of reality.

Marriage considered to be natural

Leaving aside these nominal references the composers and the redactors of the epics believed that marriage was a normal, natural and usual custom in every civilized society. Its performance was impossible only in a lawless and unorganized society.[2]

Varying Emphasis on Marriage-Obligation

(1) *Marriage not compulsory*

However necessary[3] and natural marriage might have been considered for women, it seems, that it was not a compulsory sacrament. According to older traditions cited in the epics, several accounts of old maids are found. When a suitable husband was not found for Sulabhā, she was instructed in the religion of emancipation.[4] Other saintly women like Śabarī and[5] Swayamprabhā[6] attaind regions of bliss through penances and services to others. The case of Subhrū, the daughter of Sage Kuṇi is different and traces a later society than cited in the former cases. Subhrū had hopes of attaining

1. R. C. Dutt "HCAI" Vol. I, Chap. II. p. 134-136.
2. Mbh. XII. 68. 22 न विवाहाः समाजो वा यदि राजा न पालयेत् ।
   Rām. II. 67. 11 नास्ति भार्याप्यराजके । Rām. VI. 123. 16—Even among the vanaras, where there was laxity in sex morals, marriage was recognized institution.
3. Mbh. I. 104. 36 अपतीनां तु नारीणामद्यप्रभृति पातकम् ।
   XIII. 46 14. भर्ता रक्षति यौवने ।
4. Mbh. XII. 320. 183. विनीता मोक्षधर्मेषु ।
5. Rām. III. 74 (sec.) Here Śramaṇī is used for Saintly women. As her preceptor Mātanga performed sacrifices there is nothing to prove her as a Buddhist nun.
6. Rām. IV. 50-51 (Sec.)

heaven through penances. Nārada, however, enlightened her that without marriage paradise was lost for her. To fulfil her object she married Śṛngavat by offering him half of the merit of her penance.[1]

(2) *Penances performed for getting accomplished husbands*

In these changing circumstances it was natural that Vedavatī was instructed by her father to do penance in order to get Vishṇu as her husband.[2] Śrutāvatī's case is very much like that of Vedavatī's.[3] Such girls did not mind performing penances for an extra-ordinary husband even if their youth or life passed away. This indicates that they did not mind foregoing marriage in case their ambitions for extra-ordinary husbands were not fulfilled.[4]

(3) *Marriage obligatory but not compulsory*

Similarly parents were anxious to get suitable matches for their daughters but the future of the girl was not sacrificed on the altar of marriage. Parents sometimes refused suits from prospective grooms even though there was the risk of the daughter having to remain unmarried.[5] The fear of refusal made the suitors hesitant in making their offer as in the case of Kaikasī[6] and Sāvitrī.[7] Well may Sītā narrate to Anusūyā that unable to get a suitable match for her, her father felt like a rich man who had lost all his wealth but we cannot easily believe it. In that case he would not have organized a 'Swayamvara' with such a stiff condition. Janaka and Drupada arranged 'Swayamvaras' to get by that means heroes full of strength and skilled in archery, as most qualified for the hand of their daughters in that heroic age. A Brāhamaṇa father like sage Vadānya had other ways of testing the man who

1. Mbh. IX. 52. 3 ff.
2. Rām. VII. 17. 8-18.
3. Mbh. IX. 48. 3 ff.
4. Rām. VII. 17. 22 त्रैलोक्यसुन्दरी भीरु यौवनं तेऽतिवर्तते ।

Mbh. IX. 48. 3-62 Śrutāvatī could only get Indra in her next life.

5. Rām. VII. 17. 10-11.
6. Rām. VII. 9. 7. पुत्रि प्रदानकालोऽयं यौवनं व्यतिवर्तते । प्रत्याख्यानाच्च भीतैस्त्वं न वरैः प्रतिगृह्यसे ।
7. Mbh. III. 293. 27, 32-36.

sought for his daughter's hand and only after it had been proved to his satisfaction that his prospective son-in-law had a chaste and noble character he consented to give away his daughter.[1] Had marriage been a compulsory sacrament, the standard of merit of the bridegroom would have been relaxed, as is the condition described by some Sūtra and Smṛti writers.[2]

(4) *Absolute importance of marriage*

In the later didactic portions the marriage of girls assumed still greater importance. The foremost duty of a father came to be the marriage of his daughter.[3] Failure in performing this duty amounted to great sin (Mahāpātaka) of Brahmahatyā,[4] and spelt great disgrace to the defaulting father.[5] For a daughter was a pledge entrusted by the maker which the father must keep carefully for her husband.[6] In the great Epic it has been repeatedly stated that falsehood spoken to bring about a marriage was not a sin.[7] Nobody was to hinder a wedding in any case.[8] Those who helped in bringing about a wedding were said to earn such merit as entitled them to a seat in heaven.[9] Those men who gave such articles as were needed in marriage ascended to the region of bliss.[10] It was in such a condition of society that the composer has stated that fathers like the great Janaka might have felt small because of

1. Mbh. XIII. 19-20 (sec.) Rām. VII. 12 (Sec.) Mbh. V. 98 ff (Sec.) indicate how fathers roam round the world to get suitable matches for their daughters.
2. Pāndey. R. B. "Hindu Sanskāras" p. 344.
3. Mbh. XIII. 44. 1-2.
4. Mbh. XIII. 24. 9.
5. Mbh. III. 293. 35 अप्रदाता पिता वाच्यो० ।
   cf. M. IX- 4 कालेऽदाता पिता वाच्यो० ।
6. Mbh. I. 157. 35 भर्तुरर्थाय निक्षिप्तां न्यासं धात्रा महात्मना ।
7. Mbh. XII. 34. 25 ; 109. 19 ; 165. 30 III. 209. 3 VIII. 69. 33 cf. Vas Dh. Ś. XVI. 35.
8. Mbh. XIII. 111. 81 उपस्थिते विवाहे तु यज्ञे दानेऽपि वा विभो ।
   मोहात्करोति यो विघ्नं स मृतो जायते कृमिः ॥
9. Mbh. XIII. 23. 91. कुटुम्बानां च दातारः पुरुषाः स्वर्गगामिनः ।
   and Nīlakaṇṭha comments कुटुम्बानां दातारः परविवाहकर्तारः ।
10. Mbh. XIII. 23. 98 वैवाहिकानां द्रव्याणां० ।
   Nīlakaṇṭha amplifies द्रव्याणां वध्वलङ्कारादीनां० ।

their failure to get suitable bridegrooms for their daughters. They naturally felt the disgrace that was attached to such failures in the prevailing state of belief.[1]

Reasons for importance

Marriage as a social and biological necessity was given religious sanctity even in the Vedic age. In the epics marriage as a prelude to life of the greatest importance[2] i.e. domestic life, gradually became an important and obligatory sacrament.

In the case of woman, however, the question of marriage has been inseparably associated with her status. When women by virtue of their intellectual education and religious status had a voice in shaping their future, marriage was not imperative for them. Thus Sulabhā and others could forego marriage and lead a life of asceticism and independence.[3] According to the belief of that age these women could work for the emancipation of their souls. With the passing of that religious status, however, and the disappearance of education their independence was lost. Entire dependence on men-folk, which came to be the rule, naturally led to compulsory marriage.[4] The success of women's life was considered in giving love (i.e. being wife) and being mother.[5] These positions could only be gained through marriage. It was said that the duties of women began with marriage.[6] The status of religious partner of the husband was gained by women through the sacrament of marriage. Otherwise a woman had no religious status in a society where such a status was prized. But in later societies she was an ignorant partner of a learned husband. Therefore it was natural that marriage had an educative value for her. Husbands thus assumed the position of preceptors.[7] Thus it is that all the synonyms of marriage indicate her going near the husband perhaps in the same spirit and state of submissiveness

1. Rām. II. 118. 34-36 VII. 9. 9-10. VII. 12. 11. Mbh. XIII. 44. 16. Page 52 of this chapter.
2. See chap. "Married life" Mbh. XII. 12. 12 ff.
3. Ante. page 22 and "Maid and her status".
4. Mbh. XIII. 43. 19 ; 46. 14.
5. Mbh. V. 39. 67 रतिपुत्रफला नारी ।
6. Mbh. XIII. 146. 34
7. Rām. II. 118. 2.

as that of a disciple to the guru.[1] Thus "Pāṇigrahaṇa",[2] taking of the hand, was the symbol of taking charge. 'Upayāma'[3] another word for marriage means 'acceptance' or "to take as one's own." This indicates the idea of "Upanayana", where the guru takes over the charge of the disciple.

It has been already shown that even the attainment of paradise for women depended upon marriage.[4] The religion prescribed for them was the service of the husband. Through these services women could attain heaven.[5] Naturally husband was for women a divine incarnation, a god as well, to be gained only through marriage.[6] Thus women's education, worldly duties as well as emancipation depended upon marriage but in these conditions her status was not that of an equal partner of the husband but of a disciple and devotee.

To crown all, there was the question of imperative chastity for women which will be discussed later. To guard it, it was necessary that she must have protectors throughout her life,[7] and not to have one in her youth would have been a calamity. It was through marriage that she got such a protector in her husband, to live without him was considered sin for her.[8]

It was natural that when such importance was attached to marriage for girls, fathers would have been anxious to give away their daughters as already shown. In such social conditions if sometimes a suitable bridegroom was in view the bride may have been given away a little before she attained youth, or even disparity in age of the couple may have been overlooked.

Age of marriage

The question of marriageable age for girls is one of the most debatable points in ancient social history. As the epics,

1. M. II. 67 ; Vi. Dh. S. XXII. 32 स्त्रीणां विवाह संस्कारः ।
2. Mbh. XIII. 44. 55, 49.
3. Mbh. I. 95. 14, 15, 16 etc.
4. Ante p. 37-28.
5. Mbh. III. 205. 22-23. Mbh. XIII. 46. 13 ; Vishṇu. Dh, S. XXV 13-14 forbids fasts etc. explicitly Rām. II. 24. 26. 27 ; 118. 8-10.
6. Rām. II. 117. 22.
7. Mbh. XIII. 46. 14, 8 ff ; 20. 14, 20, 21.
8. Mbh. I. 104. 36 अपतीनां तु नारीणामद्यप्रभृति पातकम् ।

particularly the Mahābhārata include many older traditions as well as later ones in the redacted portions the data on this account is contradictory. It represents various stages of a changing society. In fact all the conditions that prevailed from the time of the Ṛg-Veda to those described in the earlier smṛties are reflected in the great Epic.

Post-puberty marriage in the epics

Post puberty marriages are generally referred to in the Ṛg-Veda[1] and earlier Gṛhya Sūtras.[2] In the Ṛg-Veda there is mention of unmarried girls growing old in their parental home.[3] This condition has parallels in the Mahābhārata. Subhrū's case has already been cited and some old maids have been described as entertaining hopes of getting married.[4] These, however, must have been rare cases. The conditions described in the gṛhysūtras are also reflected in the epic stories. Maidens have been often described as full of beauty and youth, i.e. Rūpayauvana sampannā[5] and post puberty marriage is generally implied. Kuntī and Satyavatī were already mothers when married. Subhadrā must have been grown up for Arjuna would not have fallen in love with a child.[6] Knowing that her husband was blind, Gāndhārī had the sense to tie cloth on her eyes. This can never be expected of a child bride.[7] Uttarā, although she played with her dolls, had attained age before her marriage,[8] birth of Parīkshita within the year of her marriage points to the same. There, of course, could not be doubt about the maturity of Damayantī,[9] who was in love with

1. Upādhyāya, B. S. "Women in Ṛg Veda" p. 50-54.
Pāndey R. B. "Hindu Saṁskāra" 316-317.
2. Sāns. G. S. 1. 17. 5 Ap. G. S. 3. 8. 8. Khadira G. S. 1. 4. 10 Asv. G. S. 1. 8. 10 Kathaka G. S. 30. 1. A doubtful case of child marriage in Chh. Up. 1. 101 has been well explained by Dr. R. B. Pāndey "Hindu Saṁskāra", p. 318.
3. Ṛg—V. I. 117. 7 ; II. 17. 7 ; X. 40. 5
4. Mbh. IX. 52 (sec.) XII. 128-18.
5. Mbh. I. 82. 6-7.
6. Mbh. I. 219. 15 ; 220. 7.
7. Mbh. I. 110. 14.
8. Mbh. IV. 37. 28 ; 66. 12 ff ; 69. 15-16 & 72. 4. वयस्थया तया राजन् सह संवत्सरोषितः ।
9. Mbh. III. 54. 1 ff.

Nala before marriage ; of Sāvitrī[1] who went to choose her husband, of Śakuntalā and Gangā[2] who married by the Gāndharva form and of Draupadī who refused to marry Sūtaputra and took charge of her family immediately after Swayamvara even before her marriage. Draupadī's marriage was consummated after the ceremonies daily for five days.[3] Śarmishṭhā and Lopāmudrā both had attained age. Devayānī had attained youth when she was in love with Kacha, naturally so when she proposed to Yayāti.[4] A Brāhmaṇa father also states that his duty was to give away his daughter only after she had attained age.[5] According to the Rāmāyaṇa the marriage of Sītā and her sisters were consummated immediately after they returned to Ayodhyā.[6] Sītā narrates to Anusūyā that she was grown up before her marriage.[7] Kaikesī and Maṇḍodarī also were of age before marriage.[8] Thus there is not a single case to indicate that child marriage was practised.

Better status of maiden implied by such marriages

Only in such marriages the dignity of a maiden could be maintained. Only a grown up girl could exercise her right of choice and consent. In most of these cases she could not be given as a chattel to the family of her husband or as disciple or devotee to him. Here she was bestowed as a partner of her husband in performance of secular and spiritual duties. This was not her position in theory but in practice as well. She was aware of and fit to perform her duties of wifehood and motherhood successfully.

References to child marriage in the epics

The only passage in the Rāmāyaṇa where Sītā described

1. Mbh. III 294 (sec.)
2. Mbh. I. 73. 15 ff; 98. 2 ff.
3. Mbh. I. 187. 23 ; 192. 7 ff ; 198. 14.
4. Mbh. I. 82. 6-7 ; 76. 25-26 ; 78. 16-17 Acc. to Nīlakaṇṭha Śyāma is of sixteen years—a youthful maiden.
5. Mbh. I. 157. 35 बालमप्राप्तवयसमजातव्यञ्जनाकृतिम् ।
भर्तुरर्थाय निक्षिप्तां न्यासं धात्रा महात्मना ॥
6. Rām. I. 77. 14 रेमिरे मुदिताः सर्वा भर्तृभिः सहिता रहः ।
7. Rām. II. 118. 34. पतिसंयोगसुलभं वयो दृष्ट्वा तु मे पिता ।
8. Rām. VII. 9.7 ff. पुत्रि प्रदानकालोऽयं यौवनं व्यतिवर्तते ।

herself as six years old at the time of marriage, is clearly a redacted one.[1] How could Sītā who was so much worried about Rāma's safety, discuss her and her husband's age, with a complete stranger. As shown already she was grown up when married.

In one śloka from the redacted portion of the Mahābhārata the age of marriage prescribed for girls is even lower than that described by Manu.[2] Kaṇe[3] thinks that the lower age reading of the verse is correct on the basis of metre. In 'Vīrmitrodaya Sanskāra Prakāśa[4] and Udvahatattva[5] the reading is "Shoḍaśavarshām" for "Daśavarshām." It is quite possible that the former composer may not have been very particular about the metre and recommended sixteen years which was changed by redactors into ten years. Dr. Altekar had already shown how "Nagnikā" in the above mentioned verse first meant a grown up girl and later a small girl playing with dust.[6]

Disparity of age between bride and bridegroom

The above mentioned Śloka also suggests a disparity in age of bride and bridegroom, which is nowhere found in the Rāmāyaṇa, where even in the redacted portion the difference between Rāma's and Sītā's age is of seven years.[7] In the narrative part of the Mahābhārata there are rare instances of young maidens, not immature girls, given to old men in

1. Rām. III. 47. 4 उषित्वा द्वादश समा इक्ष्वाकूणां निवेशने ।
10. मम भर्ता महातेजा वयसा पञ्चविंशकः ।
अष्टादश हि वर्षाणि मम जन्मनि गण्यते ।।

2. Mbh. XIII. 44.14 त्रिंशद्वर्षो दशवर्षां भार्यां विन्देत नग्निकाम् ।
एकविंशतिवर्षो वा सप्तवर्षामवाप्नुयात् ।।
Cf. M. IX 94. त्रिंशद्वर्षोद्वहेत्कन्यां हृद्यां द्वादशवार्षिकीम् ।
त्र्यष्टवर्षोऽष्टवर्षां वा धर्मे सीदति सत्वरः ।।

3. Kaṇe, "History of Dh." Vol. II, Part I. p. 438-439.

4. p. 766.

5. p. 123.

6. Altekar "PWHC" chap. II. p. 61 referring to Mātṛdatta's commentary. Cf. Kaṇe "History of Dh." Vol. II, Part I, p. 440.

7. Rām. III. 47. 10 as quoted in note one. In the Mbh. XIII. 44. 14 Ten years old girl is to be married to thirty years old man and seven years old to twenty-one year old one, according to later reading.

marriage. Virāṭa is ready to bestow his young daughter upon Arjuna who was definitely sixty-five years old if not much more.[1] Gautāma was prepared to give his daughter to Uttanka who was very old. As such sacrifice of maiden's interest was not liked by the society in Uttanka's case, a miracle is introduced by the composer and he is transformed into a youth.[2] Elsewhere a simile describes a young maiden not liking a husband of sixty.[3] Such rare cases occur in every society. It must, however, be borne in mind that in the above mentioned two cases it was due to the accomplishments of the proposed bridegrooms that the fathers of maidens were tempted. Usually it was difficult to get brides in old age.[4]

Child marriage not the general rule

On the basis of the above mentioned scanty data (i.e. one spurious passage in the Rāmāyaṇa and another redacted śloka from the Mahābhārata, which definitely contains Dharmaśāstra material) it can not be upheld that child marriages generally prevailed even in the later societies depicted in the epics. For the didactic portions also suggest attainment of womanhood as necessary qualification for marriage, in tune with the earlier sūtras.[5] This age of marriage, just after the advent of puberty i.e. near about sixteen to eighteen years, as opposed to late marriage, has been considered even by modern researches on family happiness as the correct age for marriage. At this time the girl is physically and emotionally mature but not so intellectually and thus there are greater chances of adjustment to the new environment.[6]

1. Mbh. IV. 43. 6 पार्थ : पञ्च च षष्टि च वर्षाणि श्वेतवाहनः ।
2. Mbh. XIV. 56. 9 ff, 21-24.
3. Mbh. II. 64. 14 ; III 5. 15. पतिः कुमार्या इव षष्टिवर्षाः । Rām. II. 10. 23.
4. Mbh. I. 46.11 न च स्म लभते भार्यां वृद्धोऽयमिति शौनकः ।
5. Mbh. XIII. 44.16. त्रीणिवर्षाण्युदीक्षेत कन्या ऋतुमती सती ।
चतुर्थे त्वथ संप्राप्ते स्वयं भर्तारमर्जयेत् ॥

Mbh. XIII. 104. 124. वयस्थां च महाप्राज्ञः कन्यामवोढुमर्हति ।

Cf. footnotes Pandey "Hindu Saṁskāra" p. 322. quoting Vas. Dh. S. XVII. 67-68, 70 ; B. D. S. IV 1. 12-14.

6. Havelock Ellis ("Psychology of Sex" Vol. VI) "Sex in Society" Chap. XII. 395-397. S. Radhākṛshnan "Religion and Society", p. 170 (1947, London), Prabhu "Hindu Social Organization" p. 185-192.

A tendency of lowering down the marriageable age

Child marriages as discussed above, were not the general rule. It cannot be, however, denied that Dharmasūtras written between 600 B.C. to 300 B.C.[1] indicate a tendency of lowering down the age of marriage. This tendency as shown above is reflected in the redacted portions of the epics. Contradictory remarks, on the question of child marriages in the epics and Manusmṛti, suggest a transition period.[2] Not only in the redacted portions of the great Epic post puberty age of marrige is implied but even much later works like the "Kāmasūtra" and the "Vishṇu Purāṇa" advocate it.[3] This debatable point of pre-puberty and post puberty period was at last decided in favour of child marriages near about 100 A.D.[4]

Reasons that favoured child marriages for maidens

(*i*) *Ṛtu*

In the didactic portion even when attainment of womanhood is suggested as a qualification for marriage[5] there is a tendency of not letting maiden remain unmarried much longer after puberty. As ṛtu[6] was considered the proper time for conception, it was a sign of divine call and unavoidable duty for woman. Ṛtu was not to slip without being made use of, for it was woman's calling to bring forth. So in case a father failed to get a bridegroom, the daughter was given independence to choose for herself otherwise she incurred sin against "prajāpati."[7] Therefore it was that the father was to find

1. Cf. Kaṇe "History of Dh." Vol. II. Part I, Chronological table p. xi Dharmasūtras of Vaśishṭha, Baudhāyana and Gautama are assigned 300 to 600 B. C.

2. M. IX. 88-90.

3. Vātsyāyana 'Kām. S. III. 1.2. that a man must marry after the completion of his education (generally at 21 or 24) and the girl must be three years younger than him. She would be grown up then.

Ibid., III. 5. 29-30 is in favour of the Gāndharva form which suggests again a grown up girl. Vishṇu Puraṇa III. 10.16.

4. Y. S. I. 52. अनन्यपूर्विकां० ।

5. Mbh. XIII. 44. 16 as quoted in note 5 of previous page.

6. Ṛtu denotes the first twelve or sixteen days after menstruation (M. III. 45-50; IV. 128).

7. Mbh. XIII. 44.17 न प्रजा हीयते तस्या रतिश्च भरतर्षभ ।
अतोऽन्यथा वर्तमाना भवेद्वाच्या प्रजापतेः ॥

a worthy husband for his daughter before this event. In this competition for securing bridegrooms fathers must have been in a hurry to get their daughters married otherwise they were considered defaulters in performing their sacred duty of bestowing their daughters. So if the fathers secured a worthy bridegroom they married their daughter even at an early age.

(ii) Idea of chastity rather than the foreign invasions responsible for lowering down the age of marriage

It has been said that the custom of child marriage, was due to the foreign invasion after 300 B. C. The foreigners who invaded from north-west frontier were often wanting in proper respect for the honour of Indian women. Under these social conditions it was more convenient for fathers to get their daughters married soon, even in childhood when the question of chastity did not arise. Pre-marriage chastity has assumed great importance because the character of women in such areas may have been doubted.[1] It must, however, be borne in mind that virginity as the qualification of marriage was stressed in the earlier Dharmasūtras[2] written before the foreign invasion. Moreover, the foreign invasions might have had social repercussions mostly in the north-western part of India by about 100 A.D. So the real reason for child-marriages seems to be a rigid chastity imposed upon women.[3] The idea was that the wife was the completest possible possession of the husband. She must be given to him pure and unsullied and must continue to remain so, as through her he continues his line.[4] Thus maidens were considered to have been entrusted in the safe custody of fathers by God[5] for performing this duty.

1. R. B. Pāndey. "Hindu Saṁskāras" p. 322.

2. Earlier Sūtras Vas. Dh. S. 8. 1 ; Āp. Dh. S. II. 6.13.1 ; Gaut. Dh. S. IV, 1 ; Ap. G. S. I. 6.19.2. states that a girl chaste and virgin was to be married. Later M. IX. 47. Y. S.I. 52, Vi. Dh. S. V. 45-47 advocate the same.

3. Mbh. XIII. 146. 43.

4. Mbh. III. 12.96.

5. Mbh. I. 157. 35 as quoted in foot-note 5. page 43.

In the contemporary literature it was believed that Soma, Agni and Gandharva enjoyed the maiden. This may be an indirect reference to her physical, emotional and aesthetic growth, but due to superstition it was thought that she should be married even before she was enjoyed by these, when she was a child. cf. Kaṇe "Hist. of Dh." Vol. II Part I, p. 443.

(*iii*) *Disappearance of intellectual education*

The denial of the right of intellectual education to girls has been already mentioned. In case the maidens were allowed to pursue such specialized education the lowest marriageable age for them would have to be near about twenty-two and the highest forty-six, which for psychological and biological reasons could not have been allowed by any society. When thus the education of girls was limited to domestic sciences,[1] it was useless to waste their time at the parental home. They could secure that education from their mothers-in-law side by side could inculcate love for their permanent home in their impressionable years. They could know their family traditions better and as already mentioned the husband assumed the status of preceptor in the epics as well as in the contemporary smṛties.[2] As for the boys so for the girls also education was to begin early, which in the latter case meant marriage.

(*iv*) *To check women from joining nunneries*

The redacted portions of the great Epic were written after the advent of Buddhism. Although nothing can be asserted about the knowledge of Buddhism of the composer of the Rāmāyaṇa yet nuns were known to him.[3] In the post Buddha period women from all walks of society were taking to nunneries.[4] Since Hinduism, as reflected in the epics was against such religious activities of women,[5] therefore Brāhmaṇa priests might have thought of curbing the intellectual activities of women by prescribing the earlier age of marriage.

1. See Chap. I. "Maid, Her status and Education".
2. Rām. II. 118. 2. नार्याः पतिर्गुरुः ।

Cf. M. II. 67 वैवाहिको विधिः स्त्रीणां संस्कारो वैदिकः स्मृतः ।
पतिसेवा गुरौ वासो गृहार्थोऽग्निपरिक्रिया ॥

Another verse proves, discontinuation of religious studies M. II. 66
अमंत्रिका तु कार्येयं स्त्रीणामावृदशेषतः ।
संस्कारार्थं शरीरस्य यथाकालं यथाक्रमम् ॥

Thus there was no sense in performing upanyana without Mantras.

3. Rām. II. 29. 13 "भिक्षिण्याः ।"; III. 74.7 ; IV. 51.1.
4. "Women under Primative Buddhism" by Horner p. 167-8. Women of royal, Brāhmaṇa families as well as of unknown caste and courtezans joined the order.
5. Mbh. XIII. 46. 13.

(v) To check inter-caste and love marriages

The conversion of Varṇas into Jātis and the exclusive and conservative character of the society might have resulted in checking intercaste and inter-racial marriages. But when freedom of love and courtship was a practice before marriage this was not possible. Infant marriages may have been introduced as a device to curb this form of incontinence.

Results

This tendency of lowering down the age of marriage was disastrous for girls. Their status under these conditions was that of a chattel to be given away at the sweet will of the guardians. As an ignorant wife she was no more partner of her educated husband but her status was that of a disciple and devotee. The only purpose of their lives in such conditions was to bear children.[1] In order to fulfil this purpose assigned by providence not only were they intellectually starved but physically run down. In this fall of motherhood a people's fall was inevitable.

Order of Seniority

In the didactic portions there was a feeling of resentment in society for breaking the order of seniority in matrimony. It has been stated that a man, who marries the younger sister before her elder sister was married, is a sinner and must perform expiation.[2] As there is no penance prescribed it may be assumed that in the period when girls had the right of selection and choice such cases might have occurred. Later when the marriage of girls was assuming absolute importance, it was better to get any sister married first, irrespective of the age, in case she got a good match. But usually in marriages arranged one naturally avoided the younger sister, for if the younger sister was married first it would be difficult for the elder sister to get a husband. The suitors may think that her

1. Mbh. V. 39. 67 रतिपुत्रफला नारी ।

2. Mbh. XII. 34. 4, 15. Such younger sister was known as "Agre Didhishu" and the elder sister "Didhishu." According to Manu III. 170-76 her husband should not be called in Śraddā dinner as he is polluter of the line पंक्तिदूष्य cf. Gaut. Dh. S. XV. 16. Vi. Dh. S. XXXVII. 13.15. LIV. 16 These legislations were to discourage such marriages.

claim was overlooked because of some defect. Among the ancient Jews also there was a custom of prohibiting the marriage of the younger sister before that of the elder.[1]

The social resentment was more felt when a younger brother married before the elder brother, and for this actual penance is prescribed in the didactic portions of the great Epic as well as in the Rāmāyaṇa. He was to do kṛchha penance for twelve days, or had to perform chāndrāyaṇa and kṛchha penance and offer his wife to the elder brother and after taking his permission was to wed her again.[2] Such younger brother was known as Parivettā and the elder one Parivitta. According to the great Epic as well as Manu both brothers were polluters of the line "Panktidūshyas".[3] According to Rāmāyaṇa 'parivettā' attained hell.[4] Arjuna states that he does not want to earn the sin of becoming Parivettā.[5]

Right of selection

The right of maidens to have a voice in the selection of their life-partner is naturally inseparably associated with the question of age of marriage. As grown up maidens only they could exercise it. With the tendency of lowering down the age of marriage such right was lost to them.

Older traditions depict right of selection

Thus it is that in the older traditions when grown up maidens were married, examples of chosing life partners by them are to be found. This real self-choice was known as

1. Holy Bible—Old Testament, Genesis 29. 25-26 Jacob wanted Rachel the younger one but Laban, bestowed Leah, the elder one to him first, pleading in name of the custom.

2. Rām. IV. 17. 34-35. Mbh. XII. 34. 3-4 XII. 35. 27-30 XII. 165. 68-70. Cf. "Primitive family. Its origin and development" : In Assam the younger brother cannot marry before the unwedded elder one, but only if the elder one gives in writing. Then he cannot marry any longer. In Germany such elder brother is laughed at and has to dance in swine's trough. Cf. Vas. Dh. S. XX. 7-10 prescribes kṛchhra penance for 20 days and even the sisters who are thus married are to be offered to each other's husbands and then with their consent remarried. Vi. Dh. S. XXXVII. 15-17, LIV. 16. Baud. Dh. S. IV. 6. 7,6. Ap. Dh. S. II. 5.12. 22-23. Gaut. Dh. S. XV. 16. Y. S. I. 223.

3. Mbh. XIII. 90.10 M. III. 154.

4. Rām. IV. 17.34 नास्तिकः परिवेत्ता च सर्वे निरयगामिनः ।
Cf. M. III. 171.

5. Mbh. I. 191.8-10.

Gāndharva form of the marriage and will be dealt with later at its proper place.[1]

(i) Bride and bridegroom

It was natural that generally the initiative in proposing was taken by the young men in the cases of self choice. There were, however, some bold women like Śūrpaṇakhā, Ulūpī, Hiḍimbā, Gangā and Devayānī who took the initiative.[2] Such exceptional cases may have been the result of bold individual temperament. This, however, indicates the unusual freedom maidens had in selecting their partners.

Father's consent nominal

In some older traditions the father's consent, after the choice was made, seems to be nominal. In the case of Devayani need for her father's approval was due to the fact that Yayātī was not ready to consent to her proposal, being afraid of Śukra's curse. Damayantī and Ambā had made their choice before their Svayamvaras. The incredulous swan-episode may have been added to Damayantī's story to suit a later opinion, when pre-marital love was not approved. But it was so unbelievable that the author had to arrange a meeting between Nala and Damayantī before the marriage.[3]

Some exceptional cases

Some older traditions, however, show that previous consent of father or guardian was given for exercising the right of self-choice. As already indicated Sāvitrī and Kaikasī were given the right to choose for themselves only when their fathers received no proposal, due to the high accomplishments of both the maidens. Sāvitrī's father was afraid of impending public slur and gave her full freedom to stick to her choice.[4] This was real self-choice. Sumālī, however, thought it better to direct Kaikasī.[5] Such direction on the part of parents was

1. See "Marriage" part II. Chap. IV.
2. Rām. III. 18. 24 ff; Mbh. I, 152. 27 ff; I. 214.18 ff. Mbh. I. 77.5; 81.17.
3. Mbh. I. 81. 23-27 ; III 53-56 (sec.)
4. Mbh. III. 293. 32 ff.
5. Rām. VII. 9.10 ff.

on the increase. Another kind of Svayamvara is that of Keśinī, who to satisfy herself puts questions to the suitors.[1] In the Rāmāyaṇa we come across a strange kind of self choice when many dames came to Rāvaṇa just because they were attracted or impressed by his qualities.[2] Some of these above mentioned cases, especially the last one, are, isolated examples and it will be wrong to infer from these that any custom prevailed.

The above mentioned cases, indicate that maidens were grown-up, independent and intellectually mature to decide about their life-partner for which they were given freedom by society. Sticking to their choice, once it was made, through thick and thin, is as much indicative of their maturity in judgement as of their pātivratā ideals. For ideals are only followed blindly by those who have no independent judgement. In these cases a maiden was not given away as a chattel. As she could decide her future in a dignified way she was not a burden for her parents.

Right of selection on decline

Gradually the right of selection, granted to maidens, was on the decline. The later redactors of the great Epic and Dharmaśāstrakāras allowed the right of self choice to the daughter in case the father was unable to marry her off within three years (or three months according to some) after puberty.[3] Her father's losing authority over her and her forfeiting the claim to the family jewels clearly point out that the punishments to both were given because such self choice was unpopular and therefore the legal writers wanted to discourage it. The only example of this kind of self choice is that of Śarmisṭhā's. She had no wide choice as no body could enter Yayāti's harem and so demanded from him not only the right of ṛtu, but husbandhood as well.[4]

Epic Svayaṃvaras did not give right of self-choice

The word "Svayamvara" has been used as real "self-choice" twice only; once by Kuśanābha's daughters when

1. Mbh. V. 35. 6-7 ff.
2. Rām. V. 9. 69-71.
3. Mbh. XIII. 44.16. cf. M. IX. 90. 92.
4. Mbh. I. 82. 12-23.

Vāyu made a proposal[1] and next by Bhīshma when he was abducting the three daughters of Kāśirāja.[2] Although the word 'Svayamvara' itself means self-choice, yet this was not the case with most of the epic Svayamvaras.

Right of preference in choice given

For the maidens, the epic-Svayamvara custom gave the right of preference and not that of self-choice. In this kind of Svayamvara it was either love at first sight that made the girl choose her mate[3] or she had heard about the hero and was already in love with him.[4] When the maiden was already in love it was natural for her to dislike Svayamvara.[5]

In certain cases Svayamvara held twice

Damayantī's Svayamvara reveals another aspect of Svayamvara custom. Ṛtuparṇa, without doubting, came to attend Damayantī's second Svayamvara. This means that if no trace of husband was found Svayamvara could be held a second time.[6]

Svayamvara of Vīraśulkā

Another kind of Svayamvara in tune with the epic traditions was the one in which the girl was Vīraśulkā, i.e. her price was to be paid in the form of valour. Thus Janaka and Drupada arranged tough tests for selecting sons-in-law.[7] This was not real self choice for the girls used to be pawns. Draupadī's refusal to marry Sūta Karṇa however, indicates that a limited choice was given to the girl.[8] Such choice may not be pronounced if the maiden did not like a Kshatriya for

1. Rām. I. 32.20 मा भूत्स कालो दुर्मेघः पितरं सत्यवादिनम् ।
अवमन्य स्वधर्मेण स्वयंवरमुपास्महे ॥
2. Mbh. I. 102. 11 भीष्मस्तदा स्वयं कन्या वरयामास ताः प्रभुः ।
16. स्वयंवरं तु राजन्याः प्रशंसन्त्युपयान्ति च ।
प्रमथ्य तु हृतामाहुर्ज्यायसीं धर्मवादिनः ।
3. Mbh. I. 112. 7-9.
4. Mbh. III. 53 ; I. 102.61.
5. Mbh. V. 175.31.
6. Mbh. III. 57. 70-71 (sections) In such cases grass widows were allowed to marry Vas. Dh. S. XVII 75-76, Nārada XII. 99.
7. Rām. I. 67. 14 Mbh. I. 185. 35 ff ; I. 95. 77.
8. Mbh. I. 187. 23.

in any case if he wanted he could lift her. Draupadī's refusal and its approval by the assembly was due to the hatred for mixed classes.[1]

Thus epic Svayamvara was only a method of selection which more or less served the same purpose as matrimonial advertisements of today. The writers of law books did not mention it for it was followed only by the Kshatriya kings and not even by a particular class.[2] Hopkins forwards another reason for this omission. He thinks that as epic Svayamvara was a later development of original prājāpatya form, therefore there was no need to mention it.[3] But Svayamvara was practised even after the epics and even then it finds no place in much later smṛtis, where prājāpatya is still recognised as a prevalent form. The real reason for this omission is that it was a form of selection, the real marriage was performed according to Brāhma form after it. It is possible too that the parents resorted to this method in order to avoid unpleasantness of Rākshasa form, but in this attempt, however, they were not always successful.[4]

Parental control on increase

Gradually the right of self-choice was being limited. The Svayamvara of Vīraśulkā type was hardly worth the name. When parents organized Svayaṁvara they might have controlled it to a certain extent. Kuśanābha's daughters denounced the right of self-choice in harsh terms.[5] The didactic por-

1. Mbh. XIII. 48.1 ff; VI. 25.41 (G.I. 41); VI. 27.24 (G.S. III.24).

2. In this royal gathering Brāhmaṇas only came to witness and receive presents. (Mbh. I. 184. 5-19 ; I. 185.13—15). Dhṛṣṭadyumna only addressed the kings and princes (Mbh. I. 185.35). Arjuna who was in guise of a Brāhmaṇa only ventured to try when the kings and the princes failed. (Mbh. I. 188.1). Even after he had won the competition the princes were not ready to suffer the defeat without a fight (Mbh. I. 189. 7) Drupada's question to Yudhishṭhira seems absurd. (Mbh. I. 195.2-3) Had the Pāṇḍavas been Śūdras Draupadī would have raised objection then and there for the status of the Śūdra was far below that of a Sūta, whom she refused. (Mbh. I. 187.23) Karṇa, a supposed Sūta had right to read Vedas which Śūdras were denied (Rām. VII 74-76) ; (Mbh. V. 140.7).

3. J. O. A. S. Vol. XIII. Art III. "The social and military position of ruling caste in India as represented by the Sanskrit Epic" Edwards Hopkins Appendix on "the status of women".
See in "The forms of marriage" of next chapter.

4. Mbh. I. 102. 16 ff ; Rām. I. 66.16-23. ; Mbh. VII. 11.10 ; 144. 9 ff. XII. 4. So the amphitheatre used to be well fortified, Mbh. I. 185. 17.

5. Rām. I. 32.30. VII. 80. 9-11

tions of the great Epic favour and eulogize the Brāhma form according to which fathers bestowed daughters.[1] Fathers also considered this to be their duty.[2] Even in such a case of premarital love (which was in no way less than that of Sāvitrī for Satyavān) as of Ruru[3], his father arranged for his marriage. Sumālī's guidance,[4] refusal of Tapatī[5] and Kuśanābha's daughters,[6] Mātali's efforts,[7] all point out to increasing parental control over the question of marriage of their daughters. Nārada states that no marriage is complete without guardian's consent i.e. Kanyādāna.[8] The marriages of Gāndhārī, Uttarā and Sukanyā were performed by the guardians.

Brother as guardian for sister

The responsibility of bestowing a fatherless daughter used to fall upon the brother.[9] Vibhīshaṇa blames Rāvaṇa for not being able to perform this duty for Kumbhīnāsī.[10] It was perhaps due to the loss of independence of woman and for her helplessness that a mother's status was put very low in the lists of the guardians who were to bestow the maiden.[11] According to the Mahābhārata kinsmen also had the right to give away the bride.[12]

Reasons for disappearance of self-choice and establishment of guardian's control

Many factors may have contributed to the disappearance of self-choice for maidens as well as for the increased control

1. Mbh. XIII. 44. 3, 4 ; 93. 36 ; 94.44 ; 57.25, 32.
2. Mbh. I. 157. 35 as quoted in page 43. note 5.
   Cf. later Kālidāsa's "Abhigyāna Śākuntalam" Act. IV. 24.
   Cf. Chap. I "Maid her status and her education".
3. Mbh. I. 8.14. ff.
4. Rām. VII. 9.11 ff.
5. Mbh. I. 172. 20 ff.
6. Rām. I. 32.20
7. Mbh. V. 97.19 ff ; 98. (sec.).
8. Mbh. VII. 55. 15-16.
9. Mbh. I. 113. 6 ff.
10. Rām. VII. 25.28 यस्मादवश्यं दातव्या कन्या भर्त्रे हि भ्रातृभिः ।
11. Mbh. I. 158. 16-19 indicates inability. cf. Y. S. I. 63.
12. Mbh. XIII. 44.25 बन्धुभिः समनुज्ञाते । 26. 'ज्ञातिभिः कृतः'

of guardians over the marriage question. As will be shown later the results of Gāndharva form were not very encouraging. While Śakuntalā was abandoned at the very outset by her husband, Suśobhanā left her husband—a conduct which was considered faulty on her part even by her father. He bestowed her upon her husband again commanding her to serve him.[1] But these stories indicate that only when the guardians arranged marriage i.e. when it has sanction of the society it results in lasting relationship. It was in view of giving stability to marriage institution that great merits were attached to Brāhma form.

Other reasons were that the maidens themselves were incapable of making a suitable choice due to their ignorance which was the result of the denial of intellectual and religious education. The reduction of marriageable age, however, may have been responsible for curbing this freedom altogether. All these questions have been already dealt with.

Results of guardian's control on the future of the maiden

Human nature being what it is, it can never be asserted that future happiness of maidens was always in the view of the guardians. There were, of course fathers like Dāśarāja, who guided by the interest of his daughter took advantage of the situation and refused a royal proposal.[2] These conditions perhaps prevailed among the common people. For the royal families generally, heroism and family were of much more importance than any other consideration. In case, the bridegrooms belonged to good families they were not considered disqualified by kings for their daughters even if old,[3] blind[4] or polygamous.[5] Śalya was more worried about Śulka than the qualifications of the bridegroom.[6] Thus the bride may be bestowed as chattel sometimes by the guardians, she had no right or capacity to make any choice. Although these condi-

1. Mbh. III. 192. 9-37.
2. Mbh. I. 100. 53, 54 ff. Rām. II. 107.3 In Kaikeyī's case it may have been the same although the fact was never insisted by her.
3. Mbh. IV. 43.6 Arjuna's age ; 71.34.
4. Mbh. I. 110. 11 ff.
5. Mbh. I. 113. 9 ff.
6. Ibid.

tions indicate inferior social position of maidens yet under the circumstances when they were ignorant it was better for them to be guided by experienced opinion. Even otherwise, mostly in epic Svayamvaras where the right of selection was based upon desire, which cannot be the basis of permanent relationship, such opinion would have been better.

In arranging marriages it was natural for the guardians to look into the qualifications and disqualifications of proposed brides and bridegrooms. These are described in the didactic portions which recommend arranged marriages.

Qualifications of the bride (1) *Kula, i.e. family*

According to the composer of the Anuśāsana Parva the maiden to be wedded must belong to a high family.[1] A woman of inferior order or that is fallen away from the order of her birth should never be taken by one who is desireous of prosperity.[2] 'Mahākulas' i.e. great families as defined by Vidura are to be judged by conduct, learning and pure-marriages. Thus these include intellectual and moral qualifications. By leaving the prescribed conduct "Mahākulas" could be degraded.[3] It is stated that even for expiation of sins one should marry in 'Mahākulas', high families.[4] Now these injunctions were prescribing a code of morality from the material of Dharmaśāstras. Nevertheless, these propounders of law gave concession to human nature and weakness. They had consideration for the daughters of the fallen families for these must be married and were not to suffer for the faults of their parents. Thus it was ordained that even a low born woman who is an ornament of her sex, may be taken as wife, and women like

1. Mbh. XIII. 104. 123 महाकुले प्रसूतां च ।
   Cf. Vas. Dh. S. I. 38
   Mbh. XIII. 104. 136. महाकुले निवेष्टव्यं सदृशे वा युधिष्ठिर ।
2. Mbh. XIII. 104. 136. अवरा पतिता चैव न ग्राह्या भूतिमिच्छता ॥
3. Mbh. V. 36. 23-31, 59. cf. Baud. Dh. S. I. 5.10, 29, 26.
   Y. S. I. 54.
4. Mbh. XII. 134. 12-13. अत्रैतदाहुराचार्याः पापस्य परिमोक्षणे ।
   महामनाश्चापि भवेद्विवहे च महाकुले ॥

water and jewels can never be impure.[1] The respect of blue blood, although always a consideration,[2] could not have been enforced when society was free. In case of love at first sight, as of Śāntanu for Satyawatī and Gangā, nothing about family was known and so it was natural that in such marriages 'kula' considerations relaxed.[3]

Physical qualification (i) Beauty

Beauty is the power of woman[4] and it has been prized every where. Therefore the bride to be married was to be handsome.[5]

(*ii*) *Auspicious marks*

The conception of beauty is indicated by the "auspicious marks"[6] in the epics though the composers do not give similar accounts of the marks yet these include all the details of the grace of physical form and beauty of each limb.[7]

It was a superstitious belief that women with auspicious marks had not to suffer widowhood, were crowned with their husbands and were to have "Chakravartī" sons.[8] Mitāksharā, commenting on Yājwalka-Smṛti, states that these are signs of potential motherhood.[9]

1. Mbh. XII. 165. 32 स्त्रीरत्नं दुष्कुलादपि ।
अदूष्या हि स्त्रियो रत्नमपि इत्यव धर्मतः ।

cf. Manu. II. 238-240. Vas. Dh. S. XIII. 51-53 female offspring of an outcaste could be married without taking dowry.

2. Mbh. I. 110.6 कुलीना रूपवत्यश्च । Rām. V. 9. 72, V. 16.5.

3. Mbh. I. 97. 27 ff; 100. 47 ff.

4. Mbh. XII. 320.73. रूपयौवनसौभाग्यं स्त्रीणां बलमनुत्तमम् ।

5. Mbh. XIII. 104.135. मनोज्ञां दर्शनीयां च तां भवान्वोढुमर्हति ।

Cf. Āp. G. S. I. 3.20 and Vātsyāyana "Kām. S." suggest commonsense rule "A girl on whom his mind and eyes are reverted will bring him happiness and prosperity."

6. Mbh. XIII. 104. 135 लक्षणैरन्विता या च प्रशस्ता या च लक्षणैः ।

7. Mbh. V. 116. 2; IV. 9. 10. cf. Rām. VI. 48. 5-13. VI. 48. 2.

8. Rām. V. 48. 5 ff.; Mbh. V. 11. 20-21 Śachī, for she had such marks, was sure that her husband was alive.

9. Y. S. I. 52-53 (Mit. Com.) "Lakshaṇas" are external and internal. Sītā narrated external ones in Rām. VI.48.5-13 As internal were difficult to know people resorted to superstitions cf. Pāndey "Hindu Saṁskāra" p. 358 In "Smṛti Chandrikā" I. Saṁskāra Kānda p. 200-202 The external signs enumerated are different from the epics.

Biological objections

Maidens with certain biological defects were not to be married. One was to avoid a maiden who was deficient in limbs. A wise man was never to wed a woman who was either old or ascetic or "true to her lord" and "whose organs of generation were not well formed" (here "Ayonim" and "Viyonim" may also mean one of "unknown" or "mean birth"). A woman of yellow complexion was not to be wedded, for usually such persons are anaemic. One affected by leprosy or born in the family where there was epilepsy or consumption was not to be married.[1]

Most of these biological objections are found in the smṛtis also.[2] The considerations of wealth and health are important factors in the selection of bride and bridegroom. It is quite likely that a maiden from a diseased family may be a victim of diseases and even if she is healthy she may yet be a carrier of diseases. As one of the aims of marriage was progeny it was pointless to marry an old woman. Then again one who had left his or her āśrama was not to be wedded for such a person was considered an outlaw and had no right to join gṛhasthāśrama.

P. C. Roy translates "Varjayet"[3] as "should not have sexual congress" but it should be one "should not wed" for here in all subsequent ślokas the maiden to be married is to be discussed.[4] As will be shown in a later chapter adultery with any one was forbidden. So giving a special list of the women with whom physical congress was not to be had, was pointless. But in these disqualifications there is one dilemma

1. Mbh. XIII. 104. 131. वर्जयेद् ह्यंगिनीं नारीं तथा कन्यां नरोत्तम ।
समार्षां व्यंगितां चैव मातुः स्वकुलजां तथा ।
Mbh. XIII. 104. 132. वृद्धां प्रव्रजितां चैव तथैव च पतिव्रताम् ।
133 अयोनिं च वियोनिं च न गच्छेत विचक्षणः ।
पिंगलां कुष्ठिनीं नारीं न त्वमुद्वोढुमर्हसि ।
134 श्वित्रिणां च कुले जातां क्षयिणां मनुजेश्वर ।

2. Cf. M. III. 7-9. Y. S. I. 53, 54 ; Vi. Dh. S. XXIV. 9-13.

3. Mbh. XIII. 104-131 वर्जयेद् ह्यंगिनीं
P. C. Roy Eng. trans. 1895 Ed. p. 515

4. Mbh. XIII. 104. 133-135. indicates clearly.

i.e. तथैव च पतिव्रताम् । Does it refer to abduction like that of Sītā and Draupadī. Rāvaṇa and Jayadratha, respectively, wanted to have them as wives. Or does this refer to a widow, loyal to her deceased husband? In such a case loyalty to her former husband will obstruct her adjustment. The strange story of Mādhavi proves that only chaste maidens were not offered as brides and fresh marriages could be contracted even when previous husbands were living.[1] As the Mahābhārata includes many traditions nothing can be definitely asserted about this passage.

Qualifications of the bridegroom

It will not be out of place to describe some of the qualifications of the bridegroom because on him depended the future of the girl. The girl was not always given or sold like a chattel.[2] Generally great pains were taken in selecting a bridegroom. An accomplished person was preferred to an unqualified one, even though the latter had paid the dower.[3] As to what these disqualifications were it is not suggested.

Intellectual, moral and family qualifications

Bhīshma states that according to the Brāhma form the maiden was to be given to an accomplished person after having enquired into the conduct, disposition of the person, learning, family and acquirements. Although this form was specially meant for Brāhmaṇas yet all good people were expected to follow it. It has been already stated how far these duties were performed well by the guardians.[4] Some parents, however, were very particular about these. When Janamejaya asked for the hand of Vapushṭamā, her father gave her only after a thorough enquiry into his antecendents even though it was obvious that he belonged to a great family.[5] Thus physical, intellectual and moral qualities of the bridegroom were taken into account in accepting or rejecting his suit.

1. Mbh. V 115-120 (sections).
2. Cf. "Meyer" S. L. A. I." Vol. I. chap. IV. "Life in marriage" p. 181. Line 21 ff.
3. Mbh. XIII. 44.35-37.
4. See pp. 55-56. ante.
5. Mbh. I. 44. 8-9 ततः स राजा प्रददौ वपुष्टमां कुरुप्रवीराय परीक्ष्य धर्मतः ।

Betrothal

Sometimes the marriage was preceeded by betrothal. It was, however, a rare custom in the epics as well as in the gṛhyasūtras. It was a later feature[1] and therefore it is only in those portions of the great Epic which are thought to be recensions by scholars that the idea of betrothal was found.[2] This idea of Vāgdāna (giving the word for marriage) indicates guardians' control in arrangements of the marriages. When love and self choice were features of marriage there would have been no such need or custom. Even in didactic portions such a promise is not binding in case a better qualified bridegroom appears.[3]

The marriage ceremony proper

In the epics except in the case of marriage descriptions of Sītā and Draupadī, the data on this account is very scanty. As the epics were dealing with different kinds of material this omission was quite natural.[4] For the object of the present studies also the description of only those rites and ceremonies which relates or indicate the position of women in society, will suffice.

Rejoicing and assemblage of the people

Marriage is not only an important rite in the life of an individual but also a great social event in the community of which a person is the member. In the epics the accounts of the wedding ceremonies of the princes are found. Naturally marriage is celebrated with great public rejoicing, feast and extraordinary festivity[5] and is attended by all sorts of

1. Pandey R. B. "Hindu Saṁskāra" pp. 353-358. found in later "Prayogās and Paddhatis"

2. Mbh. I. 5. 19-31 Here Vṛta is used for betrothal and "Mantravat Vṛtā" for marriage. ; Mbh. XII. 342.62 gives idea of Umā's engagement when Bhṛgu appeared as a suitor.

3. Mbh. XIII. 44. 19-20 ; Mbh. I. 5. 19-36 may be illustrating such a case for Bhṛgu may have been more competent than Rākshasa Pouloma.

4. Most of these ceremonies are described in Āśv. G. S. I. 7. 1 ff. Pār. G. S. I. 5. 1 ff ; Ap. G. S. II. 4.10 ff Gobh. G. S. II. 1. 13 ff. ; Kha. G. S. I. 3.5 ff. etc.

5. Mbh. I. 184. 11-19 दिव्यं महोत्सवं० ।
194.12-15 ; V. 141. 14· आवाहाश्च विवाहाश्च ।
invitation always goes with wedding. Mbh. IV. 72. 28 सुरामैरेयपानानि

P. T. O. Note Continued.

people.[1] The assemblage of the people was in the vested interests of both the parties concerned. Moreover, the parents of the bride wanted all to witness the event of transfer of guardianship as well as her attaining the status of wifehood. Thus it has a legal significance also.

Therefore it was that marriage was always celebrated at the parental home of the bride. There are exceptional cases where it was performed at bridegroom's place. The reason for this kind of deviation from the custom was, in case the bride was procured by unapproved forms,[2] or due to the physical inability of bridegroom or important members of his party to take up a long journey,[3] or due to poverty of bride's party to hold a royal wedding.[4]

Patriarchical Bonds

Many of the epic marriages where guardians arrange marriages, also indicate strong patriarchical family bonds. The male head of the family either proposes or from him the hand of the daughter was demanded, to him the charge of the daughter was given.[5] Thus not only the husband but the whole family, particularly its head, was responsible for her future protection and well-being.

Although grown elaborate epic marriage ceremony was continuation of simple ceremony narrated in the Rg. Veda. X. 85. It (Epic marriage) corresponds to the Sūtra period ceremony cf. R. B. Pāndey 'Hindu Saṁskāra" pp. 352-3. Madhu-parka, Lajāhoma, Nāndi Śrāddha, Kanyādāna, Paṇigrahaṇa, all rites are mentioned in the sūtras as well as in the epics. Horoscopes are later development, were not consulted. Cf. Altekar "PWAC" but an auspicious day was fixed for marriage. Certain lunar months Uttara Phālgunī and Pushya were considered auspicious for marriage (Mbh. I. 198.5 Pushya Rām. I. 71. 24; 72. 13 Cf. Rg. Veda X. 85.13

अघासु हन्यन्ते गावोऽर्जुन्योः पर्युह्यते ।

Arjuni is Phalgunī Cf. Āśv. G. S. I. 4.1-2 suggests auspicious Nakshatra or according to some teachers it can be held at any time.

1. Rām. I. 69. 4-6 ; Mbh. I. 184. 11-19 ; 185. 13 ff.
2. Rākshasa, Paiśācha, Gāndharva, Asura will be mentioned in details later. So is Mādrī's case (Mbh. I. 113.4 ff) who was procured through Asura form, Mbh. I. 102.59 ff procured through Rākshasa form.
3. Mbh. I. 110. 16 ff. ; III. 295. 2 ff.
4. Mbh. I. 100. 100 ff ; 101.1. In this case Śāntanu may not also have proceeded alone due to the sense of shame.
5. Rām. I. 72. 1-11. Māṇḍavī, and Śruta-Kīrti were demanded from Janaka and not from their father Kuśadwaja Mbh. III 295.8. Dyumatsena's permission sought for Satyawāna. Mbh. IV. 71. 31-33 ; 72.34 Yudhishṭhira is consulted for Arjuna's marriage, and the former takes charge of Uttarā.

Racial importance of marriage

The marriage ceremonies began with Nāndī Śrāddha, as symbolic presentment to the ancestors, which makes the significance of marriage more clear. It was not merely a phase in family existence or individual affair but an event of great importance to the race,[1] in which the individuals were just instruments.

Kanyādāna

The idea of Kanyādāna, which is mentioned with certain forms of marriages in the epic,[2] was a new one. When the marriage was performed at the bridegroom's place and also according to unapproved last four forms, 'Kanyādāna' was not possible. In the Ṛg-Veda this idea is not found.[3] This new idea may have developed from the Daiva form of marriage when the girl was given as a gift to a Ṛtwik priest,[4] but it possibly had a greater ideal in view. The gift does indicate the transfer of guardianship and giving away the daughter for her future happiness but above all it was a sacrifice to be made on the father's part. The daughter was to be given for the happiness and well being of another Kula and thus to the society for performing 'Dharma', while the son was brought up for selfish motives, for the well being and prosperity of one's own family (Kula). This clearly explains the merits attached to Kanyādāna.

Pāṇigrahaṇa

It was one of the most important rites by which the status of wife was achieved by the girl. According to Manu the hand of only one's own caste wife was to be taken.[5] There is an indication of similar custom in the great Epic. Drupada may have pointed out this custom when he stated that he will

1. Rām. I. 72. 21 ff.

2. Mbh. XIII. 44. 3-4. It was only in first four forms which will be mentioned later that Kanyādāna is to be found.

3. Ṛg—V. X. 85 Sūryā is wedded at her bridegroom's place.

4. The gift of daughters to the Brāhmaṇas was thought meritorious later Mbh. XII. 234. 28, 34, 35.

5. M. III. 43, 44 also Vi. Dh. S. XXIV. 5.8.

make arrangements for his daughter's marriage according to the order to which her winner belonged,[1] or there may have been certain different rites followed by different castes. This ceremony is indicative of the guardianship of the husband over the wife.

Agni Pradakshiṇā

After taking the hand of the bride (Pāṇigrahaṇa) homa (sacrifice) and walking round the fire was done. Thus fire was the spiritual element bearing witness of new conjugal relationship.

Saptapadī

Although in some descriptions of marriages[2] Saptapadī has not been mentioned yet many more references prove that this was an important rite when the epics and gṛhya Sūtras were written. After this rite marriage was complete, final and irrevocable according to the great Epic, Sūtras and Śāstras.[3]

The bride then departed for her new home. The welcoming of the bride was again followed by sacrifices and worship of gods. The consummation of the marriage just after this points out post-puberty marriage.[4] According to Anuśāsana parva marriage could not be revoked after consummation.[5]

Presents

In the epics there is mention of various presents given not only to the couple but to the relations of the bridegroom's party. The presents given by mother's family may have been

1. Mbh. I. 195. 2-7.

2. That of Sītā, Draupadī, Uttarā. Rām. II. 73 (Sarga) Mbh. I. 198 ; IV. 72. 33 ff.

3. Mbh. VII. 55. 16 ; Y. S. 84.

पाणिग्रहण-संस्कारात्पतित्वं सप्तमे पदे ।

; XIII. 44. 55

पाणिग्रहणमन्त्राणां निष्ठा स्यात्सप्तमे पदे ।

Rām. IV. 5.16-17 ; Mbh. III. 260.35 ; 297.23 Saptapadī friendship is mentioned. All these rites have been mentioned in gṛhyasūtras Cf. R. B. Pandey, "Hindu Saṁskāra" page 352-3.

4. Rām. I. 77. 13-14.

5. Mbh. XIII. 44. 52-53 Cf. Vas. Dh. S. XVII. 74 Baud. Dh. S. IV. 1. 16. but if the marriage was not consummated she could be married agnia.

a remnant or outcome of amalgamation of some matriarchal clan into the Āryan fold. The daughter's share, after her property right had been taken away in patriarchy, may have thus been presented to her and her children, from time to time out of a sense of justice.[1]

Dowry

According to the Brāhma form the maiden was to be decorated for marriage.[2] The wealth that one was expected to give to his daughter was according to one's own status.[3] This injuction may have been prompted out of the sense of duty or justice towards the daughter who had no right of inheritance, therefore dowry was her due, it was known as "Kanyādhanam" "Gyātideyam" and sometimes "Haraṇam", "Yautakam" (seperate property).[4] The great kings might have given a portion of their wealth to their daughters out of affection. Other reasons might have prompted to the growth of this custom. The idea of Kanyādāna was recognized. Giving away gifts after 'dāna' was known as "Dakshiṇā", which had great religious merits.[5] These presents may have been naturally recomended for the Brāhma form of marriage where the daughter was given as a gift. In cases even where the bride was procured by other methods (forms), but her parental family agreed to give her away, such presents were given.[6] Although among the dowry of princesses all kinds of movable property, including slaves, is mentioned; such profuse presents were perhaps not given by the commoners. It must however, be mentioned that dowry as a part of marriage settlement, is nowhere mentioned in the

1. Mbh. I. 199. 13 ff. Kuntī was Vasudeva's sister, his son Kṛshṇa thus brings presents when the Pāṇḍavas are married. Kṛshna, Subhadrā's brother, again brings presents, (Mbh. IV. 72. 26) on the occassion of the marriage of Uttarā and Abhimanyu.

2. Mbh. I. 102. 12-13 ; XIII. 46. 2.

3. Mbh. I. 102. 12-13. अलंकृत्य यथाशक्ति प्रदाय च धनान्यपि ॥

4. Rām. I. 74.3. 'कन्याधनं' ; Mbh. I. 221. 44. "ज्ञातिदेयं", "हरणं" XIII. 45.12. 'यौतकम्'

5. Mbh. XIV. 88. 14-15. If the "Dakshiṇā" was increased the merit of gift also increased.

6. Mbh. I. 221. 31 ff i.e. in case of Subhadrā. In such dowries wealth, property, costly robes, ornaments, gems, cows, chariots, excellent beds, maid servants are mentioned.

epics, and was not an impediment in marriage. A Brāhmaṇī in the Ādi Parva, enumerating her difficulties, in getting her daughter married, in case, she was widowed, utters not a word about dowry.[1] Mātali does not think dowry to be an impediment in his daughter's marriage, the only difficulty was that of getting a suitable bridegroom.[2]

Marriage, a Sacrament

The brief account of the marriage ceremony makes it clear that the epic marriage was not a contract but a sacrament.[3] It was a union of the human beings (parties) under divine witness represented here by the spiritual element that was Agni. The divine witness was devised to ensure permanence. Human mind changes and therefore the human element alone was not considered as a sufficient basis for the performance of the union. Marriage was a spiritual union undergone for the performance of the religious duties. The husband and wife were colleagues in dharma, hence this formed the basis of permanence of the epic marriage. Thus according to didactic portions, marriage performed with sacred mantra and saptapadī, was considered indissoluble and irrevocable.[4] It was supposed that after death, even in heaven, wife or husband waited for each other.[5] As it was an eternal union[6] the restoration of a wife was considered best of all gifts.[7] It was perhaps for this reason of irrevocability of marriage that Bhīshma could not utter any thing in the Kuru court upholding the case of Draupadī, for according to him the slavery of Yudhishṭhira could not dissolve his marriage with Draupadī. Thus even when Ahalya was guilty of adultery, Gautama ordered her to repent for her sin by doing penance and attaining purity in this way. She was later received back

1. Mbh. I. 158. 14-18.
2. Mbh. V. 97. 14-21.
3. An outward manifestation of inward spiritual grace.
4. Mbh. XIII. 44. 55 ; 19. 1 ff. Rām. II. 29. 17-18.
5. Mbh. I. 74. 45 ; Rām. IV. 24. 35 II. 29.18 अद्भिर्दत्ता स्वधर्मेण प्रेत्यभावेऽपि तस्य सा । It is, therefore, that Sītā accuses Rāma cf. Rām. VI. 116. 16.
6. Mbh. I. 74.46-47 ; Rām. IV. 24.38
7. Rām. IV. 24.37.

by him.[1] Sītā's casc was different. She was forsaken due to public censure but Rāma was ever loyal to her. The marriage vow was never dissolved. The only two exceptional cases when husbands dissolve the marriage union with their wives are those of Kaikeyī and her mother. The reason for this unusual action is, however, extreme cases of selfishness where wives did not even care for the lives of their husbands.[2] As "pariṇayana" marriage was the transformation of two souls, and as "Niyojana", the two souls were drawn together under the yoke of Dharma, the eternal immutable law, which carried them upwards and therefore marriage was known as Udvāha.[3]

It was natural for sceptics to doubt the possibility of such a union. After all judging from the worldly point of view marriage, no doubt, is the outcome of desire and therefore Yudhishṭhira fails to understand how it could be meant for practising the duties together.[4] Bhishma citing an old narrative i.e. Ashṭāvakra's trial, proves that it is neither for desire nor for the beauty of flesh nor for the riches that one marries, but for practising Dharma in order to pay the debts to the Gods, manes and society and to attain the highest through the aid of these services, for the desire is incapable of being transcended but the abandoment of it leads to proper preparation for marriage i.e. 'Sahadharma.'[5]

Nevertheless, the change was coming. The history of marriage custom in any society is an index of the position of womankind. Janaka's words are of great significance. For these indicate that side by side this 'Sahadhamiṇī' conception where the dignity of wife is upheld, another idea, of wife "as a shadow", which loses its identity and has no personality, was developing.[6]

Marriage, a contract

As opposed to this sacramental character of marriage

1. Rām. I. 48-49.
2. Rām. II. 35; 42. 6-9; 14. 14.
3. Mbh. I. 198. 12, 11; XIII. 104. 24.
4. Mbh. XIII. 19. 1 ff.
5. Mbh. XIII. 19-21 (sections)
6. Rām. I. 73. 24 इयं सीता मम सुता सहधर्मचरी तव ।
पतिव्रता महाभागा छायेवानुगता सदा ॥

is the modern idea of contract, not that the idea of marriage as contract was entirely absent in the epics but it was rare and decidedly discouraged. Gangā's and Suśobhanā's[1] marriages were such. Mādhavi, the daughter of Yayāti was married four times, each time for a year according to the contract. At last a Svayamvara was held when her former four husbands were still living. Her choosing "the Forest"[2] this time may indicate that disgusted with the whole affair, she took to penances in the forest, an indication of women not liking such contracts. This story may not be true according to geneological tables,[3] but it may probably indicate the existence of such social conditions.

The idea of contract generally upheld for ameliorating the legal position of women can do nothing for promoting matrimonial harmony. The contractual character of marriage never satisfies or appeals to woman, who is mostly monogamous and gives and expects love without reserve to her life-partner. Thus sacramental character suits her inherent qualities much better. The essential fact in married life is to make it permanent and harmonious through the growth of a gradual love and an understanding, strong enough to render this most intimate of relationships possible and desirable. This cannot be made a matter of contract, which at the very outset pre-supposes non-permanent relationship. This was long before realised by the Indians when the epics were being written. This realization came from various sociological experiments taken up in the field of marriage in "forms of marriages." The Brāhma form, which recognized sacramental character of marriage was adjudged to be the best. Let us now examine these forms as adopted by a people with free and vigorous mind ready to judge a custom with boldness after a thorough, practical examination.

1. Mbh. III. 192. 32-35. In Suśobhanā's case it was thought to be bad even by her father.

2. . Mbh. V. 120. 1-5.

3. Pargiter "AHIT" "Table of Royal geneologies" pages 144-145. None of the four kings are contemporaries of Yayāti. Yayāti—6th step. Haryaśwa. 15. Divodāsa I 25, Divodāsa II 40, Śivi-26. in the table.

CHAPTER IV

MARRIAGE—PART II

(The freedom and limitations in contracting marriage or some special features of epic marriages)

Forms of marriages

The forms of marriages as described in the epics were ways of procuring (or acquiring) a wife. Some of these forms were probably practised earlier during the period of the Ṛg- Veda[1], but were not formalised or named till a later date. In the social development a particular name is given to a custom only when it becomes general, hence the belated recognition of these forms. As will be shown presently some of these may have been adopted as a result of a fusion between various races and cultures. A study of these forms will indicate how a living society accepts the challenge when confronted with unfamiliar customs and finally fits, adopts and assimilates the best in them according to its social and cultural pattern. Thus many of these unfamiliar forms of marriages were not approved by the society but all of them were legalised taking into view the weakness of human nature, or of certain people and saving innocent women from life-long suffering usually without fault of their own.

The list of these forms of marriages in various Sūtras is not always the same. Some of these mention all the eight forms while others do not.[2] Most of these Sūtras are not widely separated in time.[3] Therefore the reason for this diversity in the lists may be due to the fact that the Sūtra writers belonged to

1. Upādhyāya "Women in Ṛg-Veda", p. 65-66, 1941 ed.

2. Ap. Dh. S. II. 5.11.17-20; II. 5.12. 1-2.
Vas. Dh. S. I. 29ff. Gaut. Dh. S. IV. 6-13.
Asv. G.S. I. 6. 1-8. Baud. Dh. S. I. 11. 20. 1-9
Vi. S. XXIV. 17-26.

3. Kaṇe "Hist. of Dh." Vol II. part I. Chronological Table p. xi. tentative dates for most of the Sūtras from 800 B.C. to 300 B.C.

different schools and localities and were dealing with diverse races and thoughts. However, by the time of Smṛtis all the forms were legalised and so more or less all Smṛtis describe them though the names might vary.[1]

In the great Epic three lists of these forms of marriages are mentioned, two of them in the Ādi Parva record the eight forms and the third in the Anuśāsana narrates the five forms.[2] These eight forms in ascending order are Paiśācha, Rākshasa, Asura, Gāndharva, Prājāpatya, Ārsha, Daiva and Brāhma. According to Tripāṭhī[3], Gāndharva, Rākshasa, Asura, Paiśācha were observed by the four non-Āryan races of the same name. However, it may well be that when the composers of the codes were naming the various prevalent ways of acquiring a wife they called the unapproved (or improper) methods after the name of the races whose conduct they held in contempt. Similarly the proper forms were christened after the name of the races held in reverence.

Paiśācha

When a maiden was abducted sleeping or in a drunken state the form was known as Paiśācha[4]. The earlier Sūtra writers ignore it or allow it for the lower classes.[5] The composers of the great Epic and earlier Smṛtis, strange though it may seem, merely contented themselves with a condemnation of the Paiśācha practice but did not require that a man who has had sexual intercourse with a maiden must marry her

1. M. III. 21. Y. S. I. 58-61 Kāyā is the name given for Prājāpatya by him.

2. Mbh. I. 73. 8-9; 102. 12-16; XIII. 44.3 ff.

3. Tripāṭhī. G.M. "Marriage Forms Under Ancient Hindu Law" pages 7 to 11.

4. Mbh. I. 102. 14 प्रमत्तामुपयन्त्यन्ये Cp. M. III. 34.

Kaṇe "Hist. of Dh. "Vol. II. Part I (p. 519 propounds that Paiśācha was so called for there was in it the action like the piśāchas, who are supposed to act stealthily by night.)

5. Ap. Dh. S. II. 5. 11. 17-20. Vas. Dh. S. XVII. 73. ignores it, Gaut. Dh. S. IV. 13-15 disapproves it. Baud. Dh. S. I. 11. 20. 13-14. states it is lawful form for Vaiśyas and Śūdras as they are not particular about their wives.

while such ordinance is included in the later Nārada Smṛti.[1] The above data illustrates how a living society faces the changing situation within it with a positive outlook and is not averse to the adoption of more humane laws for the protection of the innocent. The earlier Śūtra writers perhaps described the same social conditions as depicted in the Epics when maidens like Kuntī and Satyavatī, who had been mothers before marriage, could be well married. Naturally Paiśācha form was ignored and in the circumstances it must have appeared the best thing to do. In the second stage chastity as a qualification for marriage was receiving more and more insistence. So faced with this change the earlier Smṛtis and the Mahābhārata portions, which are identical to Dharmaśāstras mention Paiśācha form, condemnation of this form was to discourage deceit and to safeguard the interest of the abducted one. By the time of the later Smṛtis virginity of a maiden came to be an absolutely indispensable qualification for marriage, so the seducer was made responsible for his crime and the interest of the maiden was thus guarded. It would be a falsification of position to maintain as some western scholars[2] do that the later writers gave a virtual recognition to fraud in this matter. The fact of the matter is that they were simply trying to meet the challenge of the time boldly with realism, upholding as far as possible the interests of innocent individuals against mere custom. In this way they were trying to harmonise their laws with the demands of justice.

Rākshasa

According to the composers of the Mahābhārata slaying and cutting off the hands of weeping kinsmen, the bride-groom sometimes forcibly takes away the girl he weds. Such wedding is called Rākshasa marriage.[3] This kind of abduction was practised not only for oneself but sometimes for others too. Thus, for instance, Bhīshma abducted Ambā, Ambikā and

1. Mbh. I. 73. 12 Cp. M. III. 21, 25. Nārada XII. 39-43. Vi. S. 29 Cp. Nārada XII. 72. S. B. E. Vol. XXXIII. page 179.

2. Macnaughton "Principles and Precedents of Hindu law" page 60.

3. P. C. Roy's Eng. Tr. "Anuśāsana Parva" Vol. X. New ed. page 17.

Ambālikā for his brother.[1] This was one of the approved forms for the warrior caste[2] and they also practised it[3] as did Bhīshma.[4] While condemning Swayamvara, Brāhma and Asura, Kṛshna upholds Rākshasa for Kshatriyas. In his opinion self-choice (i.e. Swayamvara) cannot be relied upon. The idea of acquiring any thing as a gift (Brāhma) was repugnant to Kshatriyas. No Kshatriya would like to sell his own progeny. Therefore for the brave warriors who depended upon valour Rākshasa was the best form.[5] This form particularly suited the temper and occupation of Kshatriyas[6].

From the point of view of sociology Rākshasa form is one of the primitive ones. Women as a valuable property must have been lifted by primitive men or tribes after defeating the foes. In the primitive social conditions women were useful as wives, (producers of progeny), as helping hands in agricultural operations and maintenance of cattle, as house keepers or as maid servants, all in one. That suggests the motive behind the Rākshasa form or abduction. The origin of this form of marriage in the epics, however, is different. From the legends Rākshasas are known to have been forceful abductors.[7] Rāvaṇa states that it was a virtue of Rākshasas to visit other people's wives or to take them by force.[8] If force could be used in case of married women it would have been much more so in case of maidens. For further evidence Rāvaṇa assigns a limit of one year to Sītā to agree to his proposal. In the Śānti Parva the same limit is prescribed in the case of a captured maiden, who should then

1. Mbh. I. 102. 16-17; VII. 144. 9 another case.
2. Mbh. I. 73.11 राज्ञा तु राक्षसोऽप्युक्तो Cf. M. III. 24.
3. Mbh. I. 220 7; XII. 4. (sec.); VII. 10. 33-34; 11.10; III. 224. 1-4; IV. 33. 8-9 Lover carries off the maiden but this may refer to elopment as well.
4. Mbh. I. 102. 16; VI. 122. 17.
5. Mbh. I. 219. 22 ff हरणं चापि.........को वै वेद चिकीर्षितम् । 221. 3-4.
6. Even after Swayamvara they fought for the girl Mbh. I. 102. 12; 189. 190 (sec.); XII. 4(sec.); VII. 11.33-34.
7. Rām. VII. 24. 1 ff.
Rām. III. 49. 20 ff.
Mbh. I. 5-6 (sec.); III. 157 (sec.).
8. Rām. V. 20. 5.

स्वधर्मो रक्षसां भीरु सर्वदैव न संशयः ।
गमनं वा परस्त्रीणां हरणं संप्रमथ्य वा ।

be returned if still not agreeable.[1] The above mentioned discussion points to the possibility that this form was adopted by Kshatriyas from Rākshasas. Although frequent among the warrior classes it was resorted to in a reformed way; keeping in view the interest and consent of women. Abducted maidens, if unwilling were, not to be married and Ambā who refused, was thus returned.[2] Bhīshma was blamed by Śiśupāla for abducting a virtuous girl who had set her heart upon another.[3] Married women were not seized. There were, of course, some rare exceptions. Śiśupāla was thus impeached by Kṛshṇa for this fault.[4] Jayadratha[5] was amply punished and Rāvaṇa killed[6] for kidnapping Draupadī and Sitā respectively. Although the intentions in these cases were of forcing the kidnapped women to be wives, yet as these were rare and condemned cases, it can be said definitely that among the Āryans the practice was not to abduct wives. The seizure a of maiden also was to be followed by the sacred rites with Mantra and Homa.[7] Sometimes the maiden was carried away with her consent though without the consent of her guardians.[8] In order to discourage such form it is stated that Kāyavya, who for his acts obtained great reward in the other world condemned forcible abduction of women even by robbers.[9]

Gāndharva

Next in ascending order was Gāndharva. This was a union achieved in secret, without Mantras between a willing woman and a man desiring her. The form was considered the

1. Mbh. XII. 96.5
2. Mbh. I. 102. 60 ff; XIII. 44.39 ff.
3. Mbh. 11.41.22.
4. Mbh. II. 45. 10-11.
5. Mbh. III. 272 (sec.).
6. Rām VI. 106 (sec.).

7. Mbh. I. 221. 1-14; In case of Subhadrā. An abducted maiden could be married again Cp. Mbh. XIII. 44.24ff Baud. Dh. S. IV. 1.15 and Vas. Dh. S. XVII. 73 both opine that in case the maiden was not married with sacred rites, she could be lawfully given to others.

8. Mbh. II. 45. 15-18. Rukmaṇī's marriage is referred to. According to Kumbhakonam ed. of Mbh. Subhadrā also was a party in abduction.

9. Mbh. XII. 135. 13. न च ग्राह्या बलात्स्त्रियः ।

24. कायव्यः कर्मणा तेन महतीं सिद्धिमाप्तवान् ।

best for the Kshatriyas.[1] In the Anuśāsana Parva, however, Gāndharva is defined as a form of marriage in which the guardian of the maiden gives her hand setting aside his choice in favour of hers.[2] Vaidya thinks that Damayantī's marriage was according to Gāndharva rites as defined in the Anuśāsana Parva[3], even though in her marriage there was no question of setting aside "the choice of guardian". Gāndharva was always contracted in secret. "Samyoga"—union—is the most appropriate word used for it by Manu, which conforms to the kind of Gāndharva practised in most of the epic stories,[4] that of Śakuntalā and Dushyanta as well as of Ulūpī and Arjuna. It was self choice in the true sense of the term. The initiative was taken by the young man. The cases when women used this unusual freedom have already been cited before.[5]

Although scholars have propounded theories about the origin of Gāndharva,[6] yet it must have been the most natural and the most primitive of the forms. It was for this reason that

1. Mbh. I. 73. 27.

क्षत्रियस्य च गान्धर्वो विवाहः श्रेष्ठ उच्यते ।
सकामायाः सकामेन निर्मन्त्रो रहसि स्मृतः ॥

Mbh. I. 73. 11-13.
Cp. Vi. S. XXIV. 28; M. III. 32

इच्छया ऽ-योन्य-संयोगः ।

2. Mbh. XIII. 45. 5-6

आत्माभिप्रेतमुत्सृज्य कन्याभिप्रेत एव यः ॥
अभिप्रेता च या यस्य तस्मै देया युधिष्ठिर ।
गान्धर्वमिति तं धर्मं प्राहुर्वेदविदो जनाः ॥

3. Vaidya, C.V. "Mahābhārata Mīmānsā" Chap. VII. p. 232.

4. Mbh. I. 73. 6 ff; 214. 24 ff.

5. Mbh. I. 214. 18 ff. ; 152. 27 ff. Rām. III. 18. 24; VII. 24. 26 ff Foot note "Marriage" Part I pages 50-52.

6. Acc. of Dr. Altekar "PWHC" p. 50 Gandharvas was the name of a people well known for their amorous disposition. Tai. S. VI. 1. 6.5 स्त्रीकामा वै गान्धर्वः and the same in Mait. S. III. 7.3. Tripāṭhī, G. M. opines that Gāndharvas must have been the horse breeding tribe of Kabul valley, who practised this kind of marriage. We can still have another interpretation that the 'Kanyā' was "Gāndharva grihītā" before marriage and according to this form she was directly taken from Gāndharva and not from the guardian.

in some lists it has not been recommended for any particular class.[1]

Reasons for unpopularity of Gāndharva

Gradually as more and more importance came to be attached to the sacred rites and to the guardian's consent for the marriage, the popularity of Gāndharva must have declined. No doubt the warrior class still practised this form, and the great Epic dealing with the warrior—traditions had naturally to extol it, still this form did not produce happy results and continued to lose favour. Although it gave right of consent to women yet it also betrayed their interests. Śakuntalā's story teaches a moral. She suffers for contracting Gāndharva marriage and is insulted in the audience hall of the king. This suggests that even among Kshatriyas there was a tendency to discourage it. When Samvaraṇa proposed to Tapatī she refused pleading dependence of daughter on father and so do Kuśanābha's daughters.[2] As Gāndharva took place in secret it was difficult for the society to accept the validity of this form of marriage.[3] In this free play of desire persons like Dushyanta could have taken advantage of innocent girls. Last, but not the least, when more emphasis was laid on the acquisition of merit and welfare of community as the aims of marriage it was thought better to be guided by the experienced opinion.[4] All these factors contributed to the gradual decline and unpopularity of the Gāndharva form of marriage.

Asura

When the maiden was purchased after paying a high price and gratifying the greed of kinsmen, the form was known

1. Mbh. XIII. 44. 10. cp. M. III. 23; Nārada XII. 42, 44, recommend this for all . Mbh. I. 73.4 विवाहानां हि रम्भोरु गान्धर्वः श्रेष्ठः उच्यते । Baud I. 11. 20.13-14, 16 allows it for Śūdrā and Vaiśyas they being not particular about their wives. Acc. to Vātsyāyana "Kām. S." III. 29-30 as it is founded on mutual love it is best of all marriage form, above all it is free from cumbersome formalities and trouble.

2. Mbh. I. 172. 20 ff; Rām. I. 32. 20 ff.

3. Mbh. I. 74. 116-123.

4. Mbh. I. 44. 3-4, 25, 26 In the later society 'Kula' (family) and Śīla (character) of the bridegroom were the main qualifications.

as Asura.[1] This is one of the condemned forms in the lists of the great Epic.[2] The practice of bestowing girl in return for wealth was prevalent among the ancient Assyrians. It cannot be definitely stated whether the Āryans adopted it from them or took it from Iranian Asuras or whether it was an indigenous practice.[3]

This custom seems to be closely connected with the right of "patria potestas" which was thus put to use in India long before Justinian. In certain social conditions depicted in the great Epic this usage was followed even by some royal families. In Gādhi's case one is tempted to think that the demand was made in order to avoid the marriage[4] but it is definitely stated that taking Śulka was an ancient family custom. So was it for Śalya in Mādrī's case and Bhīshma supports it as part of religion propounded by Brahmā.[5] The Madra king himself doubts[6] the morality of taking the dower but finds himself helpless in eradicating an ancient and therefore entrenched custom. That it was an ancient custom admits of no doubt, as it has been mentioned in ancient literature.[7] Promises extracted as the condition of marriage were also known as Śulka[8], although the promise extracted by Satyavatī's father has not been mentioned as such.[9]

1. Mbh. XIII. 44.7

धनेन बहुधा क्रीत्वा संप्रलोभ्य च बान्धवान् ।
असुराणां नृपैतं वै धर्ममाहुर्मनीषिणः ॥

2. Mbh. I. 73. 12; XIII. 44. 9. cp. M III. 25 the same.
3. Sale of women in N. W. India is testified by the Greek author Arrian—Vaidya "Epic India" p. 93.
4. Mbh. XIII. 4. 9-10

दरिद्र इति मत्वा वै० ।

5. Mbh. I. 113. 11. कुलधर्मः स नो वीर० ।

also I. 113. 12.

6. Mbh. I. 113.9

पूर्वैः प्रवर्तितं किंचित्कुलेऽस्मिन्नृपसत्तमैः ।
साधु वा यदि वाऽसाधु तन्नातिक्रान्तुमुत्सहे ।

4. Ṛg-V. I. 109. 2. According to Ṛg-V. a defective person pays the price. Nirukta. VI. 9. for further reference see Kaṇe "Hist. of Dh." Vol. II part I Chapt. IX. pp. 504-505.
5. Rām. II. 107. 2-3; Mbh. XIII. 2. 31 ff.
6. Mbh. I. 100. 56.

In the didactic portions the opinion of society was gradually crystallizing against Asura form of marriage. And if, as has been already noticed[1], Bhīshma did not denounce this usage, the chances here are that the redactors of the Mahābhārata, struggling against this feature surviving from the old society and anxious to change it, put diverse opinions into the mouth of Bhīshma and in this anxiety lost sight of the proper time (or chronological) sequence.

At first the claim of the giver of dower is accepted and protected

According to one set of opinions we are on firmer grounds about the claims of the giver of the dower. In case he went away after paying, a rich sonless father was to maintain the daughter for whom the money was paid. If the dower was not returned to the kinsmen of the payee the daughter was considered to belong to the giver, and may have progeny by Niyoga for him[2] or she may be united with the brother-in-law. Gradually the idea of chastity was taking hold of society and Bhīshma opines that when the maiden for whom the dower was paid, is married but whose marriage is not consummated it is better for her to take to penance.[3] It was also stated that there is no sin in giving and accepting the dower if the marriage is perfored with sacred rites i.e. with mantras before the sacrificial fire and with the consent of kinsmen.[4]

Maiden's interest assumes greater importances as compared to the giver of dower

In the stage next to this although the right of the payee was recognized yet it was held that even after receiving the dower and promising the maiden in return, she may be bestowed to another person. In such a case the person who takes her hand does not incur sin although the giver may, for giving false promise.[5] In case there appeared a more accomplished person

1. Foot note 6. p. 76.
2. Mbh. XIII. 45. 1-8 cf. M. VIII. 204 (right of the giver of dower.
3. Mbh. XIII. 44. 51-52.
4. Mbh. XIII. 44. 22-27.
5. Mbh. XIII. 44. 19-23 These lines are exceedingly terse, here only the gist, of all the ideas, is narrated.

after the acceptance of the dower, there is no sin in giving away the girl to the latter.[1] The status of wife does not arise from sale, only persons unacquainted with scriptures and indulging in slave trade regard such status as arising from sale.[2] Thus the maiden's interest assumed greater importance.

Asura form condemned

In the period that followed, opinion was definitely against taking the dower. Manu and the composers of the Anuśāsana Parva do not even approve the limitations of Ārsha, not to say of Asura.[3] To live on the proceeds of the sale of a daughter is stated to be one of the gravest of crimes,[4] such criminals are condemned to sink in the seven hells known as the 'Kālas'[5]. On the other hand it is declared that the good never bestow their daughter in return for dower.[6] No dharma could ever be served with the riches acquired by such acts (i.e. the sale of a daughter). Manu and the composer of Anuśāsana opine that whatever is agreeable should be given to a maiden[7] and no amount should be taken however small. Even a human being with whom one has no relationship of blood should not be sold, what need be said of one's own daughter.[8]

Reasons for condemnation and some exceptional cases when Asura form was allowed

To conclude, the Asura form was practised but the writers of Sūtras and Smṛtis as well as the redactors of the great Epic were fighting against it. The custom does not reflect good taste and is a slur on the family affections, where practised.[9]

1. Mbh. XIII. 44. 28 ff.
2. Mbh. XIII. 44. 34-36, 43-47. This was the opinion of many law givers as well. cp. Baud. Dh. S. I. 11. 21.2 Atri Sam. 387 Smṛtichandrikā 1. Samskāra Kānada p. 232 quoting Kasyapa. क्रीता द्रव्येण या नारी न सा पत्न्यभिधीयते । न सा दैवे न पित्र्ये च दासी तां कश्यपोऽब्रवीत् ।
3. Mbh. XIII. 46. 20 cp. M III. 53.
4. Mbh. XIII. 93. 119. 133; 94. 31
5. Mbh. XIII. 46. 18-19.
6. Mbh. XIII. 44. 31.
7. Mbh. XIII. 46. 1-3 cp. M. III. 54-55.
8. Mbh. XIII. 46. 33. cp. M. III. 51-53.
9. Mbh. I. 221. 4; XII. 234. 12; XIII. 94.31 cp. Ap. Dh. S. II 13.11; Vas. Dh. S. I. 30-37; Baud. Dh. S. I. II. 21; 2-3. M. III. 51.

According to this form the position of a woman is like that of a slave or an article to be sold. As practical social reformers, however, the writers of laws realized that it was difficult to wipe out such an ancient custom. Therefore they made certain concessions, specially to Vaiśyas who belonged to trading classes and as such were money-minded, and to Śūdras, who had less scruples in the matter.[1] It was declared that from unqualified bridegrooms dower may be taken.[2] It was stated that if the dower is demanded for adorning the girl it was not sale[3], thus they evolved a way of having the wealth returned as present to bride. Jewels are still taken by the bridegroom's party for the bride and the usage may be a survival of the Asura form.

Prājāpatya

The next method of obtaining the bride was Prājāpatya, which was perhaps named after Prajāpati, an abstract god who taught men how to live and multiply. According to this form the guardian gave away the girl to the suitor commanding them both to perform their religious and civic duties together.[4] This form then is almost identical to Brāhma,[5] but the difference between both the forms may be noticed in the definition of Prājāpatya as mentioned in thc Ādi parva i.e. "Swayamanye cha Vindate".[6] While in Brāhma bride's father invites the bridegroom, in the Prājāpatya the demand was made by the suitor and so the guardian of the girl could impose the condition,[7]

1. Mbh. I. 73. 11. cp. M. III. 24 विट्शूद्रेष्वासुरः स्मृतः ।

Against them Mbh. XIII. 44. 46-47 is directed. 'Asura' was known as "Manusha Vivāha" followed by people's caste Vas. Dh. S. 35.

2. Mbh. XIII. 44. 32 cp. footnote 4 of page 76.
3. Mbh. XIII. 44. 32-33; 46. 1-3 cp. M. III. 54-55.
4. M. III. 30. Asv. Dh. S. 1. 6.3. Y. S. I. 60.
5. Pāndey "Hindu Sanskāra" page 286-289 suggests that it was for discharging debts to Prajāpati by begetting children but that was the aim of every Hindu marriage.

6. Mbh. I. 102-14. स्वयमन्ये च विन्दते-स्वयमन्ये इति प्राजापत्यः-नीलकण्ठ

cp. Vi. S. XXIV. 22 (If she is given to a suitor, by her father it is called Prājāpatya marriage. See condition in note No. 4.

7. Haradatta. Gaut. Dh. S. IV. 5.—The commentator rightly suggests injuction to the couple in the Prājāpatya form of marriage to remain inseparable companions by performing religious duties together which rendered polygamy impossible and prohibited husband from entering 'Vānsprastha'

which may have given her perpetual position of "Patnī" (a wife who alone has the right of performing religious rites with the husband) never to be challenged. This might have rendered polygamy impossible. The epic data does not provide any practical example of this form.

This form of marriage could develop only in a cultured and free society where grown-up persons contracted marriage, for only grown-up persons could understand the implications of the conditions imposed. This type of wedding will naturally appeal to the modern mind as it secured the rights of both the parties and is suggestive of equal legal rights of women. But as it imposed a condition[1], it was placed fourth in descending order in the legal lists of marriages as well as in the Mahabhārata, for according to the Hindū ideal all gifts should be free from stipulation.

Hopkins[2] states that as in the Prājāpatya of old consent was given, it was this form only which was later transformed in the Knightly Swayamvara of the Kshatriyas. But as already shown Swayamvara was a way of advertisement only. Again in Swayamvara the noble ideals of Prājāpatya, which gave equal legal status to women, were never imposed. There was no objection to polygamy in Swayamvara.[3]

Ārsha

The next superior form was Ārsha. According to this method the father of the bride received a pair of kine or two

and 'sanyās' without the consent of wife. Samskāra Prakāśa p. 851-852.

1. सहधर्म क्रिया हेतोर्दानं समय बन्धनात् अलंकृत्यैव कन्याया विवाह : स प्रजापते : ।

Devala quoted by V. M. S. Vol. II. p. 851.

2. J. A. O. S. Vol. XIII. Art III. "The social and Military Position of the Ruling caste in India as represented by the Sanskrit Epic," by E. Hopkins appendix on "The Status of Women."

3. Ibid. Hopkins quotes Mbh. XIII. 19.2 आर्ष एष भवेद्धर्मः प्राजापत्योऽथवाऽऽसुरः । यदेतत्सहधर्मेति पूर्वमुक्तं महर्षिभिः ।
states that Ārsha, Prājāpatya and Asura were respectively for Brāhmaṇas, Kshatriyas and Vaiśyas. As swayamvara was Kshatriya custom it was successor of Prājāpatya. But this sloka does not recommend Prājāpatya for the Kshatriyas only. It is not so in any other Sūtras or Smṛitis.

from the bridegroom.[1] As the gift was limited and was meant for sacrifice it was not called bride-price. The name suggests that the form must have been prevalent among the ṛshies, who pursued agriculture. They may have been in the habit of presenting kine, useful animals for their professional needs. As the idea of Kanyādāna was gaining ground such gifts from the bride-groom were condemned by both Manu and the composer of the Anuśāsana. No practical example of this method is, however, found in the epics. The name must have been taken from the conventional lists. It may be because of this unfamiliarity that in the Ādi Parva Ārsha has been defined without name and Daiva has been given the name of Ārsha.[2]

Daiva

The method of marriage which excelled Ārsha was Daiva. In this the decorated girl was given away by the guardian, as a gift to the priest on the occasion of Daiva sacrifice. Even in the great Epic gift of girls to Brāhmaṇas has been considered meritorious.[3] In spite of its being a praiseworthy form, it was next to Brāhma as the girl was given for services rendered in the sacrifice. No practical example of this method, is found in the epics. As already shown its definition is not given correct in the Ādi-Parva which denotes further unfamiliarity with this usage.

Brāhma

The best, the purest and the first of all the forms was Brāhma. Bhīshma states, "Having enquired into the conduct and disposition of the person, his learning and acquirements,

1. M. III. 29

एकं गोमिथुनं द्वे वा वरादादाय धर्मतः ।
कन्याप्रदानं विधिवदार्षो धर्मः स उच्यते ।।

2. Mbh. I. 102. 13 प्रयच्छन्त्यपरे कन्यां मिथुनेन गवामपि ।
15 आर्षं विधिं पुरस्कृत्य दारान्विन्दति चापरे

Nīlkaṇṭha explains Śloka 13 and 14 thus

मिथुनेन गृहीतेनेत्यार्षः । आर्षं विधि यज्ञं तेन दैव उक्तः ।

3. Mbh. XII. 234. 28, 34, 35; V. 106. 19 ff. king Yayāti assigns his daughter Mādhavī to the Brāhmaṇa Gālava so that he may acquire his wonderful steeds by giving her from one ruler to another.

his birth and his actions, good people should then bestow their daughters upon the accomplished bridegrooms. This is known as Brāhma marriage. Selecting an eligible bridegroom, the father of the girl should persuade him to marry the daughter having by presents of diverse kinds induced the bridegroom to that act".[1] The composer of Mahābhārata and Manu regard this as proper (Dharmya), praiseworthy (Praśasta), and fit for Brāhmaṇas.[2] The name of the form denotes the fact. It may also be suggested that as it was the highest in order of merit it was named after Brāhman, the creator. Here the marriage was not determined by the intensity of desire or by pecuniary considerations but by the welfare of society which was more concerned about the health, family, character and economic standing of the bridegroom. In this way the maiden's happiness was also ensured. It is not very sound to leave the social question of marriage (where improvement of race is involved) to individual caprice. For any society it is really impossible to devise a perfect system of marriage. It can well be said against Brāhma form that being loveless it had no chance of success but the results tell quite a different story. This is the form practised most in India at present and it can never be said that there is a greater disharmony in Indian married life than in those of other nations. Circumstances themselves contributed to the success of this form. During the period when Sūtras, Dharmaśāstras and Epics were compiled the ideal of Pātivrata was firmly entrenched and this ideal was inculcated in girls from childhood. Thus by the time the maiden had attained marriageable age, she was fully pre-

1. Mbh. XIII. 44. 3-4 ; I. 102. 12-13.
2. Mbh. I. 73. 10-11 प्रशस्तांश्चतुरः पूर्वान्ब्राह्मणस्योपधारय।
Mbh. XIII. 44.9, cp. also M. III. 25, cp M III 24

पञ्चानां तु त्रयो धर्म्या द्वावधर्म्यौ युधिष्ठिर ।

It is interesting to note that Meyer "SLAI" p. 511 states that it was named so "not of course, on moral but on very selfish ground"by Brāhmaṇas. A remark made due to prejudice against Brāhmaṇas and ignorence of Indian social conditions.

कुलं च शीलं च वपुर्यशं च, विद्या च वित्तं च सनाथतां च ।
एतैर्गुणा सप्त परीक्ष्य देया कन्या बुधैः शेषंमचिन्तनीयम् ॥

pared psychologically for the kind of relationship that this form involves. Having been brought up to regard the husband as her ideal and almost a god, she was ready willingly to accept any thing as a matter of grace and thus there could be no question of unsuccessful married life. Besides there were also the chances of growth of that love, which grows only through lasting companionship and which can seldom grow out of sheer romantic attraction.

Forms of marriage as practised in the Rāmāyaṇa

From the evidence gathered from the Rāmāyaṇa it seems that Brāhma form of marriage was generally practised. Even if Sītā's marriage is considered according to Prājāpatya form[1] there is not much difference between Brāhma and Prājāpatya as already noticed.[2] Rākshasa form was rarely practised even among the Rākshasa race.[3] Kaikeyī's marriage does not strictly come under the purview of conventional Asura form as the condition for marriage was not money.

It cannot, however, be upheld that other forms were not practised in the society of those days but as the composer of the Rāmāyaṇa wanted to present the ideal point of view, he might have ignored other references.[4]

Forms of marriage as practised in the Mahābhārata

Brāhma, Gāndharva, Rākshasa and Asura forms of procuring the bride were prevalent when the stories of the epics were being written. There was a tendency to prefer Brāhma form. Asura, practised by a few as "Kula Dharma", was not well thought of. To the redactors of the great Epic, however, all the eight forms were known.[5] But they do not state the good results following from the practice of the praiseworthy four

1. Rām. I. 73. 24-25 Janaka's injuction to Rāma and her retaining the status of 'Patnī' throughout.

2. Page 79 Foot note 5 also.

3. Rām. VII. 9.1 ff; 12. 16 ff; 21 ff. are Brāhma marriages practised by the Rākshasas. Rarely, however, Rām. VII 24. 1 ff.

4. References of Gāndharva form cf. Rām. V. 9.68-9; III. 17.25. Vyāsa. S. N. "Rāmāyaṇakālīn Samāj" page 121. (Delhi 1958) quotes some cases of Paiśacha but these cannot be quoted as marriages.

5. A general discussion about these is presented in Appendix A.

forms.[1] Nevertheless in order to discourage the Asura form, the Putrikā who married according to this form was deemed to have forfeited her rights. It was predicted that bad progeny would be the consequence of such a union.[2]

Status of women as depicted by these forms

All these forms throw light upon the position of women. According to Paiśācha and Rākshasa, woman was considered chattel. These forms indicate a very low status of women in society. Nevertheless as already shown Paiśācha was recognized merely to safeguard the interest of women and was not practised. The Rākshasa form as adopted by the Āryans did take the willingness of the maiden concerned into consideration. It cannot be contended that the status of woman was higher according to Ārsha and Asura forms for she had a value and status of respect in her family.[3] Although among the poor people this form may have tended towards monogamy and better treatment of wife for they could not afford her cost repeatedly she was still treated as a commodity. Prājāpatya and Gāndharva did give her equality and freedom of choice. The girl was a gift according to Daiva form but must have been given away by the guardian after considering the suitability, brilliance and learning of the priest (bridegroom). The motive in Brāhma form was of a higher order i.e. it aimed at social good. But it can be argued that the girl concerned was considered a gift. Perhaps the idea underlying was that while the sons were brought up for the benefit of one's own Kula the daughter was given away to another family, in fact to society, for common weal. Nevertheless this form does indicate that her freedom of choice was on the decrease.

Limitations on marriage

So far the freedom in marriage and its gradual decline has been discussed. It may well be that the recognition of these forms was the result of assimilation of various cultures. Many

1. As is done by some Sūtrakāras. Asv. G.G. I. 6. 1-4; Baud. Dh. S. IV. 30-33. Vi. S. XXIV. 29-32. Y. S. I. 58-59 Ap. Dh. S. II. 5.12.4. Manu III. 37-44.

2. Mbh. XIII. 45. 7, 15.16.

3. Altekar "PWHC" pages 46-47.

of these forms as already shown, did not produce good results or were unapproved by society therefore there was a tendency of restricting the freedom of selection given to bride and bridegroom in this field. It was also during the period when the great Epic was being redacted that various races[1] were invading India and were being amalgamated among Indians. It may have been in this process of assimilation of and opposition to various cultures that a tendency of conservatism was developing. This may have been due to the anxiety of preserving whatever was thought to be good in the old culture or due to the experience gained by the society in marriage. This conservatism led to certain limitations in the field of marriage. Thus Asavarṇa i.e. intercaste[2] marriage, although practised before were gradually being discouraged. Marriages between Sagotra, Samānpravara and Sapiṇḍa[3] were also prohibited. This was all in tune with the Dharmaśāstras.

Inter-Racial marriages

The kernel of the epic stories does not indicate restriction in marriages as far as race distinct from Varṇa, (caste) is concerned. The marriages among the Āryans and the non-Āryans, though not common, had no stigma attached to them. Thus Ulūpī, a Nāga by race and Hiḍimbā, a Rākshasī married Arjuna and Bhīma respectively. Jayadratha had wives of many races.[4] Some of the non-Āryans kings may have had the same social status as Kshatriya kings and may have been gradually amalgamated in them due to these inter-racial marriages.

Śūdra-Āryan Marriages

The majority of the non-Āryans, however, sank to the low status of the "Dāsas" who were later on known as Śūdras. In the Ṛg-Vedic society marriage among the Āryans and the 'Dāsīs' were not uncommon[5] and illegal. Even later in the

1. In the Mahābhārata we come across the names of the various races.
2. Mbh. XII. 47. (sec.).
3. Mbh. XIII. 44. 18.
4. Mbh. I. 214. 13 ff. 155 (sec.) XI. 22. 10-11.
Rām. VII. 9 (Kaikasī and Viśrava).
5. Ṛg-V-I-18. 1 ; I. 112. 11. Some respectable Vedic personages like Auśija, Kavaśa and Vatsya were Dāsīputras. Same conditions prevail during the Sūtra period. Baud. Dh. S. I. 11.20.14 remarks that men of warrior caste and people's caste were not particular about their wives.

Manusmṛti it has been stated that the low-born Akshamālā and Sārangī united with Vasishṭha and Mandapāla respectively.[1] The composer of the great Epic also refers to these marriages.[2] But no stigma is attached to them.

Inter caste marriages mostly Anuloma, Āryan-Śūdrā marriages discouraged

Gradually social conditions were changing. Inter caste marriages although at first allowed were being discouraged. A Brāhmaṇa was allowed to have four wives, evidently of four castes but his caste was inherited by the Brāhmaṇī and Kshatriyā wive's progeny. Similarly the Kshatriyas could marry within their caste or lower than theirs but their caste was to be inherited by the issues born of the wives of their own and the Vaiśya caste.[3] In the case of Vaiśya, however, his progeny by Śūdrā woman did not inherit his caste. After this in the next stage marriage of an Āryan with Śūdrā was discouraged.[4] A Brāhmaṇa was allowed to marry the women of the three upper castes. A Kshatriya was permitted two wives that of his own and Vaiśya caste but a Vaiśya was allowed to marry in his own caste only.[5] To discourage, even these marriages the children of the lower caste wives were not given equality in inheritence.[6] Such marriages, when a man married a woman of lower caste, were known as Anuloma, and were sanctioned by law. In spite of this there was a growing dislike for Brāhmaṇa-Śūdrā connections.[7] Thus Śūdrās could be taken by regenerate classes for pleasure but not for having progeny or practising Dharma, i.e. she was denied the status of Patnī-wife. Although these above mention-

1. M. IX. 23.

2. Mbh. V. 117. 11; I. 229. 15-6 although the latter does not sound authentic. Mbh. I. 106. 23-29; 115. 41-44 Dāsīputras like Vidura and Yuyutsu, son of a Vaiśyā-maid servant, are respected in the Kuru court.

3. Mbh. XIII. 48. 4-8 cp. Baud. Dh. S.I. 8. 16. 2; I. 9.17. 2ff. Vi. S. XXIV 1-4; Vas. Dh. S. I. 24; M. III. 12-14. Gaut. Dh. S. IV. 2-5; 12-17.

4. Mbh. XIII. 44. 13; 47.8-9; 48.5.

5. Mbh. XIII. 44. 11-12. Cp. Pāraskara G. S. I. 4. 8-11. Y. S. I.57

6. Mbh. XIII. 47. 11ff. cp. Vas. Dh. S. I. 25-27.

7. Mbh. XIII. 44. 13.

रत्यर्थमपि शूद्रा स्यान्नेत्याहुरपरे जनाः ।
अपत्यजन्म शूद्रायां न प्रशंसन्ति साधवः ॥

ed laws indicated a very low position of Śūdrā woman in Āryan families they also speak ill of the society which could allow a woman to be had for pleasure like an article of enjoyment yet denied her the rights as well as abjured the highest caste men from the responsibilities which are always attached to such pleasures in the civilized world. A Brāhmaṇa's position was only degraded in case he married a Śūdrā but perhaps it did not in case he had extra-marital relations with her[1], and he had to perform expiation only when children were born of such a marriage.[2] The reason for toleration of the Āryan-Śūdrā marriages in the Ṛg-Veda and subsequent ages in the beginning may have been paucity of women among the Āryans. Although the Āryans thought themselves superior still they tolerated Ārya-Dāsī relations. Later when there was no paucity of women, Brāhmaṇas thought of discouraging such marriages. Because it was difficult now to eradicate this system, they made rules prohibiting such unions amongst Brahmaṇas. So while Brāhmaṇa-Śūdrā relations are condemned so much, nothing is stated about Kshatriya-Śūdrā or Vaiśya-Śūdrā relations. It may be presumed that such marriages took place, as Baudhāyana states.[3] It was natural for Kshatriyas and Vaiśayas to have marriage relations with Śūdrās as in their daily life either as conquerors, administrators, traders or agriculturists they were constantly coming in contact[4] with Śūdrās. The above account proves that the Varṇas (castes) were not endogamous during the progress of the great Epic, although it was so advocated by the Dharmaśāstra writers.[5]

1. Mbh. VII. 71.2-3. states that a Brāhmaṇa who married Śūdra degraded his position and Śrāddha performed by him had no efficacy.

आहोस्विदन्तन्तो नष्टं श्राद्धं शूद्रीपताविव ।

Mbh. XIII. 44. 12; 47. 8-9; Mbh. XIII. 23.18; 126.25 Such a Brāhmaṇa was also known as Vṛshalīpati; no gifts, made in honour of gods and manes, were to be given to him. Mbh. V. 37. 12-13. He is classed with the greatest sinners-Brahmahans.

2. Mbh. XIII. 44. 13; 47. 8-9; 48.5 degraded position of such a son.

3. See footnote 5 page 85.

4. It may be due to this contact with Śūdras which made Kshatriyas and Vaiśyas to forget their Āryan code of conduct and therefore it is the tendency of Dharmaśāstrakāras as well as of didactic writers of the great Epic to address the code of conduct to the Brāhmaṇas and frame rules for them only.

5. M. III. 4, 43; Nārada XII. 4.

Pratiloma

As opposed to Anuloma was Pratiloma marriage according to which a lower caste man married a higher caste woman. In order to discourage this form, the composers of the didactic portions of the great Epic, consider the progeny born out of such a connection, outside the pale of the four varṇas (castes).[1] Fear of rebirth was also shown to deter people from such marriages.[2]

Inter-caste marriage in vouge in the epics

In the epic-stories, however, Anuloma and Pratiloma were both practised.[3] It must be due to the fact that these stories depict an older society, although Brāhmaṇa—Śūdrā relations are condemned in these also.

(i) *Brāhmaṇa-Śūdrā relations and Pratiloma in narrative parts*

Garuḍa thought it improper to kill a sinful Brāhmaṇa who had married a Nishādī woman, indicating thereby that marriage with such a woman did not degrade the legal and social position of such a Brāhmaṇa.[4] There is another example of a Brāhmaṇa who married a widow Śūdrā but such relations when mentioned in the didactic portions were condemned all right.[5] The parents of Mātanga illustrate a case of Pratiloma.[6] Devayānī's was Pratiloma marriage. The case of Yayāti being afraid of Śukra's curse, as well as Kacha's curse to Devayānī, may have been added by the redactors to whom such a marriage was repugnant.[7]

1. Mbh. XIII. 48 (sec.) Cp. Vi. S. XVI. They were assigned mean occupations. This is also in tune with the dictum of the great Epic as well as the writers of law Cp. Baud. Dh. S. I. 5. 10. 26 that by neglect of lawful marriage, by which (Savarṇa) one's own caste is meant, families are degraded.
2. Mbh. XIII. 111. 89-91.
3. Mbh. III. 180. 31-37; 171.5 ; 173. 16 ff.
4. Mbh. I. 29. 1-3 न हि मे ब्राह्मणो वध्यः पापेष्वपि रतः सदा
5. Mbh. XII. 168. 32-34 (story from 168-173 sec.).
6. Mbh. XIII. 27.17 Another possible case may be of Prabhāvatī, sister of Brāhmaṇi Rūchi, married to the king of Anga. see Mbh. XIII. 42.8.
7. Mbh. I. 81. 20, 23, 33, 34; I. 77. 19.

(ii) *Marriage with mixed classes*

Either Draupadī's objection[1] for marrying Karṇa is an interpolation or regenerate classes did not like to marry among the mixed classes to which Karṇa was supposed to have belonged. It is really strange that Draupadī had no objection for Arjuna whose parentage was not known and he may have been a Śūdra in the guise of a Brāhmaṇa.[2]

(iii) *Anuloma in practice*

As for the Anuloma marriage there is no dearth of examples. Brāhmaṇa-Kshatriya marriages were quite common. Although many examples of these are found[3] they were gradually being discouraged. Intellectually the Brāhmaṇas may have been superior, but Kshatriya fathers hesitated to give away their daughters, born and bred up in luxury, to poor Brāhmaṇas. When Agni came in the form of Brāhmaṇa to demand the hand of Duryodhana's daughter, he thought "Poor he is and not of my caste"[4], although it was considered meritorious to give away daughters to Brāhmaṇas.[5] In spite of its conservative and idealist tone references hinting at inter-caste marriage are also found in the Rāmāyaṇa.[6]

1. Mbh. I. 187. 23.
2. Mbh. I. 192.14-16 For Drupada suspects this—

पञ्चालराजस्तु विषण्णरूप–
स्तान्पाण्डवान प्रतिविन्दमानः ।
धृष्टद्युम्नं पर्यपृच्छन्महात्मा
क्व सा गता केन नीता च कृष्णा ॥
कच्चिन्न शूद्रेण न हीनजेन
वैश्येन वा करदेनोपपन्ना ।
कच्चित्पदं मूर्ध्नि न पङ्कदिग्धम्
कच्चिन्न माला पतिता श्मशाने ॥

3. Mbh. III. 122. 12-29; 97. 3ff; 115.20-31; 116. 2-9.
4. Mbh. XIII. 2.22.
5. Mbh. XII. 234. 28, 34, 35; XIII. 137. 16, 23. 25, 26; III. 186. 15; cp. Y. S. I. 133 and Kāṇe "Hist. of Dh." Vol. II. part II. chap. XXV. p. 856-857.
6. Rām. II. 63.50 शूद्रायामस्मि वैश्येन जातो नरवराधिप ।

Sociological basis for Pratiloma and Anuloma

The reason for not allowing Pratiloma are sociological. A man does not often rise above to the social level of his wife, and this may be due to the male pride. In such cases the wife being adjustable sinks to the level of her husband. It is therefore better if the husband is of the higher caste, for the wife is capable of rising to higher level. Thus by checking Pratiloma the chances of the wife's sinking to the lower level would be checked. These Anuloma marriages indicate that Āryans intermarried and intermixed, but slowly the gulf between the Varṇas (castes) was widening.

Tendency towards caste endogamy

Gradually inter-caste-marriages were coming to be hated. In the didactic portions such marriages were not recommended.[1] There was a horror against the mixing of the castes (Varṇasankara). The reason for the unpopularity of Pratiloma has already been mentioned. As for Anuloma the Kshatriya's pride may have revolted against the inequality given to their daughters in a Brāhmaṇa household, which may have been the feeling of lower classes when their daughters were married to a higher caste.[2] Indications of dissatisfaction of princesses when

1. Mbh. XIII. 48.1

अर्थाल्लोभाद्वा कामाद्वा वर्णानां चाप्यनिश्चयात् ।
अज्ञानाद्वापि वर्णानां जायते वर्णसंकरः ॥

Mbh. XIII. 104. 132-133

तथा निकृष्टवर्णां च वर्णोत्कृष्टां च वर्जयेत् ।
अयोनिं च वियोनिं च न गच्छेत् विचक्षणः ॥

Mbh. V. 33. 117 समैर्विवाहं कुरुते न हीनैः समैः सख्यं व्यवहारं कथां च ।

Mbh. I. 131. 10 ययोरेव समं वित्तं ययोरेव समं श्रुतम् ।
तयोर्विवाहः सख्यं च न तु पुष्टविपुष्टयोः ॥

Mbh. III. 180. 31-32 ; VII. 66.4 अनन्यासु सवर्णासु पुत्रजन्म च मे भवेत् ।

I. 192. 14-16 Drupada fears that Draupadī might have been won by Vaiśya or Śūdra. Mbh. XII. 69.93; XIII 48.1 ff. cp. Y. S. I. 56. M. III.4.

2. Mbh. XIII. 47. 31-40 cp. M. IX. 86-87; III. 12-14. cp. chap. on "Married life" also Mbh. III. 97. 17-19; 116.6-14 Vi. S. XXVI. 1.3.

married to poor ṛshies are found in the great Epic.[1] In the matter of inheritence also the sons of lower caste wives were not given equality.[2] These various apparent reasons must have led to the unpopularity of inter-caste marriages. Still deeper reasons which prompted the legislation against inter-caste marriages are to be found in appendix 'B'.

Pravara and Gotra limitations in contracting marriages

After race and Varṇa was the Samānapravara and Sagotra limitation in contracting marriages. In the Epic stories, which were depicting earlier social conditions and were not meant for propounding law or morality, nothing is stated against Sagotra and Samānpravara marriages. In the Anuśāsana parva these marriages are forbidden on the authority of Manu.[3] Nothing about pravara has been mentioned in the Mahābhārata and the 'Gotra' is used in the sense of surname in the story part[4] of the great Epic and that of spiritual brotherhood in the didactic portions.[5] In Sītā and Draupadī's marriage Gotra in the modern sense is not mentioned.[6] These restrictions on marriages were not of much importance when the original stories of

1. Mbh. III. 97. 16 ff; 116. 2-8. may be cited as a possible case.

2. Mbh. XIII. 47. 11-20, cp. M. IX. 149 ff. Y. S. II. 125 ff; II. 25-27; I. 38-40. Gaut. Dh. S. XXVIII, 35 ff, Vi. S. XVIII. 1-5.

3. Mbh. XIII. 104. 131

समार्षां व्यंगितां चैव मातुः स्वकुलजां तथा ।

Mbh. XIII. 44. 18.

असपिण्डा च या मातुरंसगोत्रा च या पितुः ।

इत्येतामनुगच्छेत तं धर्मं मनुरब्रवीत् ।।

This Manu may be older than the composer of the present "Manusmṛti" for even in Sūtra literature there is penance prescribed for such a marriage but not in the Mahābhārata.

4. Mbh. I. 81. 8-10 cp. Pāṇini 4.1. 162 अपत्य–पौत्र–प्रभृति गोत्रम् ।

Mbh. I. 185. 37—नाम्ना च गोत्रेण च कर्मणा च ।

5. Mbh. XII. 296. 17-18—मूलगोत्राणि चत्वारि समुत्पन्नानि पार्थिव ।

6. It is said that the kings in Draupadī's swayamvara were introduced by Gotras (see note 2 above), no Gotras in present sense are mentioned in the relevant chapter—see Mbh. I. 186. Therefore, here, Gotra may mean surname. Sita's was in fact Sagotra marriage both she and Rāma discended from Ikshwāku. Where names of the ancestors of both the parties are enumerated nothing is said of the Gotras in present sense.

the epics were written. Even in the recensions where these are mentioned, there is no sin attached, or punishment prescribed for such marriages, as was done in the later metrical Smṛtis.[1]

Sapiṇḍa restrictions

In the Vedas, there is no evidence against Sapiṇḍa marriages.[2] Even marriages within Kula, prohibited in the Mahābhārata[3] were within the memory of the Ṛg-Vedic times[4] although not actually practised. Śatapatha Brāhmaṇa referst to the union of cousins in the fourth generation.[5] Later the composers of the Dharmaśāstras were, however, against such marriages.[6] In spite of this Sapiṇḍa marriages are even now performed in the South. Gautama and Baudhāyana refer to it as a peculiar custom of the South and the former condemns it as a sin.[7] Manu prescribes Chāndrāyaṇa penance for this sin.[8] All this shows that the kernel of the epic story depicts older social conditions than the Dharmaśāstras. The marriages of Arjuna and Subhadrā as well as of Sahadeva and Vijayā[9] indicate that marriages with maternal uncle's daughters were contracted and there was no Sapiṇḍa restriction imposed when epic stories were written and enacted. By the time the didactic portions were written this change in society occurred.[10]

1. The whole question is a complicated one and is dealt with in details in appendix 'C'.

2. Y. S. I. 52. Sapiṇḍa means one who has the same Piṇḍa or particle of the body. Sapiṇḍa relationship according to one verse of Manu after fifth generation, according to another, seventh. The numbers of generations are given differently by Smṛtikāras. (Raghunandana Udvahatattva p. 574).

3. Mbh. XIII. 44. 18; 104. 31 Vyāsa S. N. "Rāmāyaṇa Kālīn Samāj" p. 135.

4. Ṛg. V. X. 9-14 Yama—Yamī episode.

5. Śat. Br. I. 8. 3. 6 S.B.E. Vol. XII. p. 238.
Śat. Br. X. 10—not agnate but cognate marriages were prevalent among Indo-Āryans. Also Smṛti Chandrikā quoting Vājśaneyī Saṁhitā.

तस्मात्समादेव पुरुषादत्तां-चाद्यश्च जायते ।
उत तृतीये सङ्गच्छावहै चतुर्थे सङ्गच्छावहै ।

6. M. III. 5. Y. S. I. 52-53.
Pandey "Hindu Sanskāra", p. 300-303.

7. Baud. Dh. S. I. 1.2.3 and such laws were to be followed in particular localities cp. Gaut. Dh. S. XI. 20.

8. M. XI. 172-173; Ap. Dh. S. II. 5. 11. 16 forbids such marriage.

9. Mbh. I. 219-220; I. 95. 78, 80.

10. Kāṇe "Hist. of Dh." Vol. II. Part I. Chap. IX. p. 460—Tantravartika of Kumārila page 210—Kumārila wants to prove that Subhadrā was not the daughter of Vasudeva but the daughter of his mother's sister, and says

Exogamic Restrictions

Nothing, however, can be stated how these exogamic taboos came to be applied in the field of marriage. The psychological origin of these lies in the horror of incest taboos. As the joint family took hold of the Hindu society sept and Sapiṇḍa exogamy might have been introduced. Experience and observation might have also taught that there was fear of defective progeny in case cousins or blood relations, with bad traits (which are sometimes latent and recessive) are united in marriage. This risk was too great to be taken on the genetic side. As samānagotras and samānapravaras were also supposed to be the progeny of the same ancestors, therefore such marriages were banned.

Effect of these limitations on the status of women

The status of women by these limitations, especially the samānapravara and sagotra ones, must have deteriorated, for these restricted the choice of the bridegrooms who were to be found within the castes but must not belong to the same gotra, pravara and piṇḍa. This difficulty in procuring good bridegrooms, which was encountered by the parents, must have made the daughter a burden, which certainly deteriorated her position.

Plight of a fatherless and brotherless girl in the field of marriage

When the didactic portions of the great Epic were written a fatherless and brotherless girl had less chances of getting married,[1] for a brotherless girl was known as putrikādharmiṇī,

that such female cousins, one degree or several degrees removed, were spoken of as sisters. The argument of Kumārila well illustrates the method of dealing with inconvenient texts adopted by Mīmānsākāras like Kumārila when the text ran counter to their cherished customs but in the Mahābhārata Subhadrā is the daughter of Vasudeva and sister of Kṛshna. See Mbh. I. 219. 18
दुहिता वसुदेवस्य वासुदेवस्य च स्वसा ।

1. Mbh. XIII. 44, 15 यस्यास्तु न भवेद्भ्राता पिता वा भरतर्षभ ।

This objection was an old tradition found from the time of Ṛg-Veda to the time of Smṛtis. Ṛg-V.V. 124.7; II.17.7; Nirukta III. 5. ; M. III. 11 and Y. S. I. 53 Vas. Dh. S. XVII. 16. Vi. S. 15.5 Gaut. Dh. S. XXVIII 18-19 states अभिसन्धिमात्रात्पुत्रिकेत्येकेषाम् ।

Acc. to some teachers she could be mentally made putrikā without any contract with the bridegroom. Therefore it is that Manu and Mbh. forbade marriages with putrikā. In Arjuna's marriage, however, there is a contract. Mbh. I. 215. 25. Other example in the Mahābhārata, Mbh. I. 66. 12ff.

i.e. "invested with the character of a son". Her sons were thus accounted as maternal grandfather's sons. As the Hindu marriage was contracted for continuation of the line, its very purpose was defeated by marrying a putrikā. This, however, does not seem to be a serious objection when the kernel of the epic stories was enacted or was being written.[1] Not only Chitrāngadā who was third wife of Arjuna (thus he had not to depend only upon her for progeny) but Kuntī, Śakuntalā, Sītā were all brotherless. Apart from the objections of the law givers marriage with the brotherless and fatherless girl was avoided because she had no proper protectors in her maidenhood[2] and so her character may have been subject to odium.[3] Her hand was demanded by incompetent persons as she had no father to look after her interest.[4] As already stated dowry and money were not counted in marriage settlement and therefore even when a brotherless girl was an heiress, she had less chances of marriage and to discourage marriage with such a girl her son was given a low status in society by the didactic writers.[5] Thus when the didactic portions of the great Epic were written, a brother and father living at the marriageable age of a girl, enhanced the chances of her marriage which were otherwise diminished if they were not alive.

Polygamy and Polyandry

Polygamy and Polyandry are two peculiar features of marriage as they are a deviation from normal married life i.e. monogamy. Although monogamy was an ideal even in the

1. Mbh. I. 215. 23 ff ; I. 111. 2 ff; I. 72-73 (sec.)

2. Father as protector Mbh. XIII. 20.21 46. 14. पिता रक्षति कौमारे भर्ता रक्षति यौवने । पुत्राश्च स्थाविरे भावे न स्त्री स्वातन्त्र्यमर्हति ।

Mbh. V. 176. 5-8 विषमे च पिता गतिः । Brother the giver of maiden. Rām. VII. 25.28 Cp. Y. S. 63 father, grandfather, brother and mother each is entitled to give away a girl in the absence of the former guardian.

3. According to old Ṛg-Vedic tradition it is said that a brotherless girl runs after men. Ṛg-V. 124. 7.

4. Mbh. I. 158. 14-19.

5. Mbh. XIII. 23. 20 पुत्रिकापूर्वपुत्राश्च श्राद्धे नार्हन्ति केतनम् । पुत्रिकापूर्वपुत्राः अस्यामुत्पन्नः पुत्रो मदीय इति नियमेन या दीयते तस्यां च यो जातः स पुत्रिकापूर्वपुत्रः । स पितृगोत्राद्भ्रष्टो मातृगोत्रोपजीवित्वान्निन्द्यः ।—नीलकण्ठ ।

epics[1], polygamy was a common practice among Kshatriyas.[2] Thus kings had no objection in bestowing their daughters as second and third wives[3] and sometimes many sisters were married to the same person.[4] Among Brāhmaṇas, polygamy was allowed by law[5] yet they did not practise it[6]. Polygamy does indicate that woman was thought to be property to be collected by man. In giving a daughter as second and third wife the parents did not have consideration for her future happiness and even her rights (as will be shown in the next chapter), for only the eldest wife had certain religious rights with the hus band. But polygamy was taken so much for granted that even an old hero with four wives was thought to be a competent bridegroom for a very young princess,[7] for in those heroic ages to be fourth wife of a hero was of greater prestige and status than to be first wife of a young prince with no such reputation.[8]

It may be said that as opposed to polygamy polyandry is mentioned in the great Epic which apparently gives same right to woman as polygamy to men. But there is only a single case of polyandry and in that also the father is most unwilling to give away his daughter. To draw any conclusion about Draupadī's status is very difficult as she has been shown as

1. Example of Rāma who was an ideal king page 446 of M. N. Dutta's translation of Rām. II. 104.4. 65. 43

2. Even Dharmarāja is married twice Mbh. I. 95. 76 although Devikā, has not been mentioned any where even in XV. 25. Kṛshṇa had many thousand wives. Mbh. V. 158.8. In Mbh. VII. 65. 1-2 a man with hundred thousand wives has a 'Viruda' of high souled.

3. Mbh. I. 215 (marriage of Arjuna—Chitrāngadā) Mbh. I. 219.21. Kṛshṇa agrees to give away Subhadrā as third wife to Arjuna. Thus many married kings attend Draupadī's Swayamvara with a view to the contest and are introduced to her. Mbh. I. 186. 13, 21, 23, 24 Śalya, Jarāsandha and Śiśupāla.

4. Mbh. I. 66. 11 ff.

5. Mbh. I, 158. 35-36. XIII. 44. 11 ; 47.7.

6. Pargiter in "AIHT" chap. XXVII. p. 328 condemns Brāhmaṇa morality but Jamdagni, Gautama, Droṇa, Kṛpa, Jaratkāru, Vaśiśtha, Atri, the Brāhmaṇa in Vaka-Vadha. parva (Mbh. I. 158) and the Brāhmaṇa in Nakulopākhyāna all were monogamous.

7. Mbh. IV. 71. 34.

उत्तरां प्रतिगृह्णातु सव्यसाची धनञ्जयः
अयं ह्यौपयिको भर्ता तस्याः पुरुषसत्तमः ॥

8. Mbh. IV. 72. 1 ff. when Arjuna suggests that Uttarā will be taken by him as his daughter-in-law Virāta questions him why he rejected her for his wife? For further reference see appendix D.

an ideal Pativratā by the writers to whom polyandry was repugnant and unfamiliar and whatever strong opinions she may hold she is cften made to bow down to the opinion of Dharmarāja. The subsequent discussion in Appendix—E will also indicate that as Draupadi's was a single case therefore it is not proper to draw any conclusion about the status of women in polyandry. It can, however, be said that even in polyandry in case there is patriarchy, the woman is considered as property and so was Draupadī.[1]

Due to the various reasons cited above considerable freedom which was once possessed by the maidens in contracting marriage and even living unmarried, gradually diminished. The guardian's control and various limitations took possession of all her rights. Her legal position in marriage was that of chattel although loving guardians and fathers did not consider it to be so yet practically all her future happiness depended upon their mercy.

1. Saxena "Social Economy of a Polyandrous People" chap. III. pp. 28-29 Marriage and divorce laws, clearly indicate that women are considered property in polyandry. The pawning of Draupadī indicates the same status of chattel, Polyandry may have been a strong tradition but it was not liked. Mbh. XIV. 18. 14; I. 158. 35-36.

CHAPTER V

MARRIED LIFE

(The woman and family life)

Importance of Married Life

The life according to the Epics was divided into four Āśramas[1], in which a person exerted for the attainment of four Purushārthas of life.[2] In the Great Epic the three opinions about the Āśramas i.e. Bandha, Vikalpa and Samuchchaya,[3] are to be found, although these were not as yet assigned any specific name. Samuchchaya means to follow the four Āśramas in order[4], an idea which permeates throughout the Great Epic. Those who follow Vikalpa were for option, that is, one may take straightaway to Sanyāsa after the studies or may enter Gṛhasthāśrama i.e. married life, for every Āśram if followed properly led to the highest aim i.e. the attainment of Brāhman.[5] In fact the Āśramas are compared to the flights of steps. One had option to walk firmly through all or to jump over them but the destination[6] was the same. According to Bandha, Gṛhasthāśrama was the best of all the Āśramas[7], the weightiest of all.[8]

The social conditions as depicted in the Great Epic indicate that the idea of Bandha had to fight a strong tendency

1. अश्राम्यति अस्मिन् इति आश्रमः ।
2. धर्म, अर्थ, काम, मोक्ष ।
3. For these names see Kaṇe "Hist. of Dh." Vol. II, Chap. VIII. part I. p. 424.
4. Mbh. XII. 234. 6-7.
5. Mbh. XII. 242. 13; 234. 3-5; 352. 2-3.
6. Mbh. XII. 242. 15.

   चतुष्पदी हि निःश्रेणी ब्रह्मण्येषा प्रतिष्ठिता ।
   एतामारुह्य निःश्रेणीं ब्रह्मलोके महीयते ॥
7. Mbh. XII. 12. 6, 11, 12 (whole sec. also).
8. Mbh. XII. 12. 12.

   आश्रमांस्तुलया सर्वान् धृतानाहुर्मनीषिणः ।
   एकतश्च त्रयो राजन् गृहस्थाश्रम एकतः ।

pp. 21.22 of Eng. tr. of P. C. Roy Mbh. XII. 64.6; 66.15 Mbh. XIV. 44. 17; Rām. II. 106.22. चतुर्णामाश्रमाणां हि गार्हस्थ्यं श्रेष्ठमुत्तमम् ।

of renunciation, which was slowly gaining ground[1]. Renunciation although, open to all was mostly followed by the Brāhamaṇas, due to its rigid discipline and was thought to be suitable for them.[2] Even for the Brāhmaṇas for whom the danger of renunciation was the most, this new tendency was discouraged, for the masses were being influenced by anti-Vedic religions i.e. Jainism and Buddhism. On the Brāhmaṇas fell the duty of preserving and following the old pattern of the Vedic society. Thus the tendency of Dharmaśāstras of addressing the code of conduct to the Brāhmaṇas only, even if it was considered proper for all the classes, is also followed by the didactic portions of the Great Epic. In innumerable passages of the Śānti Parva, the Brāhmaṇas are advised to enter domestic life on concluding their studies.[3] The other three orders generally did not take to the life of renunciation.[4] Nevertheless, whenever kings thought of adopting Sanyāsa, they were jeered at by their relatives and wives[5] and were dissuaded from that path. Angāraparṇa chides the Pāṇḍavas for not entering the life of domesticity after finishing their studies.[6]

There were two main reasons for the great importance attached to domestic life. As already stated it was believed that man was born with three debts viz. to the ṛshis (Ṛshi ṛṇa), to the deities (Deva ṛṇa) and to the ancestors (Pitṛ ṛṇa) which he could repay, and had to repay,—respectively by studying the Vedas, by offering sacrifices and by begetting children.[7] It was only in the domestic phase of life that the two debts to the deities and to the ancestors (manes) could be repaid. This part of life was considered to be the best, the root and refuge of all the Āśramas[8] and was a prop even of Sanyāsa. Without it no other phase of life was possible.[9] It was like a mother in giving shelter to all. As the sea received all rivers so it

1. Mbh. XII. 296 (sec.); 24 (sec.) ;
2. Mbh. XII. 23. 15; 57.3 राजानं चाविरोद्धारं ब्राह्मणं चाप्रवासिनम्।
3. Mbh. XII. 234. 6, 7.
4. Mbh. XII. 62. 2; 63. 1.
5. Mbh. XII. 8-17 (sec.); 18.3 ff.
6. Mbh. I. 170. 60 अनग्नयोऽनाहुतयो–अनग्नयः दारहीनत्वात्—— Nīlakaṇṭha cp. Ram. II. 75.35; I. 18.51.
7. Mbh. XII. 28. 55.
8. Mbh. XII. 234. 6-7; 295. 39 cp. M. VI. 90. is the same.
9. Mbh. XII. 269. 5-8.

welcomed every one.[1] It was said that in the family life one performed great penance,[2] of course, by serving the society. Therefore, domestic life, as an essential element of social responsibility, was almost compulsory.

Wife's place in the family—her great importance

The family as traced in the Epics is patriarchal and patrilineal; sons inherit the name, wealth and kingdoms of fathers. As already stated marriages also indicate these strong patriarchal bonds.[3] The single vague reference to undeveloped matriarchy that occurs, has been made disparagingly.[4] Naturally husband was considered the senior partner in the home although theoretically the husband and wife were "Dampati" which etymologically means joint owners.[5] Nevertheless, woman's altruistic spirit, economy, artistic propensities, above all her vocation of motherhood—all centripetal functions—essential for the smooth running of a good home, always give her all the power which she well deserves. Thus she was considered the light and life of the home.[6] It is stated that a householder's home, even if filled with sons and grandsons, daughters-in-law and servants was to be regarded a void and wilderness without a wife.[7] According to old Vedic tradition which continued even in the Epics the wife was considered to be

1. Mbh. XII. 269. 6.
Mbh. XII. 295. 39

यथा नदीनदाः सर्वे सागरे यान्ति संस्थितिम् ।
एवमाश्रमिणः सर्वे गृहस्थे यान्ति संस्थितिम् ॥

M. VI. 90 is the same.

2. Mbh. XII. 66. 23; 269. 7.
3. Supra. Chap. 2. "Marriage" p. 62.
4. Mbh. VIII. 45. 13

न चैवास्मात्प्रमोक्षध्वं घोरात्पापान्नराधमाः ।
तस्मात्तेषाँ भागहरा भागिनेया न सूनवः ॥

5. Mbh. XIII. 146. 39-40

6. Mbh. V. 38. 11 पूजनीया महाभागाः पुण्याश्च गृहदीप्तयः ।
Mbh. I. 74. 52 ff.
Cp. Ṛg V. I. 66. 3 ornaments of home.

7. Mbh. XII. 144. 5-6, 17. cp. Ṛg. III. 53.4. जायेदस्तं मघवन्त्सेदु योनिस्तदित्त्वा युक्ता हरयो वहन्तु ।

a true friend of man given by God,[1] for she was man's half, his religious partner, giver of joy and sons, through whom he attained immortality.[2] At home every thing appertaining to religion, pleasure, wealth, careful nursing of offspring for perpetuating the race—all depended upon her.[3] It was natural for such importance to be attached to the wife in view of the central position she occupied in her domestic life.

In the didactic portions of the Great Epic woman in general has been dehumanized due to ascetic influence but even such an influence did not harm the position of a wife, for woman as wife has been praised and respected. The difference between woman and wife sometimes reaches ridiculous heights. A Nāga for instance describes his wife as chaste, devoted and auspicious and at once asks her whether she had neglected her duties due to the 'unclean' (dull) understanding natural to a woman[4] and then in the next chapter states that he is specially lucky in getting such a wife.[5] There is no dearth of such typical passages in the Great Epic where a wife as such is extolled and trusted and women are scorned and distrusted. In the conditions depicted in the story part of the Epics husbands regard their wives with tenderness and affection. The Brāhmaṇa husband was not ready to sacrifice his wife saying, "Thou art my helpmate in all good

1. Mbh. I. 74. 41 भार्या श्रेष्ठतमः सखा । I. 157. 31. सखायं विहितां देवैः ०।

Rām. I. 77. 27-28; 12. 68-69.

Cp. A. Br. VII. 3. 13 सखा ह जाया।

Raghuvaṃśa VIII. 67. गृहिणी सचिवः सखी मिथः प्रियशिष्या ललिते कलाविधौ।

Sam. Nilkāya I. 6. 4. भरिया च परमा सखा ।

Tait. Sam. VI. 8. 5. Thus according to older traditions a man was incomplete till he married. Acc. to Bhavabhuti's "Mālatī Mādhava" VI, 18. "The wife is to the husband and vice versa the dearest friend, the essence of all kinship, the fulfilment of all desires, a veritable treasure, the very life itself" प्रेयो मित्रं, बन्धुता वा समग्रा सव कामाः, शेवधिर्जीवितं वा। स्त्रीणां भर्ता, धर्मदाराश्च पुंसामित्यन्योन्यं वत्सयोर्ज्ञातमस्तु ।।

2. Mbh. I. 74. 37 ff.

3. Mbh. XIII. 46. 10 ff.

4. Mbh. XII. 359. 3-4. अथ त्वमसि कल्याणि देवतातिथिपूजने। पूर्वमुक्तेन विधिना युक्तियुक्तेन तत्समम्। न खल्वस्य कृतार्थेन स्त्रीबुद्धया मार्दवी कृता ।

5. Mbh. XII. 360. 19,

deeds, self denying and always affectionate to me as mother. The Gods have given thee to me a true friend and thou art my prime stay.........I cannot abandon thee my wife so constant in thy vow to save my life."[1] The same tenderness of feelings, the same love flows through Rāma's lips when Sītā is abducted, he says, "Coming within the compass of my remembrance, the loss of my kingdom, the death of my father, the separation of my mother, culminated in grief. Repairing unto woods, O, Lakshmaṇa, in Sītā's company my grief was assuaged, nay I did not suffer physical afflictions even, without Sītā these sorrows have grown anew, like unto the forest fire flaring again by means of fuel.[2]" This was the general idea about a wife before the Great Epic was recast. This reveals the true picture of a wife as a friend to man in distress and a medicine to which there was no equal.[3] It was such a wife, who was true saha-dharmiṇī[4] and gave her husband psychological protection and security through her care.[5]

The transition of wife from Sahadharmiṇī to docile Pativratā and the position of woman under the two ideals (a) A Sahadharmiṇī.

The dignity of wifely position in the story part of the Epics naturally inspired confidence and the Epics are full of stories when princesses born and bred in luxury happily followed their royal or rshi husbands to the wilderness of the forest.[6] They could gladly bear all woes and hardships with an even temper. Sītā, Sāvitrī, Damayantī, Sukanyā, Lopāmudrā are all examples of Himālayan self-confidence, which Indian women later lost completely for they were not true sahadharmiṇīs. Even in great troubles the Epic heroines retain perfect balance of mind. Yudhishṭhira, knowing that Karṇa was the brother of the Pāṇḍavas, killed by them, loses heart. He is ready to renounce the kingdom. While Draupadī, whose loss as a mother

1. Mbh. I. 157. 30-34.
2. Ram. III.63.5-6 p. 655 of M.N. Roy's translation.
Ram IV. 54. 7-17 Even the non-Āryans, the Vānaras, could not live long without their wives. Rāma respected their feelings cf. Ram. VI. 120. 5-6.
3. Mbh. I. 74. 41, 43 ff; XII. 144. 15.
4. Mbh. XIII. 141. 43; दम्पत्योः समशीलत्वं धर्मः स्याद्गृहमेधिनः। XII. 144. 13. cp. Āp. Dh. S. II. 6. 14. 17-19.
5. Mbh. XIV. 90. 46 ff.
6. Rām. II. 40; Mbh. III. 116. 2-3; 123. 26; 115. 29-30; 113. 22; 97. 7-10. II. 79. 3.

was greatest in the Pāṇḍava camp reminds Yudhishṭhira of his Kshatriya duties,[1] and another Kshatriyā queen of Videha brings back her husband to the path of duty.[2] These women often discussed with their husbands and chid and corrected them whenever they did not see eye to eye, yet they were perfect pativratās[3] and were known as such, for generally speaking a pativratā is one who is devoted to her husband and is his companion through thick and thin.

Difference between Sahadharmiṇī and the later Pativratā conception of an ideal wife (b) Pativratā

In the didactic portions, however, this position of sahadharmiṇī or friend was lost and the whole conception of pativratā gradually changed. The wife as portrayed in the narrative part of the Epics played the role of sahadharmiṇī by guiding the husband and retaining independent judgement. Due to lack of education, loss of religious status and child marriages she lost her judgement and her personality was naturally immersed in the personality of her husband who was learned, while she was ignorant. So the husband, as already stated, came to command the same respect from the wife as the preceptors commanded from their disciple.[4] According to the redactors of the Mahābhārata as well as the idealist tone of the Rāmāyaṇa the husband was not only a friend but an ideal, principle, preceptor and the very God[5] of the wife. She was to worship him with single-minded devotion. Her position was later not of a friend but of a devotee. Both these attitudes are found intermingled in the Epics probably because the redactors have changed the old stories to suit the new conditions. The devotee wife, who also did her house-hold duties carefully was known as pativratā—a real sharer of the husband's cult.[6] So here for convenience in further references sahdharmiṇīs, will be

1. Mbh. XII. 14. 7 ff.
2. Mbh. XII. 18. 3 ff.
3. Mbh. III. 1. 6.
4. Rām. II. 118. 2. नार्याः पतिर्गुरुः।
5. Rām. II. 39. 31 स्त्रिया भर्ता हि दैवतम्। II. 62. 8; 117. 22, VI. 119. 36; Mbh. III. 206. 30. XII. 148. 7. XIII. 8. 20.
6. Mbh. XIII. 123. 21 'पतिधर्म' is used for all duties towards house-hold and for such a lady who performs these पतिव्रत-भागिनी is used in Mbh. XIII. 146. 53. 59.

used for the wives who were friends and guides of their husbands and paṭivratās for those who were devotees, for the word has been used to cover the broad aspect of a wife's duties.

The mental attitude and training of Pativratā

The life of a true pativratā was to be of unremitting service of a constant round of duties towards parents-in-law, husband, house-hold, servants, guests, together with other religious and economic obligations. The sacrifice of her own interests and even personality, for her husband and his family, was by no means an easy task. Therefore she was to be trained for it from the very childhood. In the family which is the first training ground and where the behaviour of the child receives its first shaping influence, the pātivrata ideal was carefully inculcated from the very childhood. As already referred to the parents and the Brāhmaṇas prepared the plastic or impresionable mind of a girl for this ideal.[1] Later when she was married mothers-in-law, other elderly ladies and friends also gave the same sermon.[2] In fact the composers of the Epics seize every opportunity to describe the duties of women, perhaps, thinking that as women were frail and fickle-minded they must be reminded of their duties constantly. Thus not only the elders and friends advise but the younger also instruct their elders.[3] Lest bad company may spoil, in the redacted portions of the Mahābhārata a pativratā was advised that even among women she was to form attachments carefully only with such females as were high born, sinless and devoted to their lords.[4]

Duties and responsibilities of a wife (a) towards the elders

In the joint household of which the Epic-brides became members their duties towards the parents-in-law were of great importance. An attitude of deference towards the parents-in-law, which was the heritage of the Vedic age, was still maintained.[5] In many respects, in case she had administrative capacity like that of Draupadī, the Ṛg-vedic position of the empress

1. Rām. II. 27. 10; 117. 7-9; 29. 18 ff.
2. Rām. II. 117. 15 ff. Mbh. III. 233 (Sec.).
3. Rām. II. 21. 60; 24. 25 ff. Rām. VII. 47. 17-18.
4. Mbh. III. 234. 10 cp. Vāt. Kāmasūtra IV. 1. 9.
5. Upādhyāya "Women in Ṛg. V." p. 138; 144 ff. for mother was always respected in family.

of the household was also maintained.[1] Usually the daughters-in-law looked after the household in a subordinate position.[2] Serving at the feet of the father-in-law and the mother-in-law, waiting upon them with drinks and clothes was an important duty of a daughter-in-law. By these services she gained ascetic merits and heaven for herself.[3] Yudhishṭhira's message to the daughters-in-law of the Kuru family indicated that society expected them to be kind and considerate to their fathers-in-law.[4] In the didactic portions daughters-in-law, in order to show their reverence, were not expected to order the servants in the presence of their parents-in-law. When Daityā women imbibed such defect Śrī (the Goddess of prosperity) is supposed to have left them[5]. Humiliating the mother-in-law was considered to be a great sin.[6] Husband's putative father (father through Niyoga) was also accorded the same respect.[7]

Whatever is prescribed in the didactic portions, is also supported by the stories of the Epics and therefore in this respect the former practice and the later theory were the same. Thus Sāvitrī attended upon her parents-in-law and went to the forest with Satyavān after obtaining their permission.[8]

Sītā and Draupadī served their mothers-in-law with care and affection.[9] Sītā in her distress always thought of Kauśalyā which indicates her affection.[10] Draupadī, even when she was queen herself prepared unguents for Kuntī.[11] The elder brother of the husband, was in many cases head of the family and was to be accorded the services and obedience due to such a head, even otherwise he commanded the same respect[12], and was served by the younger sister-in-law, with the humility worthy of a disciple.

1. Ṛg. V. X. 85. 46 cp. Mbh. III. 233; II. 52. 48.
2. Mbh. III. 233. 33; XIII. 123. 10.
3. Rām II. 26. 30-32, 35.
   Mbh. III. 233. 38; XIII. 123. 10; 146. 15 XIII. 146. 57
   cp. Vat. Kāma Sūtra IV. 5.
4. Mbh. V. 30. 35.
5. Mbh. XII. 228. 76.
6. Mbh. XIII. 93. 131; 94. 38.
7. Mbh. XV. 29. 37; 30. 1.
8. Mbh. III. 295. 20; 296. 23 ff.
9. Rām. VII. 42. 27. Mbh. III. 233. 33;
10. Rām. V. 25. 11. VI. 32. 11; 48. 20-21.
11. Mbh. IV. 20. 23-24.
12. Mbh. XV. 27. 16; XV. 19. 6; XIV, 69. 9. Uttarā wants to take Yudhishṭhira's permission for dying.

With all the respect enjoined for him, the father-in-law was not feared and kept at a distance. Dhṛtarāshṭra when leaving for the forest mode of life (Vānaprastha) was surrounded by his daughters-in-law and the Pāṇḍava ladies uttered loud wails when he left.[1] There could be no better homage paid to the father-in-law than that of the daughter-in-law of the Brāhmaṇa in Nakulopākhyāna "Thou art the senior of my senior, since thou art deity of my deity. Thou art verily the God of my God......... My body, life-breath and religious rites have all one purpose viz., the service of my senior. Through thy grace, O, learned Brāhmaṇa, I shall obtain many regions of happiness hereafter'[2]. All these examples indicate the respect and affection of the daughters-in-law for their fathers-in-law.

(b) *Duties towards the husband*

The wife's duties and obligations towards her husband were of utmost importance. All her duties according to the Mahābhārata began with married life when she became the religious partner of her husband.[3] He was to her all in all. The supreme good of her life was to fulfil her duty towards him for he was her lord.[4]

1. Mbh. XV. 15. 3-4 वधूजनवृतो राजा ।

2. Mbh. XIV. 90. 76 ff. page 196 of P. C. Roy's Eng. translation (New Ed.)

3. Mbh. XIII. 146. 34

स्त्रीधर्मः पूर्व एवायं विवाहे बन्धुभिः कृतः ।
सहधर्मचरी भर्तुर्भवत्यग्निसमीपतः ॥

4. Rām. v 16. 26 भर्ता नाम परं नार्याः शोभनं भूषणादपि ।

Rām. II. 39. 29.

नातन्त्री वाद्यते वीणा नाचक्रो विद्यते रथः ।
नापतिः सुखमेधेत या स्यादपि शतात्मजा ॥

Rām. II. 39. 30 मितं ददाति हि पिता मितं भ्राता मितं सुतः ।
Mbh. XII. 148. 6-7 अमितस्य तु दातारं भर्तारं का न पूजयेत् ॥

Rām. II. 27. 6.

न पिता नात्मजो नात्मा न माता न सखीजनः ।
इह प्रेत्य च नारीणां पतिरेको गतिः सदा ॥

Rām. VII. 48. 17-18.

पतिर्हि देवता नार्याः पतिर्बन्धुः पतिर्गुरुः ।
प्राणैरपि प्रियं तस्माद्भर्तुः कार्यं विशेषतः ॥

Rām. II. 24. 12 ff; 61. 24; 29. 7; 27. 4-6; 117. 22; 118. 2-9.

Her loyalty towards her husband started from the moment the choice of the groom by her or for her was made; that is to say even before she was actually married.[1] She was never to waver from her loyalty and never to find fault with her husband. She must follow him in prosperity as well as in adversity. He may be well-disposed or ill-disposed towards her, wicked, libidinous, poor or sickly he must be obeyed and loved.[2] Her affection for him was to be like that of a mother for her child, the highest and the most selfless.[3] She was to be sweet in speech for such a wife was the joy of the world.[4] Even if the husband should lose his temper, she must not. She should be ever cheerful.[5] She must never entertain the thought of another man, for even this very thought polluted her.[6] This was not all but a truly devoted wife must not cast her eyes upon the moon or sun or a tree that had a masculine name ![7] Her loyalty and human weakness were to be extremely guarded, for Satyabhāmā is advised by Draupadī that she must forego all excitement and carelessness in the presence of men, concealing her inclinations by observing silence and she was not to converse in private even with her sons Pradyumna and Sāmba[8]. The loyalty of wife to husband was taken so much for granted that according to the notions of the times it was only during anarchy, evil times or when the destruction of a race was drawing near such a loyalty c.ased.[9]

It was not for a pativratā to question the command or the will of her master. Lakshmaṇa while leaving the renounced Sītā, in the wilderness of the forest, advises her to spend her days happily, keeping Rāma always in her mind. To the modern

1. Mbh. III. 294. 26-28 in case of Sāvitrī.
2. Rām. II. 27. 5; 117. 21-23.
3. Mbh. XIII. 146. 44.
4. Mbh. V. 33. 82. प्रिया च भार्या प्रियवादिनी च···षड् जीवलोकस्य सुखानि राजन् ।
5. Mbh. XIII. 146. 42; XIII. 123. 9.
6. Mbh. III. 116. 7-8 ff.
7. Mbh. XIII. 146. 43 न चन्द्रसूर्यौ न तरुं पुंनाम्ना या निरीक्षते ।
8. Mbh. III. 234. 10. मदं प्रमादं पुरुषेषु हित्वा, संयच्छ भावं प्रतिगृह्य मौनम् । प्रद्युम्नसाम्बावपि ते कुमारौ, नोपासितव्यौ रहिते कदाचित् ॥
9. Mbh. XVI. 2. 11.

mind it may sound ironical but not to Sītā, as depicted by the redactors, who had the mental make-up of a pativratā.[1] A bad husband could order his wife to do any thing howsoever improper or unrighteous but she was to perform it as a sacred duty in adversity regardless of the consequences.[2] As there was complete submission without any wish for reciprocation the ideal pativratās themselves felt unhappy if the husband's life was sacrificed for them even in distress, a duty which he was expected to perform by the society. Their devotee attitude belittled themselves as insignificant objects unworthy of such a sacrifice.[3]

Through some of the passage the redactors of the Epics have tried to give the impression that such an ideal was followed in the period when the Epic stories were being enacted.[4] Thus the ideal pativratā, Draupadī, waited upon her husbands with the devotion of a slave so that her days and nights were equal.[5] Suppressing and finally leaving all human weakness,[6] Draupadī served her husbands steadfastly. She did nothing which was disagreeable to them even in little matters and waited upon them with single-minded servile devotion.[7] This ideal behaviour of pativratā has been reiterated by Śāṇdilī and Pārvatī in the Anuśāsana parva.[8]

Wifehood vs. Motherhood

Although motherhood is supreme and is so recognized at one place in the Great Epic,[9] yet according to the Epic ideal a woman's love for husband must outweigh that for her child, she had been advised to love her husband as a child.[10] Generally the Epic women wanted to adhere to this ideal.[11] Kausalyā wavers as was natural in her case but regains her balance.[12] The only exception is Kaikeyī, who preferred the

1. Rām. VII. 48. 17 ff.
2. Mbh. XIII. 146. 57-58 (Duty in distress).
3. Rām. VI. 32. 28; Mbh. I. 158. 24, 27.
4. Mbh. III. Sec. 233-234. Draupadī's advice to Satyabhāmā is in the Vana parva. Most of its parts are redacted according to the scholars.
5. Mbh. III. 233. 55-57.
6. Mbh. III. 233. 19, 27, 29.
7. Mbh. III. 233. 19 ff. (whole sec.).
8. Mbh. XIII. 123. ; 146 (sec.).
9. Mbh. I. 233. 31.
10. Rām. II. 35. 8. Mbh. XIII. 146. 44.
11. Mbh. XIV. 80. 7. Rām. IV 21. 13.
12. Rām. II. 61. 2 ff.

kingdom for her son to the life of her husband.[1] Circumstances, however, prove that she was not much to blame.

In favour of this ideal of wifehood preached in the Epics it must be said that however powerful motherhood may be it is after all the instinct of reproduction in action which is as strong a force in animals. As civilization advances it does not lose its place but other important duties and functions are also attached to womanhood. Foremost among these is the duty of love or wifehood which is to be cultivated. Valuable to each life and each generation is a wife who ranks higher in art, literature and with finer spirits. A perfect beloved is an ideal form created by a developed intellect. Wifehood thus is a specialized object of human feelings and fastidious emotions. The worth of wifehood in a society can best be estimated by the completeness with which women fulfil the inspirations of love with the devotion which reached its highest in the pātivratā ideal.

Proshita-patikā

According to the ideals described by the redactors a pativrāta was to live in great simplicity when her husband was absent. She was expected to decorate herself to please her husband and for this object only ornaments were given to her by her relatives.[2] Śāṇḍilī describing her ideal behaviour says "when my husband is away on any business, I remain at home engaged in diverse kinds of auspicious acts to bless his enterprise. During the absence of my husband I never use collyrium or ornaments; I never dress myself beautifully or use garlands and unguents, deck my feet with lac dye or my person with ornaments."[3] Draupadī also states that the separation of her lords was never agreeable to her and on such occasions she used to undergo penance.[4] Rāma persuading Sītā to stay back while he would be away in the forest recommends the same behaviour.[5]

1. Even in her case if the events are followed carefully she is not much to blame for there was an atmosphere of suspicion against her and her son and no one except Vasishṭha trusted them cp. Rām. II. 37. 30 ff. We do not find any legislation against 'Patighni' in the legal portions of the Great epic although it is in subsequent legal literature cp. Y. S. I. 70-72 Vas. Dh. S. XXI. 10. for there were no such women described in the Epics.

2. Mbh. III. 233. 30 ff; XIII. 46. 3-4 cp. Vāt. Kāma Sūtra IV. 1. 13, 23 ff.

3. Mbh. XIII. 123. 16-7 cp. Vat. ; Kāma Sūtra. IV. 1. 43.-44.

4. Mbh. III. 233. 30-31.

5. Rām. II. 26. 29-30.

Sītā lives up to this ideal when the separation was forced on her by Rāvaṇa. She never decorated herself at Lankā. Hanūmān saw her in few dirty ornaments, soiled clothes and wearing a single matted braid, grown thin by fasting and full of tears.[1] Damayantī in Chedi kingdom lived, divested of all her ornaments, in great simplicity.[2]

General behaviour

The general behaviour of an ideal woman was to be marked by tenderness, delicacy, gentleness, serenity and self-control. She was never to laugh a loud except in jest.[3] Smiling and cheerful faces of women were ideal of the Epic composers.[4] She was never to indulge in any passion.[5] She was not to linger at the house gate or even in the pleasure garden attached to the house.[6] This segregation was not due to any 'purdah' system. It was thought respectable for the aristocratic ladies to be aloof from the public gaze. They sought retiring modesty for they thought that aloofness and seclusion lends charm to women. An ideal pativratā was not only to serve her husband but also her co-wives restraining her jealousy.[7] Thus by her complete self-denial she was to sweeten the life within the sphere of her influence.

Respect and reward for such behaviour

It was a belief of society that the goddess of prosperity (Śrī) resided in such a woman.[8] As for a pativratā the highest reality was considered to be the duties towards her

1. Rām. V. 19. 20-21; 15. 20-24, 34; 16. 26. The description is given in fullest details in Rām. V. 11.2; 28. 12;

Rām. V Sargas 15 and 16.

Mbh. III. 281. 1.

2. Mbh. III. 68. 13 ff. cp. M. IX. 74-75. Vi. S. XXV, 9-10. Veda-Vyāsa Smṛti II. 52-all enjoin upon wife whose husband was away to lead life of simplicity.

3. Mbh. III. 233. 28.

4. Mbh. XIII. 123. 7.

5. Mbh. III. 233. 19; 234. 10.

6. Mbh. III. 233. 28.

7. Mbh. III. 233. 19-20 प्रणयमीर्ष्याम् ।—नीलकण्ठः ।

cp. Kālidāsa's "Abhijñāna Śākuntalam" Act. IV· प्रियसखीवृत्तिं सपत्नीजने ।

8. Mbh. XIII. 11. 14.

husband, such women who served their husbands well were known as "Brahmachāriṇī,[1] Here this word was connotative of chastity and not celibacy. It was true otherwise also for the husband was considered to be a means of wife's spiritual fulfilment.[2] It was a belief that through the services rendered to the husband and duties performed at home a pativratā attained the highest heaven.[3]

The Epics are full of praise for the pativratās. In fact the aim of the Rāmāyaṇa is to depict the greatness of Sītā's character.[4]

Such ideals dwarfed woman's personality

To the modern mind there is nothing much to appreciate in this kind of one-sided loyalty, which was complete slavery for women. Not that a man is not advised, in the Epics, to be loyal to his wives but it must be borne in mind that while for a woman the idea of chastity was very rigid,[5] a man could have many wives.[6] The artificial seclusion imposed upon her must have dwarfed her personality, which develops only in relation to society.[7]

Extra-ordinary even supernatural powers of Pativratā

According to the belief of the Epic societies extra-ordinary powers were attributed to a wife as a result of her pativratā character, which was nothing less than a penance. She could protect her chastity, and even burn her abductor if she pleased.[8] Kṛshṇa attributed immense destructive powers to the angry looks of Gāndharī, which she did show by burning Yudhishṭhira's

1. Rām. II. 27. 13; Mbh. XI. 23. 36.

A man loyal to his wife was also known as Brahmachārī cp. Mbh. XII. 193. 11;XIII. 90. 28-29 conjugal fidelity was the reality which such husbands and wives followed.

2. Rām. II. 39. 24.
3. Mbh. III. 205. 22-23; XIII. 46. 13.
4. Rām. I. 4. 7. काव्यं रामायणं कृत्स्नं सीतायाश्चरितं महत् ।
5. Mbh. II. 72. 5-7; III. 116. 7-8; Rām III. 2. 21.
   Rām. V. 37. 62 ff.
6. Sufra Chap. II. Marriage pp. 17.
7. Mbh. III. 234. 10 ff.; 235. 28.

Mbh. XIII. 146. 43, cp. Vāt. Kāma Sūtra. IV. 1. 9 She was to form her attachments carefully.

8. Rām. III. 37. 14; VI. 111. 22-23; 118. 18; V. 22. 20
   MBh. III. 62. 14, 24; 63. 38-39.

toe.[1] Her curse exterminated the whole race of Lord Kṛshṇa.[2] While demnation of another Satī made Araṭṭā women unchaste.[3] Through Sītā's prayers fire became cold.[4] The Aświns pleased by Sukanyā's single-minded devotion transformed her old decrepit husband into a handsome youth.[5] Sāvitrī could even bring her dead husband back to life. Such was the force of her pātivrata dharma.[6] All this appears unbelievable to us but we can at least understand that it might have been propounded in order to encourage the ideals of pātivrata. The propaganda value of it is undeniable.

The investing of pātivrata with such extraordinary almost supernatural powers was perhaps, an indirect recognition by the composers of the Epics of the infirmity of the human mind. They apparently knew that it would be difficult to keep up this one-sided loyalty. Great rewards[7] were thus promised to pativratās in the form of these powers and competences. As it would be shown in a later chapter it was even difficult and unnatural for such pativratās as Sītā, Draupadī, Maṇḍodarī, Kausalyā to accord to this ideal and to be always docile and agreeable to their husbands even if they went wrong.[8] The cases which seem a lapse from this ideal are probably illustrations of human nature in women asserting itself in spite of religious training in childhood.

Thus in the Great Epic itself there are many instances when the wives act, most of the time naturally, against the theories propounded by the redactors. Contrary to their teachings and

1. Mbh. IX. 63. 64-65
शक्ता चासि महाभागे पृथिवीं सचराचराम् ।
चक्षुषा क्रोधदीप्तेन निर्दग्धुं तपसो बलात् ॥
Mbh. XIII. 123. 21 Śāṇḍilī had been attributed with powers of appearing and disappearing.
Rām. VI. 111. 66. पतिव्रतानां नाकस्मात्पतन्त्यश्रूणि भूतले ।
2. Mbh. XI. 25. 39-46.
3. Mbh. VIII. 45. 11 ff.
4. Rām. V. 53. 28. ff; 22. 20.
5. Mbh. III. 123 (sec.).
6. Mbh. III. 293:299 (sec.).
7. Mbh. XII. 73. 2 Regions of bliss gained which were not even seen by Śakra ; XIII. 123. 1 ff; IX. 50. 43.
8. Infra Chap. "An Estimate of some important characters of the Epics character of Sītā and Draupadī, Mbh. II 75. 2 ff. Rām. III. 77; Rām. IV. 33. 51 ff. These cases show that some wives wanted to save kingdoms from impending calamities to which their husbands were leading them.

expectations wives do expect their husbands to earn for the family. Sometimes they do so notwithstanding the fact that the husband is blind.[1] Lopāmudrā wanted luxury to be provided for her by Agastya.[2]

Dissatisfied wives

It was but natural for some women, specially for princesses not to have any aptitude for penance and hard life. When these were married to poor Brāhmaṇas with rigid vow, they may have been dissatisfied although there are examples of Sukanyā and Śāntā who worked hard to serve their poor husbands[3]. Pushkaradhāriṇī and Reṇukā only helped their husbands for they were afraid of their curse, not from a sense of duty.[4] It may have been due to such discontent that some of these wavered in their loyalty towards their husbands and were sometimes seduced, as may be in the case of Reṇukā, Ahalyā and Ruchi[5]. Some disloyal wives were abandoned by their husbands.[6] A bad Brāhmiṇī made her husband renounce the world and preach the theory of renunciation.[7] Not to speak of others when pativratā Anusūyā left her husband's protection in anger and disgust, she received a son through penances by Mahādeva's grace and received his protection.[8]

Bad wives

So we must not get away with the idea that women universally accepted the near or full slavery represented in the pātivrata ideal and were always devoted to their husbands and household duties. It may not have been possible to incite Draupadī against her husbands through the spies but in general

1. Mbh. I. 104. 30 ff. according to ideals they are not expected to do so, see Mbh. XIII. 123. 19.
2. Mbh. III. 97. 17-19.
3. Mbh. III. 113. 24 ff; 122. 27, 28; 123. 6 ff.
4. Mbh. XII. 272. 6-8; XIII. 95. 6-15.
5. Mbh. III. 116. 6-14; XIII. 40-41 (sec.) Rām. I. 48.17 ff. VII. 30. 28 ff.
6. Rām. I. 48. 30-32; II. 35. 26; 42. 6-9.
7. Mbh. XII. 176. 3 ff.
8. Mbh. XIII. 14. 95 (Nīlakaṇṭha comments) पतिद्वेषिण्योऽपि स्त्रियो महादेवं प्राप्य कृतकृत्या भवन्तीतिभावः। as it is stated in Rām. II. 117. 22 स्त्रीणामार्यस्वभावानां परमं दैवतं पतिः। It may well be that Mahādeva having a "Viruda" of a non-Āryan deity cared a little for Āryaswabhāva.

it was not an unthinkable proposition.[1] According to Karṇa women like to have many husbands.[2] Even in the Rāmāyaṇa, with its idealistic tone, there are references to unchaste and unfaithful wives.[3] The redactors of the Great Epic testify to the existence of termagants[4] bad[5], selfish[6], unchaste[7], self willed[8] and wicked wives, who treading on the path of sin injure their husbands, causing bad diseases.[9] This shows the existence of some bad wives. That may well be the case. Whatever the ideal, it takes all sorts to compose a society. But it may also show that notwithstanding the careful training for pātivrata initiated from the very childhood some women revolted in overt and covert fashion against this one-sided ideal and refused to accept that status which was in fact a denial of status.

All this however, should not detract from the position of nobility and grace which the Epic women have been considered to enjoy. The epic women should not fear any comparison, and some of them as Sāvitrī, Damayantī and Sītā will always be revered as extra-ordinary examples of conjugal fidelity and domestic grace. Even among the commoners the wifely devotion can be measured from the utterances of Kapotī and the Brāhmaṇī[10] in the Ādi Parva.

Religious duties and partnership

As the religious status in ancient India was of the same importance as political status in any modern state, the wife's status in the household can also be judged by the religious duties she had to perform. It was a virtuous wife who was believed (supposed) to keep balance in the performance of worldly duties i.e. trivarga (dharma, artha, kāma) i.e. religion, profit and

1. Mbh. I. 201. 9; 202. 6-8.
2. Mbh. I. 202. 7-8.
3. Rām. II. 39. 20-23;
4. Mbh. XII. 139. 89
   गृहस्नेहावबद्धानां नराणामल्पमेधसाम् ।
   कुस्त्री खादति मांसानि माघमां सेगवा इव ॥
5. Mbh. XII. 139. 93-94 कुभार्यायां कुतो रतिः Rām. II. 75. 35 स्वेषु दारेषु दुःखितः is however a curse.
6. Mbh. I. 233. 7 ff.
7. Mbh. III. 4. 21.
8. Rām. III. 13. 5-6.
9. Mbh. III. 233. 10, 17.
10. Mbh. XII. 145. 2 ff.; XII. 148. 1 ff; I. 158 (sec.).

desire, which were otherwise considered to be difficult to achieve due to their opposite nature.[1] A patnī had the right to perform sacrifices with her husband,[2] in fact sacrifices could not be performed without her. Thus in the absence of Sītā, Rāma had to perform sacrifice along with her image.[3] These sacrifices were performed perhaps by all the chief queens of a king as is shown in the Rāmāyaṇa. Wives also performed śrāddha with their husbands.[4] Thus in many parts of the Epics we find the wife being accorded somewhat equal status in religious matters with her husband.[5]

In the later recensions of the Great Epic the religion of sacrifices was on decline. The followers of the new school of renunciation regarded women as numberless leeches of the world.[6] Along with this attitude it was due to impurity[7] attached to women that the wife lost the right of performing śrāddhas and sacrifices. The rights of the senior-most wife belonging to the husband's caste were now restricted in keeping the articles used in religious performances or otherwise[8] by the husband. She could worship deities and pitṛs (gods and manes) and offer them flowers, pour libations in order to attend fire, and cook food for śrāddha, with cleanliness according to

1. Mbh. III. 313. 101-2. धर्मश्चार्थश्च कामश्च परस्परविरोधिनः । एषां नित्यविरुद्धानां कथमेकत्र सङ्गमः । यदा धर्मश्च भार्याश्च परस्परवशानुगौ । तदा धर्मार्थकामानां त्रयाणामपि सङ्गमः ॥
cp. Rām. II. 21.59.

2. 'Amarkosh' of Nirṇaya Sāgar Press 1929 ed. p. 204. line 1-2 पत्नीति "पंत्युर्यंज्ञसंयोगो यया दंपत्योः सहाधिकारात् ।" पत्युर्नोयज्ञ संयोगे— Pāṇinī IV.. 1. 33. This right as well as duty was coming down from the time of the Vedas. cp.Ṛg. I. 72. 5. संजानाना उपसीदन्नभिज्ञु पत्नीवन्तो नमस्यं नमस्यन् । Ṛg I. 72. 3; V. 3. 2. Jaminī VI. 1. 2 1. They were supposed to enjoy, the fruits of action together. As quoted by Kāṇe "Hist. of Dh." Vol. II. Part I. chap. XI. pp. 556. 558.

3. Rām. I. 14. 34-35; 13. 41; VII. 99.8. Mbh. XIV. 89. 2-4. Husband and wife according to Sūtras as well as Epics did sacrifice together.

4. Mbh. XII. 42. 5; XV. 15. 2; Rām. II. 103. 21 ff.

5. Mbh. XIII. 141. 43 दम्पत्योः समशीलत्वं धर्मःस्याग्दृहमेधिनः ।

Cp. Ap. Dh. S. II. 6. 14. 16-20 जायापत्योर्नविभागो विद्यते । पाणिग्रहणाद्धि सहत्वं कर्मसु तथा पुण्यफलेषु द्रव्यपरिग्रहेषु च ॥

Rām. II. 27. 5; VI. 128. 51-61; 48. 6. It is therefore that Tara blames Vāli. Ram. IV. 23. 26-27.

6. Mbh. XII. 301. 70 ff. पुत्रदारजलौकौघं ।

7. Discussed in the chapter "Attitude towards women".

8. Mbh. XIII. 47. 32-34.

the notions of the times.[1] Her religious duties thus were completely restricted towards the husband, home and hearth.[2]

In the performance of trivarga the religious duties have been described. Next in importance are her household duties, the performance of Artha—worldly object of a gṛhastha.

Greater responsibility of wife in prosperous homes

The prosperous homes had heavier and more numerous responsibilities than ordinary homes and those were naturally to be discharged by the housewife. Aged relatives and high born persons fallen in adversity, friends and issueless sisters might have to be maintained[3] by such a household. In this sphere of "Family Duties", the mother-in-law was probably the supreme guide. She always kept an overseeing eye on the daughter-in-law.[4] An ideal woman looked after the needs of relatives and dependents.[5] A queen like Draupadī regulated numbers of numerous horses and elephants of the royal household. Draupadī regulated the income and expenditure of the king and his wealth. She used to carry the heavy burden day and night, forgetting her thirst and hunger. From her description it appears that to manage a royal household was really a difficult task.[6]

Treatment towards the servants

The housewife was expected to be kind towards the servants. She took food after she had fed them.[7] Draupadī who had many thousand maid servants, knew the names and features of all of them. She was well aware of all their habits and

1. Mbh. XIII. 141. 37-43; 146. 49; 123. 10 देवतानां पितॄणां च ब्राह्मणानां च पूजने ।
(cp. Vāt. "Kāma Sūtra." IV. 1.3.) Mbh. XIII. 127. 13; 92. 15; 23. 4.

2. Mbh. XIII. 46. 13; III. 295. 22-23. cp. the same Slokas in Markaṇḍeya Purāṇa 16. 61 and Hemādri Vratakhaṇḍa part I. p. 362—as quoted by Kāṇe "Hist. of Dh." Vol. II part I. Chap. XI. p. 577 and footnote no. 1348.

3. Mbh. V. 33. 70 चत्वारि ते तात गृहे वसन्तु, श्रियाऽभिजुष्टस्य गृहस्थधर्मे । वृद्धो ज्ञातिरवसन्नः कुलीनः सखा दरिद्रोभगिनी चानपत्या । 40. 9. Mbh. XIII. 104. 113, more or less the same.

4. Mbh. III. 233. 33 ये च धर्माः कुटुम्बेषु श्वश्र्वा ते कथिताः पुरा ।

5. Mbh. XIII. 123. 15; 146. 52.

6. Mbh. III. 233. 47-58.

7. Mbh. XIII. 146. 49-50.

activities, as also of other classes of attendants viz., cowherds, shepherds etc. This shows the amount of interest a good housewife took in her servants.[1]

(b) *Duties towards guests*

Indian hospitality is proverbial. It was not merely a personal or family virtue but an important social duty. The strenuous duties involved in hospitality were among the important functions of a wife.[2] Exercise of hospitality not infrequently involved severe tests. A guest might turn up at any odd hour.[3] He had to be attended to with the utmost attention and courtesy. People and families often risked starvation to the point of death in order to provide for their guests.[4] So much so that one did not consider oneself absolved from this duty even in such resourceless conditions as in a state of exile in the forest.[5] Thus Sītā offered fruits and roots to Rāvaṇa in the forest considering him a Brāhmaṇa guest.[6] The Brāhmaṇa guests were served with special devotion and concern.[7] The loyalty to the Brāhmaṇa guest was so important that even the chastity of a wife was sacrificed for the entertainment of such a guest.[8] In such cases while the wife herself suffered from the feeling of impurity, she was declared chaste and pure in order to encourage such deeds of hospitality where these were necessary.[9] Such was the obedience commanded by the Brāhmaṇa guests that king Kauśika and his wife, Vāsudeva and Rukmiṇī were yoked on to cars and put to severe trial. Their plight was no better than that of the slaves in the Roman Empire.[10]

1. Mbh. III. 233. 48-52.
2. Mbh. XIII. 159. 3 ff. Special importance of Brāhmaṇa guests. XIII. 146. 52; 123. 10.
3. Mbh. III. 163. (Sec.) Draupadī's difficulty. 6 ff.
4. Mbh. XIV. 90 (sec.).
5. Mbh. III. 3. 82-83; 262. 22; 263. 1 ff.
6. Rām. III. 46. 32; note No. 1 also.
7. Mbh. III. 233. 42-47.
8. Mbh. XIII. 2. 42 to 47.
9. Mbh. XIII. 2. 60, 81, 82 August Bebel "Women in Past Present and Future" "The habit of offering wives and daughters for the night hospitality, existed among many races." p. 19.
   Rām. III. 46. 35. Mbh. V. 40. 10-11 provide description of auspicious things that were to be kept by the householders for worshipping guests.
10. Mbh. XIII. 52-53 (Sec.); 159. 16-30.

Other social and public obligations

As already stated domestic life was an essential feature of social structure. Many social responsibilities were to be performed by the householder. The wife as the mistress of the house had to share the major burden of these. She was to provide food to the weak, the poor, the blind, the orphan and the pitiable,[1] to yatis, brāhmachārīs and in fact, to any one who was hungry and thirsty.

The household duties—Looking after kitchen and meals

A woman's sphere of activity was her husband's home. Goddess of prosperity dwelt in such women who were attached to their homes, otherwise their fame suffered.[2] Ceaseless labour and arduous duties, done in a humble, resigned spirit, kept her busy and upright from early morning till late at night. She had to leave the bed at dawn to keep the house clean. She used to wash the floor with cowdung.[3] Her duties towards fire, deities and manes (Pitṛs) were then performed.[4] She looked after the kitchen, of course, assisted by her mother-in-law.[5] Delicious, good food and meat was to be prepared for offering to deities and not for one's ownself.[6] In the preparation of food, drinks and articles of enjoyment the wife was expected to renounce every thing which the husband did not like.[7] The food was kept ready and clean in order to be served at the pro-

1. Mbh. XIII. 146. 52. ब्राह्मणान् दुर्बलानाथान्दीनान्धकृपणांस्तथा । विभर्त्यन्नेन या नारी सा पातिव्रत-भागिनी ।
These were duties to be followed in the gṛhasthasram Mbh. III. 2.52-56.

2. Mbh. XIII. 11. 12 परस्य वेश्माभिरतामलज्जामेवंविधाँ तां परिवर्जयामि ।

Mbh. I. 74. 12 नारीणां चिरवासो हि बान्धवेषु न रोचते ।
कीर्तिचारित्र-धर्मघ्नस्तस्मान्नयत मा चिरम् ।

Mbh. V. 30. 34 सुसंगुप्ताः सुरभयोऽनवद्याः कच्चिग्दृहानावसथाप्रमत्ताः ।

Mbh. V. 39. 80 विप्रवासमलाःस्त्रियः ।

3. Mbh. XIII. 146. 48.

4. Note 1 of page 115.

5. Mbh. V. 38. 12 मातुर्दद्यान्महानसम् ।

6. Mbh. XII. 36. 33; XIII. 115. 54; III. 2. 58 In V. S. Agrawāla "Pāṇini Kālīna Bhārata" chap. III. p. 122 the same delicacies described in the Mahābhārata are described in details.

7. Mbh. III. 233. 32; XIII. 123. 14. cp. Vāt. "Kāma Sūtra." IV. 1. 10.

per time.[1] After the offering of food to deities, pitṛs and guests[2] had been made, pregnant women, old men and children of the household were to be fed.[3] The housewife, herself was to eat only after the members of the household, including the servants had taken their meals.[4] In the Rāmāyaṇa we come across the custom of husband and wife taking food together.[5] In the didactic portions of the Great Epic, it seems, the wife was the last to take her meals.[6]

To encourage active, meticulous supervision of the household it was stated that the goddess of wealth resided in the woman who kept every thing in the house neat, clean and in proper order[7] and she left those who were lazy.[8] This must have been a great impetus to work for Gṛhalakashmī is still a title coveted by Hindū housewives.

So far we have described the general duties of the housewife, which may have varied according to personal capacity and the nature and importance of particular household.[9] Due to the character of the Epics we only get a picture of the performance of the duties by the Kshatriya ladies. It can be just stated that the general duties of Brāhmaṇī, Vaiśyā and Kshatriya ladies may have been the same except for some assistance given to the husbands in their varied services as would have been natural.

The duties of child-bearing—'Kāma' Sublimated

The central Purushārtha in trivarga was kāma i. e. the legitimate enjoyment of life, in a crude sense it was sexual life between a husband and wife. Although kāma (desire)

1. Mbh. III 233-26 cp. Vāt "Kāmasūtra" IV 1. 18.
2. See pages 115 and 116.
3. Mbh. XIII. 157. 13.
4. Mbh. XIII. 146. 49; 141. 41-43.
5. Rām. II. 96. 1. 2; VII. 42. 18-19.
6. Mbh. III. 3. 83-84; XIII. 146. 49. Although Yudhisṭhira says (III 2. 60) that the householder should eat after everyone has been fed but such practice was not adhered to even by him see III. 262. 21 ff. Mbh. XIII. 93. 131; 94. 38 एकास्वादु समाश्नातु । indicates that it was a great sin for housewife to eat without offering food to others.
7. Mbh. XIII. 11. 12.
8. Mbh. XIII. 11. 13.
9. Mbh. III. 233. (Sec.) indicates that for ordinary wife, who had not the superintending capacity of Draupadī, to perform these duties would have been impossible. Moreover in ordinary households there may not have been such duties to be performed.

was one of the dominant factors[1] in marriage, it was to be sublimated by producing progeny for paying the debts to the ancestors and was regarded as a racial duty. The old Upanishadic idea of not cutting the thread of progeny still persisted.[2] The success of a wife thus lay in being the mother of sons.[3] The manner of inquiring after the welfare of princes was, "Have thy wives borne children"[4] This was Dharma for women. Śarmishṭha wanted to be saved from Adharma by Yayāti.[5] The wives also thought that the mission of their life was complete after giving birth to children and they could then gladly leave for another world.[6]

Of such importance was the duty of child-bearing that a barren wife was thought to be useless.[7] She was not to be approached by her husband and was to be abandoned.[8] It was of course a cruel com and as women without children were to be without the love and attention of their husbands.

The duty of bearing children varied according to the castes. While a Kshatriya was to have heroic sons, it was a curse for a

1. Rām. IV. 33. 54-7; IV. 1. 68; II. 53. 9; IV. 30. 45, 54, 58; V. 14. 18; VI. 13. 2-4; VI. 5. 13, 14, 20.

2. Tai. Up. I. 10. 1 प्रजातन्तुं मा व्यवच्छेत्सीः p. 348 Upanishad Bhāshya Poona 1927. Son saved father from Punna-hell according to Epics and Hindū thought Rām. II. 107. 12 and Mbh. I. 74. 39.

3. Mbh. II. 5. 111, 112 रतिपुत्रफला दाराः० V. 39. 67 is more or less the same.

4. Rām. II. 100. 72.

5. Mbh. I. 82. 21

अधर्मात्पाहि मां राजन्धर्मं च प्रतिपादय ।
त्वत्तोऽपत्यवती लोके चरेयं धर्ममुत्तमम् ॥

Nīlakaṇṭha has wrongly interpreted "Adharma" here as "choosing other person than Yayāti" अधर्मात् त्वदन्यवरणजद्व्याभिचारात् Śarmishtha was a maiden and was free to choose any body after Ṛtu even according Dharmaśāstras and didactic portions of the Great Epic (Mbh. XIII. 44. 16. M. IX. 90). She had no other choice as she was living in Yayāti's harem. "Apatyawatī" clearly indicates an aim of begetting children. Here P. C. Roy's Eng. Translation of I. 82. 24. śloka is correct.

6. Mbh. I. 158. 7 ff.

यदर्थमिष्यते भार्या प्राप्तः सोऽर्थस्त्वया मयि ।
कन्या चैका कुमारश्च कृताहमनृणा त्वया ॥

7. Mbh. XII. 78. 41.

8. Mbh. XIII. 129 2-4 P. C. Roy to make its milder translates Yoshita a s woman but as intercourse with other people's wife is forbidden in the same śloka "Yoshita" here cannot wife.

Brāhmaṇi[1]. The children were to be trained according to the tradition of the caste, so that they may fulfil their assigned task in the social set up.[2]

Although Manu allows remarriage by the husband in case no progeny or even daughters were born to the wife[3] such instructions are not to be found in the Epics. According to one passage the wife was to have both sons and daughters.[4] Even in the case of Daśaratha it would be wrong to say that he remarried as his wives had no sons, for the kings generally adhered to polygamy. Still such ideas as that of Manu are reflected in the didactic portions of the Epics.[5] The detailed description of woman as mother will be given in the next chapter.

Her rights and benefits in the family

So far the duties of the wife in the household have been dealt with. She had not only arduous duties to perform but also some rights and benefits in the family in which she was married.

Treatment accorded to her by the elders

(a) *Rights and benefits in relation to mother in-law*

In her newly married life the bride was first accorded a very affectionate welcome by her mother-in-law, with blessings and greetings.[6] One may, however, contend that even the most tyrannizing mother-in-law can give a hearty welcome but it is rather difficult to share the authority at home and affection of son with another woman. In the Epics, we come across not only exemplary but also affectionate and sweet relations between mothers-in-law and daughters-in-law. Here Dharma with its quality to hold and not to break, came to the aid of the mothers-in-law

1. Mbh. XIII. 93. 132 अभोग्या वीरसूरस्तु ।
2. Mbh. XI. 26. 5. तपोर्थीयं ब्राह्मणी धत्त गर्भं·········
शूद्रा दासं पशुपालं च वैश्या, वधार्थीयं क्षत्रिया राजपुत्री ।

Mbh. VII. 77. 17. footnote on p. 105 IV. Vol. (a śloka with same meanings) Mbh. Poona ed.

3. M. IX.81. बन्ध्याष्टमेऽधिवेद्याब्दे दशमे तु मृतप्रजा ।
एकादशे स्त्रीजननी मद्यस्त्वप्रियवादिनी ॥
4. Mbh. I. 158. 7.
5. Mbh. XII. 78. 41. Barren wife was useless.
6. Rām. I. 77. 11. 14; Mbh. I. 199. 5-12; 192. 4.

for it was the basis of all relationships then.[1] It prescribed every body's duty, by adhering to these naturally everyone's rights were secure. There was no question of authority, of rights, which are, of course, a great impediment to understanding, but duty and love made renunciation easy. Neither were the mothers-in-law in the Epics confronted with the difficulty of handing over charge of the house to a child-bride, which may have been later a problem. Thus Kuntī after acquainting Draupadī with domestic tradition gave her the charge even before she was legally married.[2] At Indraprastha too Draupadī and not Kuntī managed the household of the Pāṇḍavas.[3] The young blood was given a chance to learn while the old people remained to give advice and guide. In their leisure whatever knowledge they gathered from the Brāhmaṇas and ṛshis was imparted to the new generation.[4]

The relations between Sītā and Kausalyā, Draupadī and Kuntī are affectionate.[5] With motherly affection these mothers-in-law decorate their daughters-in-law[6], are worried on their account more than that of their sons.[7] Kuntī was never able to forget the insults meted out to Draupadī in the Kuru court and as her sons tolerated these she loved them no more. Her epithets for Draupadī show her love and regard for her[8]. When she finally retires she advises her sons to be agreeable to Draupadī[9]. Gāndharī does not so much refer to her sorrow in the loss of her sons as to the widowhood of her daughters-in-law.[10]

(b) *In relation to Father-in-law*

A father-in-law as the head of the family had his duties towards the daughter-in-law[11]. He was duty bound to protect

1. From the root धृ । धारणाद्धर्ममित्याहुर्धर्मेण विधृताः प्रजाः Rām. VII. 59.7 (२ प्रक्षिप्त)
2. Mbh. I. 192. 4 to 7; 193. 9; Rām. II. 26. 1-5 Sītā had her separate palace.
3. Mbh. III. 233. 34 ff.
4. Mbh. XIII. 64. 3, 36 Devakī questioned Nārada on gifts and gave that knowledge to her daughters-in-law. Ram. II. 118.7.
5. Mbh. IV. 20. 25; Rām. II. 39. 24 ff.
6. Rām. VI. 128. 17.
7. Mbh. V. 137. 17-20. Rām. II. 61. 4-6.
8. Mbh. V. 90. 44, 45, 47, 49, 50.
9. Mbh. XV. 16. 15.
10. Mbh. XI. 17. 24; XI. 18. 2, 6; 22. 15.
11. Mbh. V. 38. 12. A king has been advised to give the duty of protecting inner apartment to his father पितुरन्तःपुरं दद्यात् but it seems strange.

(*Contd. on page* 122)

the daughter-in-law. Thus the father-in-law in "Nakulopākhyāna" recognized his duty of protection of the daughter-in-law.[1] Along with the duty of protection he had to maintain high dignity and was not to be protected by her.[2] There was great affection and tenderness felt for a daughters-in-law. Arjuna feels great pity for Uttarā[3] and so does Daśaratha for Sītā.[4] Dhṛtarāshṭra, who treated Kuntī as his daughter-in-law wanted her to stay back and not to accompany him to the forest.[5] Thus the relations between the daughters-in-law and the parents-in-law were ideal and affectionate. In them the daughter-in-law found her experienced guides and guardians.

Husband's duties (1) *Protection*

It was, however, to the husband that the charge of the wife was given after marriage and in coverture her happiness mostly depended upon him. As the duty of protection of the wife fell upon him he was known as Pati.[6] It has been stated that the wife has no protection like that of her lord.[7] However weak a man may be he was to protect his wife according to the eternal way of Dharma.[8] In every civilized society man being the stronger partner in married life has to perform this

Although he may have been the most trusted but usually he himself might have been the king before his son.

1. Mbh. XIV. 90. 72-75.

2. Mbh. V. 37. 5. वध्वाऽवहासं श्वशुरो मन्यते यो । वध्वाऽवसन्नभयो मानकामः । परक्षेत्रे निर्वपति यश्च बीजं······एतान्नयन्ति निरयं पाशहस्ताः ॥

P. C. Roy translated मानकाम as 'boasteth' but it perhaps should be "wants to be respected", for being protected by one who is to be protected was unchivalrous.

3. Mbh. VII. 72. 58-59. While later uneducated parents-in-law thought their widowed daughters-in-law as inauspicious and thus the cause of their son's death.

4. Rām. II. 38. 6. II. 39. 15-16.

5. Mbh. XV. 18. 4 ff. XV. 17. 18-21; XV. 27. 17. Elder brother of the husband was respected as the father-in-law. His position is that of the head of the family after his father's death. Bhīsma, Dhṛtarāshṭra and Yudhishṭhira held such a position. Younger brothers-in-law treated elder sisters-in-law with great respect. Rām. II. 45. 28; VII 48. 19-22.

6. Mbh. I. 104. 30. पालनाच्च पतिः स्मृतः ।

Mbh. XII. 266. 37 पात्या चैव स्त्रियः पतिः

7. Mbh. XII. 148. 7 नास्ति भर्तृसमो नाथो ।

8. Mbh. III. 12. 68; cp. Rām. II. 30. 8.

duty. In the Epics the husband is advised to protect his wife for the purity of his line.[1]

Āpaddharma

In certain conditions as anarchy[2] and adversity[3] the protection of the wife, however, may not have been possible. So Nala left Damayantī during adversity.[4] Viśwāmitra also wandered wifeless in the famine.[5] The Epic heroes, however, could not have accepted this practice so patently unchivalrous and so utterly wanting in heroic quality. Thus Rāma and Bhīma did protect their wives in adversity.[6] There is an injunction to the kings to rescue their wives at the risk of their own imprisonment.[7] It was a dreadful thing for a hero like Bhīma that Draupadī rescued him and his brothers from slavery.[8]

Methods of protection recommended

In the didactic portions distrust of women deteriorated the position of the wife. Husbands are thus warned to protect wives well as the task was supposed to be difficult due to their fickle character.[9] The misogynist and ascetic opinion was to keep wives under control by keeping them poorly attired[10] and

1. Mbh. III. 12. 69 ff cp. M. IX. 9 तस्मात्प्रजाविशुद्ध्यर्थं स्त्रियं रक्षेत्प्रयत्नतः । Ram II. 100. 49.

2. Mbh. I. 160. 4-10 The Brāhmaṇa in Vetrakīya was not thus able to perform this duty had not Kuntī and Bhīma come to his rescue. Therefore in order this duty of protection of wife may be possible one is advised first to choose the king and country and then a wife Mbh. XII. 57.41. Importance of royal protection for women Mbh. XII. 68. 15, 32.

3. Mbh. V. 37. 18

आपदर्थे धनं रक्षेद्दारान् रक्षेद्धनैरपि ।
आत्मानं सततं रक्षेद्दारैरपि धनैरपि ।

I. 158. 26-27 and M. VII. 213 is the same.

4. Mbh. III. 62 (sec.)

5. Mbh. XII. 141. 26-27.

6. Mbh. III. 161. 48-49. Kubera is pleased with Bhīma that he has endangered his life for his wife. III. 157. 46 ff. IV. 22-23 (sec.) Rām. IV. VI. kāṇḍas.

7. Mbh. XII. 131. 8.

8. Mbh. II. 72. 1 ff; V. 160. 112 ff;—161. 30 ff.

9. Mbh. V. 35. 72; 33. 85; XIII. 43. 22

Mbh. V. 33. 86 षडिमानि विनश्यन्ति मुहूर्तमनवेक्षणात्
गावः सेवा कृषिर्भार्या······

Mbh. V. 37. 1-6 describes this almost impossible task.

10. Mbh. V. 34. 39-40 स्त्रियो रक्ष्याः कुचेलतः ।

confining them at home.[1] So much was the wife distrusted in youth that it has been stated that only an old wife was to be applauded.[2] It is, however, interesting to note that in a story cited to prove that wife could not be protected, Indra is shown as seducer and is thus more to blame.[3] This represents the typical attitude of a renouncer who, being unable to check weakness in man, blames woman for its cause.[4]

Duty of supporting the wife

According to the Great Epic the wife was to be properly supported by the husband. A man who was able to perform this duty has been declared successful in life.[5] A husband was "the giver of plenty" for the wife.[6] He was known as Bhartā (i.e. the supporter) and wife who was to be supported[7] was known as Bhāryā. When he was unable to perform these duties he was not to be considered so.[8] Therefore the husband is enjoined not to take any thing without sharing it with his wife.[9] A woman's duty at home is more important and she is incapable of physical exertion to earn in certain periods of her life. Thus the duty of supporting the wife is prescribed for husbands in every civilized society. In the Epics it was entirely his duty, therefore the wife has been declared without wealth.[10] There was a flaw in this injunction. A

1. Mbh. V. 39. 80 विप्रवासमलाः स्त्रियः ।
2. Mbh. V. 35. 69 जीर्णमन्नं प्रशंसन्ति भार्यां च गतयौवनाम् ।
3. Mbh. XIII. 40. 14-15.; 41 (sec.)
4. Mbh. XIII. Sec. 40 and 41.
5. Mbh. V. 39. 83 अन्नपानजिता दाराः सफलं तस्य जीवितम् ।
Mbh. VII. 174. 43.
6. Rām. II. 39. 30; Mbh. XII. 148. 6-7 अमितस्य च दातारं भर्तारं का न पूजयेत्
7. Mbh. XII. 266. 37 भरणाद्धि स्त्रियो भर्ता ।
Mbh. I. 104. 30 भार्याया भरणाद्भर्ता ।
8. Mbh. XII. 266. 37
भरणाद्धि स्त्रियो भर्ता पात्या चैव स्त्रियः पतिः ।
गुणस्यास्य निवृत्तौ तु न भर्ता न पुनः पतिः ।
9. Rām. II. 75. 33; 30. 15; 27. 14.
Mbh. VII. 73. 33-34.
10. Mbh. I. 82. 22
त्रय एवाधना राजन्भार्या दासस्तथा सुतः ।
यत्ते समधिगच्छन्ति यस्यैते तस्य तद्धनम् ।
V. 33. 64 Cp, M. VIII. 416. is the same.
Mbh. XIV. 90. 46-48.

husband may misappropriate the money his wife received from her rich father. In order to check these tendencies it was considered sinful to draw sustenance from the father-in-law and wife or desire maintenance from them.[1]

There are only five examples in the Great Epic when the wife was not supported. Chitrāngadā was Putrikā-dharmiṇī, therefore she stayed in her parental home.[2] Hiḍimbā's was a contractual marriage[3] and Ulūpī was already living at her father-in-law's home.[4] Jaratkāru's case was peculiar for even before marriage her husband dictated the terms of not supporting her.[5] Nevertheless such was the importance of this duty that Pradweshī threw her husband into a river for he failed in his duty as his wife's protector and supporter.[6] According to the belief of the times whosoever was not able to accomplish these duties was to suffer in this world and in the next too.[7]

Behaviour towards the wife

For all her unremitting services and selfless sacrifice a wife was to be respected by the husband. He was expected to be pleasant and sweet-tongued towards his wives.[8] One who condemned and cursed his wife had always to regret it,[9] and one who spoke ill of his wife has been stated to be foolish and was expected to go to hell.[10]

A man was allowed to have many wives but he was enjoined to treat each one of them equally[11] although it was natural to favour one of them.[12]

1. Mbh. XIII. 93. 125 भार्योपजीवी is a curse
Mbh. XIII. 94. 22 ......भार्याया चैव पुष्यतु ।
श्वसुरात्तस्य वृत्तिः स्याद्यस्ते हरति पुष्करम् ।
2. Mbh. I. 215. 23 ff.
3. Mbh. I. 155. 19-20.
4. Mbh. VI. 90. 7-10 Also note No. 1 p. of the Chap. "Widow"
5. Mbh. I. 47. 1-2.
6. Mbh. I. 104. 30 ff.
7. Mbh. IV. 21. 40-43; XIV. 90. 45 ff; XIII. 23. 71; cp. 23. 82.
8. Mbh. V. 38. 10-11. Such behaviour was adhered to, see Mbh. XII. 148. 4-5; V. 36. 61; 37. 5.
9. Mbh. XIII. 93. 70.
10. Mbh. V. 37. 1-5 (in the lists of foolish persons.)
11. Soma is cursed for being partial to one wife.
Mbh. IX. 35. 45 ff; XII. 342. 57 ff.
12. Thus Kausalyā's case is the most touching one. Rām. II. 20. 32 ff; 72. 12; 9. 24-26. Rām. VII 58 .7 shows Devayānī's plight.

Wife's rights in relation to others

Not only upon the husband and father-in-law but upon all men of the family the duty of protection of women was enjoined. It is stated that knowing the frailty, the good and bad qualities of women, Manu, while leaving for heaven, made them over the care and protection of men. As all acts necessary for the needs of society depended upon women they were to be worshipped, honoured, cherished, treated with affection and protected. In the homes where women were respected deities were filled with joy and where they indulged in tears of grief families became extinct and all acts there became fruitless.[1]

Wife's conjugal rights

It has been already stated that the marriage was not so much a pursuit of pleasure and enjoyment as of Dharma or being free from the debts of manes. It was believed that progeny was born when wives were approached only in their season.[2] In order to encourage men to do so such men who adhere to this rule are praised, given high place in society[3] and happiness here in this world and hereafter is predicated for them.[4] Unbelievable stories are cited in the Mahābhārata to illustrate this point.[5] It was considered a disgrace to neglect wives in season.[6] This right to Ṛtu, as it was known, was very important for women for through this she was supposed to fulfil the duties enjoined upon her by Providence. So much so that if a girl demanded such a right from a man, she was to be married,[7] for otherwise a maiden could not be approached.[8]

CONCLUSION

The wife was the central figure of domestic life, which was her career, her profession, her joy and her duty. Married-life was Strī-Dharma and she also thought it to be Svadharma. Dharma is rather an abstract and illusive term, but its general

1. Mbh. XIII. 46. 8-12.
2. Mbh. XIII. 93. 124; 94. 27.
3. Mbh. XII. 193. 11; 110. 9; XIII. 90. 28.
4. Mbh. XIII. 157. 10. 11.
5. Mbh. I. 63. 51 ff. Story of king Vasu. Mbh. I. 64. 10. In an ideal reign such behaviour was adopted by men.
6. Mbh. III. 293. 35. Rām. II. 72. 52, 55.
7. Mbh. I. 82. 13, 24; 83. 32-33.
8. Mbh. XIII. 104. 131, 108; XII. 90. 32.

meaning is duty in an ethical sense. Svadharma is something inherent in an individual, in fact one was bound to follow one's own dharma the dominant note of one's own being, that which distinguished one from other human beings. Here Svadharma meant one's right response to environment according to one's psychological development. Home, i. e. married life in the Epics is the field where woman was to perform her duties and services to humanity and was to have fulfilment of her life by killing her selfish interests,[1] for the power of woman lay in serving others.[2] At home, as has been already shown she had to perform unremitting duties towards elders, husband, dependents and society. It was on the whole a life of sacrifice and not of individual pleasure or convenience. Most of the Epic heroines had the strength of character, immense energy, resolute mind and forceful personality to perform these duties as the husband's true friend, philosopher and guide, sahadharmiṇīs as they were termed.

The position of the sahadharmiṇī was lost by the time the didactic portions were written. The ascetic ideal and later that of docile pativratā, disparity in age and education between a woman and her husband pulled down her position from sahadharmiṇī to that of slave and devotee. This fall was not sudden and even in the narrative part we may find traces of this degraded position easily. From many accounts this conclusion is irresistible to the modern mind that the wife was as a rule considered no better than a piece of property by the husband. Thus she could be pawned, abandoned on slightest suspicion, given away to any one. A true friend, thus, is one who can easily offer his wife.[3] Epic heroes many a time show true friendship by asserting that they could sacrifice their wives along with other possessions for amity.[4] Against this suggestion it may be contended that in this way the husbands used to emphasise their identity with their wives. But the argument would be difficult to sustain in view of the fact that the wife has many times been mentioned along with property as if she was one of the posses-

1. Mbh. XIII. 146. 35 ff.
2. Mbh. V. 34. 75 शुश्रूषा तु बलं स्त्रीणां···।
3. Mbh. V. 45. 12.
4. Rām. VII. 34. 40-41; III. 10. 19; VI. 41. 4; 10. 50. Mbh. VI. 122. 25.

sions.[1] Besides this if there was such an identity of interest the wife could also make similar statements to express her sense of identity. But there is not even a single expression of that kind in the Epics. How could she give away her very god ? This argument of identity of interest would appear thinner still when we remember that his honour was much more precious for a man than his innocent wife.[2] Had it been such an identity of interest Rāma would have renounced his kingdom for Sitā. A wife and even such a wife, who was considered to be slave, friend, wife, sister and mother all in one,[3] could also be abandoned for the sake[4] of the son, or could be troubled.[5] A husband like Nala could abandon his wife and then later blame her for infidelity. Not to say of others but even Rāma who held monogamy as an ideal was influenced by such ideas for he thinks that in every land one could find wives but not a brother[6]. How could he even hope to get a woman like Sītā ?[7] Arjuna proves this dictum by getting wives from many countries. All this goes to prove that one of the reasons for the deterioration of the position of the wife was polygamy. The custom was taken for granted by the society and by women also.[8] Nevertheless it was an encroachment upon a wife's right to conjugal fidelity. The competition of winning over the love of the same person made even

1. Mbh. I. 158. 26-27 आपद्धर्मप्रमोक्षाय भार्या चापि सतां मतम् ।
Mbh. V. 37. 18
आपदर्थे धनं रक्षेद्दारान्-रक्षेद्धनैरपि ।
आत्मानं सततं रक्षेद्दारैरपि धनैरपि ।
Rām. II. 34. 47. नैवाहं राज्यमिच्छामि न सुखं न च मैथिलीम् ।

2. Rām. VI. 115. 2 ff.; VII. 45. 2 ff; 47. 12-14.

3. Rām. II. 12. 69.

4. Rām. II. 12. 11.

5. Rām. II. 12. 69-71, 11. ; Mbh. III. 62, 29; 70. 8 ff; 71. 6; 76. 22-24; 74. 25 ff.

6. Rām. VI. 101. 15
देशे देशे कलत्राणि देशे देशे च बान्धवाः ।
तं तु देशं न पश्यामि यत्र भ्राता सहोदरः ।

7. Rām. VI. 49. 5-6.
किं नु मे सीतया कार्यं लब्धया जीवितेन वा ।
शक्या सीतासमा नारी मर्त्यलोके विचिन्वता ।
न लक्ष्मणसमो भ्राता सचिवः सांपरायिकः ॥

8. Mbh. I. 158. 35.

sisters jealous of each other not to say of other co-wives.[1] Sometimes in the aristocratic families due to good breeding[2] or as a result of sympathy between two sufferers[3] such jealous feelings were suppressed although rarely. Often the competition of winning over the love of the same person, the domination of the favourite wife over others,[4] the prospective fear of life being miserable due to the succession of a co-wife's son (in royal families[5]), must have contributed to great misery in married life. To crown all these miseries in polygamy a junior or low-caste wife had no religious or social status in the family.

Polyandry theoretically gave the same rights to women as were accorded by polygamy to men. But as there is only one practical example this custom was almost non-existent. When the pātivrata ideals were making headway, it was natural that a woman having many husbands or lovers was looked down upon by society and was talked disparagingly.[6] A story cited[7] proves that it was not possible to practise polyandry due to the greater intensity of sex-jealousy among men.

Neither was a wife's status any better in polyandry. The historic example, of the husband's utter neglect of his duty and wife's right, is the pawning of Draupadī[8]. This may have been a right of "patria potesta" for Pushkara suggested the same to Nala but in this case even a weak husband like Nala, refused. This clearly indicates that in polyandry when a wife

1. Mbh. IX. 35. 49; Mbh. I. 20 to 27 (sec.)
rarely as in the case of Jarāsandha's father both the sister-wives were tolerated equally. Mbh. II. 17. 17 ff. Other cases of jealousy Mbh. I. 221. 17 although Draupadī herself preached against it in Mbh. III. 223. 19-20. Mbh. I. 233 (Sec.); Mbh. I. 125. 19-21; 124. 6. संरम्भो हि सपत्नीत्वाद्वक्तुं कुन्तिसुतां प्रति । In Mbh. XIV. 81. 4 suspicion of such jealousy indicated.

2. Mbh. I. 221. 23 ff; XIV. 81. 6; Daśartha's queens work in unity Rām. I. 14. 34-35; II. 84. 6; VI. 127. 14 respect of eldest cowife—religious and other rights. Mādrī respects Kuntī and does not refute her right Mbh. I. 125. 23 ff; II. 79. 19-20. Kuntī recognizes it.

3. Rām. II. 4. 32, 39; II. 44 (sec.) clearly proves such alliance between Kausalyā and Sumitrā.

4. Rām. II. 12. 70.

5. Rām. II. 8. 37. 24, 26.

6. Mbh. II. 68. 35; Mbh. V. 40. 7; XIII. 38. 19, 25, is all stated disperagingly. Unfamiliarity with this custom is proved by different opinions for it in the Kuru court cp. Mbh. I. 202. 4-16 and I. 201. 16.

7. Mbh. I. 208-212 (sec.) cp. Āp. Dh. S. II. 10. 27. 4-9 states that polyandry was impossible to practise due to the nature of men.

8. Mbh. II. 65. 33-38.

was the property of so many, her rights were not so much respected as in monogamy.

Whatever may have been Draupadī's legal status after being lost at stakes morality and humanity demanded a better treatment. Although Dhṛstarāshṭra's admonition to Duryodhana indicates that a Dharmpatnī, —a wife who was a religious partner—was to be treated well. It indirectly shows that a wife, who did not possess such a status and was just Dārā could be treated otherwise.[1] The fact that the Kuru elders witnessed the treatment meted out to Draupadī, which is revolting even in thought not to speak of reality, shows further the degraded culture in which women were not at all respected.[2]

Husband's right to inflict capital punishment on the wife, even for little suspicion shows that he was the master of her destiny.[3] The same is proved by the insults she had to bear for keeping his vow of hospitality.[4]

For a wife to have a position in the family and conjugal rights just because she was instrumental in producing progeny, is surely unreasonable and illogical. The plight of a barren wife has already been described. The irony indicating this status is complete when Draupadī becomes an instrument in releasing her husbands from the bondage of slavery. Instead of being grateful to her Bhīma states "How can a son born from this insulted wife of ours, prove serviceable to us ?" This was the height of male vanity and utter neglect of woman's dignity when indirectly one of the Pāṇḍavas was responsible for Draupadī's insults.

Nevertheless due to the ancient traditions the old ideals were not altogether forgotten. Even in the didactic portions where so much has been written against women,[5] it has been also stated that she is to be treated with affection and in homes where woman is respected the very deities are filled with joy

1. Mbh. II. 71. 25

हतोसि दुर्योधन मन्दबुद्धे, यस्त्वं सभायाँ कुरुपुङ्गवानाम्
स्त्रियं समाभाषसि दुर्विनीत, विशेषतो द्रौपदीं धर्मपत्नीम् ।

2. In case the elders were utterly helpless against Duryodhana their walking out from the court would have been effective or even sitting on "prāyā" which was a custom those days. Mbh. X. 11. 15.

3. Mbh. III. 116 (sec.) Reṇuka was killed by her husband's order.

4. Mbh. XIII. 2. 6 ff Story of Sudharśana Oghāvatī.

5. Mbh. XIII. 38-40, 43 (sec.)

and live there.[1] Even in these redacted portions the essence of happiness in married life was agreeableness of both husband and wife. For it has been well-said :—

> यो भर्ता वासिता तुष्टो भर्तुस्तुष्टा च वासिता ।
> यस्मिन्नेवं कुले सर्वं कल्याणं तत्र वर्तते ।।[2]

1. Mbh. XIII. 46.5

> पूज्या लालयितव्याश्च स्त्रियो नित्यं जनाधिप ।
> स्त्रियो यत्र च पूज्यन्ते रमन्ते तत्र देवताः ।।

2. Mbh.XIII.122.17
Manu III. 60.

Chapter VI

WOMAN AS MOTHER

Mother, the creator

A woman as the mother occupies a place of great honour and prestige in the Epics. The very epithets used for her are a recognition of her importance as a mother. Thus she is called, "Dhātrī" for she carries the body of a child in her womb, "Jananī" for she gives birth to the baby and is its creator. In the heroic age for giving birth to heroes she was respected as, "Vīrasū".[1] Of the two parents the mother's role was greater and more significant. Against the argument that the desire for children is cherished by both the parents it was maintained that the fruition of the desire depends more upon the mother.[2] She was the cause of the body of the child as the fire stick is that of fire.[3] He was born from her limb and heart,[4] in fact he was considered to be her own body.[5] Therefore even in patriarchal societies of the Epics the mother was as much master of her children as the father.[6]

The high status of motherhood

The position assigned to the mother by society was great and according to a section of opinion, she is placed higher than

1. Mbh. XII. 266. 32-33. कुक्षिसंधारणाद्धात्री जननाज्जननी स्मृता ।
2. Mbh. XII. 266. 34. दम्पत्योः प्राणसंश्लेषे यो ऽभिसंधिः कृतः किल ।
तं माता च पिता चेति भूतार्थो मातरि स्थितः ॥

Cp. Meyer "SLAI" V. p. 205 "The man in sexual union really seeks only his pleasure, but woman seeks the child, which rule will always be true."

3. Mbh. XII. 266. 25.
4. Rām. II. 74. 14. अंगप्रत्यङ्गजः पुत्रो हृदयाच्चाभिजायते ।

Rām. II. 35. 17, 18, 28. Here daughters are said to be like mothers.

5. Mbh. XII. 266. 33. माता देहमनन्तरम् ।
6. Mbh. I. 105. 31-32.

the preceptor and father[1] and higher even than the whole earth.[2] There was no preceptor like her.[3] She was in fact the highest preceptor (Guru).[4] She is mentioned first among the three 'Atigurus' and this rule holds good from the time of the Upanishads.[5]

The mother has been compared to "Dakshiṇāgni" one of the three holy fires to be tended,[6] for casting off the three fires was a great sin.[7] At one place she has been described as one of the five fires to be tended carefully by everyone.[8] For the follower of the Vedic sacrificial religion, which the Epic Āryan was, fire was an object of reverence for, through its agency gods were propitiated.[9] Fire has other attributes also. In the history of human civilization it has contributed towards the preservation and protection of mankind just like a mother. Its purifying quality was also an attribute of the Epic mother, for as will be shown later when a son diverted from the path of duty

1. Mbh. XIII. 105. 14 दशाचार्यानुपाध्याय उपाध्यायान्पिता दश ।
दश चैव पितृन्माता सर्वां वा पृथिवीमपि ।
गौरवेणाभिभवति नास्ति मातृ-समो गुरुः
माता गरीयसी यच्च तेनैतां मन्यते जनः ।
Mbh. XII. 108.17 is the same cp. M II. 145 the same with a little variation.

2. Mbh. III. 313. 60 माता गुरुतरा भूमेः ।

3. Mbh. XIII. 106. 65 नास्ति वेदात्परं शास्त्रं नास्ति मातृसमो गुरुः ।
Mbh. XIII. 62. 92-93. नास्ति भूमिसमं दानं नास्ति मातृसमो गुरुः ।
cp. Atri Sam. 150. Ap. Dh. S. I. 4. 14. 6.

4. Mbh. XII. 342. 18 नास्ति सत्यात्परोधर्मो नास्ति मातृसमो गुरुः ।
Mbh. I. 196.16. गुरुणां चैव सर्वेषां माता परमको गुरुः ।

5. Tait. Upa. I. 9. 12. Mbh. XII. 108. 16. M II. 145. Vas. Dh. S. XIII. 48. Y. S. I. 35. Gautam. Dh. S. II. 51. Vishṇu S. XIX. 1-2. XXXI 1-2. Mbh. (K. XIV) 110. 60 Mother is above all.

6. Mbh. XII. 108. 7. पिता वै गार्हपत्योऽग्निर्माता ऽग्निर्दक्षिणः स्मृतः ।
गुरुराहवनीयस्तु साग्नित्रेता गरीयसी ॥
Cp. Vi. S. XXXI. 8. V. S. Agrawal, "Pāṇini Kālīn Bhārata" p. 363 states that, "Dakshiṇāgṇi was not tended after sacrifice". But as mother was always to be served we cannot attach these meanings here. Here, "Dakshiṇāgni" means most important fire in the sacrifice used for cooking sacrificial viands.
Cp. Ap. Dh. S. II. 3. 7. 2. p. 116. S.B.E. II. Gobhila G. S. IV. 4. 5. Julius Jolly (S.B.E. Vol. VII) Translates it as ceremonial fire.

7. Mbh. XIII. 93. 126 त्रीनग्नीनपविध्यतु—is a curse

8. Mbh. V. 33. 74 पञ्चाग्नयो मनुष्येण परिचर्याः प्रयत्नतः ।
पितामाता ऽग्निरात्मा च गुरुश्च भरतर्षभ ॥

9. Cp. Ap. Dh. S. II. 7. 16. 1. sacrifices taken to heaven.

mothers inculcated the sense of righteousness. Motherhood made women resplendant.[1] A wife who had children was to be respected and protected at all costs.[2]

A barren woman's plight and status in the family and in society further indicates the practical importance of the status of motherhood to women. In a polygamous society where the son was to save the father from the torments of hell, barrenness often imposed the presence of a second wife, a rival in her love, to which after all, a woman gives first place. Moreover, a woman had to lead a life of dependence, therefore, barrenness also meant subjection to the co-wife's son, the heir to his mother's hatred, in old age.[3] To crown all these troubles there is a religious belief mentioned in the didactic portions according to which a women was deprived of her conjugal rights and thus accursed in the family, in case she had no progeny.[4] All these motives weighed by intellect must have led to the desire of being a mother, above all of a son.[5]

For the Epic woman motherhood was not merely the operation of a self preserving, self satisfying and self-creating instinct but even more so of a deep sense of social responsibility which lifted motherhood to the level of a sacred duty. The religion and philosophy of the Epics have never hesitated in informing her that as a living being her primary function was to continue the race. The bride on the wedding day was blessed with joyous promise of being, "Vīrasū", "Jīvasū" and "Jātaputrā".

Efforts to attain the status of motherhood

All these reasons led women to do their utmost to attain the status of motherhood. They would shirk no penance, hesitate at no sacrifice to be able to attain the status of mother.[6] Thus even the mother of Śakra[7], not to speak of ordinary women passed through great austerities to attain the qualification. The

1. Rām. I. 18. 11.
2. Mbh. I. 157. 33-34; 74. 48 ff; XIV. 90. 45 ff.
3. Rām. II. 8. 4.
4. Mbh. XII. 36. 27; 78. 41; XIII. 127. 13-14; 129. 2. 4.
5. Mbh. I. 116. 11 ff, Mbh. I. 158. 7. indicate that the daughters are desired with the sons and not without them.
6. Mbh. XIII. 83. 26; Rām. II. 20. 52.
7. Mbh. XII. 7. 14.

cases of Śarmishṭhā[1] and Mādrī[2] prove the same point while Pārvatī's cursing the Devas for denying her the right to motherhood further reinforces it.[3]

Number of children

Old opinions die hard.[4] Thus some mothers adhering to old Vedic traditions wanted to have many children.[5] But opinions were changing gradually. Perhaps historical conditions also might have influenced the attitude in the matter. Their being less in number was no longer a serious question for the Āryans, as they have no more to fight deadly wars with the non-Āryans. The Kauravas and the sons of Sagara with their evil character must also have discouraged the tendency of having many sons. According to new opinion in the Epics it was fatal to have many sons and it was believed by some that only in an evil age several sons were born.[6] It seems, above all, women in the Epics were gradually realising that motherhood in order to deserve admiration must be responsible and dignified. Therefore, mothers who wanted excellent sons and aspired to pay full attention to their physique, education and character-building, desired only one or two sons.[7]

Mother, responsibilities towards her

(a) (*Towards the expectant mother*)

As begetting children was considered to be a great social as well as a religious duty, the expectant mother in her delicate condition was given care, protection and respect by society. It seems there were maternity homes for the common people. When enumerating the special duties of kings, Bhīshma states that although fire should not be ignited during the day one exception to this rule was in maternity homes.[8] On the road one was to

1. Mbh. I. 82. 2 । अधर्मात्पाहि मां राजन्धर्मं च प्रतिपादय ।
   त्वत्तो ऽपत्यवती लोके चरेयं धर्ममुत्तमम् ॥
2. Mbh. I. 124. 4 ff. Mādrī takes initiative.
3. Rām. I. 36. 22 ff. ; Mbh. XIII. 84. 73-74.
4. Mbh. III. 84. 97; Rām. II. 107. 13.
5. Mbh. I. 110. 9-10 ; 16. 8 ; 115. 8 ; III. 297. 45.
6. Mbh. XIII. 93. 128; III. 188. 41.
7. Mbh. I. 16. 9; III. 99. 22.
8. Mbh. XII. 69. 48-49 कर्मारारिष्टशालासु ज्वलेदग्निः सुरक्षितः ।
   "अरिष्टंसूतिकागृहं तद्रूपासु शालासु—" नीलकण्ठः

stand and give way to pregnant women.[1] Moral law (Dharma) ordained that by slaying a woman big with child one incurred the great sin of Brāhmaṇicide. If a man killed a pregnant woman knowingly he incurred doubly the sin of Brāhmaṇicide.[2] Foetus murder as sin has been referred to many times.[3]

In the family the greatest possible care was taken of the expectant mother. All her wishes were to be fulfilled. This was because of the belief that not only physique but also the child's character and capacity for learning were formed in the womb.[4] Thus Ambikā's and Ambālikā's fears during conception ruined their children.[5] The mother's attitude influenced the child.[6] Even the food she ate had an effect on the child's mental make up. Due to this belief different kinds of "Charus" were given to produce a good Brāhmaṇa and a good Kshatriya child.[7] Therefore it was necessary that the expectant mother was kept cheerful and satisfied. Rama and Drupada attend to the wishes and comforts of their pregnant wives.[8] Although Jaratkāru is an exceptional case, for she is not supported by her husband in her pregnancy, yet her brother Vāsuki adored her with gifts of wealth at that time.[9] To protect the health of the child in

1. Mbh. XIII. 104. 25-26. पन्था देयो. . . . .गर्भिण्यै दुर्बलाय च ।
2. Mbh. XII. 165. 55 एवं तु समभिज्ञातामात्रेयीं वा निपातयेत् ।
द्विगुणा ब्रह्महत्या वै आत्रेयीनिधने भवेत् ॥
"आत्रेयीं प्राप्तगर्भां—"नीलकण्ठः

Cp. M. XI. 88. Gaut. Dh. S. 22. 12.

But Ātreyī is also one who has bathed after temporary uncleanliness, for if her husband approaches her he will have offspring. "Atra"=At the time. "ye"=to approach. According to Vas. Dh. S. XX. 34. 36 Brahmahatya occurred only in case of Brāhmaṇātreyī. Acc. to Baud. Dh. S. II. 1. 1. 12. in case of all Ātreyī murders the sin was that of Brahmahatyā. The verse may throw an interesting light on the position of women in the Great Epic, the sin of slaying a pregnant woman was double-Brahmaṇicide and therefore her status at least legally was equal to a Brahman. A sharp contrast is presented by Vas. Dh. S. XX. 34-40... When the sin of killing Ātreyī of each class was equal to sin of killing a man immediately below her caste.

3. Mbh. XII. 108. 30, 31 तेषां पापं भ्रूणहत्याविशिष्टं । Although there were transgressions to this rule Mbh. I. 178; 19-23; (Haihaya); X.15-16 (see); XIV. 66. 9; (Uttarā's case).

Kaṇe, P. V. "Hist. of Dh." Vol. III chap. XV p. 398-399 even a Brāhmaṇa was to be killed for this sin. The exemption of the Brāhmaṇas from sentence was otherwise universal and unanimous.

4. Mbh. I. 106. 17, 9.
5. Mbh. I. 106. 9, 15.
6. Mbh. I. 106. 10, 17.
7. Mbh. XIII. 4. 28 ff.
8. Rām. VII. 42. 30-31 Mbh. V. 188. 11-12.
9. Mbh. I. 48. 15.

the womb a pregnant woman is told not to grieve even on her husband's death.[1] It was believed that woman during the delicate days of pregnancy and soon after delivery was harmed by evil supernatural spirits. Therefore she was to be protected from all such possible dangers.[2] Auspicious things, portents of good luck, weapons for protection, fire for heat, old and experienced women for nursing and looking after and physicians for medical care, were present in Uttarā's lying-in-room.[3]

(b) *Responsibilities towards mothers in general*

It is natural that the social code of conduct prescribed proper veneration and respect for mothers. According to old tradition from the hoary past the teacher gave parting advice to students to revere mother, father and preceptor. The mother was naturally first in the list.[4] In the same strain Bhīshma advises Yudhishṭhira that parents were to be worshipped with respect and even if their command was unrighteous it was to be obeyed without hesitation.[5] Its application in case of mother was still more emphatic. A mother's bidding was never to be disobeyed[6] or even found fault with.[7] Where a mother deserved punishment one's failure to award it was not accounted as a sin. She enjoyed impunity. But if she was injured in thought or deed, one incurred the sin of foetus murder. She was never to be injured, never to be slain.[8] Sons were to comport themselves kindly towards the mother[9], and to support her.[10] In the Epic society where heroes were respected, those sons who served their parents well, were considered as heroes.[11]

Manners towards the mother

In consonance with prevalent manners, parents were to be

1. Mbh. XIV. 61. 39-44. Kuntī to Uttarā.
2. Rām. VII. 66. 3, 5, 10. Mbh. XIV. 68. 6; 70. 2.
3. Mbh. XIV. 68. 3-7 कुशलैर्जनैः' is translated as physician by P.C. Roy.
4. Tait. Up. I. 11. 2. मातृदेवो भव पितृदेवो भव. .
"The Upanishad Bhāshya" p. 348 Vol. II. part I Asteker & Co. Poona 1927.
5. Mbh. XII. 108. 3, 4; Mbh. XIII. 104. 145.
6. Mbh. XII. 108. 5.
7. Mbh. XII. 108. 10.
8. Mbh. XII. 108. 20-21. अवध्या हि सदा माता ।
9. Mbh. V. 30. 32-33.
10. Mbh. XII. 108. 31.
11. Mbh. XIII. 75. 22-26.

saluted every morning.[1] While bidding farewell or meeting parents, children used to touch their feet.[2] One was not to eat before the mother had eaten.[3]

(c) *Good results of serving the mother*

High status of the mother as well as encouragement to children is reflected in good results attending on one who served the mother. It was believed that by serving the mother fame in the three worlds, honour, religious merit (धर्मफल) and heaven were gained.[4] No other merit in life was superior to the one earned by serving the mother.[5] Whatever was given in honour of parents acquired significance, hundred and thousand fold.[6] The last injunction was perhaps to persuade people to perform the duty of Śrāddhas (rites after death) for the welfare of the parents.[7] It is stated that even uncontrollable destiny could be controlled through the services rendered to parents.[8] Adoration of the mother was equal to the adoration of Vishṇu.[9] Such persons, as are devoted to parents overcome all difficulties.[10] Through services to parents, Śravaṇa, son of a Śūdrā woman attained heaven[11] and Kāyāvya, a robber, achieved great success.[12]

Persons who served their parents were considered competent to point out the path of duties even to those Brāhmaṇas who gained miraculous powers by performing austerities.[13]

Bad results of disregarding parents

The high status of the mother has again been illustrated

1. Mbh. XIII. 104. 43.
2. Mbh. XIV. 59. 19-20; I. 155. 37; Rām. VI. 127. 46; III. 104. 18; 18. 2.
3. Mbh. XII. 108. 10.
4. Mbh. XII., 108, 3, 8, 25, 9, 10, 16; 129. 9 ff.
5. Mbh. XII. 161. 9 'नातिमातरमाश्रम: XIII. 23. 93. Rām. II. 30. 33, 34, 37.
6. Mbh. XII. 108. 15.
7. Mbh. XV. 39. 15 ff. Rām. II. 103. 20 ff; 76. 23; 77. 14.
8. Rām. II. 30. 33.
9. Mbh. XII. 345. 26-27.
10. Mbh. XII. 110. 6.
11. Rām. II. 63. 50; 64. 49 Subhadrā wishes such regions for Abhimanyu. Mbh. VII. 78. 31.
12. Mbh. XII. 135. 6.
13. Mbh. III. 206. 44-45. Sec. 207; 216.

by the bad results of neglecting one's duties towards one's parents. The evil consequences that were said to befall one who disregarded the mother were also terrible. Śrī is said to have left the Dānavas for this fault,[1] which means that prosperity wanes if parents are not well attended. Such persons who did not take care of the parents never earned any good name or merit.[2] Those who cast off parents without any fault were considered fallen persons[3] and were more or less boycotted by society.[4] Yama's regions and vile rebirth were predicted for the person who disregarded parents.[5] Patricides and matricides went to unwanted regions.[6] Such predictions may sound ridiculous to the modern mind but for the persons living in the various societies depicted in the Epics, these were real dangers for they did believe in the theories of eschatology, of transmigration and Karma.

It was taken for granted that there was no release from a mother's curse.[7] There were means of averting or neutralising other curses but none for the ones pronounced by a mother.[8] All these predictions and fears must have forced even undutiful children to perform their duties towards a mother well.

Feelings and regard for the mother

The feelings and conduct of the heroes of the Epics indicate that the mother was highly regarded. Her love and affection was always repaid with a deep sense of gratitude. The Pāṇḍavas' great regard for Kuntī is effectively drawn in many a vivid and touching scene. Their visit to the hermitage, farewell to their mother, their lamentations, weeping bitterly like children when she was burnt in the forest, Bhīma's deep feelings-all show their unspeakably tender regard for Kuntī.[9] Yudhishṭhira

1. Mbh. XII. 228. 56.
2. Rām. II. 75. 45-47.
3. Mbh. XII. 165. 62. Acc. to Vi. S. XXXVII. 6, 7 abandoning mother is a minor sin for which penance and sacrifices were to be performed. Surely this is later opinion than that of Āpasthambha and the Great Epic.
4. Mbh. XII. 165. 36, 39.
5. Mbh. XII. 108. 12-13; XIII. 111. 58-63. Rām. VII. 15. 22.
6. Mbh. VII. 73. 25.
7. Mbh. I. 22. 1.
8. Mbh. I. 37. 3-5 cf. Mārkandeya Purāṇa CVI 28-32 although acc. to L XXVII. 31 she never curses her child.
9. Mbh. XV. 21. 1 ff. ; 36. 27-28, 35 ff; 37. 8, 18 ff; I. 151. 21-27.

refers to the protection and love accorded to them by Kuntī with deep gratitude.[1] Even the ideal hero of patriarchal society, Rāma, who turned down his mother's proposal for obeying his father[2] is very anxious for his mother's plight when he is leaving for the exile.[3] He requests his father so to behave towards his mother that she may not die smitten with the grief of his separation.[6] Later in the forest he thinks himself to be a worthless son for having left his mother in a sorrowful plight and wants Lakshmaṇa to go back and look after her,[5] for he himself had to obey the father. All this goes to prove that even if according to some opinions a father was to be respected more the natural feeling towards a mother could not be ousted by this kind of upbringing.

On the mother was placed the greatest confidence and she has been referred to as the best adviser.[6] The children thus recognised her value as an educator. Even the arch-villain, Duryodhana listens rather to his mother than to his father. He obediently comes, "filled with longing for his mother's words."[7] Mother's grace was solicited as a great boon.[8]

It was natural in the circumstances for children to have a pious and keen sense of filial duty. It has been shown that one of the reasons put forward for the adherence of the Paṇḍavas to polyandry, even in the teeth of social opposition, was their desire to carry out the command of their mother.[9] Yudhishṭhira in his message to Kuntī says that he has been dreaming of the time when he will be able to make his mother happy.[10] For the fowler in the Vana Parva, parents were supreme gods. He served and pleased them in every way.[11] Similar is the case of Śravaṇa[12] and Kāyavya.[13]

1. Mbh. XV. 38. 7 ff.
2. Rām. II. 21. 22-26ff. Rāma's disregard of mother's proposal.
3. Rām. II. 31. 11 ff. को भजिष्यति कौसल्यां सुमित्रां वा यशस्विनीम् ।
4. Rām. II. 38. 14-16.
5. Rām. II. 52. 34-36 ; 53. 18 ff.
6. Mbh. IV. 4. 52; V. 154. 24 ff.
7. Mbh. V. 129. 7, 10, 17 स मातुर्वचनाकाङ्क्षी प्रविवेश पुनः सभाम्।
8. Mbh. XIII. 15. 6· मातृतश्च प्रसादं ।
9. Mbh. I. 191. 2, 16; 195. 30; 196. 16-17.
10. Mbh. V. 83. 37 ff.
11. Mbh. III. 214. 18-29.
12. Rām. II. 64. 50. Mbh. VII. 78. 31 points the same.
13. Mbh. XII. 135. 6.

Breach of the Rule (1) *by Villains*

There are some cases of transgression of the rule which emphasise the supreme duty towards the mother. When Duryodhana[1] and Rāvaṇa[2] are disobedient to their mothers, their disobedience can be well understood, for in them the composer wanted to show arch villains, and so they disregarded their parents.

(2) *In order to show importance of the royal protection*

In the didactic portions to show the importance of the royal protection it has been stated that in its absence man disregarded and even injured their aged parents.[3] This is, however, not supported by any evidence, for when the Pāṇḍavas were living in the lawless forests, Kuntī is well cared for.[4] Even in Ekachakra where the king existed only in name, filial affection in the Brāhmaṇā's family is not lacking in any way.[5]

(3) *Due to love for high qualities.*

Disregard for mother is sometimes the outcome of a love for truth, justice, loyalty and brotherly affection, in which case it is justifiable, for it is meant to uphold the intrinsic human values so important for the stability of society. Although Rāma blames Bharata for such disregard none will think ill of such unnatural behaviour.[6] The didactic portions also place truth above parents.[7] Yudhishṭhira's opposition to Kuntī is also due to the extraordinary circumstances when he thinks that she was going to sacrifice Bhīma for the Brāhmaṇa family.[8] Karṇa's loyalty to the Kauravas can also be appreciated for after all Kuntī had only been his "Jananī" by giving him birth but she did not perform the more important duties of maintainer and educator for him.[9] It must, however, be said to the credit of the didactic writers that no possible human failing escaped their observation.

1. Mbh. V. 129-130 (Sec.).
2. Rām. VI. 34. 20
3. Mbh. XII. 68. 18; 228. 56 Śri leaves the Dānavas for this fault.
4. Mbh. I. 151. 21 ff.
5. Mbh. I. 158-161 (Sec.).
6. Rām. II. 112. 27 same are the feelings of Lakshmaṇa towards Kaikeyī.
7. Mbh. XIII. 107. 50.
8. Mbh. I. 162. 6-11.
9. Mbh. V. 140. 12 ff.

To warn mothers and to prepare them for any possible disappointment, sons after marriage are enumerated among those sinners who forget all obligations to their former well-wishers.[1]

Pāraśurāma an Exception.

Paraśurāma killed his mother at his father's command,[2] his four elder brothers having refused to do so.[3] But very tender and humane are the boons he demands from his father, namely his mother's life as well as her losing the memory of his improper act of killing her.[4] Chirkārin is less resolute and saves his mother by his reflective temper[5], although he does not blame his father for such a command. But it must also be borne in mind that in the Āryan patriarchal set up of society where there is a conflict between the commands of the mother and those of the father, the duty towards the latter is considered greater. Rāma prefers to obey his father against his mother's wishes.[6]

Feelings and conduct towards the step-mother

It will not be very correct to state that the sons show a pious spirit towards the other wives of the father in the Epics.[7] Jealousy among co-wives was generally transmitted to the children. Even the hero Rāma is no exception and betrays such feelings, although the composer sometimes paints him as an ideal.[8] However, in the royal families with higher cultural background relations between step-sons and step-mothers were generally cordial.[9]

Duties of the daughters towards the mother

In accordance with the patriarchal character of society, woman's duties towards her father-in-law and mother-in-law were

1. Mbh. V. 33. 87. षडेते ह्यवमन्यन्ते नित्यं पूर्वोपकारिणम् ।
   आचार्यं शिक्षिताः शिष्याः कृतदाराश्च मातरम् ॥
2. Mbh. III. 116. 14. Ram. II. 22. 33.
3. Mbh. III. 116. 11
4. Mbh. III. 116. 17.
5. Mbh. XII. 266 (Sec.).
6. Rām. II. 21. 24, 25. Rāma further cites Paraśurāmas's example-30 ff.
7. Meyer. J. J. states so in "SLAI" V. p. 209.
8. Rām. II. 53. 14-18, 13-17; 52. 61; IV. 2. 18 ff.
9. Rām. VI. 119. 25-26; II. 112. 27; Mbh. III. 145. 8; VI. 91. 27.

more important than towards her mother. Among the numerous passages only once the ideal woman is expected to look after her parents.[1] Like a pot from the potter's house she was completely severed from her parental home.[2] So she had no chance of serving them. However, fleeting glimpses of a daughter's love for the parental home[3] as well as her readiness to sacrifice for them[4] have been presented in the Vaka-vadha-Parva.

The position of the widowed-mother

The duty of looking after the widowed-mother was also performed well, not only by sons, but even by step-sons. Writers on law and the didactic portions of the Epics place a widow under the dependence of the son. If a son did not protect his widowed mother he was to blame[5] and incurred the sin of foetus murder.[6] But this was only economic dependence. Otherwise the widowed mother or step-mother is generally revered and holds a position of importance as the head of the family. Dependence upon the son must also have varied according to the personal factor. Satyavatī seeks Bhīshma's permission for retiring to the forest. Yudhishṭhira once or twice acts as the head of the Pāṇḍava family.[7] All this indicates harmony and amicable relations in the family. Nevertheless Kuntī throughout is the deciding factor in important matters.[8] Even Hiḍimbā seeks her permission for obtaining Bhīma.[9] Satyavati's advice and approval on important matters of family and state is always sought by Bhishma.[10]

1. Mbh. XIII. 146. 51.
2. Mbh. III. 22. 47-48, 50 with the exception of Subhadra and Kareṇumatī none of the daughters even visited their parental home. Rāma VII. 47 Even in adverse circumstances Sītā does not take shelter with her mother. Mbh. III. 61. 21 ff.; sec. 65 Damayantī first resists such suggestion later does take shelter when she has no husband to follow.
3. Mbh. I. 157.27 इह जाता विवृद्धाऽस्मि पिता चापि ममेति वै ।
4. Mbh. I. 159. 1 ff.
5. Mbh. III. 293. 35 मृते भर्तरि पुत्रश्च वाच्यो मातुररक्षिता । Cp.M.IX 4. Rām. II. 61. 24 द्वितीया गतिरात्मजः repeats the same idea. Mbh. I. 151. 12-13. Kuntī naturally exhorts the Pāṇḍavas that although a pious lady and mother of five Pāṇḍavas, she is suffered to remain thirsty. Cp. Āp. Dh. S. I. 10. 28. 9. son must serve his mother even though fallen.
6. Mbh. XII. 108. 31.
7. Mbh. I. 128. 12; I. 155. 5 ff.
8. Mbh. I. 196. 15-16; 195. 30; V. 90 (sec.), ff.
9. Foot note 7.
10. Mbh. I. 102. 1, 4, 60, 72, 73; 103. 3ff.; 110. 3; Mbh. V. 173. 6, 22 ff; 174. 4; cp. 176. 49; 175. 1; 176. 52; ,178. 72ff; V. 186. 12.

Mother-worship indicates reverence towards the mother

The evidence of mother worship in the form of various idols comes down from the pre-historic times and is found throughout the lands between the Mediterranean and the Indus valley. This practice was based upon the cruder emotions and instinct of the primitive man and must have been excited by awe and wonder for the supposed malefic[1] as well as creative powers in women. Therefore, with the advancement of civilization and knowledge it was bound to disappear, as it did, in the other countries. In India, however, it developed fully and was the result of the reverence and refined sentiments inspired by the human mother, who was nourisher and protector.

In the Great Epic glimpses of both the sentiments are to be found, the one inspired by awe and fear of the creative power, the other by noble sacrifices and good qualities of the mother. The former was coming down from antiquity and the latter developing from the time of the Ṛg-Veda[2] and was still in the process of further evolution, for the rituals and philosophy of motherworship as described in the Purāṇas are not to be found in the Epics.[3]

Among human beings the creative element is represented by the woman, i.e. the mother. It was for this reason that this element was anthropomorphized by the ancients, in the form of godesses, and not gods. It is, therefore, that in the Great Epic for obtaining children and prosperity, godesses in form of Gṛhadevī and female spirit on trees are recommended to be worshipped.[4] Such worship must have been the outcome of fertility rites of old and reverence for the mother as creator.

Ignorance of the rules of maternity and child welfare, led the primitives to believe that some evil spirits endanger life and kill the new born baby. These spirits in the Great Epic have been described as "Mātṛkās" i.e. mothers, for primitives may have thought of propitiating them by according the position of

1. About this malefic influence, vide infra. "The Attitude towards women".
2. Ṛg. V. V. 84; X. 63.3; I. 24.1; 159; 160; 185.
3. Vaidya "Mahābhārata Mīmānsa" pp. 19, 454. and other scholars think such passages to be redacted in the Epics but as awe inspiring sentiment was old and even the nobler sentiment is there in the Ṛg.V. (vide note 2) these passages may be reflecting a process in evolution. cp. The critical edition also pronounces Durgā hymn in the Virāta and and Bhīshma parva as interpolated portion.
4. Mbh. II. 18. 2ff; Mbh. III. 231. 16.

the all compassionate mother, who would thus protect from harm. As knowledge of child welfare advanced with civilization naturally fear of such evil spirits decreased. This is signified by the legend of Skanda, where Mātṛikās were sent to kill the baby Skanda and were not able to do so. They lost their power and joined the armies of the Devas. This may further signify the worship of these aborigines godesses taken in the Hindu pantheon, while their losing power signifies gradual decline of such ideas.[1]

In the hoary past, in the primitive insecure conditions the fierce emotional energy of women and mothers may have been aroused and used sometimes for the destruction for the welfare of her children, the race and other interests. A delicate creature like woman, rising to such great energies, must have made the primitive to personify her in the forms of goddesses. Thus the goddess Kālī is the slayer of Evil symbolised in Mahishāsura.[2] From descriptions in the Great Epic[3] it appears that she was awe-inspiring and a fierce goddess of the aborigines, whose abode might have been the Vindhyas and was gradually assimilated by the Hindū Pantheon.[4] Her weapons denote her as an agent of death and destruction. But the lotus, the symbol of peace, is also held by her.[5] She is fond of meat and blood but also subsists on herbs in another form.[6] This mingling of old in the new iṇ her also indicates the idea of mother not only as a destructive power for doing away with evil but also as a peaceful non-violent force.[7] But as an agent of destruction she destroys only evil. Death and Disease represented as goddesses are for only killing those who should not live.[8] They exercise their power for human welfare, just as a mother applies her anger for the correction of the child.

Women and mothers have also been considered as inspirers. Therefore, the Energy or "Śakti" was personified in the mother goddess Umā. She goads even the great god Mahādeva, to fight for his rights. This whole legend may signify that it was

1. Mbh. III. 230. 16. ff. (whole section).
2. Mbh. IV. 6. 15.
3. Mbh. IV. 6. 17.
4. Mbh. IV. 6. 17.
5. Mbh. VI. 23. 7; Mbh. IV. 6. 8.
6. Mbh. IV. 6. 17; VI. 23. 9; III. 84. 13-17.
7. Mbh. IV. 6; VI. 23 (Sections); III. 84. 13 ff.
8. Mbh. XII. 257-258. (Sections); VII. 53-54 (Sec.); VII. 59. 63.

through the coming of this great goddess into Hindu religion or Āryan fold that her consort Mahādeva was accepted and worshipped as a god. Later this Umā, Kālī or Durgā was recognized as the supreme mother goddess.[1]

Mother as nourisher, responsible for the traits of nature in her child is represented by the idea of mother-goddesses Śrī and Lakshmī. The two distinct goddesses in the Ṛg-Veda as well as the Great Epic were later amalgamated into one.[2] Goddess Earth, a pre-Āryan Goddess of prosperity, was also added to the conception of Śrī.[3] Various legends prove that worship of this goddess was perhaps prevalent first among the Daityas and Asuras and was later taken up from them by the Āryans.[4] All fine sentiments of children towards the human mother as well as good qualities of the mother are personified in Śrī. Thus she is considered as Faith, Intelligence, Affluence, Victory, Immutability, Patience, Success, Prosperity (Bhūti), Swāhā, Swadhā, Reverence, Fate, Memory, Contentment, Advancement and Forgiveness.[5]

The role of mother as an educator is recognized in the mother goddess of learning, Swaraswatī.[6]

These accounts indicate that mother worship in the Epics was at first the outcome of dread and fear of mysterious power of creation in women. Gradually it was taken up by refined people and was inspired by mother's love and sacrifice. Her role as a nourisher and sustainer was represented in the form of Lakshmī, of protector and inspirer in Durga and Kālī and of educator in Saraswatī. All this goes to indicate the greatness and position of the human mother in whom all these attributes

1. Mbh. XII 283. 28-29; 284. 31-54; III. 39. 4. 72; Rām. I. 35. 15-21. Umā has been always mentioned along with her consort Mahādeva. Cp. Vaidya's "Mahābhārata Mīmansā" p. 19 cp. 'Great women of India' Ch. III. p. 63 etymology of her name. The idea of Umā is very old—in Kenopanishad Cp. R. C. Dutt "A History of Civilization of Ancient India". Vol. I. Bk. II. Chap. VII. p. 188.

2. Ṛg-V., V. 18. Mbh. II. 11. 41. Cp. धर्मयुग नवम्बर १३, १९५५. डा. मोतीचन्द "सौन्दर्य और ऐश्वर्य की देवी पद्मश्री ।" for the origin see Mbh. I. 66. 50, 51; I. 18. 44; XII 59. 131-133; XII. 90. 26.

3. Mbh. XIII. 91. 25; 62. 6.

4. Mbh. XII. 222 (Sec.); 228. 27; 223. 3ff.

5. Mbh. XII. 228. 21-23, 83, 84; 225. 7-8; III. 229. 3-4; 37, 32, 33; 3. 64; I. 199. 6; VII. 94. 44. IX. 46. 64.

6. Mbh. XII. 335. 35; 318. 6; III. 37. 33.

were combined and who was all compasionate, inspiring man to worship her qualities. It was the integration of all good qualities in her that later inspired the Purāṇa writers to amalgamate all the above mentioned goddesses into one supreme or compassionate goddess Maheswarī (Magna mater).

The association of mother's name with that of son does not exactly come under the purview of mother-worship, but apparently it was dictated by simple sentiments of reverence towards motherhood as well as the fame and influence of some particular mother. Thus due to Sāvitrī's fame her descendents are known as "Sāvitrī-putrakās".[1] It is not generally indicative of matriarchy, although it may be a custom surviving or borrowed from some matriarchal clan, for in the Epics patriarchal clans freely addressed sons after mothers. It will be wrong to state that this custom was due to "Resultant uncertainty of paternity or maternity in that of polygamy or polyandry."[2] In the cases cited in the Epics the names of both the parents are known. If the rules of Niyoga are followed closely, there would be little reason for uncertainty of paternity in that system.[3] In the Great Epic there is a case when a son is named after his foster mother[4] and thus it cannot be said that naming after mother was due to uncertainty about the father. It must have been because of her importance or influence in the family or due to her fame.

Responsibilities of the mother : Her high status in cosequence of her onerous responsibility

(a) *Mother's role as maintainer, excellent rearing*

The high status accorded to the mother has been traced so far and it has been shown how from the hoary past she has been worshipped as creator of the race. As civilization advances the

1. Mbh. VIII. 5. 49 Cp. Pāṇini V. 3. 116.

2. Sarkār. S. C. "Some Aspects of Early Social History of India". Chap. "Traces of the Primitive Sex." Cp. for the same discussion opinion of Dr. Shastrī and Indra's" The Status of Women in Ancient India" p. 69-70. Relations with special customs p. 81. line 14 ff.

3. See Chap. on "Niyoga",it has been already established by the Indian scholars like Kaṇe "Hist. of Dh." Vol. III. Chap. XXVII, p. 643 ff. and Jaiswāl "Manu and Yāgyawalkya" Chap. on "Family Law" that even in the list of twelve kinds of sons there was no uncertainty of paternity.

4. Mbh. XII. 218. 15-16.

mother's role as creator of the race begins to be regarded less and less in the exaltation of women's position, than is the case in primitive society, for knowledge now brings the understanding that every normal woman is a potential mother. Her greatness now is seen to lie not so much in bearing a child as in excellent rearing. Her task therefore is to develop the physical, mental and emotional powers of the child, in a perfect balance, and thus give to society and the race an integrated person, capable not merely of adjusting himself to the social problems, but of going further and uplifting humanity. Thus her vocation in the new light is that of a maintainer of the race and she is no doubt well fitted for it by nature, for in woman is implanted a strong altruistic instinct, a spirit of suffering and sacrifice for the sake of posterity. The Epic women were aware of this role. Her better designation than "Jātaputrā" is "Jīvasū", "Jīvaputrā" and "Vīrasū."[1] It is not enough to be a mother of sons: she had to be a mother of living sons and heroes. As mother was the nourisher of the limbs of her children she was known as "Ambā" and for her tender care and services as "Śuśrū."[2] A parrallel between mother and earth has been often drawn because of the fact that the earth suffers without protest when ploughed but gives instead life-giving corn to nourish people. So does the mother nourish and sustain children while she herself may be undergoing unspeakable sufferings.[3] For similar qualities of sustaining and maintaining the cow and the mother have been compared to each other.[4] To the western mind this simile may appear curious but for the Hindūs the cow is the most sacred

1. Mbh. I. 199. 12 "Jātaputrā" comes last in Kuntī's blessings while Mbh. I. 199. 7. Jīvasū, Vīrasū comes first. Mbh. XII. 266. 32. वीरसूत्वेन वीरसू: Rām. VII. 128. 109 Jīvaputrā.

2. Mbh. XII. 266. 32-33 अंगानां वर्धनादम्बा वीरसूत्वेन वीरसू : ।
शिशोः शूश्रूषणाच्छुश्रूर्माता देहमनन्तरम् ॥

3. Mbh. XIII. 62. 11, 26. यथा जनित्री स्वं पुत्रं क्षीरेण भरते सदा ।
अनुगृह्णाति दातारं तथा सर्वरसैर्मही ॥

This tradition of comparing the mother and the earth is very old Cp. Ṛg. V. I. 160; 159. Athar. V. 12. 1.1-18 "Great Women of India" Chap. III. to show the respect to womanhood Indian soil has been known as "Mātṛbhūmi" Mother is even weightier than carth Mbh. III. 313. 60. माता गुरुतरा भूमेः ।

4. Mbh. XIII. 76. 7.

animal and is a giver of property and wealth. Nothing but good emanates from her.[1]

Mother as Protector

The psychological protection given by the mother to the child through her affection is extremely significant not only for the children but even more for society. This affection by giving children security helps the development in them of a friendly attitude towards their environment and society in general.

For the father the children are mere offsprings, the mother feels joy, affection, and delight in the child from the moment of conception.[2] The expectant mother, disregarding the objects that are cherished by her seeks the good of the child and undergoes many troubles.[3] In the Great Epic a glowing tribute is paid by Chirakārin to this protection given by mother through her affection and care which rendered life, care-free and full of zeal. His utterances are an epitome of the gratitude felt by children towards mother. Thus mother is considered to be the best refuge. Due to the shelter given by her one feels protected and does not grieve. Age, poverty, misfortune do not weigh upon him. She is cooling and faithful like a shadow. There is no defence like mother, no one as dear as she. The child may be able or disabled, weak or robust but she protects him with the same care and love. When the mother dies one feels old, unhappy and the world appears like an empty desert.[4] It is

1. Mbh. XIII. 82. 24-25 in the excreta of cow goddess of prosperity abides. It is known for its cleasing power. In the Anuśāsana Parva chapters 76 to 83 are devoted to its praise.; Ram. II. 74.27; 75. 21, 30 considers killing or hitting as a cow a great sin. Ram. I. 26. 5; III. 23. 28 Every thing is done for its welfare "Gobrāhmaṇahitāya" cp. "Kaṇe Hist. of Dh." Vol. II part II Cp. XXII. p. 772-775. importance and reverence of the cow.

2. Mbh. XII. 266. 35 मातुर्भरणमात्रेण प्रीतिः स्नेहः पितुः प्रजाः ।

3. Mbh. XII. 7. 14; I. 115. 41.

4. Mbh. XII. 266. 26 ff. मातृलाभे सनाथत्वमनाथत्वं विपर्यये ।
न च शोचति नाप्येनं स्थाविर्यमपकर्षति ।
श्रिया हीनोऽपि यो गेहमम्बेति प्रतिपद्यते ॥
पुत्रपौत्रोप्रपन्नोऽपि जननीं यः समाश्रितः ।
अपि वर्षशतस्यान्ते स द्विहायनवच्चरेत् ॥
समर्थं वाऽसमर्थं वा कृशं वाप्यकृशं तथा ।
रक्षत्येव सुतं माता नान्य पोष्टा विधानतः ॥
तदा स वृद्धो भवति तदा भवति दुःखितः ।

therefore that all the protectors and well-wishers, even chastisement properly applied has been compared to the mother.[1]

Mother's affection an—unparalled sentiment

The admirable Epic-mothers were stirred with deep feelings of affection and tenderness for their children. They could suffer any amount for them. To Kuntī, widowhood, loss of property, and enemies were not so painful as separation from her sons.[2] Yudhishṭhira's greetings to her contain references to her womanly virtues, motherly tenderness and pity for her bitter lot.[3] As Kuntī lost her husband early she had to protect her children through much anxiety, care and suffering.[4] The disappearance of Bhīma gave her many anxious moments.[5] Her love for Sahadeva, the youngest of the sons and step-sons is immense. A mother's love for her youngest is proverbial.[6] When the Pāṇḍavas leave for the exile in the maddening agony of separation Kuntī is so overwhelmed that she cannot restrain her emotions. While herself leaving for the forest with touching tenderness she requests Yudhishṭhira not to be hard on Sahadeva.[7] When Arjuna competed in the tournament tears trickled down her eyes and mixing with the milk of her breast, wetted her bosom.[8] When Rāma left for the forest Daśaratha's queens weep as cows bereft of their calves.[9] Kausalyā rushes after the

तदाशून्यं जगत्तस्य यदा मात्रा वियुज्यते ॥
नास्ति मातृसमाच्छाया नास्ति मातृसमागतिः ।
नास्ति मातृसमं त्राणं नास्ति मातृसमा प्रिया ।

Mbh. III. 9. 16. Rām. II. 74, 22 ff Mother always worries for her weak children and those who are in difficulties.

1. Mbh. I. 157. 31; XII. 56. 44-45; 69. 103; 139. 105; 35-12.

2. Mbh. V. 90. 69. न मां माधव वैधव्यं नार्थनाशो न वैरता ।
तथा शोकाय दहति यथा पुत्रैर्विनाभवः ॥

3. Mbh. V. 83. 37 ff.

4. Mbh. I. 126. 8-9; 151. 12ff; II. 79. 13; V. 90 (whole sec.).

5. Mbh. I. 129. 11ff.

6. Rām. I. 61. 17. Richika's wife is not ready to give her youngest son Śaunaka for sacrifice.

7. Mbh. II. 79. 28; XV. 16. 10.

8. Mbh. I. 135. 13-14.

9. Rām. II. 41. 7 विवत्सा इव धेनवः—a pet and vivid expression often used in such circumstances in the Epics Cp. Mbh. VII. 78. 18; Rām. II. 74. 29.

chariot.[1] All these scenes and many more are vividly drawn by the Epic writers. Mothers express their tender affection for children by embracing and smelling their foreheads,[2] the greatest sign of tender love.[3] After all nothing is dearer to mothers than their children.[4] The story of Bhangāśwana confirms the point that mother's affection for children was much greater than that of father.[5]

Affection or care of children who were not reared.

The mother had love not only for the children who were rocked in the cradle and attended to during infancy but in an equal measure for those who were Kānīna and were deserted in childhood. Distance could never break the bonds of affection as is the case with Satyavatī, Gangā and Kuntī.[6]

Mother and the daughter

It is due to the heroic and patriarchal character of societies traced in the Epics that much is not found about the mother's love for the daughter. The solitary example of a Brāhmaṇī getting worried about the future of her daughter also indicates the short comings of a society where perhaps it was impossible for a widowed-mother to protect and settle her daughter honourably.[7] Of the pangs felt by Sītā's and Draupadī's mothers, while they were departing for their new homes, nothing is mentioned, although their condition must have been much more pathetic than that of Kaṇwa.[8] Gāndhārī is very much worried on account of the widowhood of her daughters-in-law. But there is no particular anxiety shown in such a condition for her daughter.[9] So much was the life of mother concentrated upon sons due to the patriarchal pattern of society that

1. Rām. II. 40. 44;
2. Rām. II. 72. 4; 75. 4; 20. 21; Mbh. XV. 36. 48-49.
3. For in Rām. VII. 71. 12 it is said उपाघ्रास्यामि ते मूर्ध्नि स्नेहस्यैषा परा गतिः ।
4. Rām. II. 74. 15ff. 24 नास्ति पुत्रसमः प्रियः ।
5. Mbh. XIII. 12. 46-47;
6. Mbh. I. 105. 26-27; 136. 27; 137. 23.
   Mbh. V. 178. 67 and 86 ff. Mbh. XV. 30 (sec.).
7. Mbh. I. 158. 16 ff.
8. Cp. Kālidāsa "Abhigyāna Śākuntalam". Act IV. 8.
9. Mbh. XI. 22. 14; Cp. 17. 24 to 25 ; 18.2;

Satywatī, Gādhi's wife, wants a better virtuous son to be born to her rather than to her daughter. Her selfishness is due to the fact that her husband's Kula (race) was much more important for her.[1]

Step-Mothers

The Epics deal mostly with royal and aristocratic families. As has been already shown in the previous chapter[2] the step-mothers were generally kind and affectionate to their step-sons due to good breeding.[3] In this respect the ideal behaviour of Kuntī towards Sahadeva has already been cited.[4] The only transgression to this rule on Kaikeyī's part is not due to her own nature but due to the atmosphere which made her feel insecure.[5]

Penances performed for the well-being of sons

For the well-being of sons mother performed various penances, kept fasts and offered prayers. Kausalyā and Kuntī propitiated the deities with fast, penances and various rites and ceremonies.[6] A Daitya's daughter Pulomā and the mighty Asura-woman Kālakā by performing various austerities got boons from the creator (Brahmā) that their offsprings will never suffer misfortunes.[7]

Grief at the death of son

Grief at the death of a child was quite natural; pathetic pictures of sorrow felt on such occasions are drawn in the Great Epic. Even righteous Gāndhārī goes mad with grief, to say nothing of Subhadrā and Uttarā.[8] However, a hero's mother was expected not to grieve for her son who died a glorious death in the battle-field.[9] The didactic portions, with ascetic outlook on life, stress the foolishness of such a grief in the world

1. Mbh. XIII. 4. 29-35.
2. Vide Supra M. Life pp. 109 ff.
3. Mbh. I. 125. 27-28 III. 235. 10-12.
4. Ante p. 150.
5. See Chap. "An Estimate of some Important women characters of the Epics", p. .
6. Rām. II. 20. 48; 25 (whole sec.) Mbh. V. 83. 37 ff.
7. Mbh. III. 173. 7-11.
8. Mbh. XI. 14. 14 ff; 15.21 ff, 29-30 burning the toes of Yudhishṭhira; 15. 22-23; VII. 78. 1ff. XIV 61. 5ff. XIV. 69. 5 ff.
9. Mbh. VII. 77 and 78 (sections).

where everything is fleeting and mortal. An ideal Brāhmṇī mother, Gautamī is resigned to her fate.[1]

Exceptional mothers

There are some cases of exceptional mothers also. Bharata's wives kill their sons for they were unlike their father and hence disliked by him. These must have been strange mothers.[2] Although Gangā's case is similar but the explanation is provided. In heaven she had promised immediate release of the Vasus from the earth.[3] As it sounds incredible it can only be said that both the cases are examples of irresponsible motherhood. Sometimes the Apsarās abandon their children to their fate. They had no family ties and such cases are rare and insignificant.[4]

Mother as an educator

The emotional outbursts of affectionate feelings and toilsome austerities and prayers performed do not, however, imply that the mothers just wanted their children to live happily and comfortably at all costs. They were well aware of other duties imposed upon motherhood by a civilised society, i.e. the duty of an educator. For the fulfilment of their duty they did not mind sacrificing sons. Kuntī was well aware of a Kshatriya's duty of protecting the Brāhmaṇas. She orders Bhīma to go to the Rākshasa Vaka in order to save the Brāhmaṇa's family,[5] although Yudhishṭhira was stunned at her resolve of sacrificing her son.[6]

Kuntī's message to the Pāṇḍavas, delivered through Śrī Kṛshṇa, requires them to develop Kshatriya qualities in their character. She wants them to fight for the kingdom and not to receive it as a gift. For this purpose she holds up the example of Muchukunda who refused the gift of a kingdom. To instil courage in their hearts she cites the story of Vidulā, who was another Kshatriya queen to prefer the death of her son to his

1. Mbh. XIII. 1. Mbh. XII. 153 Meyer regards this story as a changed version of the first one to glorify Śiva cp. "SLAI" p. 106 ff.
2. Mbh. I. 94. 20-21.
3. Mbh. I. 96. 19-20.
4. Mbh. I. 8. 8ff; 72. 9ff.
5. Mbh. I. 161; 162. 6 ff. कथं परसुतस्यार्थे स्वसुतं त्यक्तुमिच्छसि ।
6. Mbh. I. 162. 6 ff. calls the act "Lokavedaviruddam".

defeat. A spirited mother like the Kshatriyā Vidulā, might have herself been able to lead the armies but she does not want glory for herself. A mother's life was one of complete self-effacement. She was not the queen, and as a queen-mother her energies were now concentrated in educating her son, the king, in his duties.[1] Similarly Kuntī wanted her sons to fight for their rights, for when the kingdom was won she retires to the forest to serve her elder brother-in-law and sister-in-law. When she is reminded by her sons that it was under her advice and for her that the kingdom was won, she replies in a most dignified manner that she wanted the kingdom not for herself but for them. She wanted them in this way to assert their rights and independence.[2] In her opinion it was unbecoming to grieve for a Kshatriya's son who died fighting gloriously in the battle.[3] Loftiness of mind and heart and an understanding devoted to a righteous cause were, to her way of thinking, a nobler possession than worldly kingdoms and prosperity. Thus she was, as her parting advice to her sons shows, a much tried, a much loving mother but not a faint-hearted one.[4] Even her beloved son Sahadeva is sent back by her for his love would have been a hindrance in her penance.[5] Sumitrā does not hesitate for a moment and sends her son away to serve the elder brother.[6] If Kausalyā wanted Rāma to stay back, it was only because she felt the injustice of what he was being ordered to do and that in his agreeing to do it, he was following the Brāhmaṇa virtues rather than the Kshatriya virtues. Draupadī's behaviour too points out a Kshatriyā mother's anxiety and pride for her son. She wants Yudhishṭhira to be free so that her son may be saved from the odium of being called a slave's son.[7] Fathers like Dhṛtarāshṭra may sometimes spoil their sons but mothers were more anxious for their right development. Dhṛtarashṭra was of the opinion that although a bad son, Duryodhana could still be controlled by Gāndhārī alone.[8]

1. Mbh. V. 132-136 Vidulopākhyān.
2. Mbh. XV. 17. 1-21.
3. Mbh. XIV. 61. 34-35.
4. Mbh. XV. 17. 21 धर्मे ते धीयतां बुद्धिर्मनस्तु महदस्तु च ।
5. Mbh. XV. 36. 37-42.
6. Rām. II. 40ff.
7. Mbh. II. 71. 28ff.
8. Mbh. V. 129. 1ff.

The Brāhamaṇī mothers, however, were not less solicitious about the proper development of their sons and daughters. They knew well how to guide their sons for the high office society had ordained for them. This is borne out by the manner in which Upamanyu's mother sublimated his dissatisfaction by turning him into a devotee of Mahādeva and thus leading him towards the path of penance and contentment.[1] As already quoted, mothers like Gautamī were unaffected even by the sudden death of their sons.[2]

Mother as an integrating force

In the Epics where the family was the basic unit such mothers were an integrating force in society. The father was just instrumental in bringing forth the child. The sphere of his activities, as is always the case, was outside the home. The mother was the centre and pivot round whom the family life, particularly the life of children, revolved. She was not only the creator and maintainer of her child and the race but educator as well, who instructed her child according to the duties assigned to him in society. It was aptly said that "there was no sacred lore like the Vedas, there was no preceptor like the mother."[3] For it was she who determined the development of the child. Like the learning imparted by the preceptor[4] what was imparted by her was eternal and indestructible. While the father's gifts to his children, like property and dowry were transient, her silent contribution in forming their character helped the children and society permanently.

1. Mbh. XIII. 14. 128 ff.
2. Mbh. XIII. 1 (sec.).
3. Mbh. XIII. 106. 65. नास्ति वेदात्परं शास्त्रं नास्ति मातृसमो गुरुः । Cp. Atri samhita. 150.
4. Mbh. XII. 108. 20; XIII. 105. 19. आचार्यशिष्टा या जातिः सा दिव्या साऽजरामरा ।

CHAPTER VII

NIYOGA[1]

INTRODUCTION

Niyoga Explained

No account of women's life in the Epics would be complete without the mention of the practice of Niyoga. According to this custom the wife or widow of a sonless person was allowed to produce progeny through the agency of another person. Such sons were known as "Kshetraja" (born of "Kshetra" or field i.e. wife)[2] and had a legal status in the family.

Niyoga practice in the Great Epic

This practice is not directly hinted in the Vedas. But the need for such a custom may not have been then felt partly because the Āryans were a virile race and partly because there was a custom of widow marriage.[3] The aristocratic society as traced in the Mahābhārata had become lascivious and lost its virility, for the wives of such impotents like Pāṇḍu and Vichitravīrya had need to resort to this usage. This inability of the great kings was not frankly admitted by the composer and was naturally attributed to some curse. Nevertheless the stories do betray such facts.[4]

1. Niyoga has been mentioned as levirate by some Indian authors but it is wrong, for levirate was marriage with deceased brother's widow—Holy Bible St. Methews 22. 24.

2. Mbh. I. 105. 2 also refers to wives as Kshetras; XIII. 49. 12-17, 3 Meyer "Sexual Life in Ancient India"Vol. I, chap· IV, page 172 ff. Foornote quotes several examples of primitive races when husband has no sex-jealousy in the modern sense if the wife has relation with another man. It is the unauthorized use of property, which means wife also, what angers him. He himself can give his wife for pleasure and progeny to others . Even among semi-civilized societies husband gives his wife for intercourse to others for getting progeny. The civilized Greeks and Romans also support this practice—see Indra "The Status of women in Ancient India", p. 136-137.

3. Upādhyāya "Women in Ṛg-Veda" p. 98-100. It was perhaps rarely practised in coverture.

4. Mbh. I. 102. 66-71 dies of extreme lasciviousness which resulted in tuberculosis. Mbh. I. 118. 31. Pāṇḍu's incapacity is attributed to curse but his name betrays that he might have been anaemic and must have lived on hills for better health. The luxurious life of aristocrats is also proved by constant warning given to the kings for over indulgence in women.

In the Great Epic Sudeshṇā, Kuntī, Śāradaṇḍāyinī, Madayantī and Madrī practised Niyoga in coverture while Ambikā, Ambālikā and the Kshatriya ladies practised it in the state of widowhood. These are the direct cases of Niyoga. In addition there are numerous indirect cases which hint at similar practice.

Motives and basis of Niyoga

In most of the above mentioned cases Niyoga was practised in coverture.[1] Therefore the custom might have arisen out of the husband's desire for progeny for securing his spiritual and family interests. Such convenient custom might later have been extended for the benefit of widows, for when chastity (celibacy) had become the main qualification of marriage even widowers might have declined to marry them.

The basis of Niyoga may well be in the fact that woman was considered as a piece of family property. Gautama definitely supports Niyoga on this basis though it has been criticized by Āpastamba, who does not support it on this basis.[2] When a person was not able to produce progeny due to his inability or death it naturally became the sacred duty of his brother and in his default of nearest gens, to use his property i.e. wife for the spiritual benefit of the deceased or the incapable. For lack of sons was a great calamity for the spiritual and temporal welfare of a man and his family, more so in cases of kings and their dynasties. So to produce sons or to appoint some one to produce them for an incapable and deceased person was to help him out of spiritual perdition and to save his dynasty from collapse. When widow marriage was no more practised the extension of the Niyoga practice to widow also, eliminated the danger of a widow going astray.

Thus this service was rendered from the motives of kindness[3] according to the notions of the Epic-societies. Niyoga for pecuniary considerations was forbidden by law.[4] But as the

1. Mbh. 104. 6 ff. 105 (sec.) Ambīkā and Ambālikā and the Kshatriyā ladies are rare cases.

2. Gaut. Dh. S. XXVIII. 32, 23 recognizes Niyoga Ap. Dh. S. II. 10. 27. 37 criticises it.

3. Mbh. I. 120. 33. तस्यामेवोत्तमानुग्रहाज्जातः प्रणीतः ।— Nīlakanṭha comments.

4. Vas. Dh. S. XVII, 65 रिक्थलोभान्नास्ति नियोगः ।

Great Epic in the narrative parts describes many prevalent popular practices which are not to be found in the law books, so, it seems, that material considerations were not completely absent from the practice of Niyoga.[1] The practice of giving money, however, is not substantiated by any instance so the money given may have been in the form of Dakshiṇā, for the spiritual benefit rendered by the Brāhmaṇas.

Niyoga as restricted by law and as practised in the Mahābhārata

Niyoga practice as depicted in the Great Epic sometimes deviates from the rules prescribed by Dharmasūtras and Śāstras. The reason being that the Great Epic as a traditional epos preserves many customs prevalent among the people while the Sūtras and the Śāstras were propounding law and were trying to adhere to ideals. To forestall indiscriminate sex relations Niyoga was hedged round with many restrictions by the law givers. The person who was to perform Niyoga was to be appointed by the elders i.e. husband or his elder brother.[2] So is the case in the Great Epic but as it describes Niyoga in coverture husband appoints the agent.[3] Refusal of Uttanka to perform Niyoga for his preceptor's wife even when requested by females of the house, indicates that when husband was living none had the right to appoint any person for the Niyoga of the wife.[4] Most peculiar is the case of Śārdaṇḍāyanī who goes to the public square and catches hold of the first Brāhmaṇa for Niyoga.[5] Here injunctions of the lawgivers are not followed. As the sole aim of Niyoga was progeny it was to be performed during the season of the woman concerned; according to Vasishṭha it should be within sixteen years of

1. Mbh. I. 105. 2. For Bhīshma suggests to invite a virtuous Brāhmaṇa for Niyoga by giving him money. Mbh. I. 120. 33 परिक्रीत: रेतो मूल्यदानेन तस्यामेव जनित: । नीलकण्ठ । cp. J. R. A. S. p. 716 ff, 1897 Winternitz "Notes on the Mahābhārata."

2. Gaut. Dh. S. XVIII. 4-14 गुरुप्रसूता । Vas. Dh. S. XVII, 56. 61-65; Y. S. I. 68-69; M. IX. 59 सम्यङ्नियुक्तया: ।

3. Mbh. I. 103. 10 मन्नियोगान्महाबाहो धर्मं कर्तुमिहार्हसि ।
Mbh. I. 103. 23; 105, 1-2 Bhīshma's permission. Mbh. I. 120.38 सा वीरपत्नी गुरुणा नियुक्ता—here husband appoints गुरुणा-भर्त्रा—Nilkāntha. Mbh. I. 122. 30-31; 124. 5 ff. In Kuntī's and Mādrī's case husband permits.

4. Mbh. I. 3. 86 ff.

5. Mbh. I. 120. 39 ff.

puberty.[1] In the Great Epic Niyoga was practised in season and perhaps Vasishṭha's instructions were followed, for if Ambikā and Ambālikā were married just after puberty, as used to be the case generally, they live with Vichitravīrya for seven years. Niyoga for them was performed within one year of their state of widowhood.[2] The life of mortification[3] and sacrifices performed[4] before Niyoga also prove its religious sanction. Satyawatī, however, does not agree to the life of penance for her daughters-in-law as it would take time.[5] The descriptions of Niyoga in the Mahābhārata show that even unwilling woman had to agree for the benefit of the dynasty of the husband.[6] This, however, is against the injunction of Baudhāyana.[7]

The persons invited for Niyoga or who could perform Niyoga

(1) *The Brother-in-law* :

As for the persons appointed for Niyoga there is a great difference between the opinion of the law-givers and the narrative part of the Great Epic. The appointed person according to law-givers was either to be the younger brother-in-law of the woman concerned or Sapiṇḍa of her husband.[8] Pāṇḍu agrees with this in principle, to be exact, it is rather the composer who agrees to this theory.[9] But it is worthy of note that in none of the cases cited above 'devara' or 'sapiṇḍa' was appointed. Meyer thinks that "Uttama devara certainly points out to a

1. Gaut. Dh. S. XVIII 4-8 नर्तुमतीयात् cp. Mbh. I. 64. 6; 120, 39; 106. 1. Vas. Dh. S. XVII. 59-64.

2. Mbh. I. 102. 70 ताभ्यां सह समाः सप्त विहरन्पृथिवीपतेः ।

Mbh. I. 104. 42-45. Vyāsa wants Ambikā and Ambālikā to perform penance for a year to which Satyawatī does not agree. Baud. Dh. S. II. 2. 4.. 10 says that a barren woman, one who has borne sons, one who has past child—bearing age, one whose children are all dead and one who is unwilling, are not allowed to have Niyoga as the spirit of this practice will not be fulfilled by them. Cp. Vas. Dh. S. XVII. 57.

3. Mbh. I. 105. 42; Cp. Baud. Dh. S. II. 2. 4. 7.

4. Mbh. I. 120. 39; 105. 54 refers to meals to the Brāhmaṇas, deities and guests.

5. Mbh. I. 105. 43 ff.

6. Mbh. I. 120-122 (sec.) Kuntī was unwilling. She was persuaded and so was Ambikā Mbh. I. 105. 50 ff.

7. See note 2 above.

8. M. IX. 59. देवराद्वा सपिण्डाद्वा ।

2. Mbh. I. 120. 35 उत्तमाद्देवरात्पुंसः कांक्षन्ते पुत्रमापदि ।

Brāhmaṇa"[1] but no such meanings are attached to 'devara', a term which is explained as "Dwitiyo Vara" by Nirukta.[2]

The appointment of brother or Sapiṇḍa of the husband for Niyoga must have been an outcome of an old custom, followed by many ancient people.[3] In a much older tradition, certainly pre-Vedic, cited in the Great Epic, the younger brother-in-law could approach the elder sister-in-law even when her husband was alive. Mamatā's case is illustrative of this point. Her objection in the situation was that she was pregnant, otherwise Bṛhaspati was not wrong[4] in approaching her. During the Ṛg-Vedic[5] era a widow was married to her younger brother-in-law, a fact not unknown to the author of the Śānti Parva.[6] Certain passages in the Great Epic suggest the kind of relation between the younger brother-in-law and sister-in-law which would be considered as so many breaches of the moral law according to present standards.[7] Even in the Rāmāyaṇa where these relations are of a higher type[8], such ideas are not altogether wanting.[9]

(2) *Brāhmaṇas*

In the Great Epic Niyoga is generally performed through the agency of the Brāhmaṇas[10] and Pāṇḍu's request to Kuntī is for a Brāhmaṇa. But Vyāsa's claim according to Satyavatī is due to his being a brother-in-law,[11] a right which Meyer thinks as "thin and thread bare"[12]—while Ludwig and Holtzmann

1. Meyer "SLAI" IV. p. 162. Line 9 ff.
2. Nirukta III. 15. exposing Ṛg. X. 40.
3. Holy Bible St. Mathwes 22. 24 (among Jews they marry elder brother's widow) Westermarck "History of Human Marriage" Vol. III p. 207-220, 1921 ed.
4. Mbh. I. 104. 9 ff.
5. Ṛg. V. X. 40. 2.
   को वां शयुत्रा विधवेव देवरं मर्यं न योषा कृणुते संधस्थ आ।
6. Mbh. XII. 72. 12. पत्य भावे यथैव स्त्री देवरं कुरुते पतिम्।
7. Mbh. I. 213. 32; III. 61. 3 Pushkara suggests Nala to pawn Damayantī.
8. Rām. IV. 6. 22.
9. Rām. III. 45. 8, 24-25.
10. Mbh. I. 120. 39 ff; 122. 21 Examples of Śārdaṇḍāyanī and Madayantī; 122. 23. Paddu's own birth. I. 120. 22 perhaps hints at the same. I. 120. 37. सदृशाच्छ्रेयसो वा त्वं also means the same. Cp. Vis. S. 15. 2 नियुक्ताया सपिण्डेनोत्तमवर्णेन Sapiṇḍa or better class born person.
11. Mbh. I. 105. 17; 31-34.
12. Meyer "SLAI" IV. p. 167. footnote I.

think that in reality Bhīshma had performed this duty for Vichitravīrya.[1] If the elder brothers-in-law were never appointed for Niyoga Meyer would be right; and Pāṇḍu's words point out the same.[2] But the difficulty is that Bhīshma was ordered by Satyawatī for performing Niyoga with Ambikā and Ambālikā[3] and he was the elder brother-in-law ; Ambikā also expected and thought of Bhīshma.[4] So to infuse virile Brāhmaṇa blood or to have good progeny through the great and learned brother-in-law[5] such as Vyās, even elder brothers may have been sought for. It must be borne in mind that the Great Epic compiles all sorts of customs and local dynastic usages

1. Holtzmann 'Das Mahābhārata' quoted by Meyer p. 167 foot note I. The basis for this argument are that Bhīshma has been addressed as a grandfather by the Kauravas and saved the Kuru dynasty from ruin Mbh. V. 31. 9-10; XI. 23. 24 but in a joint family he was like a grandfather and his saving the dynasty may refer to Vyāsa's appointment.

S. C. Sarkar IV. SAESHI p. 171-172 propounds a theory that the Kshetraja princes may have been begotten by the three relatives i.e. Bhīshma, Valhīka and Vyāsa on the three wives of Vichitravīrya on the same ground that they were addressed as grandfathers by the princes but Vyāsa as well as Bhīshma were half brothers of Vichitravīrya. Brother's son is always mentioned in the lists of sons i.e. Mbh. I. 120. 34 ज्ञातिरेताश्च Therefore Bhīshma and his half brothers were naturally referred to as grandfathers by the Kauravas. Similarly Gāndhārī was referred to as "Jyesṭṭha Mātā" by Yudhishṭhira. On the basis of merely mode of address we can not infer that Dhṛtarashtra and his half brothers were Kshetraja sons of Bhishma and Valhika.

2. Mbh. I. 120. 35.

3. Mbh. I. 103. 10 तयोरुत्पादयापत्यं संतानाय कुलस्य नः ।
मन्नियोगान्महाबाहो धर्मं कुर्तुमिहार्हसि ॥

Mbh. I. 103. 11. राज्ये चैवाभिषिच्यस्व भारताननुशाधि च ।
दारांश्च कुरु धर्मेण मा निमज्जीः पितामहान् ॥

Two distinct alternatives are given. The second Sloka does not mean marriage with younger brother's widows, which was never a rule and as widows perhaps they could not be "Dharmadaras" although "Bhāryas" they may have been. Even Mbh. XIII. 44. 52-53 which according to Meyer (SL AI. p. 168. footnote) supports the marriage with brother-in-law, but in fact it only supports Niyoga with younger brother-in-law. "Praviśet" or Likhantyev" does not support marriage and even if it does it is for a widow whose marriage is not consummated. S.C. Sarkar "SAE SHI" page 191 thinks that Satyawatī had no scruples against remarriage of her daughters-in-law with Bhīshma but even if she is taken to be unscrupulous she had nothing to gain by Ambikā and Ambālikā's marriage to Bhīshma. In that case Bhīshma would have a legal son and her son Vichitravīrya would have been deprived of the spiritual benefit of having a son.

4. Mbh. I. 105. 16-17; 106.3 Ambikā thinks
श्वश्र्वास्तद्वचनं श्रुत्वा शयाना शयने शुभे ।
साचिन्तयत्तदा भीष्ममन्यांश्च कुरुपुङ्गवान् ।

5. Mbh. I. 105. 17-34 Satyawatī thinks Vyāsa to be the brother of Vichitravīrya.

which may not be found in the legal literature.[1] Vyāsa was a "Mātṛbandhu" and as half brother, nearest Sapiṇḍa, fit for being invited for Niyoga even according to some authors on law.[2] Of course he had no relation with the Kuru family, from the time of his birth. But the Epic society is to be judged from different standards. Karṇa, who was placed in similar circumstances, was offered the throne and even Draupadī as a bait to[3] change sides, thus indicating that Karṇa was considered one of the family. Vyāsa had thus a claim of kinsman as well as of a Brahmaṇa for there is no other example of a Sapiṇḍa being appointed for Niyoga in the Mahabharata.

Basis of Brāhmaṇa appointment

In the cases of Sudeshṇā, Śārdaṇḍāyanī and Madayantī the appointment of the Brāhmaṇa-ṛshis for Niyoga of queens was due to the belief that a son born through ascetic energy excelled others in capacity.[4] Most of them like Vyāsa may have been outstanding ascetic personalities. In the case of Dīrghatamā not much can be said about his morality, at least from the present standards. His wife and ascetics of his āśrama abandoned him for they did not like his ways, although the Great Epic upholds even such a morality.[5] But so much was the faith and confidence in the Brāhmaṇa ability for producing a better progeny that sometimes a Brāhmaṇa could be caught hold of from a public square and be appointed for Niyoga.[6]

For performing such duties Brāhmaṇas have been blamed as unscrupulous, sexual and full of vices[7], mostly by the foreign

1. Jacobi's dictum "The Mahābhārata could not have become the national epos of India, if it has been merely an illustration of the Dharmaśāstras with all its legal antiquities" quoted by Winternitz J. O. A. S. 1897 "Notes of the Mahābhārata" p. 759.
2. Gaut. Dh. S. XVIII. 156. 6.
his claim also I. 105. 14-16. "Bhartuh Kshetreshu"
3. Mbh. V. 140. 8-15.
4. Mbh. I. 64. 7 ff ; 104. 44; 105. 2; 120. 22, 39.
5. Mbh. I. 104. 26 ff. The Epic composer supports cp. Mbh. I. 104. 25 धर्मात्मा च महात्मा च वेदवेदाङ्गपारगः । and for his abandonment by the ascetics the composer blames them. Mbh. I. 104. 27 क्रुद्धा मोहाभिभूतास्ते । commentator Nīlakaṇṭha adds मोहाभिभूतत्वं—अपापे पापदर्शित्वात् ।
6. Mbh. I. 120. 39. पुष्पेण प्रयता स्नाता निशि कुन्ति चतुष्पथे ।
वरयित्वा द्विजं सिद्धं हुत्वा पुंसवनेऽनलम् ।
7. Cp. Parjiter "AIHT" chap. XXVII. p. 328 specially line 15ff cp. Hopkins "Religions of India" chap. XIV. "Early Hindusism" p. 351-352. cp. Meyer "SLAI" p. 173-174 foot note I quotes such influence of the Brāhmaṇas although it is rare in India.

scholars for whom it is really difficult to imagine the hold that the Brāhmaṇas had upon ancient Indian societies. It is wrong to think on these lines. If the Brāhmaṇas were degraded they could not have been revered or even permitted to enter their inner-apartments by the Kshatriyas. There is no need to think that Brāhmaṇas were appointed for Niyoga because the Kshatriyas were afraid of their curse. They had option to appoint a Sagotra or a Sapiṇḍa in default of a brother. Even in the case of Madayantī it is wrong to think that she was under the influence of Vaśishṭha and therefore persuaded Kalmāshapāda to agree for her Niyoga.[1] She checked Kalmāshapāda from approaching her as she wanted to save his life from the effects of the curse. It has been already shown that even marriages with lower caste husbands were not allowed. A woman was not thus to degrade herself and therefore it was in keeping with these views that the Kshatriyas, when they wanted better progeny appointed the Brahmaṇas who were their superiors.[2] Due to their penance and asceticim the Brāhmaṇas might have been considered as non-moral or amorals. Such persons were really fit because they would not be left with any feeling for the women for whom they were appointed.[3] It is on account of the change that has taken place in the standards for judging such matters that we consider Niyoga as immoral; for the Brāhmaṇas it was nothing good or bad. If the results of certain actions on their part saved a dynasty from spiritual and temporal ruin or gave psychological satisfaction of motherhood to a wife of an impotent or a widow, they were ready to help if appointed. Kumārila, later explains that Vyāsa could do so (perform Niyoga) on account of his austerities and others like him could do so, an elephant could devour branches of trees without harm but another doing

1. Mbh. I. 182. 9 ff. Sarkar S. C. "SAESHI" p. 163 IV. "and partly to the growing pretentions of the priests." On p. 168 he remarks "There is a great confusion about the story of Mitrasaha, Kalmāshapāda in the Purāṇas and the Mahābhārata" Cp. Pargiter "AIHT" chap. XVIII "The Vaśishṭhas" p. 207-209. The simple story is quoted in Rām. VII. 65.

2. Mbh. I. 167. 2 ff;94-21 ff. Draupada appoints a superior Brāhmaṇa for his queen's Niyoga although he had sons. Mbh. I. 94. 22. So does perhaps Bharata. Cp. Kautilya as quoted by Altekar "PWIHC" p. 173 permits an old king to raise a new son by Niyoga, if his own son turned out to be wicked and incompetent.

3. cp. M. IX. 62.

so would meet death.[1] Vyāsa's later interest in the Kauravas and the Pāṇḍavas might have been due to his respect for his mother, or it might have been just a normal case of a Brāhmaṇa advising the great kings on morality. His interest did not flow from the fact that he was their Niyoga father.[2] Sarkār, in his crusade against the Brāhmaṇas, citing another case states that the connection of Uddālaka's wife with his disciple[3] was given the better name of Niyoga later on, for before the birth of Śwetaketu married women were allowed free sexual relations; for Uddālaka himself agrees that such a practice is the eternal one.[4] It is, however, wrong to state as Sarkār does that "Niyoga of this type is but a form of general licence that prevailed amongst the Brāhmaṇa-settlements"[5] But it has been already shown, that the general licence[6] described in Śwetaketu's story had been just invented to give an importance to the origin of marriage.[7] In the single example also, i.e. the disciple performing Niyoga for the preceptor's wife, the Mahābhārata deviates from the Sūtra and Smṛti rules where no such 'Niyoga' is permitted. Another story of Uṭṭanka also proves that disciples used to refuse such services if unappointed. The Brāhmaṇa morality did not allow so called general licence.[8]

The Devas

The Devas were appointed only in the cases of Kuntī and Mādrī. As the situation is patently incredible the fact might well have been that the Devas was the name of a people. There may be some grain or truth in Sarkār's statement that they were contemporary princes.

The Atharvan mantra imparted by Durvāsā to Kuntī may have been some sort of charm—hypnotism—by which a person

1. Kaṇe "Hist. of Dh." Vol. III. chap. XXXII. p. 846 cp. similar is the explanation given to Kuntī for justifying Surya's morals—Mbh. XV 30.24

सर्वं बलवतां पथ्यं सर्वं बलवतां शुचि ।
सर्वं बलवतां धर्मः सर्वं बलवतां स्वकम् ।।

2. Cp. Sarkar S. C. "SAESHI" IV. p. 175 wrongly attributes it to his being Niyoga father.
3. Mbh. XII. 34. 22.
4. Mbh. I. 122. 14.
5. Sarkār. S. C. "SAESHI" IV p. 175.
6. Mbh. I. 122. 12.
7. Chap. on 'Marriage' p. 37.
8. Mbh. I. 3.86 ff. for Utanka it was "Akārya".

whether willing or unwilling, came at the beck and call of the person who used it.[1] That is why, perhaps, only Kuntī could use it for Mādrī; for Kuntī alone had the knowledge. These mantras may have been uttered for some kinds of fertility rites.

Niyoga-Indirect cases

(1) *Boons*

If the boons of the ṛshis or Brāhmaṇas are taken as indirect references to Niyoga practice there is no dearth of it in the Epics, for the boon giving ṛshies were either fathers as in the case of Kaśyapa or putative fathers.[2] Thus Damayantī and her brothers[3], Sagara[4], Duryodhana and his brothers[5], Sanjaya's son[6] were all born through the boons of ṛshies and may refer to instances of Niyoga. But in the case of Gāndhārī it would be strange if her husband as well as her sons were Niyoga—putras of Vyāsa. It may appear preposterous to the imagination of present-day society but such relations were considered no relations in those days. The boon which Anusūyā received from Rudra may too have been of a similar nature.[7]

(2) *Sacrifices, charms and fruits*

It will not be out of place here to mention sons born by

1. Mbh. I. 124. 9 ff; III. 305. 11-18. अकामो वा सकामं वा स समेप्यति ते वशे । ; III. 360. ।।.

2. Mbh. I. 2. 101 कृष्णद्वैपायनाच्चैव प्रसूतिर्वरदानजा ।
धृतराष्ट्रस्य पाण्डोश्च पाण्डवानां च संभवः ।

P. C. Roy. (Eng. Tr. 1919 p. 19.) translates it as "through the potency of Vyāsa's blessings." Sons as boons of Brāhmaṇa-husbands and Brāhmaṇas, prove the same. Cp. Mbh. I. 16. 6, 10. The sons of Śarmishṭha as boons of a ṛishi also hint a false case of Niyoga to appease Devayānī. Devayānī did not inquire further for such boons might have been common, Mbh. I. 83. 3-7.

3. Mbh. III. 53. 7-9.

4. Rām. II. 110. 16 ff through the grace of ṛshi Chyavana.

5. Mbh. I. 110. 7-9; 115. 8.

6. Mbh. VII. 65. 21 ff. Through Nārada, a little difference in XII. 31. 15 ff.

7. Mbh. XIII. 14. 98 विना भर्त्रा च रुद्रेण भविष्यति न संशयः ।
वंशे तथैव नाम्ना तु ख्यातिं यास्यति चेप्सिताम् ।।

Ingeniously, commentator Nīlakaṇṭha twists the facts, चरुद्रः चरोर्द्रवः—पानमात्रेण तव पुत्रो भविष्यतीऽत्यर्थः । when Niyoga was extinct this was a good device to cover up the unpleasant custom in which the commentator excels further. In this way he could save the reputation of pativratā Anusūyā, a paragon of virtue, as well as that of Rudra. The ingenuity of the commentator is not a new phase, in ancient literature when even legends were reconstructed to suit the times.

the performance of sacrifices by eating sacrificial "Charu" i.e. viands and fruits given by ascetics.[1] Meyer associated this with some kind of supposed magic[2], which is highly improbable. Sarkār associates all this with probable cases of Niyoga[3] but this will make Niyoga a very common practice while it is clearly stated that it was a law in distress (Āpad-Dharma)[4]. It may be said that from the time of Atharvaveda[5] "Mantroushadhi" (i.e. charm and medicine) go together. Medicines given with Mantras (charms) and sacrifices may have provided a religious air to the whole affair, and may have had some psychological effect.[6] The kings often led vicious and luxurious lives, the austerities performed or regulated life led after being initiated to sacrifices might have restored their health and given them progeny. The sacrificial viands may have been given for some kind of hormone treatment, with which the Brāhmaṇas were familiar.

With all that may be said against the above mentioned argument, the fact remains that a pure Brāhmaṇa Upayāja declined Drupada's invitation to perform sacrifice for him so that he may get better sons.[7] Upayāja suggests his brother Yāja instead, for he says, the latter did not mind impurity. A good Brāhmaṇa could never otherwise have an objection for sacrificing, which was his duty. He could never think that sacrifice should be performed by an impure Brāhmaṇa. In fact, great and good Brāhmaṇas, like Ṛshyaśṛnga, were called to perform such sacrifices.[8] The story seems to have been changed by the redactors. The slokas may be hinting at a case of Niyoga to be performed to which a celibate Brāhmaṇa may have had an objection.[9]

1. Rām. I. 15-17; Mbh. XIII. 4. 27 ff; II. 17. 18-37
2. Meyer "SLAI" p. 156 ff. attributes this to magic.
3. Sarkār S. C. "SAESHI" Chap. IV on "Niyoga".
4. Mbh. I. 120. 35 कांक्षन्ते पुत्रमापदि; 111. 6 Mantra was given to Kuntī for Āpaddharma.
5. Mbh. I. 111. 6; III. 305. 20 Kuntī's mantra was Atharvan.
मन्त्रग्रामं तदा राजन्नथर्वशिरसि श्रुतम् ।
6. Like a modern psychiatric treatment or blank doses of homoeopaths.
7. For Draupada had sons already. Mbh. I. 167. 3 (whole sec.)
जातान्पुत्रान्सनिर्वेदाद्दिग्बन्धूनिति चाब्रवीत् ।
8. Rām. I. 10-12 Ṛshyaśṛagya (a great Ṛshi called for the sacrifice of Daśratha.)
9. Mbh. I. 167. 16-19.

According to Sarkār Śāntanu was also born of Niyoga performed by Mahāvisha.[1] It is highly improbable, for if rebirths and incarnations are taken as cases of Niyoga every body in the Great Epic according to this theory would be born of Niyoga, for all characters there are born as incarnations of some god or goddess.[2] Moreover Pratīpa had sons Devāpi[3] and Vāhīka, thus he was in no need of Niyoga.[4] Another reason put forward for Śāntanu being a son of a Niyoga is that Pratīpa had grown old when Śāntanu was born. The reason for Pratīpa's old age may be different. This story seems to have been quoted wrongly in the Mahābhārata for in the Ṛg-Veda[5] Śāntanu and Devāpi are cousins, sons of Ulāna and Ṛshtisheṇa, who were Pratīpa's sons. The old traditions might have been forgotten by the composers.

According to the Mahābhārata Bharata also had a son Bhūmanyu through Bharadwāja.[6]

No cases of Niyoga in the Rāmāyaṇa

The Rāmāyaṇa though belonging more or less to the same period as the Mahābhārata gives no account of Niyoga custom. Considering its idealistic tone the omission is natural.

Objections and opinions about Niyoga

From the above-mentioned account it will be clear that Niyoga in the Great Epic was performed for the spiritual and dynastic interest of the impotent or deceased. Jolly, however, is of opinion that Niyoga apart from serving the spiritual ends was done with economic motives.[7] Witernitz quoting a missionary report writes that proverty, paucity of women and the joint family system were responsible for polyandry as well as Niyoga.[8] It can not also be said that the Pāṇḍavas were uncouth foreigners and

1. Mbh. I. 96. 5-8; 97. 18 does not hint it.
2. Mbh. I. 67 (sec.) Anśāvatarana Parva.
3. Mbh. I. 95. 44.
4. Pargiter "AIHT" chap. XILI. p. 165-166. thinks this story is quoted wrong.
5. Ṛg. V. X. 98 Devāpi is called Arshtisheṇa, son of Ṛshtisheṇa and Śāntanu AULĀNA.
6. Mbh. I. 94. 22 लेभे पुत्रं भरद्वाजाद्भुमन्यु नाम भारत ।
7. Jolly "Recht and Sette" Eng. Trans. p. 156-157.
8. J.R.A.S. 1897. Notes on the Mahābhārata pp. 716-732.—Winternitz.

Niyoga implies non-Āryan Himālayan influence. All the opinions are open to doubt and do not seem to be correct.

Criticism

As for Jolly's opinion Niyoga was certainly not performed for economic motives from the point of view of the guardians and the widow who was going to have progeny. It may have been the case to some extent with the Brāhmaṇas who received wealth[1] although this is not substantiated by any example. As already shown such service was rendered for kindness and the Brāhmaṇas prompted by pecuniary motives in the matter must have been insignificant in number.[2] In the Great Epic Brāhmaṇa agency in Niyoga was approved not only with spiritual and dynastic interest but also from the eugenic point of view. As for the Pāṇḍavas being foreigners there is no ground to think so, for Niyoga was practised by the Kuru dynasty even before them, e.g. by Vichitravīrya's widows. It may however, be contended that in desiring to have more than five sons Pāṇḍu was to some extent influenced by the morality of the Śataśṛnga people, known for laxity of morals and polyandry. (Śataśṛnga may have been the area of the Punjab hills from Kulu, Spiti, Lahul to Jaunsār Bāwar in the U.P. where still similar conditions prevail). Pāṇḍu might have lived there in exile and this explains the extraordinary Niyoga of Kuntī and Mādrī,[3] for the writers on law do not sanction Niyoga with different persons and for a number of sons. Nevertheless the fact remains that while people living in foreign countries adopt some of their manners and customs as did Pāṇḍu they do not thereby forget their own customs altogether. The history of colonization proves it.

It cannot be said, however, that poverty, paucity of women and the joint family system were responsible for ployandry as well as for Niyoga. These reasons have no relevance to the cases mentioned in the Mahābhārata where those having recourse to

1. Mbh. I. 105. 2.

2. Mbh. I. 104. 7; 105. 17; Cp. Vas. Dh. S. XVII 65. लोभान्नास्तिनियोगः ।

3. For the Pāṇḍavas connection with Jaunsār Bāwar area see K. M. Munshī's introduction p. i and iv ff to Saxena's "Social Economy of a Polyandrous people." also pp. 44, 55.

Niyoga were the royal families with rich luxurious courts. The Kshatriyā-ladies' Niyoga with the Brāhmaṇas cited as an old tradition in the Great Epic was due to paucity of men. Similar condition must have prevailed due to constant warfare when the Epic story was being enacted. The description of polygamy, many thousand slave-girls given in dowry to the Brāhmaṇas as gifts and in the court of Yudhishṭhira at Indraprastha do not indicate the scarcity of women. The hold of the joint family too does not seem to be strong[1], or at least it was not completely developed as yet. Therefore Niyoga was practised for spiritual or dynastic interests in the Epics.

This does indicate a very low status of women, for women even when unwilling had to resort to Niyoga at the command of their elders or husband.[2] In case of Ambikā and Ambālikā they were only informed when the person was already appointed.[3] The woman concerned was considered to be the property of the family for producing progeny. The benefit she could have out of this repugnant custom, from present day standards, was that she must have had natural love and respect due to a mother from a Niyoga-born-son than from an adopted one.[4] Her position was thus secure in the family. If the adoptive son was given for pecuniary consideration by his real parents, the latter were bound to exercise their influence but even if a Niyoga father had any such intentions he would not be able to realize them. In case the Kshetrin father was living his influence would predominate; even if the mother was a widow the Niyoga —father was to have nothing to do with the family, for he was to behave like a father-in-law to the widow.[5] In that case the widow's influence would be much more over the son. The system must have helped in giving the widow and the wife of an impotent the psychological satisfaction of fulfilling their instinct of motherhood.

1. There are identical condition in the Sūtras and Gaut. Dh. S. XXVII. 4. opines विभागे तु धर्मवृद्धिः ।

2 Mbh. I. 105. 54; 121 (sec); 122. 27 even unrighteous deed ordered by husband was to be performed although Baud. D. S. II. 2. 4. 7 states that Niyoga should not be performed with unwilling woman. Law, here, may be prescribing the ideal behaviour which was not followed in practice.

3 Mbh. I. 105. 50 ff.

4 An adoptive son may be influenced by his real father.

5. Cp. M. IX. 62.

Its decline and collapse

Even in the narrative part of the Great Epic the practice of Niyoga seems to be losing ground. As it was difficult to oust this custom, it seems, reformers may have begun by limiting the number of the male progeny. Dīrghatamas, when appointed had sixteen sons altogether.[1] This constant relationship for producing a number of sons amounts to nothing but a general licence and is as good as a marriage. This must have been repugnant to reformers. Kuntī states that a woman who begets the fourth son through Niyoga is "Swairiṇī"[2]. Gautama permits two sons by Niyoga while Manu opines for one son only.[3] In the didactic portions the opinion was definitely against the practice of Niyoga.[4] In the list of foolish persons enumerated by Vidura is one who scatters his own seed in another's field.[5] In the comparative legal literature the same conditions are found. Gautama and Baudhāyana approve of it.[6] Āpastamba and Manu although they began a crusade against Niyoga, had to mention the practice and lay down some rules for it, because they recognized the fact that customs die hard.[7] Nevertheless, Āpastamba and Baudhāyana, in order to persuade people against Niyoga opine that there is no spiritual welfare for the widow's husband from Niyoga-born-sons.[8] The same idea has been added in the Ādiparva, a clear case of interpolation as the ślokas have been inserted in between the prose pas-

1 Mbh I 104 44 ff

2 Mbh. I. 123. 77 page 254. P. C. Roy's in Eng. Trans. states "a woman having intercourse with four different men" is not correct for then to have five sons from the same person would be correct but नातश्चतुर्थं प्रसवमापत्स्वपि वदन्त्युत । means four child births.

3. M. IX. 60 but Vātsyāyana "Kāmsūtra" allows two. Cp. Gaut. Dh. S. XVIII. 8 also allows two.

4. Mbh. XIII. 44. 52-53; I. 95. 31.

5. Mbh. V. 37. 5-6.

6. Gaut. Dh. S. XVIII. 8.

7. Ap. Dh. S. II. 6. 13. 4-7 quoting Aupagundhanī says that such a son cannot inherit, indirectly states that there cannot be any spiritual benefit by a Niyoga—born-son. Cp. Mbh. I. 95. 30-31. भस्त्रा माता पितुः पुत्रो येन जातः स एव सः । रेतोधाः पुत्र उन्नयति नरदेव यमक्षयात् ।
Vas. Dhs. XVII. 6-11. is definitely against Niyoga. Recognizes brothers son or cowive's son as one's own son.

8. Ap. Dh. S. II. 6. 13. 1-7, 4-5; Baud. Dh. S. II. 2. 3. 33 quoting Aupagandhanī, which S. Rao Shāstrī, in "Women in the sacred laws." p 20, thinks later interpolation.

sages.[1] Manu thinks the custom beastly.[2] Bhīshma, in the didactic portions opines against Niyoga practice.[3] Giving reasons for the change Dr. Altekar states "society had developed a finer sense of the marriage ideal and conjugal fidelity. It began to feel that Niyoga procedure was primitive and beastly."[4] Whatever theories may have been propounded it appears that the sense of conjugal fidelity developed only in case of women and not in the case of men as concubinage and polygamous society bear witness to the fact. Woman[5] is by nature monogamous and it has been shown that even when the custom of Niyoga was prevalent, the one who had to perform it did not like it.[6] The queens, as was natural sometimes, did not like to unite with the poor, dreadful, awful smelling and even blind and old Brāhmaṇas with matted locks.[7] Moreover, it was the ideal of pātivrata, reaching its climax in the Satī custom that finished the institution of Niyoga as an unchaste practice and betrayal of the marriage vows. In the Great Epic the husbands who had their dynastic and spiritual interest to serve persuade their wives to the practice of Niyoga even when they did not like the idea.[8] In the Rāmāyaṇa where pātivrata ideal is nearly perfected, there is no mention of this custom and even if there were such cases, the stories have been entirely changed beyond recognition. Widows as described in the Rāmāyaṇa lead chaste, austere and celibate lives.

1. Mbh. I. 95. 30 (as quoted) in Supra. p. 170. note 7.
2. M. IX. 66.
3. Mbh. XIII. 44. 52.
4. Altekar "PWHC" p. 174.
5. Mbh. V. 30. 38 (concubinage). cp. even as late as Sūdraka 'Mṛchha—Kaṭika' Vasantasenā, also, vide infra. 'Adultery and Extra Marital Relation.'
6. Mbh. I. 121-122 (sec.); 104. 44 ff.
7. Mbh. I. 104. 46; I. 106. 5, 15.
8. Mbh. I. 122; 123. 77.

Chapter VIII

WOMEN AS WIDOW

There is little material in the Epics directly showing the position of widows in societies of the different ages depicted in the Epics. This paucity of material, adequate enough to admit of generalisation, is a great handicap to the investigator. The importance of the status of widows in society to a writer of social history can hardly be exaggerated, for, even if a society adopts a contumelious attitude towards its women, the mother, the daughter and the wife are generally loved because of certain natural instincts. In addition, the wife is ever useful, for on her depends the progeny and hence future happiness. Naturally, when in a man-dominated patriarchal society the mother, wife and daughter are respected, it is because of the position and love they get from their protectors in the family. The case of widows is different. Even when their parents are living, in a patriarchal form of society they have to depend upon their husband's families. Thus a widow is left to the care of those who have no natural love for her nor any instinct to guide them in their duty towards her. On the contrary sometimes these guardians have their own interest to serve against that of the widow. The widow being so handicapped, the treatment meted out to her is a good criterion by which to judge a culture and its attitude towards women.

Social Attitude

An object of pity but not considered inauspicious

While dealing with the pātivrata conception it has been already shown that the husband was the very god to his wife. As a logical sequal to this, a widowed woman was a luckless creature and an object of pity. Thus all the utterances of widows are full of self-pity. But in the Great Epic a widow's sorrow is compared to the sorrow of a person who has lost his son and this statement is forwarded by an enumeration of eight other types of sorrow.[1] Therefore, we may safely conclude that a widow's grief was not considered to be the greatest sorrow by the society. She may, believing in the theory of 'karma', think that her sorrow or plight was the result of her "Karmas".[2] It is, however, significant to note that she has not been enumerated among the sinners.[3] No "Vidhawa Dharma" has been prescribed for her as in the Purāṇas & later Smṛities. She is not excluded from auspicious ceremonies as an inauspicious creature, which was a position assigned to her by later writers.[4] Kuntī accompanies Draupadī to witness her mariage[5] and was the first to give her blessings.[6] Before the coronation of Rāma, Sītā is decorated by Daśaratha's wives.[7] It may be argued that these were mothers-in-law but in view of the negative evidence we can say that they were not considered inauspicious persons and excluded from the ceremonies as is the case among orthodox Hindūs at present.

Her sorrow not described to be greater than that of a mother who lost her child

It is strange to notice that a widowed woman though pitied by the society, was not so much condemned by it as she was by her own self. May be she had future fears and dread of her forlorn state. A woman who lost her child needed much more consolation and is consoled much more than one who has lost her husband. The consolation given to Subhadrā by Śrī Kṛshṇa and Kuntī on her bereavement is much greater than that given to Uttarā.[8] Uttarā in her turn bewails much more for the still-born child.[9] than for her husband. Kausalyā feels equally sad for her son's exile and her husband's death. It is of course not fair to compare the affections of a mother with

1. Mbh. II. 68. 81-83.
2. Rām. VI. 111. 30; VI 32. 9, 30;
Mbh. I. 121. 27-29; VII. 73. 24-45; XIII. 93. 17-35; 94. 16-43-; XII. 111. 46 ff.
3. Mbh. XIII. 111. (section).
4. Skandha Purāṇa III. Brahmaraṇya 7. 50-51 अमंगलेभ्यः सर्वेभ्यो विधवा स्यादमंगला—Kātyāyana quoted in Vīramitrodaya Sam. p. 626-627 —Both quoted by Kaṇe Vol. II. Part I. chap. XII. pp. 584-585.
5. Mbh. I. 194. 3.
6. Mbh. I. 199. 5-12.
7. Rām. VI. 128. 17.
8. Mbh. VII. 77. 9 ff.; 78 whole sec.; XIV. 61. 4. and 24 ff.
9. Mbh. XIV. 68. 12 ff.; 69. 1 and 5 ff.

those of a wife, but in the Epics and specially in the Great Epic, one cannot help noticing these obvious comparisons.[1]

Widowhood—A great calamity

Nevertheless, it may be stated that the state of widowhood was a great calamity. The reason for it is more or less self-evident. Women were known as 'Abalās' i.e. those without power, and therefore they depended upon their protectors.[2] Although a woman was proud of all her protectors[3] there was no greater protector than the husband and therefore, his death was the greatest calamity for her.[4] Thus Maṇḍodarī thinks that it was a great blow to her when her son died but after Rāvaṇa's death she felt as if she herself had been slain.[5] After the husband's death, society provided the widow a protector in a son[6] and failing that in a king[7] but she was still known as masterless[8] i.e. Vidhawā. When her master was living it was below the dignity of any woman to live with her son or even to depend upon him even though she might have hated her circumstances. Rāma at once rejects Kausalyā's proposal to accompany him like an insignificant widow.[9] The protection given by a son was not thought to be perfect and therefore it has been stated many times, in both the Epics, that even if a widow had many sons she was an object of pity for herself and her relatives.[10] She has been compared to a Vīṇā without strings and to a car without wheels, thereby meaning that all that is responsible for vibration and motion i.e. the urge for life was

1. Rām. IV. 24. 42-44; VII. 111. 121 ff. Rāma and Vibhīshaṇa console Tāra and Rāvaṇa's wives respectively a little and they at once attend funerals and go home.

2. Mbh. XIII. 46. 8 स्त्रियः पुंसां परिददे मनुर्जिगमिषुर्दिवम् ।
अबलाः स्वल्पकौपीनाः सुहृदःसत्य जिष्णवः ।

3. Rām. VI. 111. 39

4. Mbh. XII. 148. 7 नास्ति भर्तृसमो नाथो॰ ।

5. Rām. VI. 111. 57

6. Mbh. III. 293. 35 मृते भर्तरि पुत्रश्च वाच्यो मातुररक्षिता cp. M IX. 4.

7. Mbh. XII. 86. 23 cp. Nārada XIII. 29
पक्षद्वयावसाने तु राजा भर्ता स्मृतः स्त्रियाः ।

8. Amara Kosha p. 207. 11. विगतो धवो यस्याः इति विधवा ।

9. Rām. II. 21. 61 कथंस्विदन्या विधवेव नारी ।

10. Rām. IV. 23. 12.

lost to her.[1] Her hopes and happiness were shattered for ever even if she had a hundred sons.[2] A widow feels uprooted and her honour destroyed.[3] Widowhood was a great calamity feared by the women of aristocracy.[4] The widows used the word "Anāthā" for themselves[5] and for such state i.e. widowhood "Paśchimāvasthā"[6] which has often been translated as "the later state" but it implies much more, and just as the sun going to the west loses its splendour and light, so does the widow.

Similes prove her plight

All the similes used to denote her condition also prove her pitiable and unprotected plight. She has often been compared to a creeper on a huge tree after its destruction[7], like a plantain tree cut asunder.[8] These similes are vivid and through them we can envisage the utterly fallen, helpless and forlorn state of the widow. Many times weeping widows have been compared, in their state of helplessness, to the herd of she-elephants around their leader sunk in slough.[9] Kausalyā feels like one who, without a caravan has lost the way.[10] The husband was the real splendour of the wife; deprived of him, though beautiful, she did not look so.[11] Therefore anything shorn of splendour, glory, beauty or of protector has been compared to a widow. Ayodhyā looked such without Daśaratha.[12] Bharata thinks that

1. Rām. II. 39. 29. नातंत्री वाद्यते वीणा नाचक्रो विद्यते रथः ।
2. Rām. IV. 20.8. निरानन्दा निराशाहं० ।
   II. 39. 29 नापतिः सुखमेधेते या स्यादपि शतात्मजा ।
3. Rām. VI. 110. 20.
   Rām. IV. 23. 9.
4. Rām. VII. 25. 42.
5. Mbh. XVI. 5. 5. ; Rām. II. 66. 8; IV. 20. 15; 23. 7; 24. 40
आर्तामनाथां० । VI. 48. 17.
6. Rām. VI. 32. 8; 111. 38.
7. Rām. IV. 22. 30 महाद्रुमं छिन्नमिवाश्रिता लता ।
8. Rām. VI. 32. 6 छिन्ना तु कदली यथा ।
   Mbh. XI. 17. 1 छिन्नेव कदली वने ।
9. Mbh. XI 23. 8. वसिता गृष्टयः पङ्के परिमग्नमिव द्विपम् ।
10. Rām. II. 66.4 विपथे सार्थहीनेव नाहं जीवितुमुत्सहे ।
11. Rām. V. 16.26 भर्ता नाम परं नार्याः शोभनं भूषणादपि ।
    एषा हि रहिता तेन शोभनार्हा न शोभते ।
    Rām. VII. 25. 42; Mbh. IX. 59. 28-30; 42. 16.
12. Rām. II. 66. 24

the earth has been widowed and does not shine without Daśaratha.[1] Sītā wishes the widow-plight for Lankā.[2] After the death of Vṛshṇi heroes and Kṛshṇa, Dwārikā looked like a widow.[3]

Superstitions about widowhood, prove its dreadfulness

Sad and sorrowful as the widow's plight generally was, it was natural that some superstitions were built round it. The theory of 'Karma' and rebirth was generally believed. Widows naturally thought that it was due to the bad deeds done by them in their previous births that they had to suffer widowhood,[4] It was also believed that one who had auspicious signs could not be a widow. As has been already stated[5] these auspicious signs judged the worth of the girl during the time of her mariage. These were deciphered by the astrologers known as 'Lākshaṇikā'[6] i.e. "the readers of the signs". When Sītā was shown the supposed dead bodies of Rāma and Lakshmaṇa, she wonders how the words of these wise "Lākshaṇikās" had come to be false.[7] When the end of the Vṛshṇis was near Vṛshṇi ladies in their dream saw a lady of black complexion and white teeth, entering their homes laughing and running through Dwārikā, snatching the auspicious threads from their wrists.[8] All this proves the dreadful plight of the widow.

Widow gives full expression to her sorrow

In both the Epics we find widow giving full expression to their grief.[9] The sorrow, itself was, of course, of the profoundest kind and the society under consideration seems to suffer from no inhibitions where expression of grief was concerned, for even the heroes and aristocrats uttered loud wails.

Restraint expected from hero's wife-Greater danger of widowhood for her

Inspite of the outbursts of emotions, restraint was expected

1. Rām. II. 76. 9.
2. Rām. V. 26. 29-30.
3. Mbh. XVI. 5.4.
4. Mbh. I. 121. 29 संयुक्ता विप्रयुक्ताश्च पूर्वदेहे कृता मया । तदिदं कर्मभिः पापैः पूर्वदेहेषु संचितम् ।
5. Rām. VI. 48. 6-14. These signs are described.
6. Rām. II. 29. 9. ; Rām. VI. 48. 2.
7. Rām. VI. 48. 2-4. ज्ञानिनोऽनृतवादिनः।
8. Mbh. XVI. 3. 1.
9. Mbh. XI. 12. 10; 24. 6; 26. 4, 9; Rām. II. 76. 21 ; 65. 24; VI. 32. 3; 49. 9; 110. 5.

from a hero's wife. According to the religion and philosophy of the age it was the highest duty of a Kshatriya to die fighting. Such a glorious death was not to be mourned. And it is rather strange to note that as soon as wives of heroes are reminded of their duty, they regain their composure, and are ready to attend the funerals of their husbands.[1] This stoic and dignified behaviour would be inconceivable in the present conditions. Tārā, in her sorrow, states that nobody should bestow one's daughter upon heroes, for in the age of sanguiniary wars, a hero's life was always in danger and his wife ran an ever present risk of widowhood.[2]

Widow accompanied funeral processions

Strange again it may sound to us but widows in those days used to follow funeral processions[3] in carriages, seated according to their ranks.[4] This was an old practice coming down from the Vedic age. Gradually on account of imposition of certain restrictions and the curtailment of freedom, women became more delicate, dependent and emotional for want of intellectual education. Thus later it become impossible for them to attend the funerals and the practice was entirely abandoned. In the Epics, however, the widow at the cremation grounds circumambulated the pyre.[5] Generally the task of burning the pyre was performed by the surviving male relations, for even in those days it was too cruel a duty to be performed by women. In case of those ladies whose families were wiped out by wars, the wives and daughters-in-law had to perform the hard task.[6] After the corpse was burnt they had the right to perform watery rites[7] (तर्पण). Judging from

1. Rām. IV. 24. 42-43 न शूरपत्न्य: परिदेवयन्ति । Supra Page 174 note no. 1.

2. Rām. IV. 23. 8.

3. Rām. IV. 25 33-35 ff. II. 76. 19-20 In Punjāb they still attend funeral procession but a Punjābī woman is the most hardly among Indian women.

4. But going on foot in Rām. VI. 111. 110-111 may be due to negligence of Vibhīshaṇa.

5. Rām. II. 76. 20.

6. Mbh. XI. 25. 19 एतास्तु द्रुपदं वृद्धं स्नुषा भार्याश्च दु:खिता: ।
दग्ध्वा गच्छन्ति पाञ्चाल्यं० ।

7. Rām. II. 76. 23; Mbh. XVI. 7. 27.

modern standards it must be said that the behaviour of widows of the Epic heroes was more free from inihibitions, courageous, composed, dignified and indicates their strength of mind.

Sati not a common practice

All these descriptions prove that Satī, or widow burning was not at all common when the Epics were composed. The wives of Daśratha, Vāli and Rāvaṇa survived them. There is only one case of Satī in the Rāmāyaṇa.[1] The Uttara Kaṇḍa where it has been referred to, is a later redaction, in the opinion of Indologists. In her extreme sorrow, consequent upon her supposed widowhood Sītā requested Rāvaṇa to kill her and gain the merit of joining a wife to the husband. Tārā made a similar request to Rāma. There was no need of making such a request had there been Satī custom in existence. These words show that suicide, was not thought to be meritorious. In a fit of emotion the widows express the wish for joining their husbands but this was due to the shock they felt.[2] It had nothing to do with the idea of Satī. To our thinking, Hopkins is wrong in stating that Rām. V. 26.7 implies Satī.[3] This with "Nāham Jīvitumutsahe" has been a favourite style of expressing their deadly sorrow by the widows. Only once does Kausalyā hint at Satī custom, when she says that she will embrace the king's body and will enter fire,[4] but even she does not perform 'Satī'. There was no need of committing 'Satī' according to the Rāmāyaṇa because the merit of joining the husband in heaven, which devolved upon a Satī, according to the later writers[5], was gained by surviving

1. Rām. VII. 17. 15.
2. Rām. IV. 24. 37-38.
3. Rām. V. 26. 7 धिङ्मामनार्यामसतीं याहं तेन विनाकृता ।
मुहूर्तमपि जीवामि जीवितं पापजीविता ॥

Hopkins "The Great Epic of India" publishers. Yale University press, New Heaven. 1920 Ed. chap. 2, page 81 para. 1. lines 7-8 "lament that being not Sutte they live an evil life and not thus dying" Here "Asatī असती simply means—not true to the husband Rām. V. 26. 7; Rām. II. 66.4 VI. 116. 18. नाहं जीवितुमुत्सहे । is most common phrase used repeatedly ; Mbh. VII. 24.11; X.4. 26; XVI. 8.23; with many variation कथं जीवितुमुत्सहे also नहि शक्यामि जीवितुम् ।

4. Rām. II. 66. 12.
5. Mbh. XII. 149. 15.

wives also.[1] Daśaratha's widows united with him in the heaven were greatly delighted.

Satī in the Mahābhārata

The first case of Satī in the Mahābhārata is that of Mādrī in the Ādi-Parva, which according to scholars is mainly redacted. As the story part of the Great Epic corresponds to the Sūtra period and nowhere in the Gṛhyasūtras do we find Satī sanctioned, this must be a later redaction. Mādrī may have died of a shock as both, (of hers and Pāṇḍu's) the bodies were later taken to Hastināpura.[2] It might not have been possible had she committed Satī. But as Bombay[3] and Kumbhakoṇam editions[4] also describe Mādrī as performing Satī, Śarīra' here may mean bones.[5] Any how it is interesting to note that Kuntī thinks that performing 'Satī' was of religious merit and being the elder wife it was her privilege, but Mādrī had her own reasons. Firstly her desires were not as yet satisfied. Secondly, Pāṇḍu died without fulfilling his desire for her, so it was her duty as a wife to bring satisfaction to him in the next world. Thirdly, in case of survival she would not be able to look after Kuntī's children as her own, but if Kuntī survived she would do so in the case of Mādrī's children. But the tone of the words seems to be apologetic. From her tone of conversation we do feel an awareness on Mādrī's part that she was encroaching upon Kuntī's rights. She wants to get Kuntī's sanction; whether this was granted by Kuntī, we are not told by the composer.[6]

One case of Brāhmaṇī Satī

The only case of a Brāhmaṇi Satī[7] in the Mahābhārata is also found in the Ādī-Parva. The circumstances correspond

1. Rām. VII. 99. 16-17.
2. Mbh. I. 126.32 इमे तयोः शरीरे द्वे० ।

Then in 127 section there is the description of funeral procession.

3. Mbh. (B. Ed.) I. 150. 10 ff.
4. Mbh. (K. ed.) I. 134.
5. The composer may have been unwilling to leave the opportunity of describing a solemn, splendid public funeral I. 127. 5 ff.
6. Mbh. I. 125. 23 ff. The episode reminds one of the account given by Strabo and Didorous where the two widows of an Indian officer Ketus combat for the honour of being allowed to become Satī.
7. Mbh. I. 182. 22 Āngirasī.

to the case of Mādrī and Pāṇḍu. The Brāhmaṇa ladies did not practice Satī even long after the Mahābhārata gained its present shape.[1] This may be the latest redaction for justifying Vasishṭha—Madayantī-Niyoga, long after Niyoga was out of date.[2]

Sahamaraṇa and Anumaraṇa theory

In the Ādi-Parva only the ideas underlying 'Sahemaraṇa' and 'Anumaraṇa' are to be found, although the names are not given.[3] Some portions of undermentioned ślokas may refer to the wives like Sāvitrī but that was an exceptional case. To our way of thinking these ideas contain the nucleus which was later shaped and elaborated into 'Anumaraṇa' and 'Sahamaraṇa' by the writers of the Purāṇas and the Smṛtis.[4]

The development of Satī custom in the Great Epic

The Strī Parva is full of lamentation and funerals, but there is not a single case of Satī. The weapons and chariots of the warriors were burnt with them. In the Mausala Parva Vasudeva's four wives Devakī, Bhadrā, Rohiṇī, Madirā ascend his funeral pyre[5] and as a result attain the region of felicity with Vasudeva. At the time when these portions were composed the attractive rewards of being Satī were being hinted at to encourage the custom. However, the notion

1. Kaṇe "Hist. of Dh. " Vol. II. Part I. page 630.

2. According to some opinions Satī custom was introduced by the Sythians. V. A. Smith "The Oxford History of India" p. 665. P. Thomas. Art. on "The Institution of Suttee" p. 18-19 in "The Illustrated Weekly of India". Dt. March 2, 1958. And thus Brāhmaṇa's adopted it very late.

3. Mbh. I. 74. 45-46. संसरन्तमपि प्रेतं विषमेष्वेकपातिनम् ।
भार्यैवान्वेति भर्तारं सततं या पतिव्रता ॥
प्रथमं संस्थिता भार्या पतिं प्रेत्य प्रतीक्ष्यते ।
पूर्वं मृतं च भर्तारं पश्चात्साध्व्यनुगच्छति ॥

4. Same in Mbh. XII. 149. 13-15 Parāśara S. IV. 28
व्यालग्राही यथा व्यालं बलादुद्धरते बिलात् ।
तथा सा पतिमुद्धृत्य तेनैव सह मोदते ॥
Daksha Smṛti IV. 18-19 (page 80 of Smṛti Samuchchaya) has the same Sloka.

5. Mbh. XVI. 7. 18.

that among the funeral rewards of a Satī was winning a seat in heaven for her and her husband does not seem to have appeared as yet. The context does not show it for it is a later conception.[1] Satī, as an example to be followed has been cited in the later portions of the Mahābhārata. It has been a favourite method of Indian writers and composers to propound their theories through simple animal stories. It is a sure method to impress and convince the reader and is also recognised by modern educationalists. Through the example of Kapotī (she pigeon) the truth of Satī is brought home to the reader. A pigeon dies for the observance of the duty of hospitality and the she-pigeon dies after him. This is an example of "Anumaraṇa"[2] and as a result of the act she sports with her husband in heaven. It has been also stated that if in this way a woman performs Satī she shines like the she-pigeon in heaven.[3] So by the time this portion of the Śānti Parva was written meritorious result had come to be attached to the custom of Satī in order to encourage it.

Cases of group-suicide by widows due to insecure position

The cases of group-suicide by widows due to insecure position must not be, however, taken as examples of Satī. The case of Kṛshṇa's wives[4] burning themselves was neither "Sahamaraṇa" nor "Anumaraṇa".[5] It appears that the sense of insecurity made them feel that it was difficult to live up to the ideal of chastity. Even the protector, to whom Kṛshṇa handed them over, was old, weak and useless, for he could not sâve some of their co-wives when they were taken away or voluntarily followed the robbers.[6] This case of group-suicide by women may be cited as the earliest example of protecting honour by burning on an occasion of foreign invasion.

Another case of group-suicide in the Great Epic is that of the wives of the Kauravas. Ending life by drowning into the

1. Mbh. XVI. 7. 24.
2. Mbh. XII. 148. 10-12.
3. Mbh. XII. 149. 15 ff.
4. Mbh. XVI. 7. 73.
5. "Brahmapurāṇa quoted by Aparārka p. 111; Madana Pārijāta p. 198 Anumaraṇa is performed when husband dies and is cremated at a place where the wife was not present and she later hearing of his death, resolves to burn herself and enters fire with his ashes or Padukā or even without any thing." As quoted by Kaṇe "Hist. of Dh." Vol. II. part I, p. 628.
6. Mbh. XVI. 7. 45-58.

river Ganges. i.e. "Jalasamādhi" was one of the later ways of committing suicide.[1] From the religious point of view it was highly meritorious. Why did the Kaurava ladies commit suicide after such a long time at the instigation of Vyāsa ? It might have been due to the insignificant and miserable existence they were dragging after the death of their husbands. The widows of the conquered could never feel secure under the protection of a conqueror as will be shown presently.[2] It may be due to disgust that they committed suicide.

Reasons for Satī custom and its appearance among Indian Āryans

Taking into account the above mentioned discussions it seems that the number cases of sati as compared to the number of widows that survive is insignificant. The custom was gradually developing. The burning of the widowed, beloved wife and the weapons along with the dead warrior was, however, a primitive custom.[3] This was due to the belief of many ancient people, that the dead needed their things specially their beloveds and wives in the other world to fulfil their desires. This belief is reflected in the statement of Mādrī[4] as well as in the attempt of the Kīchakās to burn Draupadī along with Kīchaka.[5] This custom also prevailed among European Āryans, Brynhild's sacrifice on Sigurd's funeral pyre proves the same.[6] This custom of burning with the funeral pyre of the husband may have been abandoned by the Indian-Āryans due to the paucity of women who were also needed for producing many heroic sons in those periods of sanguinary warfare.[7] The custom may have

1. Mbh. XV. 33. 20-21., Mbh. IX. 39. 33-34 refers to the death at the banks of Saraswatī at Pṛthudaka.
Mbh.III. 85. 83 suicide at Prayāga and certain holy places. Mbh.XIII. 25. 62-64 suicide at the Himālayas but otherwise in I. 179. 20 suicide is forbidden. For further discussions see "Hist. of Dh. "Vol. II. part II. chap. 27. p. 924-928. Even in 20th cen. Swāmī Rāmathīrtha ended life by "Jalasamādhi".

2. See p. 193 as well as footnote 3 of the same page of this chapter sub-heading "Treatment Accorded by Conquerors".

3. Macdonell "HSL" Chap. V. p. 126. Macdonell "Vedic Mythology" p. 165. "Indian Inheritance" Vol. II. p. 231 refers to this system in S. E. Asia. (Bhartīya Vidyā Bhawan publication, Bombay. 1956.)

4. Mbh. I. 125. 23 ff.

5. Mbh. IV. 23. 4 ff.

6. "Teutonic Myths And Legends" by Donald Mackenzie, p. 322-337 "Brynhild And Gudrun".

7. Macdonell "Vedic Mythology" p. 165;p. Ṛg. X. 18.8 hints to this custom.

been again taken up when the above mentioned conditions did no more prevail in India. But it seems that it was taken up not so much for the old memory of the usage as for the sake of the pātivrata ideals. The custom may also be due to the property rights of husband over wife after marriage, till eternity.[1] The willingness of a woman to burn herself alive may have been prompted by the approbation of such an act by the then society or public opinion. The better world hereafter, promised by the moralist to a Satī, may have caused such a custom to flourish to such an extent.

Remarriage

Another course that could be taken by a widow was remarriage. Among the Āryan widows, however, examples of remarriage are not to be found in the Epics. There is no proof of marriage of even the disloyal widows of Kṛshṇa.[2] They went with robbers voluntarily. Satyawatī's proposal to Bhīshma "Dārānścha Kuru Dharmeṇa......"[3] was not for marrying the younger brother's widow for there was no custom of marrying the younger brother's widow even among the Ṛg-Vedic Āryans.[4] The proposal was for Bhīshma's marriage. Still there is some material at our disposal to prove that among certain classes widow-marriage, coming down from the Vedic age was still prevalent. The words 'Punarbhū', 'Parapūrvā', 'Anyapūrvā' in the Mahābhārata,[5] used even by some Smṛtis[6], prove that widows married. Although the custom was becoming unpopular it did exist.

1. P. Thomas "Women And Marriage In India" London 1939 p. 90-1 states on the basis of "Arth sāstra" that the practice of Satī was introduced in order to check queens from poisoning or killing their husbands. From Epic-evidences such conlusions cannot be drawn.

2. Mbh. XVI. 7. 59 ff.

3. Mbh. I. 103. 11 see chap. on Niyoga.

4. Upādhyāya B. S. "Women in the Ṛg. Veda" p. 95.

5. Mbh. I. 120.33. Paunarbhava; V.175. 5,8 Ananyapūrvā, Parapūrvā, Anyapūrvā. XIII. 90. 15 a person born of Punarbhū polluted the row of Śrāddha invitees but he was still a "Dwija".

6. Vas. Dh. S. XVII. 2 mentions two kinds of "Punarbhūs" while the first one is not remarried, the second one who remarries leaving out-cast, impotent, mad husband or marries after his death cp. Parāśara who gives permission of remarriage under certain conditions. Most elaborate account of Punarbhū is found in Nārada XII. 44-45 ff. Vi. S. XV. 9 is later opinion when widow-marriage was completely banned for he thinks that Punarbhū is not legally married more than once but had lived with another man before legal marriage.

Traces of the custom of remarriage

The composer of the Śānti Parva was so very familiar with the practice of a widow marrying her Devara (younger brother-in-law) that he used it in a simile, which indicates that Devara was the first choice or option[1] of the widow.[2] It was perhaps thought to be very hard and virtuous to remain loyal to one's husband after his death, for Subhadrā bewailing the death of her son wishes those better worlds for him which are attained by the ascetics of the rigid vows through brahmacharya (i.e. celibacy) or by those women that adhere to but one husband.[3] Does this not clearly hint that remaining loyal to one husband was rather difficult or rare ? There appears another indirect reference in Mārkaṇḍeya's statement that in Kaliyuga (i.e. a bad age) even wives of heroes, will take protetion of other persons in their husband's life time.[4] So forsaking the husband when he was alive was considered immoral, thus marriage after the husband was dead may be implied. In the Rāmāyaṇa Kumbhīnasī's statement that the husband's death was a great calamity for a 'Kulastrī'[5] or high-born lady may also lead us to infer that for ordinary woman it was not so, as she could have been remarried. This point is further reinforced by Karṇa's words[6] to the effect that Draupadī may choose another husband for it was well known that women, specially those who are slaves, are not censurable if they take freedom in selecting husbands. When among slaves a married woman would choose another husband while her husband was still living it would have been easier for the widow. Among low-caste Hindūs, widow marriage is still prevalent, although the ceremonies of the first and the subsequent marriage are a little different. Thus it could safely be concluded that among the majority, that is, among the lower-caste people, widow marriage may have

1. Mbh. XII. 72. 12 पत्यभावे यथैव स्त्री देवरं कुरुते पतिम् ।
एषः ते प्रथमः कल्प आपद्यन्यो भवेदतः ।

2. Mbh. XII. 72. 12 एषः ते प्रथमः कल्प०

3. Mbh. VII. 78. 26 एकपत्न्यश्च means पतिव्रता in Nilakaṇṭha's commentary.

4. Mbh. III. 188. 64.

5. Rām. VII. 25. 42.

6. Mbh. II. 71. 3. अन्यं वृणीष्व पतिमाशु भाविनि ।
यस्माद्दास्यं न लभसि देवनेन ।

Also Mbh. V. 29. 43.

been quite prevalent. The aristocratic ladies, did, however, think that remarriage was a sin.[1]

Non-Āryan widows marry Āryan men

There are instances of non-Āryan widows marrying Āryans. In the Śānti Parva there is a story of a Brāhmaṇa Gautama who marries a Śūdrā widow.[2] This was not allowed by the composers of the didactic portions i.e. by the later moralists. They forbid an Āryan marrying a Śūdrā, (certainly not to say of a widow Śūdrā) and such a Brāhmaṇa was considered as an out-caste.[3] We cannot be sure whether this story is another version of Dīrghatamā's Niyoga, for the circumstances are somewhat different. But though there is no stigma attached to the Arjuna-Ulūpī marriage[4] we find it there in Gautama's case if we follow the whole story. The cases however, must have been very rare.

Didactic portions opine against widow marriage

The later opinion in the Mahābhārata is so much against widow marriage that Bhīshma thinks it is preferable that a virgin widow, whose marriage is not consummated, performs penance throughout life, although some are of the opinion that she may unite by Niyoga with her younger brother-in-law.[5] This is certainly an indirect pronouncement against widow marriage, which must have been considered worse than Niyoga. Widow marriage, though mentioned in some form in the Great Epic was slowly dying.[6] There might have occurred stray

1. Mbh. III. 76. 30 ff.
2. Mbh. VI. 90. 8-10 "Snushā" may have been used here for the daughter- in-law and not the daughter of Nāgarāja and therefore Irāvana may have been forsaken by his paternal uncle Aswasena Mbh. XII. 168. 33.
3. Mbh. XIII. 93. 127. उदपानप्लवे ग्रामे ब्राह्मणो वृषलीपतिः ।
तस्य सालोक्यतां यातु बिसस्तैन्यं करोति यः ।

Let him live with that Brāhmaṇa, who resides in a village which has only one well from which water is drawn by all classes, and who has married a Śūdrā woman. Mbh. XIII. 94. 23 is similar.

4. Mbh. I. 214. 13 ff.
5. Mbh. XIII. 44. 52-53.
6. Mbh. 72. 12. But unpopularity of the custom is clear as even proposal by Kratu Ugrayudha for Satyawatī's widow marriage is not even mentioned in the Mahābhārata Cp. Harivaṃśā 20 p. 1085-1112 (Eng. Trans.) It is interesting to note that here the main objection of Bhīshma was not that the proposal was made but as it was sent, when the funeral ceremonies of Śāntanu were not yet over. Therefore it was haughty and inconsiderate.

cases which were extremely unpopular and against them the jurists propounded their theories. It has been also stated that the daughter could be given away only once.[1] This was not only the opinion of the ideal patrivratā Sāvitrī but at another place it has been said that one who gives away his daughter in marriage twice is born a worm in the next life[2], and Arjuna's oath as well as Duryodhana's utterances point to the same.[3] In the list of those who polluted the row of participants while partaking of the Śrāddha food were not only those who married women that had already been once married but also those born of such marriages.[4] And yet a Paunarbhava was considered a 'Dwija'.[5] Definitely these regulations were to discourage widow-marriages. The importance of chastity, as a necessary qualification for marriage, which has been dealt with elsewhere, and the pātivrata ideals must have further discouraged widow marriage.[6]

We also come across Dīrghatamā's reforms against re-marriage or Niyoga.[7] As the promulgator himself had no moral scruples his utterances only reflect the trend of thought in a society which was aiming at a strict monogamous ideal for women and remarriage was naturally discouraged.

Some doubtful examples of widow-marriage among the Āryans

So the custom of widow marriage was vanishing fast when the Epics were being written. Even in the case of some doubtful and rare instances of widow-marriage cited below, it cannot be maintained that these widows were Āryan women.[8]

A dubious case of widow-marriage may be of the sixteen thousand women rescued and married by Kṛshṇa from Naraka

1. Mbh. III. 294. 26; M. IX. 47 is just the same.
2. Mbh. XIII. 111. 83.
3. Mbh. VII. 73. 27 भुक्तपूर्वां स्त्रियं ये च विन्दतामघशंसिनाम् ।
Mbh. IX. 31. 45 क्षीणरत्नां च पृथिवीं हतक्षत्रियपुङ्गवाम् ।
न ह्युत्सहाम्यहं भोक्तुं विधवामिव योषितम् ।।
4. Mbh. XIII. 90. 15 and M. III. 155 and 166. It was not against widow marriage only but other kinds of Punarbhūs also. For clarification of Punarbhū, see Nārada XII. 45 ff. M. IX. 176 Vi. S. 15. 8-9 Vas. Dh. S. XVII. 19.
5. Mbh. XIII. 90. 15. पौनर्भवे द्विजे Cp. M. III. 149. 155.
6. See. Chap. on Marriage p. 47.ff, and Married Life. p. 105 ff.
7. Mbh. I. 104. 26-34 ff.
8. Acc. to Harivamśa 12 ff. Sixteen thousand of Kṛshṇa's harem were maidens of the Gods, Gāndharavas and men.

Bhauma's harem after his death.[1] Whether they were already married to Naraka we have no data at our disposal to know even from the Harivamśa. According to S. C. Sarkar when kings were conquered and killed, their wives in the harem were appropriated by the conquerors. He also states that the Kuru ladies were appropriated by the Pāṇḍavas.[2] This, however, cannot be maintained just because the palaces were transferred, for the Kaurava widows lead a chaste and austere life and later commit suicide. They are introduced as "Asīmantini" and "Śuklottarīyā."[3]

Among the non-Āryans widow marriage was practised

Rākshasas

Among the non-Āryans, however, widow-marriage was still practised. Śūpaṇakhā was a widow trying to get a husband.[4] Had Rāma, or any body in his place agreed to her proposal, her's would have been the case of widow marriage. Ulūpī was a non-Āryan widow who married Arjuna.[5]

Vānaras

The idea of chastity among the Vānaras being not very rigid as among the Āryans, Sugrīva took back Rūmā, his ravished wife for he had no scruples.[6] The Āryans had the custom of marrying the elder brother's widow, which the Rāmāyaṇa, inspite of its idealistic tone, betrays.[7] It is therefore that Rāma had no objection to Sugrīva's marriage to Tārā. Among the Vānaras, however, it was not a preposterous idea even to Tārā's former husband Vāli. He is not worried so much for Tāra[8] as

1. Mbh. V. 158. 8; XVI. 7. 38; 5. 6. ACC. to Harivamśa CXX. 12 ff. they are sixteen thousand and one hundred C XXI. 27-32 they selected Kṛshṇa as their husband.
2. S. C. Sarkar "Some Aspects of Earliest Social Life in Ancient India' p. 192.
3. Mbh. XV. 25. 16

एतास्तु सीमन्तशिरोरुहायाः शुल्कोत्तरीया नरराजपत्न्यः ।

4. Rām. III. 17. 24-28; 18. 7.
5. Mbh. VI. 90. 8-10 स्नुषा. . . .
6. Rām. IV. 18. 23 Vs. Rām. VI. 115. 2 Rāma does not even take back his unravished wife.
7. Rām. III. 45. 5 ff, 24.
8. Rām. IV. 18. 52. न चात्मानमहं शोचे न तारां नापि बान्धवान् ।

यथापुत्रं०

for Angada and perhaps even hints to Rāma to intervene for Tārā,[1] although even in a polygamous society men do not like the idea of unchaste wives, or of widows betraying the memory of their husbands. Tārā has her importance in Sugrīva's harem.[2] Angada sometimes feels like Hamlet, as was natural.[3] These ideas were certainly not the outcome of his background or upbringing, for his father had taken up Rūmā, the wife of his younger brother even when Sugrīva was alive.[4] It may have been due to the Āryan influence where gradually the elder sister-in-law was being respected like a mother.[5]

Marriage with the brother's widow, was not confined to Ancient India only; it was prevalent among many ancient people, especially the Jews.[6] It helped the domestic economy and must have saved many troubles and inconvenience, specially with regard to property which naturally would have arisen, in case, a widow chose to marry outside her family.

Living in forest for performing austereties

Yet another course taken by the Epic widow when she did not remarry or commit Satī was living in the forest and performing austerities. Satyabhāmā and some queens of Kṛshṇa, on realising the uselessness of Arjuna's protection took to penance and performed hard austerities.[7] It was just like taking to the forest mode of life after the domestic one.[8] Ambikā, Ambālikā and Kuntī stayed at home to rear the children. Later when their children got settled they too went to the forest to perform hard penance and austerities. Satyawatī,[9] after being enlightened

1. Rām. IV. 18. 57 मद्दोषकृतदोषां तां यथा तारां तपस्विनीम् ।
सुग्रीवो नावमन्येत तथावस्थातुमर्हसि ।
2. Rām. IV. 33. 31 ff. Tārā's mission and importance.
3. Rām. IV. 55. 3 ff. भ्रातुर्ज्येष्ठस्य यो भार्यां जीवितो महिषीं प्रियाम्।
धर्मेण मातरं यस्तु स्वीकरोति जुगुप्सितः ।
4. Rām. IV. 4. 28
5. Rām. IV. 6. 22 नाहं जानामि केयूरे नाहं जानामि कुण्डले ।
नूपुरे त्वाभिजानामि नित्यं पादाभिवन्दनात् ।
Rām. VII. 48. 20-21 Lakshmaṇa-Sītā relations.
6. Holy Bible St. Methew. 22. 24 ff. marriages for producing issue for brother.
7. Mbh. XVI. 7. 74.
8. Mbh. I. 128. 12 ff; XV. 15-16 (sec.)
9. Mbh. I. 128. 6-13.

by Vyāsa that bad days for their dynasty were ahead, went to the forest with Ambikā and Ambālikā and died performing hard austerities. Thus we cannot agree with Vaidya that there was no "Vānaprastha" for women.[1]

Position and mode of living at home

Many widows like Daśaratha's wives and the Kaurava's widows also lived at home. As already indicated in the previous chapter, a widowed mother had a respectable position at home. Even in the didactic portions, full of moral teachings, we do not come across any passage indicating the mode of life a widow was to lead after her husband's death. In the utterances of widows themselves some indications of the life they led are to be found. It was a life mainly of penance and austerities, so far as we can gather, but these, however, were not imposed by society to the same extent, as was the case later when Purāṇa writers and commentators prescribe their Dharma in details. The Epic widow herself felt that she had nothing to do with enjoyment any more[2] as the giver and companion of enjoyments[3] had departed. She was now counting her days to meet him in heaven,[4] her plight was now full of sorrow.[5] It could not be otherwise. Even when the husband was merely away from home a pativratā used to lead a simple and austere life,[6] therefore there could be no question of enjoyment and luxury of any kind when he was dead. The withering of a widow[7] has

1. Vaidya "Mahābhārata Mīmānsā" 7th Chap. p. 227. cp. Mbh. XIV. 35. 43; XII. 21. 15 recommends Vānaprastha for Dwijāti's. Above mentioned examples show that women could go for Vānaprasthā independently.

2. Mbh. I. 121. 26 अद्यप्रभृति मां राजन्कष्टा हृदयशोषणा: Rām. VI. 111. 58:- विहीना कामभोगैश्च शोचिष्ये शाश्वतीः समाः ।

3. Rām. VI. 111. 54. अस्माकं कामभोगानां दातारं० ।

4. Mbh. XII. 148. 3-6; Mbh. I. 121. 30

अद्यप्रभृत्यहं राजन्कुशसंस्तरशायिनी ।

22. त्वद्गतिं गन्तुमिच्छामि० ।

5. Mbh. I. 121. 30 दुःखं मामनुसंप्राप्तं राजंस्त्वद्विप्रयोगजम् । Rām. IV. 23.9.

6. Vide Supra "Married Life" p. 109 "proshitapatikā"

7. Rām. V. 26. 29 शोषमेष्यति दुर्धर्षा प्रमदा विधवा यथा ।

been used in a simile in the Rāmāyaṇa. For without the husband there was no life and it was better to die.[1]

As some of these utterances are the expression of a widow's intense sorrow at the time of her bereavement, it may be that time brought her its proverbial healing touch. There are cases such as that of Tārā who lamented profusely but remarried. Undoubtedly most Āryan widows led chaste and austere lives, even if they did not feel the same intensity of sorrow constantly. It can not however, be said that every royal widow slept on the bed of 'Kuśa' like Bhadrā Kākshīvatī,[2] for when Bhīma saw Kuntī lying on the ground after the lac-house incident his regrets show that at Hastināpura she might have slept on costly beds.[3]

Some Transgressions

As was natural there must have been some moral transgressions also on the part of widows. The word 'golaka"—his being excluded from the Śrāddha meal proves that some widows went astray and such behaviour was condemned by society.[4]

Dress and Ornaments

The dress of widows also indicated their sorrow. It was natural that in the state of their bereavement they were careless about their dress. They have been described as having dishevelled hair,[5] which was not parted[6] and without garlands and

1. Mbh. I. 121. 21, 22, 23, 28. Rām. IV. 24. 40, Rām. II. 29. 7 —पतिहीना तु या नारी न सा शक्ष्यति जीवितुम् ।

Mbh. XII. 148. 9 पतिहीना तु का नारी सती जीवितुमुत्सहेत् ।

Mbh. XII. 148. 3. शोच्या भवति बन्धूनां पतिहीना तपस्विनी ।

2. Mbh. I. 121. 30 कुशसंस्तरशायिनी ।

3. Mbh. I. 151. 26 सुकुमारतरामेनां महार्हशयनोचिताम् ।
शयानां पश्यताऽद्येहं पृथिव्यामतथोचिताम् ॥

4. Mbh. III. 200. 17 कुण्डगोलकौ ।

5. Mbh. XI. 17. 25. प्रकीर्णकेशां० 16. 18. प्रकीर्णकेशाः० 18.2 मुक्त मूर्धजाः 23. 35 मुक्तकेशीं० III. 173. 62.

6. Mbh. XV. 25. 16 एतास्तु सीमन्त शिरोरुहायाः the commentator says that it should be एतास्त्वसीमन्त शिरोरुहायाः and is supported by another

ornaments.[1] They usually dress in a single piece of cloth,[2] a custom even now followed by the orthodox South Indian widows. As the description of widows coming exclusively from aristocratic families, is to be found in the Epics, it may be a safe inference to draw that there was no check on their wearing fine clothes.[3] There is a description of a royal widow attending a public function "gorgeously dressed"[4] but otherwise they appear in white garments,[5] white being the symbol of purity and austerity. The usual custom of austere living of the widows is denoted by the fact that any thing divested of beauty and splendour has been compared to a widow. Duryodhana does not want to enjoy the earth, divested of her jewels, the Kshatriyas, it was just like a widowed woman. So looked the Kuru army without Bhīshma.[6]

The widows who performed Satī ascended the funeral pyre, fully decorated.[7] Perhaps the underlying idea was that they were going to meet their husbands in heaven and so must go in full form as they did on earth. In later ages it was not so as the widows used to ascend the funeral pyre in simple white dress.[8]

passage Mbh. IX. 23. 20 संहारे सर्वतो जाते पृथिव्यां शोकसम्भवे । वह्नीनामुत्तमस्त्रीणां सीमन्तोद्धरणे तथा । A custom which is even now followed by the widows of U.P. hills.

1. Mbh. III. 172. 22-24; 173. 64 विस्रस्तस्त्रग्विभूषणाः । III. 20. 2 निर्भूषणवरस्त्रियम् । XI. 25. 9 प्रकीर्णवस्त्राभरणा० । XVI. 7. 17 विमुक्ताभरणस्त्रजः ।

2. Mbh. XI. 24. 7 एकवस्त्रार्धसंवीता । 16. 45 एकवाससाम् । A custom still followed by orthodox south Indian widows.

3. Mbh. XI. 23. 7 एताः सुसूक्ष्मवसना० ।

4. Mbh. I. 134. 15 संप्रेष्याः सपरिच्छदाः ।

Eng. Tr. of P.C. Roy 1919 Ed. Sec. 136, p. 279 but सपरिच्छदाः may also mean "with retinue" which may nct be applied here as सप्रेष्याः stands for "with retinue".

5. Mbh. XV. 25. 10 शुक्लोत्तरीया नरराजपत्न्यः ।

6. Mbh. IX. 31. 45 क्षीणरत्नां च पृथिवीं हतक्षत्रियपुङ्गवाम् ।
न ह्युत्सहाम्यहं भोक्तुं विधवामिव योषितम् ।

Mbh. VII. 1. 27 विधवेव वरारोहा शुष्कतोयेव निम्नगा ।

for further reference vide Rām. II. 66. 24; 76. 9. VI. 26. 29; Mbh. XVI. 5. 4.

7. Mbh. XVI. 7. 22 देव्यस्ता वै स्वलंकृताः ।

8. Śuddhitattva p. 242. quoted by Kaṇe. P. V. "Hist. of Dh." Vol. II. part I. p. 633-634.

Widow's position in society

The dread of widowhood[1] even when she had many protectors has been clearly shown in the utterances of a widow or a woman at the prospect of becoming a widow. These utterances do prove that the epithet "Anāthā" was most appropriate for her. Any body could approach her, for the Brāhmaṇi in the Ādi Parva says that as birds seek with avidity a meal that is thrown on the ground, so do men solicit with impunity a woman that has lost her husband.[2] This fact is further proved by the instance of "golaka" son. To lead an honest life and to bring up children according to the family status was, in certain cases[3] rather difficult for a widow, and so it was to get her daughter married.[4] It certainly would have been a serious problem for a common Brāhmaṇī considering the fact that there was no safety even for the children of Kuntī who was an ex-queen. Bhīma, having other elder guardians, was thrown into the Ganges and nobody except Kuntī bothered about him.[5] Perhaps as an "anāthā", a widow could even be killed. When Rāvaṇa comes with the intention of killing Sītā, she wonders how this evil-minded demon would kill her, when she has a lord and was not lordless.[6]

As already stated in a previous chapter, some knaves might have cheated the widows and so it has been said that a widow, having an infant son, should not engage in any pecuniary transaction.[7] In case she borrowed money she might not repay it. She may not have the resources and so haunted by insecurity and want of money, but wanting to bring up her child well due to her affection for him, may herself be tempted to be dishonest in paying off the debt. Anyhow both implications prove that her economic position in society was quite insecure and unsound.

1. Rām. VII. 25. 42 वैधव्यं व्यसनं महत् ।
2. Mbh. I. 158. 12-13.
3. Mbh. I. 158. 15.
4. Mbh. I. 158. 16-18.
5. Mbh. I. 128-129. (sections).
6. Rām. VI. 92. 47 बधिष्यति सनाथां मामनाथामिव दुर्मतिः ।
7. Mbh. V. 37. 30 विधवा बालपुत्रा—व्यवहारेषु वर्जनीयाः स्युरेते ।
more security for bringing up her son.

Treatment accorded by the conquerors

In those days of sanguinary warfare there was danger of conquerors not treating the widows of the conquered well. There is reason to believe that such was the condition. Even Kṛshṇa's widows who followed the robbers voluntarily, drowned themselves in the Saraswatī later. It is obvious that they were not happy, for such abductors, as robbers, could not have respect for women.[1] The group-suicide of Kaurava widows has been referred to.[2] It might have been due to the insignificant and miserable existence they were dragging after the death of their husbands. Their palaces were taken away.[3] Thus they might have been forced to lower their standard of living. But economic difficulty was not all. To this was added the sense of social insignificance with which they were looked upon. Their lot being much worse for the fact of their being the widow of the conquered. Thus when the Kuru and Pāṇḍava ladies were introduced to the ṛshies each Pāṇḍava lady was separately introduced but the wives of Kauravas were introduced collectively in a summary fashion.[4] Granted that they were too many, but nevertheless wives of Duryodhana and Duśśāsana were of some importance and needed to be treated differently. This attitude of indifference was certainly not adopted entirely for the fact that they were widows. Uttarā also was a widow, but she was fully introduced. This scanty respect and honour shown to them being widows of the conquered, which may have been worse after the departure of Dhṛtarāshṭra and Gāndhārī[5], for all we know, may have been the reason for their suicide.[6] Thus the kings were specially enjoined to protect their wives well,[7] for there was the greatest dread of the conquerors for them. The widows of Nivātakavachas were terrified by the

1. Mbh. XVIII. 5. 25.
2. Mbh. IX. 31. 45; VII. 1. 27.
3. Mbh. XII. 44. 6 ff.
4. Mbh. XV. 25. 9-16.
5. Draupadī when lost at stakes was meted out dishonourable treatment. Her protectors were then living. It might have been worse in the case of the Kaurava ladies, for they were the widows of the conquered, living upon the mercy of the conquerors.
3. In Garhwāl, long after husband's death, in case the widow is not treated properly it is quite a common feature that she drowns herself into the Ganges.
7. Mbh. XII. 70.8. अनीषुं गुंप्तदारः० ।

rattle of Arjuna's car.[1] Seeing his chariot they fled in swarms, and like the sound of rocks falling on the mountain was the sound of ornaments of the terrified women. The panic stricken Daityā women entered their golden palaces.[2] We have no account as to how Arjuna treated these Daityā women but their fear was founded on the age-old dread of the conqueror and his bad treatment of the wives of the conquered. The Epic heroes like Rāma and Yudhishṭhira who looked after the widows of the conquered with care might have been very few, and as such they represent the exception rather than the rule. Rāvaṇa has in fact, been praised by Maṇḍodarī as giver of sorrow to enemy women.[3]

The king's duty towards the widows and protection provided by the composers of the Epics

In such a society, where the life of a widow was insecure, it became the duty of the king, who was protector of the weak, to protect kinless widows and to give them financial support.[4] He was especially expected to do so in the case of widows of those persons who had given their lives for him.[5] According to law the kings used to confiscate the property of the kinless dead. It was therefore in the fitness of things that he should support the dead man's widow. An opinion in the Great Epic does not comply with this view and it is enjoined upon the kings not to take money from the weeping women,[6] which must be a hint for not taking a widow's wealth. Such bad deeds are said

1. Mbh. III. 172. 22. Also the condition of the Kuru ladies when Duryodhana was defeated Mbh. IX. 29. 65-76.
2. Mbh. III. 172. 23-25.
3. Rām. VI. 111. 53 शत्रुस्त्रीशोकदातारं० ।
4. Mbh. XII. 86. 23 विधवानां च योषिताम् । योगक्षेमं च वृत्तिं च नित्यमेव प्रकल्पयेत् ।

Cp. Nārada S. XIII. 28-29 परिक्षीणे पतिकुले निर्मनुष्ये निराश्रये ।
तत्सपिण्डेषु चासत्सु पितृपक्षः प्रभुः स्त्रियाः ।।
पक्षद्वयावसाने तु राजा भर्ता स्मृतः स्त्रियाः ।
स तस्याः भरणं कुर्यान्निगृह्णीयात् पथश्च्युताम् ।।

5. Mbh. II. 5. 54. cp. Vas. Dh. S. XIX. 20. A soldier will thus lay down his life more loyally and with confidence for he will not have any worry about his family.
6. Mbh. XIII. 61. 25 न रुदन्ती धनं हरेत् ।

to be committed only in the Kaliyuga.[1] The interests of the widows have also been safeguarded by showing the fear of hell to those who cheat widows.[2] The good and ideal kings like Yudhishṭhira, Parīkhsita, Rāma and Kaikeya always performed the duty of looking after widows, which indicates their exemplary behaviour.[3]

"No widows" when a good king ruled

It has been said that when a good king rules, no widows exist in his kingdom[4] or when times are happy for a kingdom there are no widows.[5] This is rather a strange statement by which the composer may mean that in such kingdoms or times nobody was unhappy. It was natural that in the days of sanguinary wars all kings had widows in their states and king Yudhishṭhira, who had many, judged from this standard would be a most sinful king. Many orthodox scholars explain this as "nobody died untimely" which we think is not a very correct statement, for modern medical researches have proved that longevity favours women more and even when nobody met untimely death women would have survived their husbands. Only in such a case when Kshatriyā queens like, Draupadī worked day and night, looking after their husbands' unwieldy establishments that their health might have suffered, and they may have died before their husbands. But this will be a far-fetched conclusion. The above mentioned statement would be sensible only if the system of remarriage was quite common.[6] We have already shown that it was not so at least among societies described in the Epics. Nevertheless it was a superstitious belief that when kings ruled fairly according to Daṇḍaniti, in Kṛtayuga, wives did not become widows but when they failed, to give just chastisement to sinners women were widowed.[7] Kṛtayuga may here represent a bygone age when remarriage was prevalent. The composer of the Great Epic was here depicting ancient age ac-

1. Mbh. III. 190. 30 विधवानां च वित्तानि हरिष्यन्तीह मानवाः ।
2. Mbh. XIII. 23. 64.
3. Mbh. XII. 42. 10-11; Rām. VI. 128. 98; Mbh. XII. 77. 18; I. 49. 11.
4. Mbh. VII. 77. 26.
5. Mbh. I. 109. 11 when the Kuru princes were born.
6. Mbh. XII. 72. 12.
7. Mbh. XII. 69. 84. 96.

cording to hearsay from memory. It may be for this reason that in the Mahābhārata it has been said that there were no widows when Rāma ruled.[1] But in the Rāmāyaṇa itself, which is a better history and a more authentic account, all that is said is that widows were not distressed in Rama's reign.[2]

Conclusion

In the Rāmāyaṇa among the non-Āryans the custom of marrying elder brother's widow prevailed. The Āryan did not practice it although the usage was not altogether unfamiliar to them.[3] The non-Āryans also due to their contact with Āryans were abandoning this custom. From the data at our disposal from the Rāmāyaṇa it seems that the custom of Satī did not prevail.

As the Great Epic describes many strata of societies, the life and position of widows as depicted in it amounts to what was laid down for widows by the writers from the earliest Sūtra times to that of the latest Smṛtis. In tune with Gautama and Baudhāyana[4] Niyoga is recognized in the narrative parts. In recognizing "Paunarbhava" son, Baudhāyana as well as the Mahābhārata recognize widow marriage[5], it was however, allowed for widows whose marriage was not consummated,[6] although it was declining and was discouraged. In compliance with the Manusmṛti the composer of the didactic portion prefers penance for widow to Niyoga.[7] Gradually Satī was being introduced due to the ideals of chastity and pātivrata.[8] The good rewards of Satī were predicted to encourage it further. Thus like Parāśara-Smṛti the Great Epic codified all the courses open to a widow.[9]

1. Mbh. XII. 29. 52.
2. Rām. VI. 128. 98 न पर्यदेवन्विधवा० ।
3. Rām. III. 45. 6, 25 ff. Sītā taunt Lakshmaṇa.
4. Gaut. Dh. S. XVIII. 9-14.; Baud. Dh. S. II. 2. 3. 17.
5. Baud. Dh. S. II. 2. 3. 27.
6. Mbh. XIII. 44. 48-51; Cp. M. IX. 176.
7. Mbh. XIII. 44. 52-55. Cp. M. IX. 190, 54, 64, 45, 46 also Cp. Śyāmaśāstry's Eng. Trs. of Kautilya, Bk. III. Chap. II. Sūtra 152 Allows remarriage but prefers penance. Ap. Dh. S. II. 6. 13. 4 considers remarriage a sin.
8. Mbh. XII. 148. 149 (sec.) Cp. Vi. S. —. 25. 13
मृते भर्तरि ब्रह्मचर्यं तदन्वारोहणं वा. . . . ।
9. Parāśara Smṛti IV. 25-28.

In the light of these facts it can only be stated that the composers and redactors were describing the position of the widow according to changing social circumstances. Widow marriage gave place to Niyoga. Due to the ideals of pātivrata, chastity and aseceticism, Niyoga practice became repugnant. Then penance was prescribed for a widow. But when due to the various circumstances i.e. rise of pātivrata ideals, loyalty towards one husband became all important for the wife, human sacrifice, in the form of Satī was eulogized and encouraged. All these conditions find place in the Great Epic.

CHAPTER IX

ADULTERY AND EXTRA-MARITAL RELATIONS

The general stress laid on conjugal fidelity has been already discussed. The woman was always granted the right to love through which she was to fulfil her destiny of motherhood. It was for fulfilment of this destiny that under certain conditions and circumstances extra-marital relations in the form of Niyoga were recognized.[1] Notwithstanding this concession extra-marital love and adultery were considered as something immoral and perverted. Therefore, according to Epic-ideals, which reflect the Indian ideals also, love was permitted only in marriage.[2] There are, however, many tales and references in the Great Epic which may be regarded as improper from the present day moral standards. According to the composers of the narrative part these were natural human failings and have been put forward with scientific seriousness.[3] But the later redactors, born and bred in the more conservative schools of the Dharmaśāstras warn against illicit love pointing out its seriousness by evil consequences that were to befall upon adulterous persons, for such persons were not supposed to reach sacred regions.[4] Torments of hell and vile rebirths were predicted for them.[5] In order to persuade people against adultery, it was stated that persons who abstain from such a sin and were devoted to their wives attained the highest goal aspired by mankind., i.e. heaven and salvation. They are also enumerated among the list of happy persons.[6]

1. Mbh. XII. 34. 27 भिक्षितेः पारदार्यं च तद्धर्मस्य न दूषकम् । cp. Nīlakaṇṭha's commentary पतिते ज्येष्ठ-भ्रातरि भिक्षिते धर्मार्थमपि रेतः सिञ्चेति स्त्रिया प्रार्थिते सति ।

2. For further details cf. Vyāsa. S. N. "Rāmāyaṇā Kālīn Samāj". Chap. IX.

3. Mbh. I. 105. 7 ff; 63. 80 ff. Satyawatī—Parāśara relations. Mbh. I. 111. 9 ff and Kuntī—Sūrya relations.

4. Mbh. XIII. 73. 13-14.

5. Mbh. V. 33. 66; XIII. 23. 61; 104. 12; 145. 50-53; 111. 75 ff. the guilt was pronounced less in case of an elder brother's wife for Devara was 'Dwitiyo Vara" according to Nirukta III. 15 exposing Ṛg. Veda X. 40.

6. Mbh. XIII. 144. 10-15. 33; 107. 50 ff. amounts to the same; 123. 89; XII. 192. 10, 11; VII. 78. 23, 31, 32.

Adultery Classified

Adultery was classified by the redactors of the Great Epic, into many categories. The crime was considered more serious according to the reverence, social status and closeness of relation to the person against whom the sin was committed.[1] Naturally intercourse with the teacher's wife was marked out as one of the five great sins. Three out of these five great sins were irredeemable.[2] This sin amounted in turpitude to the sin of killing a person who had taken shelter, an act most unrighteous.[3] It is enumerated among the worst vices.[4] Generally violent death is prescribed for a violater of the preceptor's bed, i.e. Gurutalpin.[5] The surviving kinsmen of the sinner were not expected to observe the mourning period after his death.[6] He was only abjured from the sin if he gave away all his possessions, performed "Mahāvrata" and was killed in the battle field for the sake of his teacher.[7] Although according to one set of opinion, perhaps held by a minority as it has been mentioned only once, austerities and sacrifices could save a Gurutalpin.[8] A Brāhmaṇa Gurutalpin was, however, merely to be banished[9] and was to be degraded from his status.[10] The leniency in his case may have been due to the fact that as a Brāhmaṇa he was never to be given a capital punishment. Moreover, in this crime the honour of a higher caste woman was not violated,[11] for the preceptor was always a Brāhmaṇa.

To check the crime of Gurutalpa social boycott was inflicted upon a person guilty of such a sin.[12] Vile re-birth and

1. It must be borne in mind that according to the ancients in India, every crime committed against moral standard of society amounted to a sin.
2. Mbh. XII. 165. 34-38. Sloka 38 means all the five great sins were irredeemable. Sloka 34 points only three as irredeemable.
3. Mbh. XIII. 96. 19-11.
4. Mbh. VIII. 45. 38.
5. Mbh. XII. 35. 20 ff; 165. 49 ff "Mahāvata" which is living without water for one month amounts to death (Mbh. XII. 35. 22)cp. Nārada S. XII. 73-75; Gaut. Dh. S. XXI. 1 ff; XXIII. 8-12. Ap. Dh. S. 1. 7. 21. 8-10 widens the scope of Gurutalpa and prescribes the same punishment. Y. S. III. 231-233 Baud. Dh. S. II. 2. 4. 15.
6. Mbh. XII. 35. 20, 22 "Mahavrata" amounts to death for Nilakaṇṭha comments महाव्रतं मासमात्रं जलस्यापि त्यागः ।
7. Mbh. XII. 165. 39, 34, 35.
8. Mbh. XII. 34. 14-15.
9. Mbh. XII. 56. 32-33.
10. Mbh. XIII. 143. 25.
11. Infra, p. 201.
12. Mbh. XIII. 135. 19; 126. 28; 130. 5.

bad region after death were predicted for him.[1] The way of oath-taking and cursing indicates that society did believe in these dire consequences which were predicted to befall on Gurutalpin.[2]

So much has been said against the Gurutalpin that one really begins to wonder whether it was not quite a common crime in those days. It is likely that many of the young men who had to stay for a long time at a preceptor's place doing hard physical and mental labour without any diversion felt tempted sometimes to commit this sin. Apart from this it is difficult to say anything about the psychological causes of this crime. The education was really an ideal one and if some of the students went astray it is hard to generalise on such basis. For our purpose it is enough to conclude that great care was taken by the Epic composers and law givers to save the honour a preceptor's wife.

Dissatisfaction on the part of preceptor's wife might have led her to this temptation. Her discontent in many cases may have been due to the poor and austere life she had to lead with her husband, which she may not have liked in case she had a different temperament. Moreover, if she was a lower-caste wife of a Brāhmaṇa she had no religious status and rights at home[3]. Thus she might have felt neglected. There is no punishment prescribed for a preceptor's wife in case she went astray, the reason is clear. As the wife was her husband's property the preceptor must have followed the same conduct prescribed for a husband in the case of an adulterous wife.[4]

Agamyāgamana, and adultery between different classes

The honour of the high caste women was next in importance to that of a preceptor's wife and so was that of Agamyās i.e. those with whom marriage or sexual relations were forbidden

1. Mbh. XIII. 111. 54-56, 77-80; 145. 53; Rām. IV. 17. 34-35. Cp. M. XII. 54-67; XI. 59-52. Vi. S. XLIV. 2-3 XLV. 6. Y. S. III. 209-211, 232, 233.

2. Rām. II. 75. 44; Mbh. VII. 17. 29; 73. 25.

3. Mbh. XIII. 47. 31-36.

4. Mbh. XII. 165. 63.

according to Dharma-[1] However, Agamyāgamana, according to the law books, was as sinful as Gurutalpa.

A Brāhmaṇa was respected as a creator, ordainer, and a god.[2] Naturally according to one set of opinion adultery with his wife i.e. a Brāhmaṇī, had no expiation. One who committed such a crime was degraded and any person who associated himself with such a person for one whole year was considered among the fallen.[3] This crime was not, however, irredeemable according to another opinion as only penance was prescribed for one who had committed adultery even with the wife of a Brāhmaṇa who was conversant in the Vedas.[4] Law was very strict with a sinning woman who, leaving her husband of a superior caste, had physical congress with a vile person. In committing such a crime she violated not only conjugal fidelity but the public law as well.[5] Therefore a king was ordained to let her be devoured by dogs in public place.[6] The man who committed adultery with her was to be burnt alive. Thus both of them were expiated by death. The expiation was to be performed within one year of the commission of the sin, otherwise the sinner incurred double sin and was boycotted.[7] Miserable re-births were predicted for the Śūdra who dared approach a Brāhmaṇī.[8] In spite of such terrible ordination human frailty had its way. It was almost proverbial that an unchaste wife in the family of a Brāhmaṇa well-versed in the Vedas cannot be brought back to the path of virtue.[9]

1. The Mahābhārata does not define Agamyā although once a disciple's wife (Mbh. I. 182. 2) is described as Agamyā. Agamyāgamana i.e. approaching or marrying an Agamyā amounts to incest and Gurutalpa, violating a friend's wife, according to law books is equal in turpitude to Gurutalpa M. XI. 59 Cp. M. XI. 170-73 Baud. dh.s. II. 2. 4. 11 ff; II. 2. 4. 12; IV. 6. 6. Vi. S. XXXIV. 1-2; XXXVI. 4-5 Nārada XII.73 ff; Y. S. III.231-233.

2. Mbh. XII, 165. 19.

3. Mbh. XII. 165. 34-38, 49; Cp. M. IX. 180; Vi. S. XXXV. 2.

4. Mbh. XII. 60-61.

5. As it was violation of "Varṇāśrama Dharma" therefore came under the purview of the public law.

6. Mbh. XII. 165. 64. cp. Gaut. Dh. S. XXIII. 14, XXI. 9.

7. Mbh. XII. 165. 66-67.

8. Mbh. XIII. 111. 89-91.

9. Mbh. II. 64. 14; III. 5. 15 न श्रेयसे नीयते मन्दबुद्धिः स्त्री श्रोत्रियस्येव गृहे प्रदुष्टा ।

Adultery where caste dignity was not violated

Although to approach another person's wife was reprehensible enough,[1] adultery where caste dignity was not violated was expiatory, for men.[2] The women also were not treated harshly in such cases.[3] As marriage was considered indissoluble the husband of an adulterous woman could only deprive her of her conjugal rights and degrade her position to that of a maid servant, still she was to be supported.[4] She had to undergo certain penances.[5] It has been stated that women are cleansed even from the grave sins by abstaining from good food and pleasure for one year.[6] And whatever sins they commit in thought are cleansed by the menstrual course like a metallic plate that is brightened with ashes.[7] Different words used for sons born out of adulterous connection of a widow and married women and their condemnation point out that such lapses occurred, though they might have been rare.[8]

List of twelve kinds of sons

The twelve kinds of sons mentioned in the various lists in the Epics probably indicate that society was free and not illiberal in its outlook. A kān¯na i.e.a son born of a maiden who was taken as a wife later, a Sahoda i.e. a son of a woman who was taken as a wife during her pregnancy, or a son born of an unchaste wife, was considered as one's own son.[9] This might indicate

1. Mbh. XIII. 104. 20.
2. Mbh. XII. 165. 60, 28; 35. 25; 165. 61. In this case even taking delight in a woman's company and sitting with her in the same spot was considered adultery. Cp. Nārada. S. XII. 62 ff.
3. Mbh. XII. 165. 63; Although as already shown in case a woman violated caste dignity she was given harsh punishment.
4. Mbh. XII. 34. 30, निष्कृतिः धिक्करणं दासीवत् अन्नाच्छादनमात्रेण दूरस्थापनं तया सह रतिभोजनादिवर्जनं चेत्यर्थः ।

Nīlakaṇṭha M.XI. 177 a wife cannot be repudiated M.IX.80 only three and acc. to some four kinds of wives are to be abandoned for serious sins. M. XI. 67. it is upāpātaka for which he recommends penance Cp. Y. S. I. 72 Vas. Dh. S. XXI. 8. 12; XXXVIII, 1, 2-3, 7 Cp. Kane "Hist. of Dh." Vol. III. Chap. XXV. pp. 948, 532-533.

5. Mbh. XII 165. 61-63. M. XI. 177. Baud. Dh. S. II, 2. 4-4.
6. Mbh. XII. 35. 21 कर्मभ्यो विप्रमुच्यन्ते यत्ताः संवत्सरं स्त्रियः ।
7. Mbh. XII. 35. 27-30; cp. Y. S. I.72 M.V. 108. Vi.S. XXII. 91.
8. Mbh. III. 200. 17 cp. M. III. 156.
9. Mbh. I. 120. 32-34 पौनर्भवश्च कानीनः स्वैरिण्यां यश्च जायते । Kumbhakanam ed. I. 126. 31-32, differs slightly, Mbh. I. 74. 99; XIII. 49. 3 ff.

the importance of sons but for our purpose it points out much more i.e. many sins of women were not punished. It will be, however, too hasty to conclude that the twelve kinds of sons point out depravity of the morals. The Great Epic may be here condifying usages from all over India and among many races these practices may have been deplored. Kuntī's sense of guilt for the birth of Karṇa, throughout her life and her abandoning him indicates that there was social stigma attached to such a practice. Yet Kuntī and Satyawatī had not to suffer for their girlish pranks throughout their lives, unlike what could happen in the present society.

Maidenly honour respected

Tales of Kuntī and Satyawatī must not lead us to believe that maidenly honour was not respected.[1] The narrative part of the Great Epic depicts a society which was rather free and thus it was possible to get an unchaste maiden married.[2] But as it has been shown elsewhere the chastity of a maiden was gradually considered an imperative qualification for marriage.[3] Thus maidenly honour was not only well-guarded but to suit the existing opinion old stories were changed. So it has been stated that virginity was granted to Kuntī and Satyawatī by their adulterers.[4] It is clearly stated in the didactic portion that by pregnancy a maiden is robbed of her honour.[5]

The person guilty of violating maidenly honour has been called by the epithet of "Pāradārika"[6] for it must have been considered a crime committed against her future husband who was to receive her as chaste. The epithet may be a further indication of the fact that all guilt and punishment attached to adultery with a married woman was attached also to one who violated the chastity of a maiden. A Brāhmaṇa was degraded from his position by such an act.[7] And a king is advised to restrain himself from such a vice. The defloration of maidenly

1. Tripathi, G.M. "Form of marriages in Ancient India" p. 2 is led to think it was not.
2. Like Kuntī and Satyawatī.
3. Chapter on "Marriage", Part I. p. 47. Cp. M. VIII. 226. only a maiden could be married with Mantras.
4. Mbh. I. 63. 76-78; 11. 20.
5. Mbh. XIII. 36. 17.
6. Mbh. II. 31. 27.
7. Mbh. XII. 165. 28, 43.

virginity has been considered as being due to the negligence of kingly duties, this subject was very important and came under the purview of the public law.[1] Thus while a wife has been considered as private property of the husband, for he was to punish her in such cases, a maiden, as auspiciousness personified and an abode of the goddess of prosperity, was to be cared for by the king.[2] According to the composer of the Rāmāyaṇa also, violating the chastity of a maiden was considered to be a great sin, for which Bhārgava cursed king Daṇḍa.[3] As it was the duty of men to protect a woman thus a maiden who suffered her virginity to be deflowered incurred only one third of the sin of Brāhmaṇa murder, while the man who brought shame on her took two thirds of such a sin.[4] According to better sense of justice of those societies the stronger sex was naturally blamed more for human weaknesses.

The reasons for this liberal treatment of sinning women were many. A woman was weak—Abalā and throughout her life she was to be protected by a man.[5] Therefore her failings were due to the neglect of duty on the part of her protector. Moreover, she was the property of her husband.[6] It was the fault of the proprietor if due to his negligence his property was misused. To some extent the attitude of hating the sin and not the sinner also prevailed. Thus while there are innumerable rules and warnings against adultery, to lessen this evil, when it occurred rarely, it was tolerated.

Social stigma attached to adultery. Warnings and Rules

Social stigma was always attched to adultery. Approaching the wife of another person was considered a sin,[7] an evil begotten of desire.[8] A person who was guilty of this sin or tolerated it was assigned a very low social position and was so-

1. Mbh. XII. 90. 32. and 39.
2. Supra. Chap. I "Maiden, Her status and Education", p. 18. Mbh. XIII. 11. 14 Srī says . . . वसामि—कन्यासु
3. Rām. VI. 80. 17; 81. 6-8 cp. M. VIII. 364.
4. Mbh. XII. 165. 42-43.
5. Mbh. XIII. 46. 8, 14; 20, 14, 21.
6. Supra. Chap. V. 'Married life' p. 127-28 ff.
7. Mbh. XII. 35. 25. Rām. II. 75. 54; III. 38. 30 परदाराभिमर्शात्तुनान्यत्पापतरं महत् । cp. M. IV. 134; VIII 352 ff.
8. Rām. III. 9. 2-3; 50. 8; 72. 45 indicates the same. Ram V 21. 7; VII. 26. 29, 55, 56.

cially boycotted.[1] It was believed that gods and manes (i.e. Deities and Pitṛs) scorn sacrificial gifts made by an adulterer. According to one opinion this sin has been considered as redeemable.[2] Apart from this stigma warnings were given, rules were framed in order to check adultery.[3] Adultrous men and women were not to be trusted.[4] To warn women against bad characters it is stated that men gratified with women forgot obligations.[5] Warnings to persons not to covet the women loved by the king was, of course, on the basis of the fear of the king's punishment.[6] And to approach a hero's wife was similarly dangerous.[7] It is stated that there is nothing detrimental to a long life than this sin[8] which leads to destruction.[9]

The Kings warned against indulgence in women

As the kings were protectors of the people, they were expected to be more vigilant and to show an exemplary character.[10] But because of absolute power and immense wealth there was great danger of their being corrupted and therefore they are a specially warned against excessive indulgence in women and adultery.[11] They were to protect themselves from unknown women.[12] They had big harems where women of different lands

1. Mbh. XIII. 129. 2-4; 130. 37-38; V. 35. 46; 90. 8; XII. 165 28 the position of a man who approached other people's wife was equal to Brahmahan and stealer of Brāhmaṇa's property. He is mentioned in the list of Apankteya or Panktidushya.

2. Mbh. XII. 35. 25.

3. Mbh. XII. 193. 17; 34. 26 XIII. 145. 50 ff; 162. 47.

4. Mbh. V. 37. 30 people are warned against entering pecuniary transactions with them. Mbh. V. 33. 55 such women have no will of their own. Mbh. XII. 168. 22 friendship was only to be formed with those who do not dishonour youthful woman.

5. Mbh. V. 33. 87-88. नारीं विगतकामास्तु० ।

6. Mbh. V. 37. 28 न राजकाम्यां योषितं प्रार्थयीत ।
Cp. Y. S. II. 282. provides death for approaching queens. Nārada XII. 74.

7. Mbh. XII. 82. 51 Meyer also interpets XII. 269. 27 as a hero's wife was not to be approached but Nilakaṇṭha's commentary seems to be more correct according to the reference.

8. Mbh. XIII. 104. 21; V. 33. 65 cp. M. IV. 134 the same.

9. Rām. VI. 87. 24. दोषाः क्षयावहाः ।

10. Mbh. XII. 77. 21 thus an ideal king Kaikeya never went after other people's wife.

11. Mbh. XII. 28. 31; 140. 26; 59. 60; V. 33. 92; II. 5. 69. Cp. Kane "Hist. of Dh." Vol. III. Chap. II. p. 54-55.

12. Mbh. XII. 90. 32-33.

resided.[1] Due to jealousy among discontented concubines many of them might have acted as spies and agents of king's enemies.[2]

Conditions in Ideal Kingdoms—King's protection to save the honour of women

In the ideal kingdom of Ayodhyā, there was nobody going after other people's wives.[3] The kings of Ikshwāku dynasty banished their sons or were expected to banish them if they were guilty of such a crime.[4] According to Bhīshma, people on leaving the anarchical state formed a social compact. One of the legislations for maintaining peace passed by them was that adulterous persons should be outcast.[5] People with such vices were stated to be evil examples[6] and Dhṛtarāshṭra advises Yudhishṭhira to impose on them the punishment of fire ordeal.[7]

Adultery in Practice

So far the theories propounded by the lawgivers about adultery and its results have been discussed. Most of these were forwarded by the later redactors and contain the material of Dhramaśāstras and Dharmasūtras. It is therefore that the narrative parts of the Epics, depicting earlier societies trace quite different morals. These indicate that at least in some cases easy morals were practised even by the Āryans and aristocrats. From the present day standards it was rather a free society where the honour of married women and maidens was not so much respected as has been prescribed by the writers of the didactic portions. The Rāmāyaṇa with its idealism represents superior Āryan morals but not so in case of the non-Āryans.

1. Mbh. XI. 22. 10-11 सिन्धुसौवीरभर्तारं काम्बोज-यवन-स्त्रियः।
Mbh. XVI. 5. 6; I. 213-220 (sections) Arjuna collected wives from different lands during his exile.

2. Kauṭilya-ArthaŚāstra. B.K. I. chap. XII. 20-22. gives description of women spies. Mbh. II. 5. 21-22 among the fourteen possessions of the king to be well examined, was Antahpura also.

3. Rām. I. 6. 8-9 Cp. Vi. S. V. 196.

4. Rām. II. 72. 43-45.

5. Mbh. XII. 67. 18.

6. Mbh. XII. 88. 22 P. C. Roy's translation Vol. VII Calcutta ed. 1927, p. 206.

7. Mbh. XV. 5. 29-31.
Rām. VI. 87. 23 same as the opinion of Vibhīshaṇa.

The non-Āryans group

(a) *The Vānaras* : Among the Vānaras, Vāli appropriated Sugrīva's wife, Rūmā, while he was still living, a conduct condemned by the Āryan-Rāma.[1] Rāma refused to accept his innocent wife while Sugrīva had no scruples in taking back Rūmā after her adulterous connection with his elder brother Vāli. Still Hanumān, the Vānara, thinks that he had committed crime even by looking at other people's wives and by talking to Sītā.[2] These improved morals may have been due to his individual standard or the Vānaras also were gradually changing their morals as they were coming into contact with the Āryans.

(b) *The Rākshasas* : Among the Rākshasas as has been pointed out elsewhere kidnapping other people's wives with a motive of ravishment was quite common.[3] Despite this evidence it cannot be concluded that the morals of all the non-Āryans were much below the Āryan standard. Among the Rākshasas Vibhīshaṇa and Mārīcha did not approve of Sītā's abduction.[4]

(c) *The Āryans* (i) *Their gods, the Devas* : Judged from the modern standard there was laxity in morals even among the Āryans. The king of the Devas, who were the ideals of the Āryans, was notorious for seducing the beautiful wives of the Ṛshis. The story of Ahalyā is too well-known to be quoted here.[5] He also tried to seduce Ruchi but was not successful as she was well protected by Vipula.[6] Indra was after all in keeping with the Ṛg-vedic traditions for Śachī wants to eclipse the influence of her rivals over her husband Indra.[7]

1. Rām. IV. 18. 20; 4. 20; IV 66. 8 ff cannot be cited as case of Niyoga—for the restrictions supra, the chapter on Niyoga.

2. Rām. V. 11. 39, 45; V. 30 1 ff, 36 (sloka) Rām. IV. 66. 16; IV. 17—All indicate the Aryan influence.

3. Supra Chap. on "Marriage" Part II. pp. 71-73 The Rākshasa form of Marriage. Mbh. VII. 84. 21 Bṛhaspati's wife is stolen by Rākshasa Tāraka. Mbh. I. 5. so is Bhṛgu's wife Pulomā by Rākshasa Puloma. Mbh. III. 224. 2-4. Rām. I. 16.7; V. 20. 5; VI. 61. 20; VI. 111. 53;

4. Rām. VI. 14, 15, 16 (sec.) III. 38. 30.

5. Rām. I. 48. 28; VII. 30. 22 ff; Mbh. V. 12. 6 different interpretations were given later when the social conditions change. Kane "Hist. of Dh." Vol. II Part II. p. 1145 Foot note No. 2550 shows how the epithet of Indra i. e. "Ahalyānī Jāra" is differently interpreted by Kumārila in Tantravratika (p. 208 cp. Jai. S. 1. 3. 7) where Indra and Ahalyā respectively mean sun and night. Jāra means one who makes to disappear and wither away.

6. Mbh. XIII. 40-41 (sec.).

7. Ṛg- V. X. 159. 1, 5, 6; Griffith's translation page 596.

Indra was not even loyal to such a pativratā wife as Śachī.[1] In the Great Epic other gods follow his lead. Varuṇa according to the Ṛg-veda "has remedies for ills, releases from harm, wrong and sin" and was "the moral controller of the Universe", "the guardian of right."[2] In the Great Epic, however, he abducts Bhadrā, the daughter of Soma and wife of Utathya. Utathya's message to hand over his wife was first disregarded by Varuna but, it is said that when Utathya began to dry up the ocean i.e. Varuṇa, he gave back Bhadrā.[3] Agni was an adulterer at Māhishmatī.[4] He also gratified his desire and enjoyed Swāhā, in the guise of the wives of six Ṛshis, with whom he was passionately in love. The six Ṛshis thinking their wives to be unchaste, due to the infamy, divorced them.[5] Surya wanted to seduce Kuntī and when arguments failed he threatened to destroy her, her father and the Ṛshi who gave her the 'Mantra'. Kunti thus submitted.[6] Vyāsa later consoled her stating that for the mighty everything was moral.[7] Naturally so, for the gods on earth (i.e. the Brāhmaṇas), had to defend the gods above. Vyāsa might have been reminded of the circumstances of his own birth.

(ii) *Ṛshis* : Vyasa was Satyavatī's "Kanyāputra" through Parāśara.[8] The stories of Bṛhaspati—Mamatā[9], Dīrghatamā,[10] Uddālaka's wife,[11] although cited as old examples point out that sexual morality was not very high, at least from the present standards. Yavakrīta went with sinful motives to the daughter-in-law of Raiva although she chained him.[12] But the wives of Ṛshis-like Ahalyā and Reṇukā had to pay heavily for

1. Mbh. XII. 342. 47 ff V. 16-14 sec.).
2. The words within inverted commas are taken from Hopkins "Religion of India" p. 61-63.
3. Mbh. XIII. 154. 13-30.
4. Mbh. II. 31, 27. पारदारिकः ।
5. Mbh. III. 224. 33, 38-40; III. 225. 1-9; III. 226. 4-8.
6. Mbh. III. 306. 17 ff 307; (sec.).
7. Mbh. XV. 30. 24

सर्वं बलवतां पथ्यं सर्वं बलवतां शुचि ।
सर्वं बलवतां धर्मः सर्वं बलवतां स्वकम् ॥

8. Mbh. I. 105. 14. कन्यापुत्रो मम पुरा द्वैपायन इति श्रुतः ।
9. Mbh. I. 104. 9-23.
10. Mbh. I. 104. 25 ff.
11. Mbh. I. 122. 11 ff.
12. Mbh. III. 136. 2 ff.

their failings.[1] Thus the Ṛshis did not overlook the moral lapses on the part of their wives and sometimes guarded their morality well.[2]

Extra-Marital relations of Ṛshis and Apsarās

Śakuntalā was born of extra-marital relation of Viśwāmitra and Menakā.[3] There is no dearth of such connections in the Epics, although the stories were transformed by the redactors to suit the morals of their times. The births of Vasishṭha and Agastya[4] Kṛpī and Kṛpa[5], Droṇa[6], Rshyasṛnga[7], Śuka[8], Ruru[9], Pramadavarā[10] and even of Sītā[11], although shrouded in mystery, were the results of extra-marital relations, which will amount to adultery from the present moral standard. Nevertheless it must be said to the credit of that age that the sins of parents were never visited upon the children. If they were worthy in themselves they were always respected and revered by the society. Some of them like Vyāsa were considered to be philosophers and guides of the age.

(iii) *The Royal Morality* : Extra-marital relations could be traced among kings also. The relation between Purūravā and Urvaśī may be classified under contractual marriage. But as Apsarās were free in sex relations[12], Vasu-Ādrikā[13] and Raudrāśwa--Miśrakesī[14] relations may be considered as extra-marital. Perhaps it was also an established rule among the Apsaras to attend the person who invited them first.[15] Nahusha wanted to outrage Indraṇī's honour. His subjects reminded him that she was another's wife. But Nahusha's plea was that his predecessor

1. Rām. I. 48. 28 ff. ; VII. 30. (sec.) Mbh. III. 116. 5-4; Mbh. XII. 266. 7.
2. Mbh. XIII. 40-41 (sec.).
3. Mbh. I. 72 (sec.) Birth of Śakuntalā.
4. Rām. VII. 56. 19 ff. (Maitra-Varuṇa-Urvarśī).
5. Mbh. I. 130. 6 ff. (Jānapadī-Śaradwata).
6. Mbh. I. 130. 34 ff (Bharadwāja-Ghṛtāchī).
7. Mbh. III. 110. 35 (Vibhāṇḍaka-Urvaśī).
8. Mbh. XII. 324. 2 ff. (Vyāsa-Gṛtāchī).
9. Mbh. I. 8. 2 (Pramati-Ghṛtāchī).
10. Mbh. I. 8. 6 ff (Viswāvasu-Menakā).
11. Rām. I. 67. 13 ff.
12. Mbh. III. 46. 42 अनावृताश्च सर्वाः स्म देवराजाभिनन्दन । Rām. VII. 26. 39.
13. Mbh. I. 63. 49-64.
14. Mbh. I. 94. 8.
15. Rām. VII. 56. 16 मित्रेणाहं वृता साक्षात्पूर्वमेव सुरेश्वर ।

Indra was never prevented from such deeds against Ahalyā.[1]

These are older traditions but even during the time when the Epic story might have been enacted, such moral lapses were not altogether unheard of. Śiśupāla ravished Akrūra's wife on her way to Sauvīra, and at another time the princess of Viśālā who was the intended bride for king Karusha in the disguise of that king.[2]

(iv) *Morals of the Virāṭa Court* : Kīchaka's attempts on Draupadī point out the low moral standard of Virāṭa's court. The queen Sudeshṇā knew that Draupadī was a married woman unwilling to agree to the advances of Kīchaka. Still she helped Kīchaka in the conspiracy.[3] Virāta excused himself from the performance of his kingly duty of imparting justice by saying that he was not an eyewitness to the quarrel between Kīchaka and Draupadī and therefore, was not able to judge.[4] Arjuna was afraid of the suspicion of Virāṭa and his people for he had lived with Uttarā as her teacher for a full year. He was pure but suspicion might have lurked, due to the fact that such deeds might have occurred.[5]

Concubinage, Slave girls, female servants and their morals

In the harems the kings possessed many Dāsīs' i.e. slave girls and women, who were given away in dowry[6] śrāddhas, sacrifices[7] and as tributes[8], like chattel. In the palaces they waited not only upon the kings but also upon the guests and Brāhmaṇas. Their close personal services to kings and their

1. Mbh. V. 11. 17 ff; 12. 6-7.
2. Mbh. II. 45. 10-12 this also indicates that women could not travel safely.
3. Mbh. IV. 15 (sec.)
4. Mbh. IV. 16. 35.
5. Mbh. IV. 72. 2-4. अतिशंका भवेत् स्थाने तव लोकस्य वा विभो ।
6. Mbh. I. 221. 49-50; IV. 72. 26; I. 192. 16.
7. Given in Śrāddhas Mbh. 14. 4; 39. 20; XVII. 1. 14. XVIII. 6. 6. 12-13. given in sacrifices to the Brāhmanas Mbh. II. 33. 52; VII. 65. 6; XII. 29. 65 ff. VII. 1. 2 XII. 29. 32, 133 VII. 57. 5-7. According to Rām. I. 14. 35 it is interpreted that Daśaratha gave his queens to the Brāhmaṇas in sacrifice, but later got them back for wealth. To Brāhmaṇas and ṛshies as gifts XII. 29. 133; III. 185. 34; XIII. 63. 39 ff. III. 315. 2, 6; for services to them III. 233. 43. IV. 18. 21; XIII. 102. 11; 103. 10-12. A king who does not give them to the Brāhmaṇas is accursed. Mbh. XII. 12. 30. Rām. II. 77. 3; II. 32. 15, 16.
8. As tribute and gifts Mbh. II. 51. 8, 9; 52. 11. 29; XIV. 8. 5. 18; 89. 32; Rām. VI. 125. 44 ff; VII. 39. 11.

guests,[1] with the description of their youth, beauty, virginity, their bedecking themselves with costly ornaments and robes, being connoisseurs in the sixty-four arts, well-skilled in agreeable conversation, maddening revelry, arts of dalliance, adept in serving, their mention as wealth for being enjoyed for the rewards of good acts—leads to the conclusion that they were meant for the enjoyment of the wealthy, great and learned.[2] In the close personal services to their master, some of them who attended well, might have attracted the attentions of the master as in the case of Vaisyā Dāsī of Dhṛtarāshṭra, the mother of Yuyutsu.[3] It was perhaps such Dāsīs who could even perform Niyoga for their master as was the case of Vidura's mother. According to the Ṛg-vedic traditions the status of a slave girl shot up after the birth of a male child of the master, who was then considered her husband.[4] In the Mahābhārata Vidura's mother, as soon as she bore him for the master (by Niyoga) was liberated by Vyāsa. She was a Bhujishyā, a word which is later used for concubines by Dharmaśāstrakāras.[5] Perhaps only a Bhujishyā Dāsī i.e. concubine could produce sons for the master, for in another case, where a king's Dāsī had sons through Niyoga the putative father insisted on his claim to the sons thus produced.[6] Sons of Bhujishyās, although not heirs like Yuyutsu and Vidura, still were regarded as members of the family.[7] Śarmishṭhā's utterances prove that the Dāsīs, given in dowry to a girl, could have

1. Rām. II. 65. 7 ff; Mbh. I. 115. 42 ff; XII. 325. 34 ff. IV. 20. 25-26.

2. Mbh. XII. 325. 34 ff; VII. 72. 40; 78. 7. Rām. II. 65. 7-9; 42. 15; VII. 128. 10; II. 33. 2; 91. 53-4. Ram VI 121. 3; V. 18. 10. cp. Mbh. I. 199. 16; 221. 49-50; II. 61. 8-10. V. 86.8 (mention of virginity) 325. 33-35.

3. Mbh. I. 115. 42. Dāsīs had position of Vadhūs according to Upādhāyaya V. S. "Women in Ṛg. Veda" p. 110.

4. Upādhyāya V. S. "Women in Ṛg Veda p. 110.

5. Mbh. I. 106, 27 उत्तिष्ठन्नब्रवीदेनामभुजिष्या भविष्यसि Cp. Kauṭilya ArthaŚastra, Book III. Chap. XII. Sūtra 183 about 'Aurasa' but not "Kshetraja" sons of the master. Mbh. I. 78. 5-6. Y. S. II. 290. M. VII. 363.

6. Mbh. I. 104. 46 ff Here धात्रेयिका is used.

7. Mbh. XV. 3. 47. Yuyutsū is referred as "Aurasa" son of Dhṛtarāshṭra, by Yudhisthira. Mbh. I. 78. 5-6 ff. Kuntī stays with Vidura when Pāṇḍavas go to forest.

extra-marital relations with her husband.[1] According to the Great Epic and Manu as the maid-servants were property of a wife, they naturally belonged to her husband.[2] Sudeshṇā had her fears lest Draupadī might attract the attention of the king[3] although Sairandhrī class entered service for wages and were not slaves.[4] These Dāsīs sometimes made love to the servants of the king if they were not fortunate enough to attract his attention.[5] Their social status being that of chattel, it was natural that moral code was not strict for them and they had freedom to select a husband more than once; such a conduct on their part was not censurable.[6] The slave girls were ordered by queens to perform Niyoga on their behalf and it is strange that the Brāhmaṇas appointed, knowing the situation did not mind having extra-marital relation with such slave women even when they were Śūdrās although Brāhmaṇa-Śūdrā relations have been condemned by the later code.[7] As these Śūdrās were never appointed it is not proper to style these relations as Niyoga although considered to be so.[8]

Apsarās

It will not be out of place here to describe a class of women who were meant for the service of pleasure, enjoyment or even for lechery.

It has been already shown how these Apsarās were notorious for extra-marital relations. They were depicted as heavenly courtesans. Not to speak of heaven and earth but even Yama's, abode was not imagined to be perfect without them.[9] They were experts in dancing, singing and alluring men. As dancing

1. Mbh. I. 82. 23.

देवयान्या भुजिस्यास्मि वश्या च तव भार्गवी ।
सा चाहं च त्वया राजन्भजनीये भजस्व माम् ।।

2. Mbh. I. 82. 22., Mbh. V. 33. 64; Mbh. II. 71. 1 M. VIII. 416. More or less the same.

त्रय एवाधना राजन्भार्या दासः तथा सुतः ।
यत्ते समधिगछन्ति यस्यैते तस्य तद्धनम् ।।

3. Mbh. IV. 9. 22
4. Mbh. IV. 3. 18-20; 9. 17 ff.
5. Mbh. XII. 56. 52.
6. Mbh. II. 71. 3.
7. Mbh. XIII. 44. 12-13.
8. Mbh. I. 104. 47; 106. 30.
9. Rām. VII. 21. 20.

and singing in those days were associated with prosperity they were supposed to live in the abode of Kubera, accompanied by Gāndharvas.[1] They are known as Apsarā from their watery (Āp means water) origin.[2] It is said that they were employed, in heaven, by Indra to dance at sacrifices, to entertain the guests or he good people who attain heaven and entice great Ṛshis when the was jealous of their penances.[3] Although they were often successful in disturbing such penances, they had sometimes to pay heavy penalties for such acts.[4]

Apsarās were also invoked by the Ṛshis to entertain their guests.[5] Often they waited upon heroes and provided entertainment in sacrifices and coronations.[6] Their taking part in human affairs and extra-marital relations with mcn plainly indicates that they were not heavenly beings but might have travelled through the ocean to India and must have settled down somewhere in the Himālayas.[7] They were courtezans of the Devas whose services were sometimes lent to the Ṛshis and princes.

Prostitutes

The human counterparts of these Apsarās were courtezans. They might have been later descendents of Apsarās themselves.[8] They performed exactly the same duties for the kings as did Apsarās for Indra. Their red garments, red wreaths and red golden ornaments[9] recalled the god of Death; but

1. Mbh. III. 240. 21-22; VII. 69. 24, 25; 163. 13; XIII. 107. 64. 92.
2. Rām. I. 45. 32; Mbh. I. 65. 48-52 they are mentioned as daughters of Kaśyapa and Pradhā, but it is also stated that according to the Purāṇa they were born of Kapilā.
3. Mbh. III. 44; 45; 56 (Sec.); 46. 34; XIII. 106. 37; 107. 92, 112, 124; XIV. 10.27; I. 71. 20ff; V. 9. 9-19, Rām. I. 63. 7 ff; IV. 20. 13.
4. Rām. I. 64. 11 ff.
5. Rām. II. 91. 11 ff. 42-46.
6. Mbh. XIV. 88. 36; Rām. VI. 128. 72.
7. In the hills there is still a race of the Naiks whose beautiful daughters formerly took to dancing and prostitution in hills and plains and were trained for this profession. (vide Naik Girls protection Act. 1929 Vol. III pages 1969-72. The Uttar Pradesh Local Acts. by S. M. Hussain Lucknow 1957.)
8. Kaṇe P. V. "Hist. of Dh." Vol. III. ch. XXX. p. 801 Footnote No. 1557 Prostitutes are fifth caste descendents of Apsara Panchachūdā. She is also mentioned in Mbh. XIII 30. 2 as hetaera पुंश्चल्या पञ्चचूडया and also as Apsarā Mbh. XIII. 38. 3 ददर्शाप्सरसं ब्राह्मीं पञ्चचूडामनिन्दिताम् । Y. S. II. 290, commentary of Mitāksharā is the same.
9. Mbh. VIII. 94. 26.

in India this is also the colour of life, passion and love.[1] Famous cities were decorated by the presence of Gaṇikās.[2] These public women were open to visits of all.[3] But princes particularly took delight in them and they were often attached to the courts.[4] They had to sing and dance for entertaining kings and their guests. They welcomed the guests of honour and heroes along with maidens. The kings also, when they returned to their kingdoms were received by an escort of honour consisting of armies and hetaera.[5] They followed in expeditions of the kings,[6] and accompanied armies in the battle-fields, a sure sign of degeneration.[7] They were also engaged in alluring the Ṛshis.[8]

Some of them used to be concubines and lived among the members of the royal families. Yudhishṭhira sends tender greetings to those granters of delight along with other family members.[9] May be these were songstresses who used to sing in the palaces to awaken the princes in the morning—a custom referred to so often.[10]

In the narrative part of the Epics they are mentioned among other auspicious objects such as the maidens.[11] To welcome the heroes they go along with themaidens as already mentioned, which

1. Mayer "SLAI" page 265 foot note No. 2 discusses this at length.
2. Rām. II. 51. 21 गणिकावरशोभिताम् ।
3. Mbh. VIII. 94. 26 नारीं प्रकाशामिव सर्वगम्याम् ।
4. Rām. II. 100. 50. Cp. Havelock Ellis "Sex in Relation to Society" Vol. VI of "Studies in the Psychology of Sex" 1946 London Ch. VII "Prostitute" page 159 "yet in many respects no infamy whatever was attached to prostitution. High placed officials could claim payment of the expenses incurred in visiting prostitutes when travelling on public business. Prostitution sometimes played an official part in festivities and receptions accorded by the great cities to royal guests and brothels might form an important part of the city hospitality. When emperor Sigismund came to Ulm in 1434 A. D., the streets were illuminated at such a time as he or his suit desired to visit the common brothel. "
5. Mbh. V. 86. 15, 16; XIII. 53. 66. Rām. VI. 127. 3; Mbh. IV. 68. 24, 29. cp. Kauṭilya "Arthasāstra" Book I. ch. 27. Sūtra 123-124.
6. Rām. II. 36. 2-3; Mbh. III. 239. 22-24; II. 36. 2-3.
7. Mbh. V. 195. 19.
8. Rām. I. 9. 17; 10. 6; Mbh. III. 110. 53-54.
9. Mbh. I. 30. 38 अलंकृता वस्त्रवत्यः सुगन्धा अबीभत्साः सुखिता भोगवत्यः ।। लघु यासां दर्शनं वाक् च लध्वी । वेशस्त्रियः कुशलं तात पृच्छेः ।।
10. Mbh. V. 90. 16;XII. 325. 36 mentioned among maid servants of the king. वारमुख्याः; Ram VI. 61 6.
11. Rām. II. 3. 17; 14.39.

would be unthinkable from our present standards.[1] This only shows that they were not outcasts to such an extent as they are at present. A liberal rational society must have realised that their sin was as much as its own or it might have taken a lighter view according to which women were gradually thought to be articles of enjoyment, and as such the prostitutes were performing their true office. Nevertheless, their importance in civic life and royal patronage must only lead to conclusion that these women of pleasure were used as ornaments at palaces, courts, camps and cities. Their value and importance was that of a precious material for decoration, i.e. property and not of a human being. The composers of didactic portions framed many rules against them and the Brahmaṇas were particularly forbidden to take food provided by courtezans.[2] A gift from her was not to be accepted for she was regarded worse than butchers and oilmen.[3] A virtuous person was forbidden to make gifts to professional dancers and singers.[4] The harlots were to be held in check for they were harmful to kingdoms.[5] It has been stated that in the evil age i.e. Kaliyuga, the highways will be infested with public women.[6] This indicates a very low social position.

Gaṇikā

A Gaṇikā, however, was not a common strumpet. As she had a seat in the republican assembly "Gaṇa", she was known as Gaṇikā,[7] and was the pride, beauty and prosperity of

1. Mbh. IV. 34. 17-18; IV. 68. 24, 26, 29.
2. Mbh. XII. 36. 28 गणिकान्न cp. M. IV. 209 associates her with Gaṇas, (Republics) and says Gaṇānna (गणान्न) and Gaṇikānna (गणिकान्न) should not be taken.
3. Mbh. XIII. 125. 9.

दशसूनासमं चक्रं, दश चक्रसमो ध्वजः ।
दशध्वजसमा वेश्या, दशवेश्यासमो नृपः ।

cp. M. IV. 85 is the same. Mbh. XII. 140. 41 a list of the plaees where criminals are to be found gives brothels also here if प्रवेशेषु does not mean brothels it must be च वेशेषु (P. C. Roy) translates it so.

4. Mbh. XII. 36. 37.
5. Mbh. XII. 88. 14-15. राष्ट्रस्योपघातकाः ।
6. Mbh. III. 190. 52 शिवशूला चश्तुष्पथाः ।।
7. Cp. Havelock Ellis "Sex in Relation to Society" Chap. VII. p. 160 cp. similar origin of a "Courtezan" who had a high degree of culture and refinement, a lady following the court and observing a certain degree of

the city, i.e. "Nagaraśrī[1], being well-versed in the sixty-four arts. Later on this office was also introduced in the monarchies, for Kauṭilya states that the superintendent of the prostitute was to appoint a Gaṇikā born or not born of a prostitute family but noted for her beauty and accomplishments.[2] The Rāmāyaṇa refers to their 'samgha' (association) as well as to its leader.[3] Gaṇikā is also mentioned in the Māhābhārata.[4] According to Vātsyāyana and Bharata, she was to be the most accomplished of the prostitutes and was to be well-versed in the sixty-four arts.[5] Thus her office arose not from the need of lascivious love but from the desire for the satifaction of the artistic propensities of the people.

References to the Free Societies

There are in the Great Epic references to the free societies and some theories propounded about the freedom exercised by woman in sexual matters. These are, however, utterances of the interested parties[6] and therefore cannot be taken as authentic, Karṇa's abuse to the Madra women cannot be considered seriously.[7] Unchastity of women has been referred to several times but it is not easy to locate it in any particular country or associate it with any particular race. People are sometimes not well-informed about the different ways of living of foreign people and are misguided by wrong notions. It is very difficult for them to judge the morals of the women of other countries as

dignity—decorum and restraint had no connection with brothels. Cp. Meyer "SLAI" page 272 the counter part of an old Indian gaṇikā may be found in a hetaera of ancient Greece and Bagdad of Abbasides.

1. According to Rām. II. 51. 21 Her presence decorated the city. cp. Dwivedi, H. P. "प्राचीन भारत के कला विनोद ।"

2. Śyamśāstry Eng. tr. of Kauṭilyas "Arthasāśtra" BK. II ch. 27.

3. Rām. VI. 127. 3. गणिकाश्चैव संघशः ।

4. Mbh. XII. 36. 28.

5. According to Vat. Kam S. I. 3. 20-21 page 26. "Kāne Hist. of Dh." Vol. III. page 148 note 187 (1946) quoting Bharata's "Natya Śāstra"

अभिरभ्युच्छ्रिता वेश्या शीलरूपगुणान्विता ।
लभते गणिका शब्दं स्थानं च जनसंसदि ।।
पूजिता च सदा राज्ञा गुणवद्भिः च संस्तुता ।
प्रार्थनीयाभिगम्या च लक्ष्यभूता च जायते ।।

6. Mbh. III. 307. 15 Surya to Kuntī; Mbh. I. 122 4 ff Pāṇḍu to Kuntī.

7. Mbh. VIII. 40; 35. 40; 44. 12-14; Mbh. II. 31. 37-38 this tale may have been added to make accounts of battles more interesting.

they are not particularly charitable in their notions about women. Therefore these descriptions are not very reliable.[1]

Conclusion

To conclude, extra-marital relations and moral lapses were rare and were considered as perverted and degraded. In some stories of the Epics, these human failings are discussed with scientific seriousness. It must be said to the credit of the age that women involved in such relations had not to suffer throughout their lives. The attitude of society towards them was that of not hating the sinner. Moreover, the woman was considered as Abalā. Her protector, the man, was responsible for her moral failings. Therefore she was never given harsh punishment for her moral lapses.[2] The sins of such women were not visited upon their progeny for worth and talent was respected everywhere. Civilization, however, was slowly conquering the field of nature and ideals such as that of pātivrata were showing the way towards the ideal of monogamy for most of the women. Nevertheless, human beings in general had their weaknesses, to which the Devas and Ṛshis and kings not to speak of Rākshasas and Vānaras, were no exceptions. The moralists, specially the composers of the didactic portions were trying hard by framing rules, by warning and working upon the fear of the people, by propounding various theories of rebirths for checking adultery and extra-marital relations. All these rules indicate that much was done to save the honour of women and maidens from vile men. According to the principle of "noblesse oblige" a higher-caste woman was punished severely if involved with lower caste man in sex crime. But the same principle, however, was not applied to the Brāhmaṇa-Śūdrā relations although they were also condemned. The reason being that chastity was considered of more value and importance to higher caste women than to such men, and the general principle followed was that women were not to degrade themselves. In sex crimes where honour of the higher caste was not involved,

1. The Europeans have a much more liberal society than ours and women possess much more freedom among them. Therefore most of the orthodox Indians think that European women are depraved—a judgement which is altogether false.

2. Mbh. III. 116. 12 ff. Reṇukā and Rām. I. 48. 30 ff; VII. 30. 37 Ahalyā was the only exception.

a wife was not denied protection of the husband but was brought back to reason by expiation or slight punishment.

Certain classes, of women, however, were treated as chattel or merely as objects of enjoyment of the rich. But it must be said to the credit of the Indians that prostitution flourished in ancient India for reasons different than usual,[1] for early marriages, polygamy and concubinage were common in rich society. It seems that prostitution in the Epics arose to some extent due to the artistic needs of the people. The sincerity and refinement of the Indian civilization made it possible for a Gaṇikā to develop her artistic talents and to place them at the disposal of kings and republican chiefs who were patrons of art. Thus she gained distinction for herself. As for ordinary prostitutes although they were not considered as outcasts still they as well as professional actresses[2] had a degraded position in society.[3]

1. Havelock Ellis "Sex in Relation to Society" Vol. VI of "Psychology of Sex" Ch. VII. p. 154 "the definite way in which professional prostitution may arise are no doubt many. We may assent to general principles laid down by Schurtg, that whenever the free union of young people is impeded under conditions in which early marriage is also difficult prostitution must arise."

2. According to date assigned to the Great Epic by Winternitz and even by Hopkins (fourth century B.C. to fifth century A.D. and to 2nd Century A.D. by Hopkins) Drama must have been known by the time the later portion of the Great Epic was written. 'Nāṭaka' in Mbh. II 11. 36 does not mean verse as Hopkins thinks (The Great Epic—page 55) he contradicts himself according to the data. Some kind of open air theatre may have staged dramas in the yajyas. Actors seem to employ their wives and in these dramas and pantomines see Mbh. XII 36. 30.

3. For professional actresses see Rām. I. 5. 12 and II. 83. 15. Mbh. IV. 16. 43. Mbh. XII. 36. 30.

Chapter X

THE ATTITUDE TOWARDS WOMEN

Man's different relations to women which are factors in deciding attitude

The attitude of the ancient societies towards women was conditioned by her various relationships with man. As a wife, a mother, a sister and a daughter she was respected and loved. For her centripetal qualities of nourishing, conserving, and inspiring, she was an asset like the Brāhmaṇas, children and cows, and as such she received all protection, care, and enjoyed various types of privileges. At the same time, being a weak creature she was subjected to certain controls, restrictions and prohibitions. Woman as woman, a member of the opposite sex was an object of infatuation and admiration to a successful lover while she was the cause of wild complaints by a rejected and disappointed one. As an object of distraction, she was to be avoided and to an ascetic and a man of retiring temperament as well as to kings and heroes she was an obstacle and an object of condemnation. The Epics, comprehensive as they are in their scope and treatment depict woman in all these aspects. It is for this reason that the data about the character and position of woman is often so contradictory. The contradictions can be resolved if the matter is intrepreted in its proper context. It is also to be borne in mind that due to the above mentioned multilateral nature of woman's relationship with man he has tended to consider her as a mysterious creature and from the hoary past his attitude towards her has been guided principally by these contradictions. It will be much easier to interpret the contradictory data if the factors which guide the different attitudes of the society are explained in the beginning.

The Factors that enhance Women's prestige

(i) *Motherhood*

It was difficult for primitive man to understand paternity. Therefore it was natural for him to respect the mysterious power of fertility possessed by women, which inspired in him awe and respect for her. This power, with great self-sacrificing qualities of motherhood was woman's greatest asset.[1] It led to mother worship in all primitive and ancient civilizations from the Mediterranean to the Indus valley. In countries like Egypt and Babylon this respect was also reflected in their laws.[2] In ancient India as has already been shown mother-worship took deep roots.

(ii) *Woman as Inspirer*

Woman not only plays her great part in man's creation but by her vital charm she inspires and energizes him. Indians thus believed woman's nature to be the human manifestation of the universal Śakti (power). This manifestation was her charm. The great Indian poet puts it in his effective words, "Let no one confuse this Śakti with mere sweetness, for in this charm there is a combination of several qualities, patience, self-abnegation, sensitive intelligence, grace in thought, words and behaviour, the reticent expression of rhythmic life, the tenderness and terribleness of love; at its core, moreover, it is self-radiant spirit of delight which ever gives itself up."[3]

(iii) *Nourisher*

Another quality in woman for which she has been greatly prized by man was her power of conserving and nourishing life. Man is able to earn but in his outdoor struggle he is not able to store up his wealth for the future and the family. These functions are admirably performed by woman. She has been, therefore, considered as goddess of prosperity in Indian literature to which Epic literature is no exception.

For all these qualities as a mother and a wife she has been accorded respect in the Epics, as already shown in the earlier chapters.[4] Here it should suffice to say that the respect and kind treatment and even material gifts that she received had ulterior motives. In other words she was respected because on her depended righteousness of men[5], all the enjoyments and pleasures, the begetting and nursing of offspring and the

1. Davies. J. L. "A Short History of Women" Chap. II. p. 68 ff.
2. Davies. J. L. Chap. III. "A Short History of Women" pp. 82-89.
3. Keyserling "Book of Marriage" Chap. I. "The Indian Ideal of Marriage" by Tagore pp. 120-121.
4. Supra. Chap. on "Married life" and "The Mother".
5. Mbh. XIII. 46. 3-4, 10-11; cp. M. III. 55-62.

accomplishments of all the acts which are indispensable for society.[1] Persons desiring affluence and prosperity were required to honour them, for the presence of women so honoured was as propitious as that of the goddess of prosperity.[2] As a warning it is stated that if in some families due to the bad treatment they receive, women indulge in sorrow, no effort or deed would bear fruit and such families would soon become extinct.[3] No greater homage can be paid to women than to say that they are the light of the home,[4] mothers of the universe and the supporters of the earth with all its forests.[5]

Respect reflected in manners

The honour and respect accorded to women was also reflected in manners prescribed in the Epics. According to a passage the right to road was to be conceded to a woman and to a disabled person even prior to a man with heavy load or to a king.[6] In the didactic portions, which however, indicate a deterioration in the status of women, a Brāhmaṇa, a cow, a king and an old man are given precedence over her in this matter.[7] This attitude was, however, due to the fact that all of them were accorded great reverence in society and the Brāhmaṇas had precedence even over the queens.[8] May be these were later customs interpolated in the Epic-stories. Respect to elderly ladies was shown not only by touching their feet but by walking round them while taking leave.[9]

1. Mbh. XIII. 46. 10-11; cp. M. IX. 26.
2. Mbh. XIII. 46. 15 ; cp. Kaṇe, P. V. "Hist. of Dh." Vol. III. pp. 226-7 they are considered as auspicious creatures.
3. Mbh. XII. 46. 5-7.
4. Mbh. V. 38. 11 पुण्याश्च गृहदीप्तयः । Cp. M.IX. 26 पूजार्हा गृहदीप्तयः ।
5. Mbh. XIII. 43. 20 स्त्रियः साध्व्यो महाभागाः संमता लोकमातरः ।
धारयन्ति महीं राजन्निमां सवनकाननाम् ॥
6. Mbh. III. 133. 1; IV. 4. 5-6; III. 22. 47. Rām. II. 52. 76-77; II. 55. 18; VII. 46. 12; Rām. VI. 122. 11-12 however, proves that these manners did not show the respect to superfluous extent of taking physical help from husband and other male relatives, as is common in the western society, for Sītā feels shy.
7. Mbh. XIII. 104. 25.
8. Rām. II. 89. 13 queens follow the Brāhmaṇas. Mbh. II. 80. 7-8 Draupadī follows.
9. Mbh. I. 145. 4; V. 137. 25; 91. 1; XV. 24. 9; 35. 49. Rām. II.25. 45; 18. 2.

Woman as a weak creature

There is another side of the coin too. It was natural for primitive man to feel important for giving support and protection to women during the crucial time of her life (i.e. during child birth). Had it not been for this support the human race would have been exterminated. According to sociologists and feminists this dependence led to degradation of the status of woman. Although physical weakness is one of the reasons of degradation of woman and was responsible for her many disabilities as will be shown later it is hard to estimate its effect. In the Epics as an Abala she has been assigned a degraded position.[1] But her weakness also inspired a sense of chivalry in heroes, and so as far as one can make out "Bhīru" in the Epics, is a term more of endearment than of contempt.[2]

Privileges accorded to women due to her weakness

Injunction against woman-murder

It was as much for her assets, i.e. that of mothering and nourishing as for being Bhīru and Abalā that women were accorded certain privileges.[3] Thus she was never to be murdered.[4] Although it was an old tradition,[5] such treatment was even more in keeping with the chivalrous spirit of the heroic age. The later compilers of law also prescribed capital punishment for one who was guilty of woman murder.[6] Even a robber-chief orders his gang not to kill women.[7]

1. Mbh. XIII. 46. 8. As Abalā.
2. Mbh. I. 73. 5 Bhīru a term of endearment.
3. Mbh. XIII. 46. 8; I. 73. 4. भीरु; 83. 5. she is not only considered weak but strength in her was thought to be improper Mbh. III. 33. 81. सत्यं स्तेने बलं नार्यां राज्यं दुर्योधने तथा ।
4. Mbh. I. 158. 31-32; III. 206. 46; XII. 108. 32 points out that there is no expiation for the murder of a woman; XII. 266. 52; II. 41. 13; I. 155. 2; 217. 4 Rām. I. 25. 17 hatred for Strīvada Rām. II. 75. 36; 78. 21; VI. 92. 62 Acc. to Mbh. III. 18. 13-14. It was below the dignity of the Vṛshṇi heroes to kill a woman and old men.
5. Śat. Br. XI. 4. 32. S. B. E. Vol. 44 p. 62.
6. M. IX. 232; Vi. S. V. lines 7-8 of Smṛti Sandarbha p. 413. later Katyāyana quoted by Visvarūpa on Yājyawalka II. 281. states that even a Brāhmaṇa was to be given capital punishment in case he killed a woman. —Kaṇe P. V. "Hist. of Dh. S." Vol. III. Chapt. XV. pages 398-99.
7. Mbh. XII. 135. 13-14; Mbh. I. 158. 31-32. The Brāhmaṇī in Vaka-Badha-Parva thinks that the Rākshasa will not kill her, she being a woman.

It was ordained for a Kshatriya ruler to be very particular about punishing the murderer of a woman and a Brāhmaṇa. Such sinners were to be condemned in the assembly. It has been stated that the kingdom of a ruler, who is afraid of the above mentioned sinners, is destroyed by Rudra.[1] The protection accorded to a pregnant woman and widow has already been mentioned in the foregoing chapters.[2]

This privilege was sometimes pursued to the extreme. It has been stated that even robbers were not to be given severe punishments for in case they were given capital punishment, their wives would die of hunger which amounted to their being murdered.[3] Bhīshma did not retaliate Śikhaṇḍī's attack for he had been a woman transformed into a man.[4]

In this connection the only exception, already mentioned, was the provision that a higher caste woman found guilty of adultery with a Śūdra was to be thrown to dogs. This was a great crime against society and her husband.[5]

Transgression of the Rule

The injunction against woman murder was not always respected. There are cases of transgression. Śiśupāla blames Kṛshṇa for killing Pūtanā.[6] Rāma had some scruples, which were dispelled by Viśwāmitra who enjoined upon him the duty of looking after the welfare of the Brāhmaṇas and cows. He cited two examples of gods like Indra (Śakra) and Vishṇu, who killed Mantharā and the wife of Bhṛgu respectively for unrighteousness.[7]

There are other examples which also prove that sometimes women were killed. Janamejaya was put down by the gods for murdering a Brāhmaṇi woman.[8] In other cases also such intentions can be noticed although these did not materialise.[9] It seems

1. Mbh. XII. 73. 16-17.
2. Mbh. XII. 165.54-55.Supra.Chap. on"The Mother","The Widow."
3. Mbh. XII. 267. 10-11.
4. Mbh. V. 172. 19, 20, 21, 38; VI. 103. 7 ; 107. 80 ff.
5. Mbh. XII. 165. 64. cp. M. VIII. 371 Manu is for punishing all adulterous women irrespective of caste.
6. Mbh. II. 41. 13-17.
7. Rām. I. 25. 14-22.
8. Mbh. XIII. 6.36;I. 178. 19 ff Although it was a sin to kill a pregnant Brāhmaṇi but when embryos in their wombs were slaughtered many such women might have been killed.
9. Rām. VI. 92. 61-62 Rāvaṇa would have killed Sītā but for the advice of his ministers. Mbh. I. 147. 5 ff. the conspiricy to kill Kuntī along

that some adhered to the rule that the killing of woman in order to give pain to the enemies was admissible.[1] But facts do prove that these transgressions were exceptions. The killing of women for righteousness and for public weal can be understood. When husbands ordered wives to be murdered, for their being attracted towards other persons it was not much condemned,[2] for according to the ideas of chastity, which were held in those days, she had committed a deadly crime towards her husband. There may have been a feeling of sympathy for such a husband whose right of possession or property was thus violated. With some rational minds like that of Gautama this sense may not have been very keen as he cancelled his order later on. But if ever woman-murder was contemplated with the view that "Every thing is fair in war" it has been condemned and suppressed. Thus these exceptions clearly prove that the rule of not killing women was mostly respected.

Women to be treated with compassion

The same idea of chivalry led to compassion being shown towards the weak, and therefore, also to women. Sugrīva sends Tārā to pacify angry Lakshamaṇa, for he thinks that great men do not ill treat women. He is right in his judgment as the later events prove.[3] For the same reason Hanūmān shows mercy upon the Rākshasī Lankā.[4] A hero was expected to keep cool and smiling before women.[5] Cruel behaviour towards women has been condemned in an oath-taking.[6] A hater of women was considered to be a very low fellow.[7] It is, however, said that untruth was permissive where women were concerned still this was not considered an ideal behaviour.[8]

Nevertheless, the narrative part of the Epics depicts some

with the Pāṇḍavas Mbh. I. 153. 17 ff Hidimba's intentions to kill his sister. Mbh. XII. 266. 7 ff.

1. Mbh. VII. 143. 67-68; Rām. VI. 82. 30 is the same probably it is taken in the Great Epic from the Ramāyaṇa.
2. Mbh. III. 116. 14; XII 266. 7 ff.
3. Rām. IV. 33. 36 ff.
4. Rām. V. 3. 41 ff.
5. Mbh. VII. 100. 12; V. 38. 10 श्लक्ष्णो मधुरवाक् स्त्रीणां० ।
6. Mbh. XIII. 93. 122; 94. 29; I. 111-12. Kuntī tells Surya that whatever be the offence of a woman, she deserves pardon; Mbh. XIII. 127. 6ff.
7. Mbh. V. 43. 19; 54: 4.
8. Mbh. I. 82. 16; VIII. 69. 33, 62; XII. 34. 25, cp. Mbh. XII. 320. 72; V. 122. 9; 34. 64.

rough manners and easy morals which seem revolting to the modern mind. The dread of the ladies when a conqueror entered a conquered city does not speak much of the sense of chivalry.[1] There can be no parallel to the pawning of Draupadī, a great blot on Yudhishṭhira who committed the initial mistake. It must, however, be borne in mind that this custom was a survival of the past and is indicative of the wife's position as the property of the husband. According to the Vedic tradition a wife lost at stakes was degraded to the position of a Dāsī.[2] But the insults and the inhuman treatment meted out to Draupadī in the assembly,are revolting to any cultured mind. It goaded the Pāṇḍavas to war and a terrible revenge. This crude behaviour, not objected to and thus quietly supported by the Kuru-elders as was natural for the proteges,[3] may have been exaggerated in order to paint perfect villains or rough warriors of old, who in their jealousy forgot the finer and nobler sentiments. Nevertheless, the frequent references to the event[4] with regret and condemnation indicate that such a behaviour was not approved even by the wives of the Kurus,[5] not to say of the greater section of the civilized society,[6] for it was due to the representation of the archvillain's mother i.e. Gāndhārī, that Draupadī was granted freedom.[7] Therefore these exceptions prove that the society on the whole was for showing respect and compassion to women. The ideal, which was followed by Yudhishṭhira, the son of Dharma, was different, when the Kuru ladies were abducted by the Gāndharva, he forced his brothers to rescue them.[8]

The factors that really degraded the position of women

(i) *Impurity*

For the disparaging attitude towards women other biological reasons must also therefore be looked for. There has been a

1. Mbh. III. 172. 22 ff.
2. Upādhyāya "Wonen in Ṛg Veda" pp. 140-141.
3. Mbh. II. 67. 17, 39 ff; 70. 1.
4. Mbh. III. 4. 16 ff; 12. 62; V. 29. 36-37; 31. 13 ff; 59. 22 ff 82. 21 ff; 90. 50 ff. VII. 132. 14; 122. 3 ff; 197. 9; VIII. 73. 83 ff; 74. 22. IX. 59. 3 ff. XIV. 12. 7-12. IV. 50. 12 ff.
5. Mbh. II. 79. 32 ff.
6. See footnote 4 of this page.
7. Mbh. II. 71. 24; 75. 2 ff.
8. Mbh. III. 243. 2-6.

feeling of contamination and impurity for every waste product of the human body. This, it seems, led to the belief that woman was contaminated, impure and was to be avoided during menstrual period and child birth. It thus resulted in the seclusion of women during puberty all over the world and periodical segregation of women thereafter.

In ancient Indian literature as well as in the Epics it is narrated that Indra incurred the sin of Brāhmaṇa murder, which was divided into four parts. One of these parts was taken up by the woman. This explains her excommunication from society, like a Brāhmahan i.e. murderer of a Brāhmaṇa, during her menstrual period and was one of the reasons for the loss of her religious status.[1] As this status was different in the various societies of the Epics the whole question will be dealt with later.[2]

(2) *Object of distraction and weakness*

Despite these taboos the woman as an object of pleasure was desired by all men. But the primitive man was not able to understand the psycho-physical tiredness due to intemperance. The distraction and loss of energy which he felt due to it, was naturally associated with the malefic influence of woman, who was considered an agent of weakness. Therefore, when strength was needed i.e. during hunting and fishing expeditions her contact was tabooed.[3] The same reason may be forwarded for the advice given to warriors and kings to avoid her lest they may feel effeminate and weak as a result of excessive indulgence. There is little difference between savage and warrior-like ideas of gaining physical strength by avoiding contact with woman and ascetic idea of conserving psychic or mental strength through continence. Therefore whenever man indulged in adventurous, ambitious or world forsaking pursuits, woman as a source of distraction, alluring and arresting him in home and hearth has been painted as the cause of his degradation and was to be avoided.[4] Passages decrying

1. Tai. Sam. II. 5. 1. 5-7 page 189 menstruating woman is boycotted for she emitts the colour of guilt. Same story is repeated in Mbh. V. 13.19; XII. 343. Rām. VII. 86. 15.
2. See page 232 ff. of this chapter.
3. J. L. Davies "A Short History of Woman" Chap. II. p. 35 ff.
4. Mbh. XIII. 48. 37-38. अविद्वासंमलं लोके विद्वांसमपि वा पुनः ।
नयन्ति ह्यपथं नार्यः कामक्रोधवशानुगम् ॥

the woman will be clear if interpreted in the light of these facts.

(3) *Ascetic Attitude*

The ascetic ideal emphasized the transience of the world and preached the renunciation of all objects of desire. Naturally, it led to propaganda against woman, who was the greatest object of desire and the central figure of the family life.[1] To the composers of the Great Epic, Buddhism and Jainism were known. Even before the advent of these sects ascetics were carrying on their propaganda against the woman and her vile character. It is therefore that many parts of the Mahābhārata (thought to be of later origin by scholars) depicting the ascetic attitude to life are full of condemnation of women.[2] Nothing can be asserted about the knowledge of Buddhism on the part of the composer of the Rāmāyaṇa.[3] The ascetic way of life has not been so much stressed in the Rāmāyaṇa as in the didactic portions of the Great Epic. Therefore, the passages decrying woman are fewer and can be easily explained with reference to this context.

Jaratkāru's story clearly indicates how the position of the wife deteriorated due to ascetic ideals. Sage Jaratkāru did not marry on account of such ideals. Later when he promised to get progeny for the sake of his manes[4] he did not perform the duty of a husband. When his motive was served he left his wife without any fault on her part.[5] This shows how little regard he had for her. This instance also indicates that the importance of sons might have persuaded even ascetics to take wives. Perhaps in order to avoid such occurrences it was stated later that

Cp. M. II. 213-14 The same. स्वभावश्चैव नारीणां नराणामिह दूषणम् ।
अत्यर्थं न प्रसज्जन्ते प्रभदासु विपश्चितः ॥

1. Mbh. XII. 9. 30-31; 153. 45; 174. 33, 39-40; 176. 21-22; 178. 2, 7, 13; 120. 1-32; approve asceticism Mbh. XII. 28. 31-41. 105. 12; 110.14; 123. 7-8; 174. 7, 25-27, 33, 39, 40; 175. 17, 35; 176. 21-22; 177. 47; 178. 2, 7, 13; 195. 4; 270. 1-32; 298. 38, 40; These ideas propagate against women and home.

2. Mbh. XIII. 38-43 (sec.).

3. Jacobi thinks that the reference to Buddhism in the Rāmāyaṇa is spurious. cp. Macdonell "HSL" p. 307.

4. Mbh. I. 104. 30 भार्याया भरणाद्भर्ता पालनाच्च पतिः स्मृतः ।
XII. 266. 38 भरणाद्धि स्त्रियो भर्ता पात्या चैव स्त्रियः पतिः ।
गुणस्यास्य निवृत्तौ तु न भर्ता न पुनः पतिः ॥

5. Mbh. I. 13. 27-32; I. 47. 3, 15 ff.

through penance sons could be born.[1] It was even proponded that great Ṛshis had sons through miracles.[2]

It is interesting to note that most of the passages disparaging the character of women are not only from the didactic and later portions but are put into the mouths of those who had either renounced the worldly life[3] or were not leading normal domestic life or were like Yudhishṭhira, of a retiring tempparament. The under noted opinions will show how the charatcer of a woman was degraded in order to warn men against her.

The character assigned to women

While in Samhitā only bad women were said to be falsehood incarnate, the composer of the didactic portions of the Mahābhārata assigns this character to all women.[4] This dictum was so common that even those husbands who least deserve to pronounce it passed this judgement upon their faithful wives.[5] Most of the Epic women were pativratās but the didactic portions generally paint women as lewds betraying their husbands and going after others, even if they may be of defective limbs or otherwise undesirable.[6] Lust and wrath are

1. Mbh. XIII. 18. 6-7 we come across 'Mānasaputras' who may be mind-born thoughts.

2. Supra chapter on "Adultery and Extra Marital Relations" pages 208-209. This ascetic attitude of avoiding woman and regarding her as a gate of hell can easily be traced in the Christian monkish attitude of St. Paul, Turtillian and others. Davies. J.L. "A Short History of Women" Chap. IV. p. 114 ff. Even modern progressive writers like Bernard Shaw repeat the same old jargon, as he writes "Why man, your head is in lioness' mouth ; you are half-swallowed already..." In tune with ascetics he also thinks that the woman sacrifices the man for her purpose. "Vitality in a woman is a blind fury of creation......do you think she will hesitate to sacrifice you" p. 340 Shaw "Man and Superman" Home Libr. Club Edition.

3. Mbh. XIII. 39-43. Bhīshma, Nārada and Apsarā Panchachūḍa mostly pronounce these verdicts.

4. Mbh. XIII. 19. 6-7 ff. अनृताः स्त्रिय इत्येवं सूत्रकारो व्यवस्यति ।
XIII. 40. 12. निरिन्द्रिया ह्यशास्त्राश्च स्त्रियो ऽनृतमिति श्रुतिः ॥

The double reference is to Vedas, Samhitās and Sūtras is in tune with old tradition cp. Mait. Sam. I. 10. 17 page 88.

(quoted by Kaṇe "Hist. of Dh. S." Vol. II part I. Chapt. IX. p. 503. Baud. Dh. S. II. 2. 3. 46. M. IX. 18 निरिन्द्रिया ह्यमंत्राश्च स्त्रियो ऽनृतमिति स्थितिः ।

Tait. Sam. VI. 5. 8. 2. p. 543.

5. Mbh. I. 74. 73. Dushyanta to Śakuntalā. Mbh. III. 71. 6. Nala blames Damayantī.

6. Mbh. XIII. 38. 11-28; 19. 92-94. Rām. II. 39. 20-23.

stated to have been bestowed upon women by the creator[1] and they live upon lustful men.[2] Absence of enjoyment, therefore, was considered old age for them.[3] It is stated that the woman is unsatiable like the fire, the ocean and Yama, the destroyer. She is a sharp edge of razor, poison, snake and fire all combined into one.[4] Women were considered as creatures of illusion,[5] devoid of religion, fickle, crooked, frightful as Kṛtyā power, which brings destruction.[6]

The passages, constantly blaming women of inconsistency[7] and love for carnal pleasure[8] are numerous in the didactic portions. Sometimes to make them more convincing they are put into the mouth of women.[9] The composer, however, does not seem to be very successful in driving his point. A tale by which Bhīshma tries to prove women as false only indicates that women like Diśā, were thought to be competent to judge a Ṛshi of

1. Mbh. XIII. 40. 9-10; 48. 37-38; 39. 5-6 cp. M. II. 213-214.
2. Mbh. V. 33. 84-85 प्रमदाः कामयानेषु Mbh. V. 35. 72 प्रभवो नाधिगन्तव्यःस्त्रीणां दुश्चरितस्य च ।
3. Mbh. V. 39. 79. असंभोगो जरा स्त्रीणां० ।
4. Mbh. XIII. 38. 29

अन्तकः पवनो मृत्युः पातालं वडवामुखम् ।
क्षुरधारा विषं सर्पो वह्निरित्येकतः स्त्रियः ॥

Mbh. XIII. 38. 25 नाग्निस्तृप्यति काष्ठानां नापगानां महोदधिः ।
नान्तकः सर्वभूतानां न पुंसां वामलोचना ।

cf. Ram. II. 12. 9, 10, 100; VI. 14. 2.
Rām. III. 13. 5-6; 40. 5 is more or less the same as Mbh.XIII 38. 25.

5. Mbh. XIII. 39. 6-7 शंबरस्य च या माया माया या नमुचेरपि ।
वलेः कुम्भीनसेश्चैव सर्वास्ता येषितो विदुः ॥
6. Rām. III. 45. 29; Mbh. XIII. 40. 8-10; 39. 6-7.
7. Mbh. V. 37. 58; Rām. VI. 16. 9. विद्यते स्त्रीषु चापल्यं० ।
cp. Davies, J. L. "A short History of Women" pp. 27-33 states that women are less stable, less reliable, more changeable, more unaccountable, conservating not because of a metabolism but it is their environment which insists upon the tendency of seizing them by the throat.
8. Mbh. XIII. 40-13 शय्यासनमलंकारमन्नपानमनार्यताम् ।
दुर्वाग्भावं रतिं चैव ददौ स्त्रीभ्यः प्रजापतिः ॥
Mbh. XII. 33. 45. 2nd line cp. M. IX. 17.
9. Mbh. XIII. 19. 92-94 (Diśā's utterances).
Mbh. XIII. 38. 11 ff Panchachuḍa.

Ashtāvakra's calibre.[1] At another place although Apsarā Panchachūḍā is made to condemn the character of women yet it seems that Yudhishṭhira is not convinced.[2] The story that follows to convince him further is again ridiculous for in the case of Ruchi Indra was more to blame as he takes the initiative.[3] Although attempt has been made to arrange these episodes carefully, the disjointed accounts and repetitions betray the ascetic's eagerness to blame a woman's character in season and out of season and thus it appears most unconvincing.

Kings warned against women

In the Epics kings are warned against women who are mentioned among vices[4] created out of intoxication.[5] But this is with the object of checking the over-indulgence of the kings, in women, for many of them due to such intemperance fell victim to consumption and an easy death. Due to sensuality virtuous souls were transformed into lustful souls.[6] The despotic kings, with immense wealth, polygamous tendencies, concubinage and Dāsī system indulged too much in women which led to excessive expenditure, loss of prosperity, talk among servants and above all to destruction.[7] Women were considered as one of the causes of hostility.[8] Moreover the dissatisfied woman in such social conditions could easily be employed by foes for the destruction of such kings.[9] Therefore among the fourteen possessions of the enemies most important to be examined was the inner apartment.[10] Such was the danger of a king's life inside the

1. Mbh. XIII. 19 (sec. ff.)
2. Mbh. XIII. 38-41 (sec.)
3. Mbh. XIII. 40-43 (sec.)
4. Mbh. V. 33. 92. II. 68. 20.

Mbh. XII. 28. 31 and 37 मृगयाऽक्षाः स्त्रियः पानं प्रसङ्गा निन्दिता बुधैः ।

XII. 140. 26; 90. 30; 93. 17, 31. Ram. II. 75. 40, cp. M. VII. 47, 50 for further reference cp. Kaṇe "Hist. of Dh. S." Vol. III. pp. 54-55.

5. Mbh. III. 124. 19; 125. 8-9; XIII. 156. 27-33; Chyavana produced intoxication and divided it among dice, woman, wine and hunting.
6. Mbh. I. 102. 66 ff; 119. 3-4; V. 11. 11ff; 147. 25.
7. Mbh. II. 5. 76; III. 13. 6-7; XIII. 156. 46.
8. Mbh. XII. 139. 42.
9. Mbh. XII. 105. 12.
10. Mbh. II. 5. 21 cf. commen. of Nīlakaṇṭha quoting Nītiśāstra and P. C. Roy's tr. pp. 463; XII. 131. 8.

inner apartment that Rāvaṇa's coach was guarded by women sentries.[1]

It was due to these dangers, the character assigned to women, as well as their inability to keep secrecy[2] that the kings were advised not to be guided by women or to govern kingdom with their help.[3] Thus they were considered untrustworthy,[4] incapable of advice.[5] Any secret counsel was not to be held in their presence.[6]

Women and public administration

It was due to these reasons perhaps that women did not take part in public administration. There is, however, no mention of any such law as Salic law of Europe, in the Epics and once Yudhishṭhira has been advised to place daughters of the dead kings on the throne.[7] Vasishṭha wanted Sītā to rule when Rāma was being banished. But the proposal could not materialize as Sītā also wanted to accompany him.[8] Despite this, there is no example of women ruling kingdoms and taking part in politics generally. The political influence wielded by Gāndhārī, Draupadī and Tārā was merely due to their forceful personalities. They take part in deciding state matters and their advice is often sought in spite of the above mentioned legal injuction.[9] On the contrary it must have been due to the above

1. Rām. V. 6. 29.

2. This is attributed in the Mahābhārata to Yudhisṭhira's curse Mbh. XII. 6. 10-11.

3. Mbh. III. 150. 44; Mbh. V. 38. 43 यत्र स्त्री. . . यत्रानुशासिता। मज्जन्ति तेऽवशा राजन्नद्यामश्मप्लवाइव ।

4. Mbh. V. 38. 42 ये र्थाःस्त्रीषु समायुक्ताः सर्वे ते संशयंगताः । Therefore it is that women are regarded as incompetent to be witnesses by many law givers although allowed to be so, in disputes between women. Cp. Kaṇe 'Hist. of Dh.' Vol. III. p. 333-334, 337, 338; Rām. II. 100. 49. Mbh. II. 5.83; I. 133. 31. Mbh. V. 37. 57.

5. Mbh. II. 64. 15.

6. Mbh. III. 150. 44; II. 5. 83. 84.

7. Mbh. XII. 33. 45 कुमारो नास्ति येषां च कन्यास्तत्राभिषेचय ।

8. Rām. 37. 24. आत्मा हि दाराः सर्वेषां दारसंग्रहवर्तिनाम् ।
आत्मेयमिति रामस्य पालयिष्यति मेदिनीम् ।

Cp. Ravaṇa's proposal to Sītā Ram III. 55. 16, 26, 27.

9. Mbh. V. 67. 6-7; 129. 1 ff; XII. 45. 11; V. 173. 6 Supra chap. on "Mother" influence wielded by mother. Thus Subhadrā is given care of the kingdom and its heir Mbh. XVII. 1. 6 ff.

mentioned opinions that women had little to do with state matters in the Epics. Sometimes the influence of women in politics was really harmful.[1]

Women and their influence on social and political events

Indirectly women did influence the social and political events of the time. The whole story and the events in the Ramayaṇa evolve round Kaikeyī, Sitā[2] and Śurpanakha. The enemity between Vāli and Māyāvī, Vāli and Sugrīva was due to women.[3] The kings attacked Mithilā for Sītā.[4] Certain incidents show clearly the power they weilded.[5]

Women and Religion

In a society where reverence was accorded more for the religious rather than for the political status the attitude towards women can also be judged by the religious rights conceded to them. Here also the Epics depict many strata of society and this question must be dealt with chronologically as far as possible.

The old narratives of Sulabhā,[6] Swayamprabhā[7] and Pingalā[8] indicate that there were women ascetics and philosophers who had mastered the mysteries of life and death. They were likely to discuss their knowledge in august conferences as appears from the accounts of Sulabhā.

It has been shown elsewhere that so far as Vedic sacrificial religion, coronations and Śrāddhas[9] were concerned the wife had an important role to play. Often they performed sacrifices independently.[10] Thus to begin with their religious

1. Rām. II 21-22 sec.
   Mbh. II. 5. 76 cp. Rām. II. 10. 27 ff;
2. Rām. III. 2. 21.
3. Rām. IV. 9. 4.
4. Rām. I. 66. 21. ...
5. Rām. III. 20. 25; 33. 1 ff. VI. 66. 20.
6. Mbh. XII. 320. 79 ff.
7. Rām. IV. 51. 1-17; VII. 17. 17 Vedāvatī. Rām. II. 117. 8-12. Anusūyā.
8. Mbh. XII. 174. 56 ff; 178. 8; Mbh. V. 186. 19-20 (Ambā).
9. Rām. II. 4. 23; 5. 9; 6. 1 ff. VI. 128. 60; II. 103. 20-21, 33-34. Mbh. XII. 40. 13-14. Mbh. III. 114. 13; Mbh. XIII. 168. 20; XI. sec. 26-27; XII. 42. 5; XI. 23. 27; 27. 37.
10. Supra Chap. on "Maid" and "Married life" Rām. II. 25. 27 ff. 20. 14-19.

status was in no way inferior to that of men. The conditions in the various sacrifices described in the Epics are different, as will be shown presently, so these above mentioned conditions either depict traditions when the story part of the Epics was being enacted, or even older ones.

In the Epics Aśwāmedha, Agnishṭoma and many other sacrifices are mentioned[1], which could not be performed without the aid of wife (Patnī). By considering the nature of the actual participation the real status of women in the society can be assessed. It must, however, be borne in mind that if sometimes there is no reference to the role of the wife,[2] the omission may be due to the fact that it was beyond the province of the Epics to describe religious ceremonies in details. Moreover, when the Epic data was being reduced to writing the role of women in sacrifices was becoming formal.[3] The later composers, therefore, were writing from memory or hearsay and may not have known the details.

Wife's actual part in sacrifices was gradually disappearing

After being initiated the wife used to chant Sāma which was later done by Udgātṛ priests. She also used to pound the sacrificial rice, give bath to the animal that was immolated, lay the bricks when the altar was to be built,[4] and prepared the offering. Mention of Udgātṛs and laying of the bricks by the Brāhmaṇas[5] may indicate that the passages describing sacrifices in the Epics may be depicting the time when most of the sacrificial work was allotted to males.[6] The Pravargya cere-

1. Rām. I. 12. 8; VII. 100. 9-10. Mbh. XII. 29. is full of description of great kings who performed sacrifices XIV. 88-90; II 33 ff. (Rajsūya) Cp. Ṛg. V. I. 72. 5; Tai. Br. III. 7. 5. Asv. G. S. I. 8. 5. see Kaṇe "H. of Dh." Vol. II. part I. Chap. XI. p. 556 ff.

2. Rām. I. 13. 41 The queens of Daśaratha are initiated. Rām. VII. 91. 25 golden Sītā initiated but in Mbh. II. 33. 43. 44 and XIV. 73. 4-5 XIV. 88. 14-18 there is no mention of Draupadī's initiation.

3. Altekar "PWHC" page 239,—between 500 B. C. and the first Cen. A.D. women performed sacrifices without mantras Cp. Mbh. XII. 165. 21 also prohibits utterances of Vedic mantra for women.

4. Śat. Br. XVI, 5, 3, 1. III. 8, 2, 1-6 quoted by Altekar "PWHC" page 233 ff.

5. Rām. 1. 14. 28, 29-30 संचित: कुशलैर्द्विजै: । कुशलै: शिल्पकर्मणि ।
Mbh. XVI. 88. 31-32 Kaṇe "Hist. of Dh." Vol. II. part II, Chapt. XXXV page 1248 line 24 ff.

6. Altekar "PWHC" p. 239-40 states that although up to 250 B.C. women used to recite mantras but the practice was becoming unpopular. About the beginning of the Christian era this practice stopped altogether.

mony, an awful, mystic and recondite affair has been mentioned in both the Epics but nothing is mentioned about the wife's participation in this rite.[1] The symbolic rite of uniting with the horse[2] is shrouded in mystery and is very difficult to understand. There is no agreement between scholars on this point.[3] May be the horse symbolized the king's power and victory or prosperity with which the queen was associated. This degrading and incredible custom, from the present standard, may have been a survival of some kind of fertility rite as Aśwamedha was also performed for having progeny.[4] Although the substitution of the golden Sītā indicates Rāma's affection and love for her yet this does not speak of any active participation of women in the sacrifices. The whole description of a wife's participation does show that gradually a woman's part in sacrifices was becoming symbolic, formal and insignificant. The same conditions are described in the contemporary literature.[5]

Women given charity—An object of pity

Women appear as objects of pity for they were given gifts and food in charity along with the old and the invalid[6], although according to one passage gifts given to women were one of the sixteen useless gifts.[7]

Some of the reasons which degraded the religious status of women have been already discussed in the previous chapters, which need not be repeated here.[8] Briefly it will suffice to

1. Rām. I. 14. 4 Mbh. XIV. 88. 21; Acc. to Kaṇe "Hist. of Dh." Vol. II, part II pp. 1147-1149 at first wife was not allowed to look at the vessel in which Gharmya was put although later she was. see page 1149 foot note no. 2557.

2. Rām. I. 14. 34-35. Mbh. XIV. 89. 1-2 Kaṇe "Hist. of Dh." Vol. II, Part II, pp. 1234-1235.

3. S. B. E. Vol. 44, pp. XVIII-XXIV; Prof. Keith's "Religion and Philosophy of the Vedas and Upanishads" Part 2. p. 345-46.

4. Rām. I. 8. 8 ff.

5. Altekar "PWHC" page 239 ff.

6. Rām. I. 14. 13 बृद्धाश्च व्याधिताश्चैव स्त्रीबालाश्च तथैव च ।
Mbh. XII. 85. 33 गाश्चैव महिषीश्चैव तथा वृद्धस्त्रियोऽपि च
Mbh. XVI. 90. 14. कामैस्तुष्टा वरस्त्रियः ।

7. Mbh. III. 200. 4-8 वृथा दानानि षोडश... स्त्रीजनेषु च यद्दत्तं० ।

8. Supra Chapt. II. "Maid and her Education" p. 24-26, ff. and 33 "M. Life" p. 126 ff.

say that impurity imposed upon the woman[1], lack of education, admission of the non-Āryan woman into Āryan families, may all have been responsible for her exclusion from the Vedic sacrificial religion.[2] She took to the new Purāṇika religion[3] and satisfied her religious urge. The harm done to the woman by such excommunication was that she now began to be classed among the Śūdras.[4] Her intellectual growth was retarded as she was denied the only intellectual education i.e. Veda and Sānkhya philosophy, of that time. Women and the Śūdras were allowed to practise Yoga,[5] and they were regarded as being capable of attaining emancipation.[6] Women generally offer prayers to female divinities, tree-goddesses, rivers and invoke fate which is indicative of their helplessness as well as of superstitious nature.[7] Loss of intellectual activity and religious status may have been responsible for the loss of social status as well.

Liberty Enjoyed by Women

A discussion about the liberty enjoyed by women and its gradual deterioration will also indicate the attitude of society towards women. The life long protection[8] due to the physical weakness of women may have been imposed for their benefit.[9]

1. There was no idea of impurity attached to women in the Vedas. It may also have been taken due to the contact with the non-Aryans. This idea is first found in the Brāhmaṇas, Gopatha Br. II.23.4 (Indra "Status of Women in Ancient India" page 154) later in Taittarīya Samhita it is said that a person whose wife was in her course during the sacrifice only receieved half of merit. It is also interesting to note that this idea of impurity is only found in the later books of the Great Epic, i.e. Anuśāsana parva. cp. Āp. Dh. I. 3. 9. 13. Gaut. XIV. 30. Śat Bṛ. V. 2. 1. 17 although wife ascends with husband on the ladder against sacrificial post still she is considered impure and she is purified before the ceremony. (S. B. E. Vol. XLI, pp. 31-32).
2. Mbh. XIII. 128. 5-6; XII. 165. 21-22.
3. Mbh. XII. 3. 77; 82. 33; Mbh. XII. 284. 203 of visiting holy places, listening to stories of Itihāsa and Purāṇa.
4. Mbh. XII. 35. 39 स्त्री शूद्रं०

   Mbh. VI. 33. 32; XIV. 19. 61.
5. Mbh. XII. 165. 21-22; 239. 2 ff.
6. Mbh. XII. 240. 34. VII. 33. 32; XIV. 19. 61.
7. Mbh. II. 18. 1 ff. III. 231. 16; Rām. II. 52. 80 ff; II. 56. 19-25; Mbh. III. 30. 1. नमो धात्रे विधात्रे च० ।

   Mbh. XII. 284. 203; Rām. VII. 48.3. मामकेयं तनुर्नूनं सृष्टादुखाय लक्ष्मण । धात्रा यस्यास्तथा मे ऽद्य दुःखमूर्तिः प्रदृश्यते ।
8. Mbh. XIII. 46. 44 पिता रक्षति कौमारे.... ।
9. Mbh. I. 173. 12 (K. ed.) अनाथत्वं स्त्रियो द्वारं दुष्टानां विवृतं हि तत् ।

If a woman lost all her protectors, it was the duty of the king to protect her.[1] With such protection no idea of tutelage, confinement, seclusion or restriction to their freedom is associated. The family and the royal protection, in fact, gave them liberty of movement.

The ladies of commoners

It has been stated that it was only in a kingless country that amorous men were not able to accompany women in the woods. If the king protected well, it is said, women and maidens decked with ornaments could fearlessly wander everywhere without male relatives to attend upon them.[2] The Epic societies were mostly monarchical. This goes to establish that the movements of women were in no way restricted. Women attended courts for business.[3] They moved freely in public particularly on festive occasions or for witnessing any strange object or event.[4] On the occassion of Kṛshṇa's arrival at Hastināpur on his peace mission and when the Pāṇḍavas went out in the coronation procession, the houses were so thronged with women that they were on the point of falling. Even in the republics of the Vṛshṇis and Andhakas, it will be shown presently, that the ladies of aristocratic families used to attend festivals with the commoners.[5]

The freedom enjoyed by the royal ladies

From the narrative part of the Epics it is clear that the movements of the ladies of the inner apartments were not much confined. They followed their husbands to forests[6], wars and hunting expiditions.[7] Some of them like Satyawatī, Ambikā, Ambālikā went for penances even without any male protection.[8] Sometimes they went to the woods, to visit Ṛshi families.[9] They appeared before assemblies[10] and were coronated in public.[11]

1. Mbh. XIII. 61. 31; XV. 26. 8. Supra the chap. on the "Widow".
2. Rām. II. 67. 17; Mbh. XII. 68. 38; 67. 15.
3. Rām. VII. 53. 5.
4. Mbh. XII. 38. 3-4; VI. 121. 3-4; I. 218. 18; 219. 6, 8; II. 23. 22.
5. Mbh. I. 218. 18; Mbh. XVI. 3. 7.
6. Sītā and Draupadī, Kuntī and Mādrī followed their husbands.
7. Rām. II. 9. 16 Kaikeyi followed Daśaratha; Mbh. IX. 29. 65 ff. 30. 3; 62. 4 ff.
8. Mbh. I. 128. 12-13.
9. Rām. VII. 45. 17 ff.
10. Mbh. V. 129. 2 ff.
11. Mbh. XII. 40. 13-14. Rām. VI. 128. 60.

The ladies of royal families had their outdoor pleasures also. Subhadrā was abducted when she was returning after attending the public festival at Raivataka. The Vṛshṇi and Andhaka ladies often attended these festivities.[1] The Kuru ladies went out to the forest for picnics and for visiting their relations. The inner apartment built in one of the excursions was just to keep these ladies aloof from the public gaze so that they could freely dance, sing, laugh, drink and sport in water.[2] Sītā went with Sugrīva's wives to show them the city of Ayodhayā[3]. It has been already stated that the ladies attended Swayamvaras, funerals and tournaments. Queens sometimes had to forego their modesty and drew chariots for the Brāhmaṇas which would be unthinkable in the purdah system.[4] In grief, also, all modesty was thrown to the winds.[5]

Although Tārā's taking part in the state matters and examples of other non-Āryan women who exercise their freedom of choice to such an extent as to offer themselves in marriage indicate greater freedom exercised by royal ladies, yet they also practised seclusion.[6]

Seclusion

Despite all this freedom certain manners and passages in the Epics indicate that the custom of seclusion of women, especially of those of the royal household, was prevalent. Rāma's opinion that during calamities, wars, Swayamvaras, sacrifices and marriages there was no fault if women appeared unveiled,[7] especially with their husbands[8] suggests that this was not otherwise countenanced. It may be that even on the above mentioned occasions married ladies appeared with their husbands, i.e. their protectors. Lakshmaṇa had an objection to looking at Sītā in the absence of Rāma.[9] Maṇḍodarī's lamentations indicate

1. Mbh. I. 218-219 (sections).
2. Mbh. I. 222. 20 ff; XVI. 3. 7; III. 240. 8-9.
3. Rām. VI. 128. 22.
4. Mbh. XIII. 2. 51 ff.; 53. 30 ff; 159. 25 ff.
5. Mbh. VIII. 4. 3-4; XVI. 4. 11; IX. 29. 65 ff; XI. 16. 10-12.
6. Rām. IV. 33. 40 ff; Rām. III. 17. 9 ff; Mbh. I. 153. 5; 154. 7 ff; I. 214. 18-20; Rām. V. 5 ff. description of Rāvaṇa's Antahpura.
7. Rām. VI. 114. 28. In the śloka "Vṛttāvaraṇa" may mean veil or more probably the covered cloth of palanquin.
8. Rām. VI. 114. 29.
9. Rām. VII. 48. 21. कथमत्र हि पश्यामि रामेण रहितां वने ।

that the Rākshasa chief did not like his wives coming out unveiled.[1] Draupadī appeared properly veiled before Nārada.[2] Her lamentations in the court of the Kuru's prove that the Kuru ladies were not accustomed to appear before an assembly. Some descriptions point to the fact that these ladies never appeared before a crowd. The composers further exaggerated that they were not even seen by the sun or the wind.[3]

In the Kuru inner apartments quiet modesty was practised although such was not the case with that of Rāvaṇa's.[4] The royal ladies used to go out in closed vehicles escorted by men and Strī-adhyakshas.[5] The movement of the females confined in the inner apartments, the sight of a helpless lady in a street, were so well known to the composers of the Epics that they used these in similes.[6]

Among the young ladies of the royal household it was not a custom to talk to strangers and in case it was absolutely necessary a blade of grass was placed by them in between.[7] It was perhaps a symbolic curtain the limits of which were not to be transgressed.

Inner apartments

The description of the inner apartments also proves the isolation of ladies from the outside world. To reach the inner apartment six or seven courtyards were to be traversed.[8] In the first three "Kakshyas" chariots were allowed, the next two were crossed on foot. The last three were known as "Śuddhānta" or "Harmya"[9]

Guards

In Kausalyā's inner apartment the first "Kaksha" was occu-

1. Rām. VI. 111. 61-62.

2. Mbh. II. 208. 15 "Susamvītā" has been translated as "properly veiled" by P.C. Roy. It may only mean that Draupadī covered herself with "Uttarīya" for when she talks to Koṭika she does the same : Mbh. III. 266.1.

3. Mbh. II. 69. 4, 5, 9; IX. 29. 74, 75, 82; XI. 10. 8; XV. 15. 13; Rām. II. 33. 8.

4. Mbh. X. 10. 14. cp. Rām. V. 9-10 (sections)

5. Mbh. V. 175. 2-3 Ambā was escorted by an old Brāhmaṇa and a nurse. Mbh. IX. 29. 65-83; XII. 37. 40-41; XV. 22 20-21; Rām. II. 83. 6; VI. 127. 14.

6. Rām. V. 35. 56; Mbh. VI. 77. 60-61 प्रमदेवाध्वनि स्थिता ।

7. Rām. III. 56. 1; Mbh. III. 281. 17; 266. 2-3.

8. Rām. IV. 33. 19; II. 57. 17, 24; II. 17. 17-19.

9. Rām. V. 9-10; II. 17. 19-21.

pied by old men, second by the Veda-knowing Brāhmaṇas and the third was guarded by old men, youthful servants and female guards.[1] These "Harmyas" were well guarded by all sorts of unfit and disabled persons such as hunch-backs, lame or dwarfish women and eunuchs.[2] These persons may have been appointed precisely because of their unattractiveness as well as inability in helping the palace conspiracy and revolutions. But kings are given advice by their well-wishers not only to employ eunuchs but trusted servants, learned and old men of character[3] for these could be more loyal and self-possessed. Vidura gives a strange advice that the charge of the inner apartment should be given to the king's father[4] and it may perhaps be prompted by the distrust of others. A king's father, however, in most of the cases would not have been alive and if living could not have been free for such a job.[5] The warnings against contracting friendship with a king's wife indicates that such persons must have been punished severely.[6]

Strī-ādhyakshas

To look after the inner apartments, and the comforts of ladies even outside it[7] there were officers known as "Strī-adhyaksha", such "Mahāmātras" have been mentioned in the twelfth rock edict of Aśoka and this was perhaps an old office.[8]

Entrance allowed to a few

Only a few were allowed to enter the inner apartment and even the princes had to seek permission for entrance.[9] Trusted officials like charioteer Sumantra, envoys like Sanjaya, greatly respected Brāhmaṇas[10] revered due to their moral excellence,

1. Rām. II. 20. 11-13.
2. Rām. V. 4. 15-28; Mbh. V. 30. 39 Imbeciles included the list. Mbh. IX. 62. 5; also guarded the war camp of women.
3. Mbh. III. 150. 46. Mbh. XV. 5. 19-20.
4. Mbh. V. 38. 12.
5. But father's like Pulika & Bhattīya who placed their sons on throne may have been doing this job for their sons. H.C. Ray Chaudhari, "Political History of Ancient India" (Calcutta 1953). pp. 114-117.
6. Mbh. IV. 4. 18; XII. 131. 8.
7. Mbh. XV. 23. 12; Rām. II. 16. 3.
8. Kaṇe "Hist. of Dh." Vol. III. Appendix note 191. p. 1007 स्त्र्यध्यक्षमहामात्र (in Aśoka's edicts) p. 976. अन्तःपुरमहामात्र ।
9. Mbh. V. 59. 3 ff.
10. Rām. II. 16.11; 14. 43-44. Mbh. I. 3. 105-106. XII 325. 31; XIII. 52. 10; 159. 14 proves that the Brāhmaṇas even lived in the inner

were not stopped by the wardens. Usually to enter the inner apartment and to have a look at the ladies there, was considered a transgression of Dharma, duty, i.e. "Dharmalopa."[1]

The detailed account of Antahpuras and specially that of Rāvaṇa, although exaggerated by poetic fancy, still depicts the luxurious and free life of the inmates.[2] Numerous queens were attended by hundreds of Dāsīs.[3] Their palaces had spacious gardens, costly decorated buildings, perfumed with scents, with separate apartments for sports, painting and drinking.[4] Music, dance, wine-drinking, love-sports, point out a voluptuous life of Antahpuras particularly that of Rāvaṇa. This life indicates that the seclusion was in no way due to modesty.[5]

Seclusion, a sign of respectability

All the above mentioned facts i.e. life of the inmates of the inner apartment, inside or outside the palaces, their enjoyments, political missions, visiting and living in the forests, does not prove that there was purdāh system, confinement or restriction of freedom which developed later on. The royal ladies kept aloof from the commoners, who sometimes include unwanted and uncultured persons among their crowds. Thus their seclusion was a sign of respectability. It was meant merely to guard their chastity, to which great importance was attached by later societies depicted in the Epics. For their chastity guarded purity of their lord's royal-race as well as his property and

apartment as has been shown elsewhere they were also appointed for Niyoga. Mbh. V. 59. 3 ff cp. "Swapna Vāsavadattā" by Bhāsa Act VI. Padmāvati does not like her husband to receive ambassador of Ujjainī in her presence but he overrules her.

1. Rām. V. 11. 39-45; IV. 33. 61.
2. Rām. V. 6-11 (sargas).
3. Rām. V. 6. 42-43; II. 33. 13 and 22; IV. 33. 22-25. Mbh. III 233. 49ff; V. 59. 6; XII. 326. 3-4.
4. Rām. II. 10. 15; II. 15. 31—34, 39; II. 9. 22 ff and even an apartment for angry mood. II. 14. 29-30

Rām. II. 10. 13 चित्रगृहै० IV. 33. 14-25 दिव्यमाल्यवृत्तं० ।
V. 6. 36 क्रीडागृहाणि०; कामस्य गृहकं० । 35 चित्रशालागृहाणि० ।

Mbh. V. 59. 5-6; Rām. V. 9. 18-28; 48-55. V. 4. 28. (perfumed with scents.)

5. Rām. V. 10. 37 ff; II. 10. 12. V. 11. 4-10; Rām. V. 6. 9-12. II. 10. 15; VII. 42. 18-19; IV. 33. 38, 40; V. 5.11; 6. 41; 9.45, 57, 62. Mbh. V. 59. 4-7; XI. 20.7. Mbh. XIV. 89. 42 shows that even in sacrifices wine was distributed to women.

kingdom.[1] It is primarily due to this reason that the system of 'harems'' may have been followed by the propertied classes, although to a lesser extent it may have been prompted to check palace conspiracies and revolutions.

Some reasons for restriction of movements and thereby the fall of women

With increased emphasis on pātrivrata dharma chastity assumed greater importance. In order to keep women perfectly chaste their movements might have been restricted gradually. Other reasons for these restrictions can also be forwarded. In the later ages as depicted in the Mahābhārata, due to lack of education and therefore loss of intellectual activity and rational thinking, women became ignorant. Child marriages and thus living in unsympathetic atmosphere from an early age with ignorant mothers-in-law and cowives might have developed jealous temperament and deteriorated their character. Most of them having no other interest in life might have imbibed luxurious habits, fickle and vile character which was exaggerated by the school of renunciation to carry propoganda against women. It was stated that due to their fickle character women were to be guarded carefully throughout their lives. The theory of perpetual tutelage, entire dependence on men, an outcome of ignorance, was responsible for fetters that chained women for ages to come.

Treatment in Calamities

The importance of chastity for woman, for keeping the purity of family and property intact is also reflected in the treatment meted out to woman in the face of calamities. The place accorded to woman in society after she has suffered at the hands of enemies or ruffians, is indicative of the attitude towards her. It shows how far man (or society) is prepared to rise above sex prejudices to give her equitable, just and sympathetic treatment.

As already stated, in legalizing Paiśācha and Rākshasa forms of marriage some protection, to the maidens abducted, was given. But this legalization was ineffective sometimes. Although according to one school of opinion a girl who had set her heart upon another man was not to be abducted yet among

1. J. L. Davies "ASHW" pp. 139-140, 222 for the practice of guarding women p. 235. Dr. Johnson's opinion that all property depends upon the chastity of women.

the Mahābhārata heroes this was held good in theory rather than in practice.[1] In Ambā's case even after abducting such a maiden her mighty abductor Bhīsma was not, at first, willing to set her free.[2] He sent her back to Śālwa after being convinced by his uncle of the impropriety of the act.[3] But Śālwa refused her hand.[4] The refusal might have been prompted by the fear of Bhīshma[5] yet it was possible for him to charge Ambā with false accusation of being Parapūrvā and Anyapūrvā.[6] After this refusal by Śālwa, her fate was worse; for Bhīshma refused her even for his brother although commanded by his preceptor.[7] Had the society possessed a keener sense of justice and a balanced idea about chastity such an accusation might not have been possible and the feelings of an abducted girl might have been respected.

The Rāmāyaṇa depicts a much more conservative society. However much, Rāma may have pined for Sītā he later declares that he fought for the sake of his honour.[8] Rāma's accusation may not be representing his actual feelings.[9] Nevertheless it is a reflection of the public opinion of the time when Uttara-Kānda was being written. Even after the fire ordeal she was taken back to be exiled merely to appease the public opinion even though Rāma was convinced of her purity.

The attitude of the Pāṇḍavas towards Draupadī after her abduction has been often contrasted to that of Rāma towards Sītā. It cannot, however, be made much of. Draupadī was rescued then and there before she reached the abductor's place while Sītā was in the abductor's possession for nearly one year. So there would be no question of adverse public opinion in Draupadī's case.[10] As the Rāmāyaṇa ideals have guided

1. Mbh. XIII. 44. 40. Mbh. I. 102. 63 ff; Mbh. II. 41. 22-26; 45. 18-19.

2. Mbh. XIII. 44. 40-41 Discussion with Vāhīka who convinced Bhīshma that Ambā should be set free.

3. Ibid.

4. Mbh. V. 175. 5 ff; XIII. 44. 39.

5. Mbh. V. 175. 24 बिभेमि भीष्मात् सुश्रोणि त्वं च भीष्मपरिग्रहः ।

6. Mbh. V. 175. 5· त्वयाऽन्यपूर्वया०, 8 परपूर्वा० ।

7. Mbh. V. 178. 28 ff. Rām VII. 80 ff. Bhargava punishes Arajā for no fault of hers.

8. Rām. VI. 115. 2 ff.

9. Altekar "PWHC" chap. XI. p. 368.

10. Mbh. III. 268-272.

the Hindū society for ages, the attitude of man of making woman suffer for no fault of hers still persists. Thus it was again for the notion of extreme form of chasity recommended for woman, which was responsible for restriction of her liberty and movements, that she had no place in society, in case of calamities. This notion was the outcome of wife as a personal property and possession of the husband for his exclusive and personal use not to be polluted even by the touch of others. Moreover, the husband was her very god, only unsmelled flowers or unused offerings could be dedicated to the service of god, this idea must have prompted extreme form of chastity through which husband's race and property was also to remain pure and guarded. Some efforts were made by Dharmaśāstrakāras. To amend the wrong they enjoined the taking back of abducted women even if the abduction was followed by conception.[1] But these opinions never gained ground in Hindū society and are not reflected in the Epics.

Women as property

There are many examples in the Epics that indicate the position of women in general and of wife in particular as a piece of property.[2] This notion about women has existed from the hoary past. It was also reflected in the Rākshasa and the Asura forms of marriage. The enumeration of women along with gold and gems,[3] their being considered as an object of enjoyment,[4] also as property to be utilized in difficulties,[5]

1. Vas. Dh. S. XVII. 73. Devala Smṛti 37. 38, 47-52 (Smṛti Samuchchaya pages 86-87).

2. Rām. IV. 35.13; VI 101. 15.

3. Rām. VII. 21. 20 सुवर्ण-मणि-मुक्ताभिः प्रमदाभिरलंकृतान् ।
Rām. IV. 33. 13.
Mbh. III. 80. 20 यो धनानि च कन्याश्च युधि जित्वा महारथः ।

4. Mbh. V. 36. 55 न स्त्रीषु राजन् रतिमाप्नुवन्ति ।
Mbh. II. 5. 112; V. 39. 67 रतिपुत्रफला नारी० ।
Chapter on "Adultery and Extra-Marital Relations"

5. Mbh. I. 158. 27 आपदर्थे धनं रक्षेद् दारान्रक्षेद्धनैरपि ।
Mbh. V. 37. 18. आत्मानं सततं रक्षेद् दारैरपिधनैरपि ॥
Cp. M. VII. 213 is the same.
Mbh. I. 158. 3-4, 22, 26, 28; Mbh. V. 33. 64 त्रय एवाधना राजन्भार्या-दासस्तथा सुतः । यत्ते समधिगच्छन्ति यस्यैते तस्य तद्धनम् ।
Mbh. I. 82. 22.
Mbh. I. 71. 1; V. 45. 12.

all point out to the same conclusion. It has been stated in a previous chapter that she was considered as a piece of property of the husband.[1]

Property rights of the wife

In such a state of affairs where the wife was like a living possession to be supported and protected perpetually there would be no question of her taking to a career or possessing property. Although Āpastamba Dharma Sūtra maintains that there can be no division of wealth between husband and wife,[2] which amounts to their equal ownership, the wife in reality appears to be only a good manager of the husband's property in the Epics. Draupadī, when describing how she managed the affairs at Indraprastha, never refers to the household as "mine" or "ours" but always "that of the king" or of "Yudhishṭhira".[3] She figures as a good manager, follower and loyal servant, on whom the master could place complete confidence and not as the joint proprietor of the household. Neither Damayantī nor Draupadī had the power to check their husbands from pawning the kingdoms in the game of dice. They were, in fact, never consulted.[4] Thus this kind of identity of interest can very well be compared to the position of the wife in the nineteenth century England, "The two are called one person in law for the purpose of inferring that whatever is hers is his, but the parallel inference is never drawn that whatever is his is hers; the maxim is not applied against the man, except to make him responsible to third parties for her acts as a master is for the acts of his slaves or cattle."[5]

In the didactic portions it is clearly stated that women can enjoy the wealth given to them by husbands but have no right of giving it away i.e. they have no proprietary rights over

1. Supra Chapt. on "Married Life" conclusion pages 126-131.
2. Ap. Dh. S. II. 6.14.20 जायापत्योर्नविभागो विद्यते०
VI. 11. 29. 3 Apastamba says that both have power over common property, a similar passage in Mbh. XIII. 141. 43 दम्पत्योः समशीलत्वं धर्मः स्याद्गृहमेधिनः। but it does not refer to property rights.
3. Mbh. III. 233. 42. युधिष्ठिरनिवेशने; 49. शत दासीसहस्त्राणि०।
Mbh. III. 233. 56. पतीनां०।
4. Mbh. II. 60-65; 74; Mbh. III. 60. 17.
5. Mill, J.S. "The Subjection of Women", p. 59.

it. P. C. Roy states that this refers to childless widows[1] but it does not appear so from the context. So far as the widow was concerned from the time of Yāska to Kālidāsa[2] no property rights were conceded to her, which were later taken up by the Smṛti writers like Yāgyawalka. The Great Epic allows Niyoga for the childless widow, otherwise the husband's heirs were to look after her. Therefore no thought was given to the property rights of the widow and these lines also do not refer to her rights. These lines were perhaps to check the unlimited power of the wife-manager like Draupadī. There may have been a possibility of such wives, helping their agnate relatives with their husand's wealth, which was regarded improper in a patriarchal society.

According to the Great Epic the wife was allowed to enjoy three thousand coins given to her by her husband,[3] a thousand more than prescribed by Kauṭilya and Vyāsa.[4] This Śloka if referring to the rights of a Brāhmaṇa and his wife the amount may refer to a sum which was perhaps to be given once in three years, for a Brāhmaṇa was not allowed to hoard more than what was required for three years.[5] It cannot be, however, maintained definitely that these were laws followed by the Brāhmaṇas only. "Dwija" may include three regenerate castes. It may also refer to a tendency of the Dharmaśāstra writers to address the code of conduct to the Brāhmaṇas for due to foreign and non-Āryan contact and some internal changes in society other castes were not particular about the rules. The Brāhmaṇas were now the custo-

1. Mbh. XIII. 47. 24 स्त्रीणां तु पतिदायाद्यमुपभोगफलं स्मृतम् ।
नापहारं स्त्रियः कुर्युः पतिवित्तात्कथंञ्चन ॥

Thus wife just appears as a manager and Āpastamba's dictum does not apply here. cp. M. IX. 199 conveys the same sense. P.C. Roy's Eng. tr. of Anusāsana Parva. page 28 line 7.

2. Yāska's Nirukta III. 5 refers to widow in the South under certain conditions gets money. Kālidāsa "Abhigyāna Śakuntalam" Act IV refers to widow's property being escheated by the king, in failure of an heir. Yāska is anterior to the Epics and Kālidāsa refers to posterior conditions. cp. Kane "Hist. of Dh." Vol. II part I. p. 582.

3. Mbh. XIII. 47. 22. 23 त्रिसहस्त्रपरो दायः स्त्रियै देयो धनस्य वै ।
भर्त्रा तच्च धनं दत्तं यथार्हं भोक्तुमर्हति ॥

4. Kauṭilya "Arthaśāstra" Eng. tr. Book III chap. II Sūtra 152, but there is no limit to jewellery. Vyāsa quoted by Smritichandrikā page 28.

5. Mbh. XIII 47.22 त्रैवार्षिकाद्यदा भक्तादधिकं स्याद् द्विजस्य तु ।

dians of the code of conduct which they were expected to follow. The wife had a right to enjoy the three-thousand coins as she willed but she had only usufructuary rights over her husband's wealth or wealth given by him.[1] It seems that this right was enjoyed by the widows also.[2]

The above discussion proves that the idea of Strīdhana was still in evolution and "Saudāyika", the wealth which is given to a married woman as a present by her husband, was not under its purview.

Strīdhana

As the rich people in Europe in the 18th and 19th centuries safeguarded the interests of their daughters by providing pin-money for them, it must be said to the credit of our legislators (Dharma and Arthaśāstra writers) that they developed the idea of Strīdhana which was much more comprehensive and guarded the property rights of women in a far better way. Sir G. D. Banerjee states "nowhere were the property rights of women recognized so early as in India, and in very few ancient systems of laws have these rights been so largely conceded as in our own"[3] In the Epics are found the descriptions of rich dowries given to the princesses which include nearly every useful article for the new royal house-hold. In the Rāmāyaṇa it has been described as "Kanyā-dhanam" and in the Mahābhārata by various names "Vaivāhakam", "Parichhadam." It is known as "Haraṇam" the share taken away by the girl or "Gyātideyam" to be given by the relatives.[4] May be "haraṇam" was the wealth given to the daughter, who was abducted and hurriedly married. The wealth was sent later, as in the case of Subhadrā. The name Strīdhana to all this kind of property developed later on. The word, "Kanyādhana" may have been later changed to "Strīdhana".

Classification of Strīdhana

Katyāyana's definition of Strīdhana is most intensive. Defining it most elaborately he states that whatever is given

1. Mbh. XIII. 47.24.
2. Ram VI. 123. 36. विभूतिं चैव सर्वासां स्त्रीणां दशरथस्य च।
3. Banerjee "Marriage and Strīdhana" page 370.
4. Rām. I. 74. 6 Mbh. I. 221. 41 ff हरणं० ; 44. ज्ञातिदेयं०; III. 295. 1. 16.

before fire in marriage is "Adhyāgni" whatever a girl receives while taking leave of the father's home is known as "Adhyavāhanika", whatever is given by the father-in-law and mother-in-law while doing obeisance at their feet is known as "Prītidatta", the money given as the cost of the house-hold utensils and for beasts of burden and milch cattle[1] is known as "Śulka". Whatever is received by her over and above this from the parental house or from the husband and his father is known as "Anvādheya". In the married state whatever presents she gets from her father, brother or husband is known as "Saudāyika".[2] Now all these kinds of presents and gifts are often stated in the Epics. The reason for not giving them a specific nomenclature may have been that the idea was still developing. It is usual in the history of the social institutions that a name is given to a system or a custom long after it has been in use.

Thus Draupadī's dowry will be classified under Adhyāgni.[3] Sītā's and Uttarā's dowry as Adhyavāhanika.[4] The meaning of Śulka was quite different in the narrative parts of the Great Epic. But as Śulka according to the didactic portions was to be presented to the maiden,[5] it gradually and automatically came under the purview of the above mentioned definition of Katyāyana. The detailed account of cows, beasts of burden and utensils given in the dowry of princesses is described in the Epics.[6] Prītidāna as the gift of affection has been mentioned in the Rāmāyaṇa[7] not as a gift from the parents-in-law but one given by Anusūyā to Sītā. Perhaps this word at first denoted the gift of the elders to the younger people given out of love. Later it was taken in the technical sense. There was, however,a custom of giving gifts to the daughters-in-law when they touched the feet of their mother-in-law.[8] Its omission sometimes may have been

1. दोह्याभरणकर्मिणाम् is explained differently by Vyāsa and Dâyabhāga. Kane. P. V. Hist of Dh. Vol. III Chap. XXX p. 775.

2. Kaṇe. P. V. "Hist of Dh." Vol. III. Chap. XXX. pp. 773 ff Cp. list given in M. IX. 194-195; Vi. S. XVII 18

3. Mbh. I. 198. 17 तदा धनं सौमकिरग्निसाक्षिकम् ।

4. Rām. I. 74. 6; Mbh. IV. 72. 36-37.

5. Mbh. XIII. 44. 32-33; Mbh. XIII. 46. 1-2.

6. Mbh. III. 295. I. mentions "Bhāṇḍam Vaivāhakam" i.e. utensils.

7. Rām. II. 118. 21 प्रीतिदानमनुत्तमम् ; II. 119.12 प्रीतिदानेन० ।

8. Mbh. XIV. 88. 4 Kuntī and others give presents to Chitrāngadā.

due to the simple reason that the Epics were not concerned with the detailed descriptions of social customs.

Dominion over Strīdhana

Except for some stray references in the didactic portions, nothing about the nature of ownership of these presents has been stated in the Epics. As the house-hold things were to be utilized in the home there was, of course, no question of the nature of ownership. It seems that the wife had the right of proprietorship over her own ornaments. Kaikeyī did present a necklace to Mantharā for bringing the good news of Rāma's coronation.[1] Sītā's hesitation in presenting a necklace to Hanūmān without Rāma's permission may have been due to the fear lest Rāma should mind her giving away a souvenir presented to her by him,[2] or the hesitation might have been due to the fact that the necklace was Saudāyika i.e. gift which in those days could be enjoyed but was not to be disposed of as already stated.

Only in the case of Kausalyā it has been stated that she maintained many servants and owned a thousand villages.[3] As the idea of Strīdhana as landed property developed much later, it is quite possible that Kausalyā may have been a brotherless daughter, "Putrikā" of some Kausala feudal chief. Her father may have been Bhānumānt[4] king of Kosala for her epithet is "Kosalendraduhitā."[5]

It is also interesting to note that while on some occasion dowry was specified as "daughter's wealth,"[6] on the other occasions it was 'wealth given to the Pāṇḍavas and Saubhadreya' and not to the princess who was married.[7] This kind of specification in case of Sītā and Subhadrā may have to do something with the republican zeal of protecting the rights of the daughter. Mithilā[8] also had the same republican tendencies.

1. Rām. II. 7. 32.
2. Rām. VII. 128. 78 ff; VII. 128. 81 ff. In Rām. II. 30. 41 also Rāma gives permission.
3. Rām. II 31. 22; II. 32. 21.
4. Rām. I. 13.26 तथा कोसलराजानं भानुमन्तं० ।
5. Rām. II. 65. 23 सा कोसलेन्द्रदुहिता० ।
6. कन्याधनम्, ज्ञातिदेयं०; हरणम् as already stated Mbh. I. 221. 33-44. Rām. I. 74. 4 ff.
7. Mbh. I. 198. 15-17; Mbh. IV. 72. 36.
8. For Sītā's dowery is referred as Kanyādhana; Rām. I. 74.48.

Devolution of Strīdnana

Strīdhana according to the Great Epic is inherited by the unmarried daughters. Here the word "Yautaka" presents difficulty, dowries are not described as "Yutuka" by the Epic-composers. But whether the word is derived from "Yuta" or, "Yu", in the Great Epic it appears from the context that it means the separate property of the mother.[1] At another place also it has been used as the separate property of anyone.[2] This Yautaka in case of the mother was the property she received from her father,[3] which devolved from mother to daughter. The Dharmaśāstrakāras had in mind the injustice meted out to women so this ingeneous way was invented by them to compensate the daughter, for they might have felt that in disinheriting her great injustice was done.

The rights of Putrikā

The injustice felt by the Dharmaśāstrakāras and didactic writers of the Great Epic is also reflected in their conceding property rights to a brotherless daughter. They repeat the dictum "the daughter is like the son."[4] Thus Jaiswāl discussing the daughter's legal position in Manusmṛti states "Nowhere in the Hindū law is her legal position so tenderly defined."[5] Similar rights are conceded to the daughter in the Great Epic in identical ślokas.[6] In the tenderness and affection felt towards her

1. Mbh. XIII. 45. 12 मातुश्च यौतकं यत्स्यात्कुमारी-भाग एव सः ।

cp. M. IX. 131; Kaṇe "Hist. of Dh." Vol. III. pp. 779 "Yuta" means to join according to Madanratna and Vyavhāramayukha and "Yu" to separate according to Devswāmin.

2. Mbh. XIII. 105. 10 ज्येष्ठः कुर्वीत यौतकम् । M IX. 214.
3. Mbh. XIII. 47.25 स्त्रियास्तु यद्भवेद्वित्तं पित्रा दत्तं युधिष्ठिर ।
ब्राह्यण्यास्तद्धरेत्कन्या यथा पुत्रस्तथा हि सा ॥

cp. M. IX. 198 is more or less the same. Here the passages were describing a Brāhmaṇa's household therefore in question of inheritence Brāhmaṇi is used but it was not implicd for her only (see foot note 1,) even now in every caste the daughter takes the Strīdhana.

4. Mbh. XIII. 45. 11; 47.25 and 26. cp. M., IX. 131.
5. Jaisawāl, K. P. "Manu and Yājyāwalka" Lecture-XII. "Family law" pp. 258. Mbh. I. 159. 11; M. IV. 184-185 the same कृपणम् means distress and therefore an object of tenderness.
6. Mbh. XIII. 45. 11 यथैवात्मा तथा पुत्रः पुत्रेण दुहिता समा ।
तस्यामात्मनि तिष्ठन्त्यां कथमन्यो धनं हरेत् ॥

cp. M. IX. 130 is the same.

it was entirely forgotten that she was also a woman who had been condemned in the same Parva. Many think that in Ancient India the daughter had no right to inherit independently but only through her son. There was no sense in giving the daughter equality with the son if the right of inheritence was not to be given to her. Therefore by "Kathmanyo Dhanam Haret", the right of the brotherless daughter to succeed was recognized. Her son also had the same right.[1] Manu and the composer of the Anuśāsana Parva, perhaps did away with the difference between the appointed and unappointed brotherless daughter as the sons of both were to inherit the maternal grand-father's wealth.[2] Such daughters could themselves inherit.[3] Therefore both Manu and the composer of the Anuśāsana Parva state that lest she be a Putrikā any brotherless girl or fatherless daughter should not be taken in marriage.[4] An appointed Putrikā was declared by a ceremony.[5] A custom which perhaps gradually died out as any brotherless daughter was considered to be a Putrikā. But still an appointed brotherless daughter had a superior claim as compared with a son by adoption or purchase. Nīlakaṇṭha and P. C. Roy interpreting the below mentioned Śloka,[6] state, "when again, a person has got a daughter and she has been invested by him with the status of son, if he then happens to take a son by adoption or purchase, then the daughter is held to be superior to such a son (for she takes three shares of her father's wealth, the son's share being limited to only the remaining two)." Although nothing can be stated definitely about the distribution of the share, the Śloka clearly means that if the girl was invested with the "Putrikā status" in that case her right could not be

1. Mbh. I. 120. 33-34, XIII. 45. 11 ff.
Bṛh. XXV. 55 ff. Y. S. II. 135 Vi. S. XVII 4 ff if there are no sons and the mother is dead then the daughter inherits father's wealth Nārada XIII. 50.
2. Mbh. XIII. 45. 11 ff. cp. M. IX. 130-131.
3. Mbh. XIII. 45. 11, 12, 14.
4. Mbh. XIII. 44. 15 cp. M. III. 11.
5. Mbh. I. 75. 8. अभिसंदधे। M. IX. 127-129

अनेन तु विधानेन पुरा चक्रेऽथ पुत्रिका ।

But Mbh. XIII. 44. 15 and M. IX. 136 recognizes any brotherless girl as Putrika.
6. Mbh. XIII. 45. 14 अन्यत्र जामया सार्धं प्रजानां पुत्र ईहते ।

दुहिताऽन्यत्र जातेन पुत्रेणापि विशिष्यते ।

P. C. Roy's Eng. Tr. of Anu. Parva page 24.

overlooked even after the birth of a brother. It also implied that in case she was not so invested, she inherited nothing from her father in a similar condition. These property rights of women were well guarded. According to the Rāmāyaṇa one who steals the wealth that belongs to a woman is destroyed with his good works.[1] In the Great Epic the king is advised not to take wealth from the weeping women.[2]

Rights of daughter's son

The Arthaśāstra law, that there was no difference between son and daughter's son was also recognised by the composers of the Anuśāsana.[3] Manu echoing the same spirit slightly differs by stating that there was no difference between a son's son and a daughter's son.[4] Jaisawal's statement that on this definite point Maurya law was made absolute for all ages and Manu introduced the Artha law into Dharma[5] applies to the composer of the Anuśāsana also. The difference is that while Kauṭilya allows these rights only to the son of appointed Putrikā, Manu and the composer of the Anuśāsana concede it to the sons of all brotherless daughters, irrespective of appointment.

In case of Asura marriage which was definitely discouraged in the later didactic portions, the son of the daughter thus sold could neither inherit nor perform the funeral rites of his maternal grand father. As the father had sold the daughter he had no rights over her property.[6] The reasons forwarded for recognizing a brotherless daughter's right as an heir are that her son continued the lineage and offered Śrāddha[7] for her father's line. The daughter's son although a "Bhinna-

1. Rām. VII. 52. (2 Prakshipta). 48.
2. Mbh. XIII. 61. 25 न रुदन्ती धनं हरेत् ।
3. Mbh. XIII. 45. 13 पुत्रदौहित्रयोरेव विशेषो नास्ति धर्मतः ।
cp. Śyamsastry's Eng. Tr. of 'Arthaśāstra of Kauṭilya" BK. III. Chap. VII. Sutra 164.
4. cp. M. IX. 133 पौत्रदौहित्रयोर्लोके न विशेषोऽस्तिधर्मतः ।
M. IX. 139 पौत्रदौहित्रयोर्लोके विशेषो नोपपद्यते ।
5. Jaiswāl, K.P. "Manu and Yājyawalka" Tagore law lectures series Lecture no. XII. page 259 line 16 ff.
6. Mbh. XIII. 45. 15.
7. Mbh. XIII. 45. 13 cp. Nārada Dāyabhag 13. 47 is the same, while Yājwalka and Vishnū S. 18 recognize her right after the widow of the deceased. (Smṛtisandharbha page 437) Kaṇe "Hist. of Dh." Vol. III. Chapt. XXVII page 645 chart about the kind of sons.

gotra" was a near "Sapiṇḍa" and the religious efficacy of the funeral rights (Śrāddha) offered by him gave him a high position among the heirs, not only according to the Mahābhārata but according to other texts also.[1] Thus the right conceded to the daughter's son to inherit was by virtue of his mother's position as Putrikā.

Inheritance of sons influenced by mother

So far the property rights of married women and daughters have been discussed. Their rights of inheriting kingdoms has already been referred to (page 231) elsewhere in the chapter. It would not be out of point here to state that although the widow did not inherit herself, her caste did affect the inheritance of her sons.[2] In a similar way, out of the twelve kinds of sons any of those born of one's own wife could be heirs and could succeed to the property of the 'Bandhus', while even an adopted son was not to do so, a system which was quite in keeping with the custom of Niyoga.[3]

Conclusion

It is very difficult to draw any definite conclusion about the attitude of society towards women. The Epic writers viewed this problem from different points of view. For the race, family happiness and stability woman was an asset. Therefore she was to be respected and honoured. As she was assigned inherently a weak character she was to be protected by men. This protection at first was advantageous to her and accorded many privileges, rights and liberties. The women in the narrative parts of the Epics are depicted as quite independent. They wielded influence on men and matters of the day. An intellectual minority was in favour of their active participation in the public administration. Even the seclusion practised by the ladies of the royal house-hold was not for restricting their liberty and freedom of movement but it was an indicator of their respectability.

In the redacted parts of the Epic with too much stress on asceticism and chastity the primitive idea of woman as

1. M. IX. 131-132; Nārada XII. 43.
2. Mbh. XIII. 47 (sec.).
3. Mbh. I. 120. 34. of Śyāmśāstry's tr. of "Arthaśāstra" of Kauṭilya BK. III. chap. 7 Śutra 164.

temptress, possession and property of the man gained ground. Thus she was either to be avoided or like chattel to be kept completely under control. This finally led to the theory of her perpetual tutelage. Inferior intellectual capacity, greater vanity and weaker sexual instinct, supposedly the inherent traits of her character were the reasons forwarded for the loss of her rights, liberties and intellectual freedom. This character was, however, not simply based on biological facts and organic defects as the composers would have us believe but may have been later developed due to the cultural pattern of society which denied all intellectual, educational, religious and property rights to women. This degradation of the woman in society[1] naturally led to her deterioration in character and was rather the result than the cause of her downfall. It must, however, be noticed that the intellectuals did never forget women's assets and considered it a great thing to gain their favour, or popularity among them. As legislators they, inspite of their background which made them condemn women, were realizing the harm done to them in many spheres. Thus they conceded rights of inheritance to the brotherless daughter and gradually developed the idea of Strīdhana. They also preached that good women were like goddesses of prosperity, lights of homes and were to be respected.

1. Mbh. XIII. 106. 36 ff The whole chapter indicates that the woman was regarded as an object of enjoyment.

CHAPTER XI

SOME IMPORTANT WOMEN CHARACTERS OF THE EPICS—AN ESTIMATE

The heroines of the Epics are still considered as the torch-bearers guiding Indian womanhood on the ideal path. Their stories are so popular, so common that they are narrated in every Hindū house-hold in India even now. Although it is useless to narrate these stories here, still their deeds are such as will help us to evaluate the position and influence of women in the society when the Epics were written. Their glory is that of a perpetual blooming flower spreading its sweetness far and wide, and it has not lost its freshness even in the modern age.

Draupadī

Among the women of the Great Epic, Draupadī's character is the most striking. In order to make her appear more extra-ordinary the author introduces a miracle. She is not born like ordinary human mortals but arises from the sacrificial altar. Along with the event an incorporeal voice is heard that she is born to achieve the purpose of gods, is the incarnation of Śrī and will be the cause of the destruction of many Kshatriyas and a great danger for the Kauravas.[1] This miracle may have been introduced to show her greatness, and the strength with which she was endowed.[2]

Her Beauty

Her captivating beauty possessed all the auspicious signs but to make it more impressive it has been said that her body emitted fragrance like that of a blue lotus which permeated a distance of two miles.[3] The figure and beauty of woman in the Epics have great importance for her destiny apart from conquest over the hearts of men.[4] The Pāṇḍavas were

1. Mbh. I. 167. 44-49.
2. Mbh. III. 239.9 यज्ञसेनस्य दुहिता तेज एव तु केवलम् । II. 81. 13.
3. Mbh. I. 67. 157; I. 167. 44 ff.
4. Cp. Rām. VI. 48. 2 ff; Mbh. V. 116. 2 ff; XII. 320. 73.

attracted towards her even by the account of her beauty.[1] At her Swayamvara kings and later Jayadratha, Kīchaka, Sudeshṇā, Kotika and Kulinda were captivated by her beauty at first sight; some paid eloquent tributes and others had to suffer for the deeds they committed in order to possess her person.[2]

Her Education and character

She had her education through learned Brāhmaṇas in her father's court.[3] Her first utterance shows that at the time of her Swayamvara her individuality and personality had fully developed and her ideas were mature and fixed. She was not a submissive "Vīraśulkā" to be given away to any winner who could fulfil the prescribed condition. With her delicate beauty she combined an iron will, and thus could pronounce her choice firmly.[4]

Polyandry

We have already discussed her polyandry elsewhere[5]; here it will suffice that as the custom was rather unfamiliar to the Kurus, she had to suffer on account of this, for Karṇa thought that a woman practising polyandry could be insulted.[6] Inspite of this, she has been regarded as one of the "Pancha Kanyās", who, if remembered, purge one of great sins.[7] It was not with the number of husbands that the ancient liberal society was bothered but it appreciated the faithfulness with which these husbands were loved and served by Draupadī, through thick and thin, despite her weakness for Arjuna. She was in no way to be blamed for the polyandry she had to contract.

A good housewife

Draupadī was given the charge of the house-hold by Kuntī as soon as she entered the potter's house after her Swayam-

1. Mbh. I. 168. 1; Mbh. II. 65. 33 ff. (Yudhishṭhira's tribute).
2. Mbh. I. 187. 3; III. 264. 12 ff. III. 265. 1 ff also sloka 7-8; III. 157. 5 ff; III. 11. 17 ff. IV 14. 4 ff; IV. 9. 10 ff.
3. Mbh. III. 32. 60 ff.
4. Mbh. I. 187. 23.
5. Supra chapter on Marriage Part II p. 94-96.
6. Mbh. II. 68. 35-36
7. अहल्या द्रौपदी सीता, तारा मन्डोदरी तथा ।
पंचकन्याः स्मरेन्नित्यं महापातकनाशिनीः ।।
as quoted in 'भक्तिमार्ग प्रदीप'—प्रातस्मरणीय श्री समर्थसदन मुंबई ४ ।

vara.[1] She herself states the details of her house-management,[2] and making some allowance for exaggerations it may be taken as an authentic account, for even her great enemy Duryodhana bears testimony to her perfect management.[3] Towards the elders and specially towards her mother-in-law her reverence was so great that despite her having many slave girls she herself used to pound unguents for Kuntī.[4] She also looked after the snātaka-Brāhmaṇa-guests. To her slaves, her treatment must have been affectionate as some of them followed her even to the forest. Due to her excellent management her husbands were free from the care of their possessions.

Intellectual Attainments

It is due to her intellectual attainments that Draupadī appears unique among the Epic heroines. In the face of calmities she does not lose the balance of her mind and her reasoning power, even when clad only in a single piece of cloth she was brought before the court. Such were her perfect arguments that no body except Vidura and Vikarṇa possessed the courage, in the Kaurava court, to reply to her question. In those excited moments, she did not forget her manners and saluted those Kuru elders[5] who had not the courage to check the evil.[6] Even if in their opinion she was a slave won at the stake, there was no justification for the treatment meted out to her. This incident is really a blot on Kuru culture or the Epic culture. Due to the efficacy of her prayer she is again saved by a miracle.[7] She then saves her husbands from slavery.

Most interesting and thought-provoking is her discussion on the qualities of anger and forgiveness. To her Yudhishṭhira's forgiveness does not appear to be a Kshatriya virtue,[8] and

1. Mbh. I. 192. 4 ff.
2. Mbh. III. section 233.
3. Mbh. II. 52. 48.
4. Mbh. IV. 20. 23-24.
5. Mbh. I. 69. 1-2.
6. Mbh. X. II. 15-16; Mbh. XIV. 80. 41. for even if the Kuru elders were powerless against the obstinate Duruyodhana, they could have walked out of the court, or sat on Prāyā, as even the ladies used to do so in those days when they wanted to achieve something impossible.
7. Mbh. II. 68. 41-49 which can be interpreted as Kṛshṇa himself came and saved the situation or to the faithful, miracles do help. These passages have been considered interpolated in the Cr. ed. of Mbh. B.O.R.I.
8. Mbh. III. section 27 and 28.

when Yudhishṭhira extols forgiveness,[1] she appeals to the Creator who has clouded his sense.[2] In poverty and misfortune she doubts the justice of God,[3] but in her discussion Yudhishṭhira smells atheism[4] and tells her not to doubt. Hopkins here wrongly thinks that she then recants her opinion and therefore the section seems to him an interpolation.[5] She only acknowledges that due to sorrow she indulged in lamentations and she does not mean to disregard God or religion; but is still a believer in Karma (action), and goads Yudhishṭhira to action, through which, it is her firm conviction, success is achieved.[6] The whole discussion proves that she had knowledge of old traditions, history and the Purāṇas.[7] She is not silenced as Hopkins thinks, but he is right in stating that "She reminds one of the scene of the Upanishads where learned women cope successfully with men in display." Many times she points out the right path to Yudhishṭhira. She does not mind being disagreeable to her husbands and condemns them constantly when they fail in performance of their duties, even though such behaviour does not accord to later ideals which are preached through her by the composers.[8] Knowing that Karṇa was the brother of the Pāṇḍavas, Yudhishṭhira is ready to renounce the kingdom, but Draupadī, who had lost all her sons, is a queen to the core and thinks it to be the duty of a king and the Kshatriya to govern the kingdom and reminds him of his duty.[9]

A True Kshatriyā

True to her kshatriyā tradition, a woman of energy, Draupadī always wants to punish the offenders[10] but at the same time she is not dogmatic. She is pleased and orders the release of Jayadrath, once he has admitted that he is a

1. Mbh. III. 29.
2. Mbh. III. 30. 1.
3. Mbh. III. 30. 21 ff.
4. Mbh. III. section 31.
5. Hopkins "Religions of India" pages 384 to 386 about Mbh. III. 32. These chapters are not considered interpolated in the Cr. ed. of Mbh.
6. Mbh. III. 32. 11-12. 13 ff.
7. Mbh. III. 28. 1 ff. III. 30. 21 ff.
8. Mbh. III. 30. 32; XII. 14. 6 Contrast Mbh. III. 233-234.
9. Mbh. XII. 14. 6 ff; from secs. 12-16 Yudhishṭhira's brothers persuade him.
10. Mbh. III. 271. 45; X. 11. 20 ff.

slave of the Pāṇḍavas. She even forgives Aśwatthāmā the murderer of her sons, after the gem had been taken from him and allows him to be set free, for he is the son of the preceptor, and therefore to be revered. Her anger is that of a true Kshatriyā for it aims at humiliation of the offender, thus showing him the right path. In these cases her husbands do not take the revenge she wanted but she gives up understanding and respecting Yudhishṭhira's wishes. In the case of Kīchaka she had no other way, for the Pāṇḍavas had to remain in secret exile and so he could only be got rid of by murder.[1]

As an adviser of her husbands

Often she acted as an inspirer of her husbands[2] and it was her insult and her words which finally goaded even a peace-loving man like Yudhishṭhira to war. At the meeting at Upaplava in the council of war everyone including the fiery Bhīma, was for peace and forgiveness but Draupadī was adamant and denounced the policy of reconciliation. She discusses with flaming zeal and determination and her words carry due weight.[3] She had sworn her revenge and Kṛshṇa promises annihilation of the Kauravas.[4] Kuntī has full faith in Draupadī's guidance and sends a message through Śrī Kṛshṇa for the Pāṇḍavas to tread a path that may be pointed out by her.[5] It was Droṇa's firm belief that as truthful Draupadī was guiding the Pāṇḍavas they were sure to win.[6] Perhaps it was for the high opinion Droṇa held about Draupadī that Duryodhana thinks the former is not fighting well due to his sympathetic attitude towards her.[7] In the Great Epic she has always been referred to in glowing terms as conversant with duty, observant in practice, and Brahmavādinī, here it means knower of reality.[8]

Faith in prayer

Although she had full faith in action, she had faith in the

1. Mbh. III. 271. 43; 272. 8-18; X. 16. 34 ff. IV. 23. 5 ff.
2. Mbh. III. 11. 55.
3. Mbh. V. 82. 35-42; X. 16. 26 ff.
4. Mbh. V. 82. 48-49; III. 12. 128 ff; 51. 36 ff; 235. 4 ff.
5. Mbh. V. 90. 80.
6. Mbh. V. 139. 18.
7. Mbh. VII. 159. 87.
8. Mbh. III. 1. 6; IV. 1. 3; XII. 14. 4. VII. 197. 9.

efficacy of prayer also. Her prayers were always answered. Towards Kṛshṇa her attitude is that of a friend and devotee.[1] She worshipped him as an incarnation of Vishṇu and yogin.[2] Her character is drawn with true human weaknesses. The redactors put different words in her mouth in advising Satyabhāmā to depict her as a docile pativratā yet she is at times jealous and has her own independence.[3]

She was in reality the embodiment of Srī, i.e. prosperity for the Pāṇḍavas. Her courage to face calamities, her indignation against offenders, her loftiness in forgiving them, all point to her majestic qualities. As a true partner of her husbands she followed them to the forest[4] just as in the pleasure garden, and was a true helpmate to them. If she finds happiness in the love she gives, she also wants recompense[5] and endangers Bhīma's life just for a Saugandhikā flower. Here she has no scruples like Sītā, who makes a request hesitating and thinking that she has no right to trouble her husband.[6] She is the best example of famous verse of Kālidās about a perfect wife. "A good housewife, wise counsellor, dear companion and a beloved pupil in the acquisition of fine art."[7]

Kuntī, her maidenhood

According to the composer of the Great Epic, Kuntī was the incarnation of Siddhi,[8] she was both success as well as embodiment of steadfastness and resolution for her sons. As a child she was given by her father Śūra to his cousin Kuntībhoja for adoption, a fact which she did not like.[9] This may have been due to the natural love and affection for one's own parents or to any other reasons best known to her. She was an excellent hostess and even while a maiden she pleased the bad tempered

1. Mbh. V. 82. 21; Mbh. III. 12. 127.
2. Mbh. II. 68. 42-44. According to critical ed. of Sabhā (BORI) Parva this prayer is an interpolation.
3. Mbh. III. 233. 19-20 advises Satyabhāmā but acts contrary cp. Mbh. I. 221. 16-18; Mbh. IV. 24. 21-22; III. 264. 8.
4. Mbh. II. 79. 3.
5. Mbh. III. 146. 5-7.
6. Rām. III. 43. 21.
7. Kālidasa Raghuvanśa VIII. 67. गृहिणी सचिवः सखी मिथः प्रियशिष्या ललिते कला-विधौ ।
8. Mbh. I. 67. 60; I. 1. 100.
9. Mbh. V. 90. 62-64.

Durvāsā so much that he granted her a boon for her services.[1] But by experimenting on the validity of the boon due to her girlish inquisitiveness she had to suffer life-long agony, and in order to save her own and her father's honour she had to throw away Karṇa into the river.[2] May be for this fault alone, it became difficult to procure a husband for her later.[3]

As a wife

At the Swayamvara, Kuntī chose Pāṇḍu but we know very little of her as a wife. She along with Mādrī left the pleasures of the palace to follow her husband into the forest. Her Niyogas, her generosity towards Mādrī and ultimate jealousy have already been referred to elsewhere.[4]

Kuntī, the mother

As a mother we find her perfect,[5] but she had more torments than joys of motherhood as her lot.[6] She is an ideal mother, who wants her sons to die gloriously in the war rather than live in infamy. Her inspiring message quoting Vidulā's story, reminding Kṛshṇa of the insults of Draupadī in the Kuru court and giving him counsel for war[7] has been described in detail elsewhere. For each of her sons her exhortation is dignified, worthy of a Kshatriyā mother.[8]

Kuntī and Karṇa

There is a deep sense of pity felt by the reader in Kuntī's affection towards Karṇa, her helplessness in checking the impending combat between Arjuna and Karṇa and thus fainting. Her joy at Karṇa's coronation excites the feelings of tenderness and pity.[9] Most agoinsing is her attempt to win him over to his brothers. She does not, of course, deserve the

1. Mbh. I. 111. 4 ff; Mbh. III. 303-305; Mbh. XV. 30. 2 ff.
2. Mbh. I. 111. 22; Mbh. III. 308. 6-9 Mbh. XV. 30.15.
3. Mbh. I. 112. 2 तां तु तेजस्विनीं कन्यां रूपयौवनशालिनीम् ।
व्यावृण्वन्पार्थिवाः केचिदतीव स्त्रीगुणैर्युताम् ॥
4. Supra Chaps. on "Niyoga" and "Married life."
5. Mbh. I. 129. 11 ff; I. 156. 13.
6. Mbh. I. 137. 23; I. 151. 23. see for further details the chapter on "The Mother" pp. 150-511.
7. Mbh. V 90. 86 ff; 132-136 (section)
8. Mbh. V. 137. 1 ff; XV. 17 (sec.)
9. Mbh. I. 136. 27 ff; 137.23.

rebuke she gets from Karṇa,[1] who still respects her and keeps up his promise of not killing any of the Paṇḍavas except Arjuna, although he had ample opportunity and valour to do so.[2] After the war and Karṇa's death, Kuntī is not able to contain her sorrow. Prompted by the motive to perform Karṇa's last rites, she discloses the fact of Karṇa's birth to her sons and thus gets a curse from Yudhishṭhira for the whole womanhood.[3] To the end of her life she is tormented by the agony of the fact of Karṇa's birth, and discloses it to Vyāsa.[4] Vyāsa does not seem to mind the fact and consoles her.[5] Her relations with and feelings for Karṇa[6] are testimony of the fact that even when motherhood is cursed by the society, it is irresistible, sublime and pure.

Indifferent to the changes of fortune

Her greatness lay in the fact that she was utterly indifferent to the changes of fortune, which had been often her lot. To instil courage in her sons she goaded them to war and then left them in their prosperity for performing her duties.[7] The parting words of advice to her sons not only contain the true spirit of her whole life but are also an epitome of the teachings of the Great Epic "let thy understanding be always devoted to righteousness; let thy mind be always great."[8]

Gāndhārī

Gāndhārī was one of the noblest examples of an ideal mother and woman. She was in reality the incarnation of understanding, judgement, intellect and good sense.[9] Only

1. Mbh. V. 146. 4 ff.
2. Mbh. VII. 139. 92; VII. 167. 20; VIII. 49. 52.
3. Mbh. XII. 6. 11-12; XI. 27. 7 ff.
4. Mbh. XV. 30. 15 ff. Incidently confession was considered a sort of purification in the Epics. Mbh. III. 200. 82

वाक्शौचं कर्मशौचं च यच्च शौचं जलात्मकम् ।
त्रिभिः शौचैरुपेतो यः स स्वर्गी नात्र संशयः ॥

Mbh. III. 207. 51-52.
Mbh. XII. 267. 14.

5. Mbh. XV. 30. 21 ff.
6. Mbh. I. 136. 27 ff. I. 137. 23. XV. 30. 15 ff.
7. Mbh. XV. 17-18 (sec.)
8. Mbh. XV. 17. 21 धर्मे ते धीयतां बुद्धिर्मनस्तु महदस्तु च ।
9. Mbh. I. 67. 60.

once, to our thinking, her great sacrifice lacked understanding.[1] Otherwise even when her sons were heading towards the great calamity, she remained attached to the cause of justice and righteousness.

Her Maidenhood

Bhīshma had heard about her piety and beauty.[2] She had pleased the great god Śiva and got the boon for obtaining a hundred sons.[3] Her father hesitated a little when he received the proposal of her marriage to Dhṛtarāshṭra on account of his blindness, but considering the family of the prince he consented.[4] Thenceforward, Gāndhāri denied herself the pleasure of eyesight.[5]

Human weaknesses

Even such a great character, with high sense of justice and morality, with great qualities of intellect and understanding, is completely human, full of human virtues and frailties. She is rather greedy for sons. She had already received a boon from Mahādeva, but by pleasing Vyāsa she got the same boon again.[6] She is jealous of Kuntī's motherhood.[7] Her longing for a daughter and a son-in-law in order to attain heaven by having a daughter's son indicates her yearning not only for a daughter[8] and son-in-law but for a seat in heaven as well.

Sense of Justice

Never did she approve of the conduct of her sons towards the Pāṇḍavas. The Pāṇḍavas, particularly Yudhishṭhira had great respect for her and due to the regard the Pāṇḍavas felt for her they released Jayadratha, evcn after he abducted Draupadī.[9] Gāndhārī together with Vidura requested Dhṛtarāshṭra to release the Pāṇḍavas, recounting the various ill omens to him.[10] She even advised Dhṛtarāshṭra to abandon

1. Supra Chap. on "Maiden and her education" p. 31.
2. Mbh. I. 110. 9 ff.
3. Mbh. I. 110. 9-10.
4. Mbh. I. 110. 12.
5. Mbh. I. 110. 14.
6. Mbh. I. 115. 7-8.
7. Mbh. I. 115. 10-12.
8. Mbh. I. 116. 10-13.
9. Mbh. III. 271. 43.
10. Mbh. II. 75. 1 ff; II. 71. 24 ff.

Duryodhana. A greater sacrifice cannot be expected of a mother for here Gāndhāri considers the interest of humanity far greater, than the life of her son. Later on, when Dhṛtarāshṭra and other Kuru elders were not able to persuade Duryodhana to accept the peace proposals of Krshṇa, Dhṛtarāshṭra calls for Gāndhārī, for he thinks that in case she is not able to bring him to the right path no one else can do so. She appears before the court, her advice is full of wisdom and shows her knowledge of state-craft.[1] She even suggests the division of the kingdom.[2] Her voice was that of warning but her advice falls on deaf ears.

Her Powers

Everybody was aware of the power she gained through penances and asceticism. She is thus considered capable of giving great boons and pronouncing great curses. Duryodhana daily went to see her to seek her blessings and inspite of his repeated requests she only wished victory for the righteous cause.[3] Yudhishṭhira is scared of her curse after the war and sends Vāsudeva to console her. Śrīkṛshṇa tells her that the calamity occurred due to her and Dhṛtarāshṭra's fault and also reminds her of her wishes (for the victory of rignteous cause) which were accomplished. Her heart becomes steady and she sends Kṛshṇa to save the Pāṇḍavas from Aśwatthāmā.[4] Vyāsa also exerts his influence and requests her not to curse the Pāṇḍavas reminding her of her erstwhile wishes.[5]

Her power of penances is said to be so great that when she directed her gaze to the tip of Yudhishṭhira's toes, it is said those at once got scorched. She could see the pathetic scene of the battle field through her spiritual eye, by the grace of Vyāsa's boon. It was natural for a mother to lose her sense of forgiveness at the sight. She blames Kṛshṇa for the carnage, as he did not exert himself enough for peace. She cursed Kṛshṇa and he bowed down quietly before her will, for was not her complaint a real one when Kṛshṇa himself had sworn to Draupadī the complete annihilation of the Kauravas ?

1. Mbh. V. 129. 2 ff.
2. Mbh. V. 129. 42-44.
3. Mbh. XI. 14. 8. XI. 17. 6-7.
4. Mbh. IX. 63. 75.
5. Mbh. XI. 14. 7.

Gāndhārī's magnanimity and the Pāṇḍava family

She does not blame the Pāṇḍavas for killing her sons; such was her equanimity, but her grievance against Bhīma was for the wrong done by him. He had transgressed the rules in killing her son[1] and had quaffed the blood of his cousin like a savage. Her pathetic plea is that the Pāṇḍavas could have spared one of her sons, whose fault was comparatively less, as a crutch to the blind couple. It was really difficult for such a saintly character as Gāndhārī to understand that war has nothing to do with the human idea of pity, justice and consideration. The Pāṇḍavas could not have spared any claimant to the throne of the Kauravas. Yet for Gāndhārī for whom Kuntī and Draupadī were not the mother and the wife of her sons' murderers but women who had suffered losses like her, this was a little difficult to understand.

While envisaging the scene of carnage Gāndhārī's sympathies for Uttarā and Draupadī are the same as for her own daughters-in-law. The Pāṇḍavas and their ladies revered her for her greatness but Bhīma did maintain a grudging attitude towards the old couple. Although Dhṛtarashṭra was grieved by those insults, Gāndhārī, an adept in duty, was not shaken by them for she considered them untrue. All her demands for performance of Śrāddhas of her sons and for giving away gifts,[2] are generously granted by Yudhishṭhira. For full sixteen years she lives at Hastināpura and then with Dhṛtarashṭra and others leaves for Vānaprastha. Her final farewell to the people is full of pathos, and after performing severe austerities she dies in a forest conflagration.

Her life was that of penance, self-abnegation and of righteousness. She is an example of sublime motherhood, which does not hesitate to wish victory for the enemies of her sons for theirs was the right cause. Her weaknesses make her character real and thus render her ideals attainable by ordinary human mortals.

Minor Characters of the Great Epic

The Mahābhārata is not only an encyclopedia dealing with every aspect of ancient Hindu life, but is also rich in

1. Mbh. XI. 15. 4 ff.
2. Mbh. XV. 14. 15; 15. 2.

representations of the various types of womanhood through stories and anecdotes scattered in between the main theme. As it is rather difficult to deal with the life of each character due to lack of space, we will only try to give a summary which will help us to judge their status in society. The foremost qualities of these women are patience, fortitude, self-sacrificing spirit and pātivrata. Some of them are intellectuals aspiring for the highest reality.

Śakuntalā

Śakuntalā is a different type of woman. She was a simple country girl, who thought that her interest was fully secured when she exacted from king Dushyanta the promise to make her son his heir. Later at the court, when the king denied having married her, she utters some eloquent verses showing the importance and rights of a wife. It throws light on her education on social subjects such as the Āśramas. But when Dushyanta sticks to his course, she disclaims him and considers truth to be higher than such a husband. She is proud of her lineage and her retort to him is dignified and spirited. She does not spare him the harsh words that he deserved just because he was her husband,[1] and presents a sharp contrast to Kālidāsa's timid and delicate Śakuntalā.

Vidulā

Vidulā represents a true Kshatriyā mother. After the defeat of her worthless son she does not take up the leadership of her country. Such a Kshatriyāṇī was quite capable of leading the armies to victory, but she knew that she was no more the queen but the queen mother who had to fulfil her mission by inspiring her son and teaching him the true duty of a Kshatriya, who was to die for the protection of his people rather than to live as a defeated and dependent prince.[2]

Gautamī and others

Gautamī and Upamanayu's mother are the examples of Brāhmaṇi-mothers, for whom revenge and desire for worldly objects were sinful and who were resigned to fate.[3] Although from the modern point of view we may not appreciate the

1. Mbh. I. 74. 82 ff.
2. Mbh. V. 134-136 (sections).
3. Mbh. XIII. 1 (section); 14 (section).

hospitality offered by Oghāvatī,[1] Kauśikī[2] and Rukmiṇī,[3] to the Brāhmaṇas and ṛshis, yet according to the ideals of those times they were ideal hostesses who achieved the pinnacle of their object. The sacrificing spirit of Jaratkāru, Lopāmudrā and Sukanyā has been referred to elsewhere.[4]

Sulabhā

Sulabhā is the intellectual type who visited Janaka's court having heard in the course of her wanderings that he was well versed in the knowledge of emancipation. She is not perturbed by the rebuke of king Janaka. Her calm reply is remarkable, indicating her knowledge, understanding, depth of thought as well as her grasp of various subjects of intellectual and philosophic import. The renowned king Janaka had to recognize her superiority in wisdom by keeping silent.[5]

Sītā

Sītā has been immortalised through Vālmīki's Rāmāyaṇa. According to R. C. Dutta[6]; "There is not a Hindū woman in the length and breadth of India to whom the story of the sufferings of Sītā is not known, and to whom her character is not a model to strive after and to imitate..." Among the galaxy of Epic heroines she shines with her own peculiar lustre. She was also like Draupadī created by divine power.[7] As she was received from the furrow by king Janaka she was named Sītā.[8] Her captivating beauty possessed all auspicious marks.[9] She was gifted with remarkable qualities of head and heart. Janaka decided that her dower was to be paid in the form of valour.[10] He gave his daughter to Rāma stating that Sītā was henceforth his partner in religious performances and she would follow him like a shadow.

1. Mbh. XIII. 2. 53 ff.
2. Mbh. XIII. 52-56 (sections).
3. Mbh. XIII. 159 27 ff.
4. Supra Chap. on "Maid, Her Status and Education" pp. 20-21.
5. Mbh. XII. 320 (sec.).
6. Dutt. R. C. "History of civilization in Ancient India" Vol. I. p. 143.
7. Rām. I. 1. 26.
8. Rām. I. 67. 13-16; II. 118. 28-32.
9. Rām. V. 29; Rām. VI. 48. 5 ff.
10. Rām. I. 67. 16; II. 118. 38-42.

Her intellectual attainments

Of Sītā's intellectual attainments, which were partly imparted through religious education, there is ample evidence. She was not only literate,[1] but was also well acquainted with the Sanskrit spoken by ordinary people and also with that spoken by cultured Brāhmaṇas.[2] She could quote moral tales and Smṛtis and was well versed in the traditional lore, the Purāṇas and Itihāsa.[3] In her parental home, there was an intellectual atmosphere and she used to meet ascetic women, astrologers and Brāhmaṇas.[4] While advising Rāma, she quotes the story of Indra and an ascetic.[5] In order to desist Hanumān from killing the Rākshasīs, she cites another story of the Brāhmaṇa and the bear.[6] She was also well versed in kingly duties and statecraft,[7] and it must have been due to this fact that Vasiṣṭha could propose that in Rāma's absence she could administer the kingdom.[8]

Religious education

Janaka, who meant Sītā to be a true Sahadharmiṇī, must have imparted to her religious education. Daśaratha commanded Rāma to perform all the necessary religious rites before his installation in company with Sītā and she did accordingly.[9] She must have performed Vedic prayers regularly[10] and was well acquainted with the rituals of the time. Before Rāma departed for Daśaratha's palace she performed certain auspicious rites.[11] Along with Rāma and Lakshmaṇa, she took part in Dasaratha's śrāddha.[12] Like all women she also had premonitions; for example, she did not like going to Daṇḍaka and it ultimately led to the tragedy of her life. Here her intuition was at work.[13]

1. Rām. V. 36. 2-4.
2. Rām. V. 30. 17-19.
3. Rām. VI. 113. 41 ff; V. 24. 9-12.
4. Rām. II. 29. 8-9, 11, 13.
5. Rām. III. 9 (section).
6. Rām. VI. 113. 42-5.
7. Rām. II. 26. 4 अभिज्ञा राजधर्माणां० ।
8. Rām. II. 37. 23-24.
9. Rām. II. 4. 23-24; Rām. II. 4. 36-37; Rām. II. 6. 1-9.
10. Rām. V. 14. 49.
11. Rām. II. 16. 21, 24-25.
12. Rām. II. 103. 20-21.
13. Rām. III. 9. 13.

Some indirect testimonies of her intellectual education are provided by the similes that have been used for her in the Rāmāyaṇa. In case she was uneducated these would seem ironical, which was not the case.[1] When Rāvaṇa could not reply to her arguments and when he realised that she was not going to listen to him, he calls her "a proud learned but foolish person."[2] He realised fully that she was a learned lady. It has also been said of Sītā that like Śruti following Brahmā she followed Vālmīkī.[3] In the Rāmāyaṇa Sīta talks in the language spoken by the learned.[4]

The knowledge of pātivrata ideals

Although in practice her whole life was that of an ideal pativratā, certain passages uttered by her show her deep knowledge of the subject.[5] At her parental home she received education on this subject from her mother and then from the Brāhmaṇas, expert in Śruti and later from her mother-in-law Kausalyā.[6] In her forest exile pativratās like Anusūyā also educated her. She was nurtured in traditional stories of ancient pativratās[7] whom she often quoted, e.g. Sāvitrī, Arundhatī, Damayantī, Lopamudrā, Śachī, Sukanyā, Keśinī, Madayantī.[8] The gods[9] and even those like Kausalyā and Agastya, who were harsh judges of women, admire her devotion to her husband,[10] and think her to be the foremost of the pativratās. Her character shows the fine mingling of the conception of Sahadharmiṇī and pativratā. Although the composer due to the idealist tone, wanted to show her as a docile wife, she is not a pativratā of the slave type; had she been Rāma's shadow-like follower, she would have stayed back at Ayodhyā according to Rāma's wishes. She decides the course of her duty without consulting her husband and her mother-in-law. Nothing, not even the great dangers and difficulties of forest life described by Rāma,

1. Rām. V. 15. 31-37; 19. 10-15; Rām. VII. 96. 12.
2. Rām. VI. 31. 17.
3. Rām. VII. 96. 12.
4. Rām. V. 21. 17 व्रतस्नातस्य विद्येव विप्रस्य विदितात्मनः । Rām. V. 28. 5
5. Rām. II. 27 and 29 (sec.); II. 118. 2 ff.
6. Rām. II. 118. 8 ff; Rām. II. 39. 24 ff; II. 118.7.
7. Rām. II. 30. 6. II. 118. 210.
8. Rām. V. 24. 9. 12.
9. Rām. VI. 118. 2 ff.
10. Rām. II. 39. 20-3; III. 13. 3 ff.

could shake her resolve. When her assurances to Rāma that she will enjoy all the difficulties and privations of forest life with him fail, she takes up another course, which shows her deep insight into human psychology. Her taunts, that her father married her to a woman, in the form of a man, and Rāma wants to give her away to Bharata, to which she will never agree—touch the core of Rāma's heart and his male pride is hurt.[1] He is so much impressed by her whole discourse that he says her manner is worthy of his and her family and he is prepared to take her with him.[2] All these incidents point out to her independent judgment and action.

Her chastity and powers

Extraordinary powers are attributed to her due to her chastity, the witness of which are shown to be the gods themselves. It is stated that her effluence was such that she could not even be burnt by fire,[3] and could protect others through her prayers.[4] These powers must have been introduced by the poet to impress her chaste character.

True performer of her duties

Sītā could discuss boldly where the performance of her duties was concerned, but she did not persist in matters relating to Rāms'a conduct, for she must have believed in his freedom of action. She was an intelligent partner and whenever she thought that his conduct was not proper, she in order to emphasise and bring the truth home quoted an old story, adopting a perfect teacher's way to illustrate through examples, and also to let matters be finally decided by him.[5]

Gentle disposition

It was also due to Sītā's gentle disposition that when she requested Rāma for the deer-skin she says that it is unseemingly terrible and smacks of wilfulness to command the husband.[6]

1. Rām. II. 30. 3-8.
2. Rām. II. 30. 41.
3. Rām. V. 56. 1 ff. 55. 22.
4. Rām. V. 53. 27-33.
5. Rām. III. 9. 3 ff but in the end she says (*Śloka* 33)
विचार्य बुद्ध्या तु सहानुजेन यद्रोचते तत्कुरु मा चिरेण ।
Same was Kṛshaṇa's way in Gītā after advising Arjuna; Gītā 18. 63.
6. Rām. III. 43. 21.

Her attitude can well be contrasted with that of Draupadī for when she wanted Saugandhika flower to adorn her abode she had no such scruples.[1] Sītā's tenderness of heart and gentle nature is again manifested when Hanūmān suggests that he will take her to Rāma. Although the proposal offered a welcome prospect of meeting Rāma and was very tempting, yet she did not agree to it because she thought that it was only Rāma's right to protect her. She does not state her feelings at once, but gradually discloses them when Hanūmān does not understand her. She had such a deep understanding for others that she pardoned the Rākshasīs who had tormented her, as according to her they were only obeying the commands of their master.[2]

Human Frailties

Despite her idealism, Sītā is intensely human. Her words to Lakshmaṇa were really very harsh but they were uttered when she thought that Rāma's life was in great danger.[3]

Tormented by intense agonies at Lankā through illusions created by the Rākshasas and being treated cruelly by the Rākshasīs she twice thinks of committing suicide,[4] and is only kept away from such resolve by Trijaṭā and Saramā as well as by her faith and hope in Rāma.[5] In such a plight it was natural for her to wish for the destruction of Lankā and the Rākshasas.[6]

Simplicity

May be it was due to her apprehension for Rāma's life that she was not able to understand Rāvaṇa's evil intentions and ulterior motive in his artless description of her beauty.[7] It may be due to other reasons also. For Sītā, simple as she was, it was difficult to understand that a Brāhmaṇa in whose guise Rāvaṇa was, may have such evil intentions. This experience matured her simple nature for when Hanūmān presents himself as a messenger of Rāma she asks for a token from Rāma and Lakshamaṇa, thinking that friendship between men

1. Mbh. III. 146. 7.
2. Rām. VI. 113. 37-41.
3. Rām. III. 45. 5-8, 21-26.
4. Rām. V. 28. 17 ff; 25. 17-20; VI. 32. 30-32 ff.
5. Rām. V. 27. 8; VI. 48. 22 ff; 33. 2 ff; VI. 92. 46 ff.
6. Rām. V. 26. 30.
7. Rām. III. 46. 16 ff.

and the Vānaras was rather strange.[1] She was also suspicious that Hanūmān may be an illusion created by the Rākshasas. After ascertaining the truth of Hanūmān's mission it was natural for her to confront Hanūmān with a volley of questions to know about her dearest, of whom she had not heard since a long time.[2]

Self-sacrificing spirit

Such was her self sacrificing spirit that she had even conquered the instinct of self preservation. When she saw Rāma and Lakshamaṇa being taken away by Virādha, she requested him to eat her up and release them arguing that anyhow she will be eaten up by bears, lions and elephants after she is deprived of their protection.[3]

Presence of mind

At the time of distress she had presence of mind, and without Rāvaṇa's knowledge she threw her ornaments, wrapped in her 'uttarīya', as she saw the Vānaras, thinking that these would provide her intelligence to Rāma.[4] Again when the Rākshasīs inquired about Hanūmān, her reply was that they must be knowing better about the illusions created by the Rākshasas.[5]

Quality of Adjustment

It was for a while when Sītā was about to put on the barks as her dress that she was frightened like a dove looking at the noose, and her eyes were filled with tears.[6] It was quite natural for a princess bred up in luxury, but her subsequent stay at the forest provides testimony to the fact that once the first shock was over, she did not feel out of place or uncomfortable in the forest, for a pativratā of her calibre would feel at home with her husband, in whatever circumstances she was placed.[7] Before her departure she gave away her ornaments to the wife of a Brāhmaṇa Suyajya, to be as light as possible

1. Rām. V. 35. 2 Vānara must have been a race and so we think that it was due to her suspicion that she wanted a proof.
2. Rām. V. 36. 11 ff.
3. Rām. III. 4. 2-3.
4. Rām. III. 54. 1-3.
5. Rām. V. 42. 9 ff.
6. Rām. II. 37. 9 ff.
7. Rām. II. 55. 28 ff.

to lead a simple life in the forest.[1] She also felt quite at home with the ṛshis and their wives.[2] and looked after guests herself.[3]

Aesthetic sense

Her aesthetic sense and keen observation helped her to enjoy the life in the forest. She wanted to know about each tree, plant, bush and creeper.[4] Thus she had the capacity to enjoy in every circumstance, which is the test of true education. She collected beautiful plants and flowers.[5] The same aesthetic sense in her appreciated the uncommon skin of the golden deer, which she wanted for the decoration of her inner apartment in Ayodhyā.[6] She had to pay a heavy price for her love of beauty and decoration to which she (herself) later becomes dead in her sorrow when separated from Rāma.[7]

Her confidence in Rāma's greatness and his sense of duty

Sītā was not just following an ideal, but she was also fully aware that the object of her affection was certainly worthy of it. She could not tolerate when Rāma acted otherwise. This is clear from her speeches when Rāma was not willing to take her to the forest and also before the fire ordeal.[8] She was conscious of his greatness and virtues, had full confidence in his love for her and in his valour,[9] reminding Rāma, how he punished a crow, when it had wounded Sītā. She wanted Rāma to perform his duty[10] of protecting her and tells Hanūmān that she will not die till she comes to know of Rāma's activities.[11] Any amount of temptations from the great king of Lankā failed to win her.[12] She not only advises him to follow the path of duty but constantly reiterates her faith and

1. Rām. II. 32. 7-8.
2. Rām. II. 118 (Section).
3. Rām. III. 46. 32-35.
4. Rām. II. 55. 29.
5. Rām. II. 55. 28-32.
6. Rām. III. 43. 17-18.
7. Rām. V. 15. 20-25; V. 58. 39 also Supra, the dress of "proshitpatikā" in the Chapter "Married life." P. 108.
8. Rām. VI. 116. 5 ff; II. 27. 1 ff. II. 30. 8 ff.
9. Rām. II. 118. 4-5; III. 49. 35, 28.
10. Rām. V. 38. 15 ff.
11. Rām. V. 36. 30; 37. 6.
12. Rām. III. 55. 13 ff; V. 20. 9 ff.

confidence in and love for Rāma.[1] She continues to live in Lankā having faith and hope in Rāma and her ultimate reunion.[2]

Reunion with Rāma

The reunion was still more agonising. Rāma did not go to meet Sita after Rāvaṇa's death, like a long parted lover. After Rāvaṇa's funeral and Vibhīshaṇa's coronation the message sent by Rāma is so cold that one was tempted to think that Rāma wanted her to continue her stay at Lankā.[3] Sītā, however, choked with delight could not utter a word at the prospect of meeting Rāma.[4] She wants to meet him at once but he did not want to see her in the dishevelled condition in which she had lived while separated from him in expectations and hopes and wants her to be brought bathed, painted and decked with ornaments. Like an obedient wife she obeys his commands.[5] A sad and solemn scene follows. Rāma was more worried about his honour after the victory. Sītā faces frustration of all the hopes she had cherished in her exile.[6] Though insulted and injured she does not lose her self-possession and faces the challenge with great dignity. Her reply to Rāma's words is spirited and worthy of a queen. Rāma, she says, had addressed her like a common man addressing a common woman forgetting all her sincerity and blaming her for the facts over which she had no control. Then she wants Lakshmaṇa to prepare her funeral pyre for there was nothing left for her to live for. Rāma gives his silent consent, but it is said that a miracle occurred. The fire-god protects her, other gods with Daśaratha[7] appear and testify to Sītā's purity and Rāma then takes her back.

Her happiness again, though she was crowned as a queen,[8] was short-lived. In her prosperity she did not forget Hanumān's services and rewarded[9] him well.

1. Rām. V. 21. 6 ff; III. 56. 2 ff; 23 and 24 (sec.)
2. Rām. VI. 92. 46 ff.
3. Rām. VI. 113. 13-14.
4. Rām. VI. 113. 48 ff.
5. Rām. VI. 114. 7 ff.
6. Rām. VI. 114. 17 ff. VI. 115. 2 ff.
7. Rām. VI. 116. 1 ff; 117-118 (sections).
8. Rām. VI. 128. 60.
9. Rām. VI. 128. 83.

Her Exile

Rāma again exiled her to save his honour. His conduct was not worthy of a king, much less of a husband. It seems he was in a hurry to save his honour. He did not even inform Sītā of his intentions although if he considered her as Sahadharmiṇī he should have done so. This shows that the rights of even the most loyal wife were not cared for by the almighty husband. Now her plight was worse for she had no hopes of reunion. Despite this, she was ready to perform her duties as a queen and as a wife. Her message to Rāma does not sound so spirited as her words before the fire ordeal. It seems that as a docile wife she submits to his cruel command but here also she stoops to conquer. Her message is indicative of supreme maturity in love that does not seek reciprocation. Even towards such a royal husband, who did not give her the right of hearing, given even to hardened criminals in ordinary courts, she was performing her duty of Sahadharmiṇī. She tells Lakshmaṇa that it was her duty to stop Rāma's ill-fame.[1] As a queen mother of her subjects, she wants the same people—who were not able to appreciate her greatness and for whose opinion she was to suffer in the later period of her life,—to be treated like his brothers by Rāma.[2] She is afraid, lest Rāma's anger, in his lonely moments may fall on them. She is the personification of self-abnegation, who for the fame of her husband and satisfaction of the people sacrifices herself. Although she herself thinks that death is better for her, she lives on to save the royal dynasty of her husband.[3]

Her final Departure

Vālmīki, who through his asceticism was fully aware of her purity and greatness, was more than a father to her in her exile. He had perhaps vowed her restoration as a queen. May be with this object in view, he prepared Lava and Kuśa to sing Rāmāyaṇa before the public on the occasion of Rāma's sacrifice, and thus created public opinion in Sītā's favour.[4] Rāma was ready to take back Sītā, in case she gave proof of her innocence to the public. It seems Sītā's existence had now only one object. She wanted Lava and Kuśa to be recognized

1. Rām. VII. 48. 13.
2. Rām. VII. 48. 14.
3. Rām. VII. 48. 8.
4. Rām. VII. 93 and 94 (sections).

as Rāma's heirs. After they were received by Rāma as his sons and he had also solemnly affirmed before Vālmīki that he believed in Sītā'a purity,[1] she had no desire to live. The great Ṛshi Vālmīki had sworn her innocence before the public.[2] Thus the opinion of sages like him as well as that of Rāma was in her favour. She had now no mind to be the queen of the same people, who after all[3] were responsible for her disgrace. She had given proof of her innocence more than once, and she thought that her life's mission had been fulfilled. Sītā did not go back to Rāma and in her own way gave him a terrible punishment, which he so rightly deserved and which no one else could pronounce on him.[4] Even for the poet it was beyond imagination to unite Sītā, who was now a supreme artist in love through suffering, while Rāma, the best of men was just an amateur.

There can be no better ideal of womanhood than that of Sītā, blending the two opposite ideals of Sahadharmiṇī and gentle wife i.e. pativratā. Gentle, tender and self-sacrificing she was, owing to her dignified suffering, at once a personification of courage endurance and magnanimity. There is no trace of pity or low—spiritedness in her silent suffering which reminds us of Bhavabhūti's dictum, "Vajrādapi kaṭhorāṇi, Mṛdūni kusumādapi"[5] and prompts us to say in the words of Griffith, "And thou, in every heart enshrined, shalt live the best of womankind."[6] Sītā is indeed immortal.

Kausalyā, Sumitrā and Kaikeyī

There is nothing extraordinary about the queens of Daśaratha. They take part in the sacrifice and welcome their daughters-in-law together. But the events that follow after the announcement of Rāma's installation as the heir-apparent show the diverse personality of each, and also the part women played in the palace intrigues. Out of these, Kaikeyī was the most dominating, bold and resourceful. She has been

1. Rām. VII. 97. 3-5.
2. Rām. VII. 96. 16-24.
3. Rām. VII. 97. 3. Rāma also says that it was due to "Lokapavāda" that Sītā was forsaken "Apavāda" is not true it is defamation. It was not "Dosha" as "Nindā" as Rāma had confessed it before public.
4. Rām. VII. 97. 18 ff.
5. Bhavabhūti "Uttara-Rāmcharita" Act II. Verse 7.
6. Griffith. Eng. Translation of Rāmāyaṇa, Book VI. Canto CXXI. page 498 last two lines. Benares 1895.

blamed most for the tragedy of Rāma's exile. But to evaluate her character we will have to digress a little. Palace revolutions in any polygamous society are quite common. She had the weakness of any common woman, i.e., to secure the interest of her only son, for which she went to the extremes. Although not a sublime type of mother like Gāndhārī and Kuntī, the difference between her and Kausalyā is very small. Kausalyā had no power while Kaikeyī had it and misused it. Both failed to understand their sons. The one fails to understand that she was going to initiate a great tragedy, the other completely drowns herself in it. It is only Sumitrā, who is the personification of steadiness and is deep as the ocean, firm as the mountains, and sees men and events in their proper perspective.

Kaikeyī

Kaikeyī, being the most beautiful, youthful and perhaps the only princess among the chief queens, was the favourite queen of Daśaratha.[1] The king was completely under her control. His words while she was in the Krodhā-gāra[2] (anger-room) prove that he was ready to do any injustice for her pleasure.[3] To paint Kaikeyī more cruel than she was, the poet, at the outset, did not mention the fact, that at the time of her wedding her father was given the promise of installing her son as heir by Daśaratha, a fact later disclosed by Rāma.[4] As Rāma had already won the people by his good nature and as he was the eldest son of the eldest queen, according to the law of primogeniture it was his right to succeed, while Kaikeyī had already earned the right for her son. There were these two interests working inside the palace. Daśaratha in his old age realized the injustice of his promise. For mending matters as they stood, he prepared the ground slowly. When Bharata was away a council was called through which Rāma's installation was confirmed. Daśratha was, it seems, in a hurry to perform the ceremony. Therefore Bharata, his maternal grand- father, and to make things appear natural Janaka of Mithilā, were not called, yet it sounds strange that kings from east, west, north, south, and the Mlechas, the Āryans and those who lived beyond

1. Rām. II. 10. 30.
2. Rām. II. 10. 20.
3. Rām. II. 10. 33 ff.
4. Rām. II. 107. 3.

the forests and mountains could be called to witness the ceremony.[1] After giving the good news to Rāma,[2] he dismisses him. Again consulting the ministers, the king commands them to perform the ceremony the very next day.[3] He then again sends for Rāma at once and imparts the information to him. He was certainly not getting old suddenly nor had he decided to join the Vānaprastha mode of life but states that his death was near due to bad stars. The real reason he then discloses. He had faith in Bharata's qualities and his love for Rāma but he says that the feelings of men are not always constant, and he feels danger from Bharata's side and wants Rāma to be protected by his friends.[4] The king is talking about Rāma's friends[5] and as soon as Rāma delivers the good news to Kausalyā, she says that his rivals are defeated.[6] Kausalyā, Sumitrā, Lakshmaṇa and Sītā were all celebrating the event in the temple after the good news.[7] Kausalyā also says that her relatives will now be prosperous and Rāma will please Sumitrā.[8] There is no talk about Kaikeyī, she is excluded even from the good news. Apparently there were two distinct parties inside the palace. Kausalyā's words also indicate that she had suspicions about Rāma's installation and she thinks it was only due to his virtues and to his being born under auspicious stars that the kingdom has become his[9],—not perhaps due to the right, for the right was already promised to Kaikeyī's son, Bharata. After this there were fasts, rites and ceremonies in Rāma's apartment and the whole city was rejoicing but Daśaratha's favourite queen was not informed. If we see the whole plot in this perspective Kaikeyī cannot be blamed much. At the outset, she seems to be simple and magnanimous. When she first came to know about the news from Mantharā, she was pleased and gave her a present for bringing it to her.[10] Rāma

1. Rām. II. 3. 24-25.
2. Rām. II. 3. 39-47.
3. Rām. II. 4. 3.
4. Rām. II. 4. 24-27. Also in Rām. II. 12. 62 Although Daśaratha himself once acknowledges the greatness of Bharata रामादपि हि तं मन्ये धर्मतो बलवत्तरम् ।
5. Rām. II. 4. 24.
6. Rām. II. 4. 39.
7. Rām. II. 4. 30-31.
8. Rām. II. 4. 39.
9. Rām. II. 4. 40.
10. Rām. II. 7. 32.

also believed in her love towards him and thinks it was destiny that made her the instrument of his exile.[1]

Mantharā

Here it will be proper to digress a little to understand the coming events, which were influenced by Mantharā, who was a politician. She understood Daśaratha's policy and calls him a sweet-tounged rogue.[2] When she was not able to persuade Kaikeyī she strikes the right note that Kaikeyī will now have to serve Kausalyā whom she had insulted many times (a fact to which Daśaratha bears testimony[3]) and Kausalyā would now take her revenge.[4] Even after Kaikeyī's statement that Bharata will get the kingdom after Rāma, Mantharā calls her a fool and further explains that Bharata will be cut off from the royal line.[5] Her appeal is psychological, and Kaikeyī is completely won over.

Mantharā is also resourceful enough in instigating Kaikeyī to demand the fulfilment of the two boons. For according to Dharmaśāstras and even according to the Great Epic, one could lie at the time of marriage.[6] So Daśaratha's promise to Keikeyī's father was not of any importance when the people also had voted for Rāma's installation. But it was rather the pious duty of the king to fulfil the boons which he had given to one who had saved his life from danger. Insistance merely on Bharata's installation as her Śulka by Kaikeyī would still leave Rāma in the capital. Now that Rāma has won the heart of the public it would be impossible for Bharata to rule while Rāma was in Ayodhyā. Therefore ample time was needed to make the throne secure for Bhārta. Mantharā knew Kaikeyī's power over the king.[7] Rāma must be sent away. He must be banished. Kaikeyī admired Mantharā so much for her suggestion that she even began to praise her beauty.[8]

Kaikeyī (Continued)

Kaikeyī knew the seriousness of her undertaking and even after Daśaratha had promised to do the needful she invokes the

1. Rām II 22. 16-19.
2. Rām. II. 7. 24.
3. Rām. II. 12.70.
4. Rām. II. 8. 37 दर्पान्निराकृता० ।
5. Rām. II. 8. 21 ff.
6. Mbh. I. 82. 16.
7. Rām. II. 9. 24; Rām. II. 10. 17 ff.
8. Rām. II. 9. 38 ff.

deities as her witnesses and then demands the boons.[1] She wants nothing else but the boons and when the king touches her feet[2] she cites the example of other kings who gave their lives to fulfil their promises[3] and even threatens to poison herself. Once her jealousy towards Kausalyā was aroused she was not going to stop.[4] She did not bother about her fame, and the opinions and feelings of the family and the public.[5] She lies to Sumantrā for she wanted to confirm the boons from Rāma and then only the public was to know about it.[6] The citizens say that they will leave with Rāma and let Kaikeyī rule over empty houses.[7] The king suggests that as he is tied down to his promise, Rāma should over-throw and arrest him and rule.[8] Sumantrā accuses her and says that Kaikeyī had inherited her mother's nature, and cites a story how her mother did not care for her father's life.[9] At the suggestion of Daśaratha that Rāma should take the treasure with him she is aroused.[10] Sidhārtha's arguments did not touch her heart.[11] This shows how far power and ambition could degrade her character. She is unmoved andgives barks to Rāma. Even the pathetic sight of Sītā attempting to put on the barks does not arouse pity in her, although it melts the hearts of all women in the inner apartments.[12] Vaśishṭha recounts the noble traits of her son's character and warns her of Bharata's painful disappointment and strong disapproval of Kaikeyī's action, but she is adamant.[13]

After Rāma's departure Daśaratha leaves her with harsh words that she is neither a wife nor a friend,[14] and does not want his last rites to be performed by Bharata in case he succeeds to the kingdom. She is not only blind to outer influences

1. Rām. II. 11. 13 ff.
2. Rām. II. 12. 36.
3. Rām. II. 12. 42 ff.
4. Rām. II. 12. 45 ff.
5. Rām. II. 12. 71 ff; 35.36 (sections)
6. Rām. II. 14. 60 ff.
7. Rām. II. 33. 21 ff.
8. Rām. II. 34. 26.
9. Rām. II. 35. 4 ff.
10. Rām. II. 36. 2 ff.
11. Rām. II. 36. 18 ff.
12. Rām. II. 37. 9-15.
13. Rām. II. 37. 30 ff.
14. Rām. II. 42. 6 ff.

but even widowhood does not soften her. Hereafter she is blamed for every calamity.[1]

To her the victory was complete. To Bharata also she tells a lie in order to make him feel that his father did not care for him.[2] But when Bharata is acquainted with real situation, he insults her, and says that he would have disowned her or killed her but for the fact of Rāma's displeasure. He is determined to defeat her plans.[3] When hated and insulted by her son, whose interest she was forwarding, she realises her mistake. Her adviser Mantharā, is badly punished by Śatrughana, who would have killed her but for Bharata's intervention.[4] Even at Bhardwāja's asylum, while introducing her, Bharata slights her.[5] But she had by then realised that her success had turned into utter failure and follows Kausalyā and Sumitrā to bring Rāma back.[6]

Kaikeyī's life shows how ambition blinds a person. It also depicts a period when women took part in the palace revolutions and the favourite queen controlled the king to a great extent, but this state of affairs surely presents a sharp contrast to the Mahābhārata where women like Gāndhārī delved into politics for the sake of justice.

Kausalyā

It is a perfect statement about Kausalyā that her greatness consisted in her having been the mother of Rāma.[7] As the chief queen she had no commanding or influential voice like that of Draupadī, Kuntī or even Kaikeyī. She was neglected by the king and insulted by Kaikeyī.[8]

Knowledge of religious rites

Kausalyā thus devoted her time in performing religious rites and austerities for the welfare of her son[9], forgetting her

1. Rām. II. 48. 21 ff; II. 53. 6 ff; II. 66. 19 ff; III. 2. 18, 19; VI. 32. 4.
2. Rām. II. 72. 36-37.
3. Rām. II. 73. 17 ff; II. 106. 9.
4. Rām. II. 78. 12 ff.
5. Rām. II. 92. 24-26.
6. Rām. II. 83. 6.
7. Śrīnivāsa Shāstrī's "Lectures on the Rāmāyaṇa" 25th lecture page 459.
8. Rām. II. 12. 70; Rām. II. 8. 37 ff.
9. Rām. II. 20. 48, 52.

sorrow in the affection for her son. She had profound knowledge of religious rites. To the bearer of the good news of Rāma's installation, she gives gold, cows, jewels and other gifts,[1] and begins to worship in the temple inside her inner apartment.[2] She had remained awake the whole night worshipping Vishṇu for the welfare of her son, performed sacrifice and had grown thin on account of her fasts when Rāma came to inform her about his exile.[3] When Rāma leaves for the forest, she performs auspicious ceremonies and pronounces benedictions herself.[4] Her dictum, when she saw Ingudī fruits offered by Rāma to Daśaratha[5] for Śrāddha, indicates her knowledge of religious books for the same dictum has been quoted in other religious books also. Constant performance of these religious rites and contemplation had not given Kausalyā calmness and serenity of nature. Perpetual insults by her co-wives had marred her peace.[6]

Her pātivrata

It is stated that "Kausalyā's strongest virtue was her devotion to her husband."[7] But there was nothing extraordinary about it. It was not like that of Sītā or Sāvitrī, or even that of Damayantī, whom adverse circumstances and even the neglect of the husband did not dishearten. Barring exceptional cases like that of Kaikeyī most women in Epic homes, bred in the tradition of pātivrata, were like Kausalyā. Kausalyā was a weak character. She did not, like Kaikeyī, decide upon a course and relentlessly pursue it. She wanted Rāma to stay back. It seems that she silently agrees with Lakshmaṇa's proposal to revolt against Daśaratha but could not take the risk of civil war. In case, Rāma approved of it she would not have minded it.[8] When Rāma does not agree to the proposal she wanted to follow him, leaving her husband behind.[9] Rāma

1. Rām. II. 3. 47.
2. Rām. II. 4. 33.
3. Rām. II. 20. 14-20.
4. Rām. II. 21. 62; 25. 1 ff.
5. Rām. II. 104. 15. यदन्नः पुरुषो भवति तदन्नास्तस्य देवताः । Cp. Āp. Dh. S II. 2.3.9.
6. Rām. II. 4.39 ff; 20. 32 ff; 75. 5 ff.
7. "Great women of India," p. 158.
8. Rām. II. 21. 20 ff; 21. 2 ff (Lakshmaṇa's proposal).
9. Rām. II. 24. 9-19.

only brings her to the path of duty.[1] Her love for Rāma was indeed far greater than that for her husband.

Daśaratha's opinion about Kausalyā was always high. He considered her as an ideal wife who served him as a slave, friend, wife, sister and mother. He also realises his guilt of disregarding her, due to the infatuation he felt for Kaikeyī.[2] When Kaikeyī had at last exiled Rāma, Daśaratha takes shelter in Kausalyā's apartment. When Sumantra comes back, Kausalayā's conduct is not like that of an ideal pativratā. In her sorrow she taunts Daśaratha,[3] whose agony was greater for he gave up his life owing to Rāma's separation.

A Harsh Judge of Woman—but an affectionate mother-in-law

Kausalyā is a harsh judge of women probably because she received bad treatment constantly from her co-wives. Therefore, she considers Sītā as an exception and is all praise for her. She is an affectionate mother-in-law. She laments that delicate Sītā had to lead a hard life in the forest like a homeless one.[4]

It was quite natural for her to blame Kaikeyī for Daśaratha's death.[5] Kausalyā failed to understand Bharata's loyalty and reverence for her and Rāma, but she equally failed in understanding some traits in Rāma's character.[6] For Bharata she uses cruel words,[7] and even threatens that she will go to the forests with Sumitrā, taking 'agnihotra' with her, meaning thereby that she will not let him perform the funeral of Daśaratha.[8] Bharata had to take many oaths before she was completely reconciled, and it was due to him that she gained her rightful position as the chief queen mother. After the funeral ceremony of Daśaratha she along with other queens follows Bharata to bring back Rāma. Kaikeyī was completely cowed down and henceforward Kausalyā speaks for and leads all the queens.[9]

1. Rām. II. 21. 61; 24. 12 ff.
2. Rām. II. 12. 68-70.
3. Rām. II. 58. 29 ff; 61. 2.
4. Rām. II. 61. 4 ff.
5. Rām. II. 66. 2 ff.
6. Rām. II. 70. 8; 21 (sarga) fails to understand Rāma.
7. Rām. II. 75. 10-16.
8. Rām. II. 75. 13.
9. Rām. VI. 127. 14; 128. 44; VII. 63. 16.

Sumitrā

Sumitrā's perhaps was a political marriage. She was Karaṇī, daughter of Daśaratha's minister,[1] Vāmadeva. Badar, quoting Monier Williams,[2] says that Lakshmaṇa and Śatrughan were born earlier, but as their mother was born of a Vaiśya, Bharata was considered the elder brother. Nowhere in the Rāmāyaṇa we get such a reference. Bharata was in fact the elder.[3] But the fact that Sumitrā was not a princess did not affect the position of her sons as Anuloma marriages were prevalent and princes born of such marriages were not only considered as true Kshatriyas but if their mothers were ambitious there was nothing to debar them from the throne also, except the law of primogeniture, which does not seem to have been very much respected.[4] All this digression is to prove that it was due to Sumitrā's character and her up-bringing that her sons had nothing to do with the throne and kingly ambitions. Had she the ambition of Kaikeyī there was no social bar to check her, as Badar and Monier Williams wrongly think.

Remarkable character

Sumitrā's character was remarkable in many ways. "There is a character truly Spartan."[5] While the great tragedy shakes everybody, she is calm, steady, does not lose the balance of her mind during those weak moments and imparts strength to others. She knows well that every cloud has a silver lining. She realizes the greatness of Rāma. Her happiness and equanimity is of her own making, for she was not ambitious. To her the path of duty and righteousness was far more important than the kingdom, an advice she had given to her sons. She can be well compared to Gāndhārī, but as her sons were of like opinion, she does not suffer like Gāndhārī.

1. William, M. "Indian wisdom" p. 342. Sumitrā was a Vaiśyā woman.

2. C. Bader "Women in Ancient India", p. 93 footnote 2. Williams, M. "Epic Poetry" Para 95. 4th line.

3. Rām. I. 18. 11-13 and 21.

4. Rām. VI. 128 and 90-93 It is only after the younger brother Lakshmaṇa's refusal that Bharata is installed as heir apparent of Rāma. VII 63. 10-18.

5. C. Bader "Women in Ancient India" page 95 ff for Sumitrā's character see "Great Women of India" page 160.

Daśratha's respect for her

It may be that king Daśaratha respected her for her qualities and calmness and therefore gave her double share of 'Pāyasa' after deliberation.[1] He had such a respect for her that he is afraid of losing her confidence in case he banishes Rāma.[2] She is lucky also, due to her own nature and due to her two sons being attached to Rāma and Bharata respectively. She had no fear of Kausalyā or Kaikeyī nor had she to lose anything in case either Rāma or Bharata was installed.

Her calm and collected attitude

Throughout the event of the banishment of Rāma she is calm and majestic. She gladly sends her son to the forests advising him not to neglect Rāma.[3] The best course, she says, for the younger brother is to follow the elder brother, be he rich or poor.[4] She continues, that for Lakshamaṇa henceforth, Rāma was to be in place of Daśaratha, Sītā in hers and the wilderness like Ayodhyā.[5] Her calm and collected utterances, though rare, are not only fine pieces of poetry in the Rāmāyaṇa but also show her deep philosophy and foresight. While consoling Kausalyā she says that the latter has no cause for lamentation, for her son is endowed with great qualities and pursues the course of righteousness. Sītā follows him like the goddess of royal prosperity, and Lakshmaṇa furnished with weapons goes on guarding him. Nothing is difficult for him to achieve. Rāma will come back soon and will be installed as king. As Sumitrā's son was following the course of righteousness she had no grief on account of his self-imposed banishment. In this way Sumitrā inspired hope by her noble and soothing words and destroyed the sorrow of Rāma's mother.[6]

Tārā

Tārā, educated particularly in religious books and rites was one of the most intelligent and influential ladies.[7] Due to the obstinacy of her husband, her attempts to make peace with

1. Rām. I. 16. 28.
2. Rām. II. 12. 72.
3. Rām. II. 40. 5.
4. Rām. II. 40. 5-6.
5. Rām. II. 40. 9.
6. Rām. II. Section 44 whole.
7. Rām. IV. 15. 11 ff. IV. 16.12. IV. 33. 31 ff.

Sugrīva by giving him back his wife, Rūmā and making him heir-apparent, fail.[1] In spite of it Vāli recognizes her sagacity and recommends her counsel to Sugrīva, for Vāli must have realized later the soundness of her advice.[2] Her reasoning was perfect. Her resourcefulness later saves Sugrīva from Lakshamaṇa's wrath.[3]

Her queenly majesty is evident even when she is grieved at the death of her husband, and she musters the Vānaras who were fleeing from the presence of Rāmā.[4] She is also bold and blames Rāma for killing Vāli.[5] At the time of Vāli's demise she was greatly grieved but later marries Sugrīva,[6] for widow-marriage was probably a custom among the Vānaras.

Maṇḍodarī, Trijaṭā and Saramā

Maṇḍodarī the beautiful and majestic queen of Lankā proud of her lineage, husband and sons,[7] had also to suffer on account of her husband's obstinacy. To her thinking, Sītā[8] was not her equal in any respect. She had also warned Rāvaṇa of the wrong course he was following.[9] Her greatness also lay in her loyalty towards her husband. Tārā, Maṇḍodarī and Rāvaṇa's mother,[10] though they fail in their missions are all examples of the Epic women, who raise their voices for the cause of justice even against their husbands and sons. Trijaṭā and Saramā also belong to such a group who in the midst of darkness spread their light by consoling Sītā during her affliction.

Conclusion

We have traced the lives and exploits of the various types of women in the Epics. There is no doubt that till recently, i.e., before the influence of modern education began to be felt most of these were held as ideals by Hindū women. If culture and civilization is the result of the capacity of a society to control

1. Rām. IV. 15. 11 ff.
2. Rām. IV. 22. 12-13.
3. Rām. IV. 33. 31, 51-57; 35. 19-22.
4. Rām. IV. 19. 5 ff.
5. Rām. IV. 24. 31 ff.
6. Rām. IV. 55. 3; 33. 43.
7. Rām. VI. 111. 39-40.
8. Rām. VI. 111. 27.
9. Rām. VI. 111. 18 ff.
10. Rām. VI. 34. 20 ff.

some of the strongest and selfish impulses these ladies were in a true sense highly cultured. A few of them like Sītā and Sāvitrī had attained great heights and never faltered. If the test of greatness lies in being immune to all shocks that life might offer some of them really failed; but it is not so, for it is natural for human beings to be affected by calamities. The greatness of these women lies in the fact that when the first shock was over, after the tragic experiences, they could discriminate between illusion and reality, evil and righteousness, injustice and justice.

Chapter XII

EPILOGUE

1. *Continuity, Varieties and Contradictions*

In the foregoing pages the status of women in the Epics has been surveyed. The main trend noticed throughout was one of continuity of thought behind sharply divergent opinions. The woman is revered as mother and creator, loved as wife but is condemned as a seducer. Various reasons may be put forward for these conflicting attitudes. As far as the question of time is concerned, it has already been shown in the introduction that the Great Epic depicts all the societies that existed in the ancient India from Vedic period to that of neo-Hinduism of the Purāṇas as well as those prehistoric ones that existed merely in the imaginations of political philosophers. The Epics also deal with the cultures of the peoples[1] residing in regions covering vast geographical dimensions.[2] The constant contact of these various cultures representing various people and times generated a process of assimilation and opposition. Apart from these outward changes there are always some inner changes in every society in response to various vicissitudes through which it passes. It is, therefore, natural that the Epics as books covering the conditions of various ages and vast areas as well as the accounts of the contact of many races are full of contradictions although revealing a continuity of thought. These are reflected in the position of women also. It is very difficult to separate the old and new ideals and practices, for these works, particularly, the Mahābhārata, have undergone various recensions and while some books (Parvas) can definitely be classed as new, others contain both old and new ideas.[3]

1. Āryans, Asuras, Rākshasas, Vānaras, Śakas, Hūṇas, Chīnas, Kirātas, Yavanas, Pāraśikas, Nāgas. cp. Mbh. I.175. 36 ff; Ram. I.55. 2 ff; Mbh. II.51-52 (Sec).

2. Trans-Himālayan regions of north like Bālhika, (Mbh. II.5213) China, of south as Ceylon, of west as Persia, and of east like Assām—areall mentioned.

3. Critical edition of the Mahābhārata. (B. O. R. I. Poona).

2. *Social Status*

(a) *Place of honour* : The place of honour and respect accorded to women can easily be traced in the Epics. They were considered pivots not only of domestic life but of the entire society. They have been described as deities of prosperity to be cherished. The heroines of the Epics were capable of high, moral and intellectual attainments, of wonderful altruistic deeds for which they are still held as ideals inspiring sentiments of respect and reverence in every Hindū heart.

The birth of a female child, no doubt, was less welcomed than that of the male, but it did not arouse cries of dismay as is generally believed. On the contrary some parents desired and performed religious rites and pilgrimages so that they may be blessed with a daughter. Those not so blessed sometimes adopted daughters. A maid was not only an object of affection at home but was considered an auspicious creature whose presence was required on ceremonious occasions. Her education was well looked after, and she was assigned important duties at home. At times she saved her parents from calamities, which is indicative of her developed social individuality and altruism. A maiden had a carefree and comfortable life at home. Under the benevolent protection and care of her father or kinsmen, and in their default under the protection of the king she had full freedom of movement and development.

Although marriage, as means for the fulfilment of a maiden's natural and inevitable goal of life was always desired, she was never sacrificed at the altar of marriage. Her intellectual attainments and physical endurance made her capable of working out her own emancipation, the greatest good to be achieved by all human beings. In marriage she had freedom and possessed independent judgement to select her life partner. Even when she was given away by her parents, as in the Brāhma and the Prājāpatya forms, her dignity was fully maintained, for she was to be an equal partner in all religious and worldly undertakings of her husband. 'Kanyādāna' does not necessarily indicate her lower social status. It stands for social responsibility of parents towards the race and their child, which is also reflected in the particular care taken by parents in the selection of bridegrooms.

Marriage as sacrament secured the position of a wife in a polygamous society, for even if she was superseded and not loved by the husband she was always to be maintained. The contractual idea of marriage, although not unknown, was rare. It was discouraged and finally abandoned. It did not help in promoting better status of women, as is generally believed, but increased unhappiness in married life.

Home was the centre of the activity of women, and the wife was assigned the central place in it. In fact the wife was considered synonymous with the home. There she performed her onerous duties through unremitting services and was partner of her husband in the pursuit of the four Purushārthas, that is, Dharma, Artha, Kāma and Moksha. Gaining by advice and experience of elders and protection of her husband, she was cherished and respected, for on women depended the prosperity and future progeny of the family.

As a mother, woman occupied a place of great honour and prestige. The social code prescribed a conduct of veneration and respect towards her. She was considered the creator, nourisher, educator and the greatest preceptor of her children and thus of her race and society. The Epic mothers performed all these duties with great care and a sense of social responsibility and were regarded as an integrating force in society. Sons repaid the affection and care of the mother in a humble and respectful manner and protected widowed mothers, whose position was never degraded or neglected in the family by the fact of her widowhood.[1] Exaltation of mothers led to mother-worship and to the custom of addressing sons after the mother's name. And even the ascetic ideal which belittled all other worldly relationship did not affect the superior position of the mother. The social position of the step-mother was similar to that of the mother.

No social stigma was attached to widowhood and the widow was not considered as an inauspicious creature. No special life of austerities and fasts was prescribed for her by the composers of the Epics in form of "Vidhawādharma" as was done by the later writers of the Purāṇas. Nevertheless widows born and bred in pātivrata ideal thought widowhood as a great calamity, and led a life of penance and chastity. Sometimes they even left home

1. Mbh. V. 67.6, 7; 129.1; 173.6; I. 102.4; V.173.22 ff.

for forests to perform penances and austerities of their own accord. In Epic narratives penances were not imposed upon them. Generally they did not sacrifice themselves on the funeral pyre of their husbands. Among certain lower classes, remarriage was allowed. In the absence of her sons and kinsmen a widow was protected by the king.

The saner view of society is also reflected in the laws framed against sinning women. The lessons in constancy, faithfulness and loyalty which were preached only to the weaker sex by the later law givers, were also meant for men and applied with greater force as they were the stronger sex. Thus while the honour of women was well protected by condemning and punishing adulterous men, women were not treated harshly for similar crimes, as long as the honour of her high caste was not involved. She was considered as "Abalā" and therefore most of her failings were attributed to the carelessness of men who should have protected her. Although the husband of a sinning woman had the right to punish her, she was never to be abandoned and was always to be maintained. The attitude was that of hating the sin rather than the sinner.

The attitude of society even towards a fallen woman, that is, to a prostitute in some respects was quite different from the usual one. She was considered auspicious and her presence was required on ceremonial occasions. She was not treated as an outcast for she appeared with maidens to welcome distinguished guests and heroes. Probably prostitutes were the preservers of the sixty-four arts and specially one among them who excelled in these had a position of respect and honour in republican assemblies as well as in royal courts.

(b) *Inferior Status in Society* : The above mentioned data indicate a place of respect and honour occupied by women in society in whatever position they were placed or dragged down. But women were gradually losing this honourable position in society as well as in family. This was not due to any sudden revolution but was prompted by certain attitudes towards women from the hoary past as well as due to certain vicissitudes through which society was passing. In certain fields, deterioration in the status of women can even be traced in the Vedas, in the narrative parts of the Great Epic as well as in the Rāmāyaṇa, which is otherwise full of lofty ideals and noble sentiments. But in the didactic portion of the Great Epic it is more marked and more rapid. Many indignities and insults are heaped upon women. Woman is mentioned as insatiated with carnal pleasures, lascivious, immoral, heartless, fickle, inconstant and therefore easily seduced, root of sin and evil, greatest illusion created by the Brahman with the help of Atharvan rites for the downfall of men. She was incapable of being guarded and of keeping a secret. It was due to the inferior character assigned to women that they were to be kept under perpetual tutelage throughout their lives and were classed among possessions and property.

Causes of deterioration of the status of women

(1) *Attitude towards women from the hoary past*

The primitive man had no understanding of woman's biological functions, the suffering she undergoes for the sake of the race and the socialising and civilizing influence she wields. He was full of respect, awe and mystery for her powers of fertility and of contempt for her weakness. The psycho-physical weakness as a result of sex polarity which he felt in women's contact made him irresolute and weak for adventurous and world-forsaking pursuits. All this he attributed to the dreadful mysterious power of woman who appeared to him, not only weak herself, but an agent and mysterious source of weakness to be avoided. Still she was indispensable for social and peaceful pursuits as well as for enjoyment. So she was to be kept under complete control in order that she may not do any harm. This led to the theory of her perpetual tutelage. Thus she was captured as booty, sold, enslaved and enjoyed. Still for the sake of precaution in those periods of her life when she was thought to be particularly harmful and impure she was excluded from religious and sacred rites. This gradually led to a denial of religious and social status for her. It was not very difficult for man to keep woman under his complete control. She was weak and surrendered completely to one she cared for and loved. But for other men who wanted to lead a life of adventure or were of ascetic temperament, she was still to be avoided as a perpetual source of weakness. They warned men against women, attributed vile character to them. In the Epics all these primitive attitudes are reflected.

(2) *Particular social vicissitudes*

The attitude, which accords to woman a lower social status, changes when man's understanding develops as a result of knowledge about woman's functions and her role. This understanding sometimes leads to an exaltation of woman's position. But in ancient Indian literature the strange phenomenon is that whereas the status of women in the Vedas and in the narrative parts of the Great Epic is satisfactory, later in the didactic portions it deteriorates. This is due to certain internal changes in society, when the Āryans were fighting deadly wars with the non-Āryans and women were fulfilling all the economic needs of society and managing the family alone. They were to be producers of many heroes for the secular needs of the society. So the custom of Satī was abolished and remarriage was introduced. As useful members of society the position of woman was exalted. The religion of sacrifices (yajñas) was also in her favour, for yajñas could not be performed without a wife. The Āryans appear fully established in the North-India in the Epics and due to the development of the Dāsī-system Āryan women were not fulfilling the economic needs of society alone as before. Still Draupadī's description of her household management and the religious needs of society indicate that the older traditions and conditions as described in the Vedas prevailed. The change, however, was taking place. It has been already mentioned that specialization of Vedic education led to the denial of religious and therefore intellectual education of women. The ascetic attitude, which is not found in the Vedas and the Brāhmaṇa literature was developing. It was perhaps because of the non-Āryan contact or may be due to any other reason. The idea of impurity attached to woman was taking hold of society. All these conditions are more marked in the didactic portions. Not only was woman ignorant herself but she lost her religious or social status and was ascribed a vile character.

Being ignorant, a maiden naturally lost her power of judgment. Her freedom in the selection of her future partner sometimes led to unhappy results in married life. This and the vile and fickle character attributed to women firmly established the theory of perpetual tutelage of women. As a consequence the right of selection of the future partner passed to the guardians of maidens. It was rather difficult to find a suitable person in order to ensure the daughter's future happiness. Moreover, the various limitations and restrictions which were being imposed for contracting marriage led to further difficulty in finding out an accomplished bridegroom. Thus a daughter became a source of anxiety for parents. The competition in finding out the bridegroom, the denial of education to women, the rigid idea of chastity as an imperative qualification of the bride as well as women led to the custom of child marriage. The girl was given by some guardians as chattel and many times in anxiety of fulfilling the sacred duty of getting their daughters married the guardians did not even look to the suitability of the bridegroom.

Child-marriages and other reasons given above were responsible for the deterioration in the position of the wife. Formerly she used to be a religious partner of her husband in the true sense of the term. But it was natural for the uneducated and child-bride to look up to her educated and mature husband as a preceptor and deity. Thus at home from the position of a partner her position became that of a disciple and devotee. Her individuality, in case she had any. was submerged in that of her lord. Polygamy further deteriorated woman's position. Woman's position in the family became psychologically insecure and jealousies among cowives, danger of domination of cowife's sons in old age further added to her miseries. As even highly respected men could marry as many women as they willed, women were naturally classed with property and possessions. Apparently polyandry, although very rarely practised gave the same right to women as polygamy to men but the concrete instance of pawning Draupadī makes it clear that here also she was regarded as the property of her husbands. This was an older tradition. According to Asura and Arsha forms of marriage she was purchased as property. In Rākshasa, Paiśācha and Vīrasulka type of swayamvara she was conquered or stolen as a possession. As an illustration we may mention the fact that husbands, were always ready to give up their wives for any cause or for a beloved person or even pawned them, forced them to submit their honour and respect for fulfilling their vows or for Niyoga. Husbands even had a right to pass death sentence on their wives. The advice given to wives to obey even wrong and unrighteous commands of their husbands indicates that women were not even considered rational beings. Wife was for the enjoyment of the husband or for producing progeny for his line. If due to some physical and natural disability she was not able to do so she was denied her conjugal rights. It was with this point in view that a brotherless and fatherless girl was not to be married, for she may be a Putrikā, who was expected to produce progeny for her father's line. It is evident that society was not so much concerned about the future protection of a weak Abalā who had no one to look after. She was just a piece of property and if as property she could not serve the purpose for which they thought she was meant, they felt least bothered about the individual. Concrete instances, however, prove that this injuction was not taken up seriously. As upon her sons depended her destiny it was natural for women in their helpless condition, to perform austerity and penances for getting them. Still it must be said that wives were a little better than other property for they could not be disposed of even in cases of adultery.

Absolute chastity recommended for maidens and widows by society (and not for bachelors or widowers to such an extent) is also an outcome of man's complete sense of possession of woman for she must be dedicated to her lord in perfect purity. The idea of rigid chastity for wife is also the outcome of man's desire of keeping his line pure and securing the property of his ancestors by a son born to him. Had chastity been the outcome of a sense of purity and fidelity it would have been similarly applied to men. Men as described in the Epics could practise polygamy and keep concubines and prostitutes but slight faithlessness on a wife's part was at times punished by death sentence. Vigilant watch was always kept on her morals.

After the husband's death, even for virgin widows a life of penances and austerities was recommended in the didactic parts of the Great Epic. Such a life was followed of their own accord by the widows in the narrative part after they had settled their children and performed worldly duties but it was never recommended formerly for widows much less for virgin widows. Remarriage for widows was not practised and the extreme form of pātivrata ideal culminated in the custom of Satī, a custom not found in the Rāmāyaṇa but traceable in the Mahābhārata. The group suicide by the widows in the Mahābhārata may be due to their social insecurity and the insignificant position they occupied. Because of this insecurity the custom of Satī probably gained further ground. It was naturally considered better to die with the husband and get mental satisfaction and social approbation rather than to live and experience the bitterness that was becoming the widow's lot.

Even the ascetic ideals were not able to lower the exalted position of the mother, which was gained as a result of her sacrifices.and natural motherly instincts. But in patriarchal society her status in the family was lower than that of the father and dutiful children like Rāma disobeyed the mother's commands in case they ran contrary to the father's. The fathers even order children to punish their mothers by death. Due to lack of education mothers were ignorant. They had no voice in their daughter's marriage and were not able to settle their children well without their husband's help.

As for women following other careers, nothing much could be expected from a society which held no other fetish so firmly as the usual association of women with enjoyment and tutelage. So at home as a wife and mother she was to administer to a man's need and outside home the only career she could adopt was for attending to his need of service and enjoyment. Even here she was dependent and possessed. Thus the careers followed by women were of menial slaves who were trained in the sixty four arts in order to provide their services and of maid servants who were paid like Sairandhrī. These had no social status.

Another class was that of Apsarās, concubines and prostitutes. These were used for enjoyment and entertainment of the wealthy and learned. Although Gaṇikās held a somewhat higher place and prostitutes appeared on ceremonial occasions yet in the didactic portions they have been assigned a low social status and are described as harmful to the nation. A class of professional actresses also existed but they too were assigned a very low social position.

Freedom of Thought, Movement and Action

The status of the woman in society and the social attitude towards her can also be judged by the freedom of expression, movement and action given to her. In these fields the same tale is repeated. Women in earlier portions of the Epics and in the narrative one possessed these freedoms but gradually they were being denied these by the time the didactic portions were written. Sulabhā and Draupadī could discuss deep metaphysical subjects and took part in learned discussions with great ease. Even when faced with great calamity in the Kuru court Draupadī does not lose her balance of mind and challenges the Kuru elders with her doubts, which they were unable to remove. The great Yudhishṭhira was many times confounded by her.

To welcome guests and heroes, to witness processions and strange objects and to attend theatres women appeared in public. The royal ladies used to reside in secluded inner apartment to ensure privacy. They observed some kind of purdah when they appeared in public[1] except on certain occasions when they were allowed to appear without veil. But all this is only indicative of a sign of respectability, a device to avoid the uncultured masses, for purdah in the Mohammadan sense of the term never existed in the Hindū period. These royal ladies went out for picnics, attended fairs and festivals in hilarious mood and went to witness tournaments. Their enjoyments did not only include dancing, singing, painting and other arts but they had drinking bouts as well. They went to the forest alone by themselves for performing penance and austerity.

It was only during the periods of anarchy that maidens and women could not move about freely. In normal peaceful times women and maidens decorated fully with gold ornaments could go out to forests and the outskirts of the city for enjoyment. In these excursions it was natural that they were sometimes courted[2] by lovers. Even at their homes, some of them were seduced and went astray.[3] But liberty was not a licence and such relations were always condemned and in the ṛshi society they were badly punished. Still a free and living society also took a milder view of these undesirable and rare occurrences, and the sinner had not to suffer life long for such human failings, although sin was always condemned.

There are certain references that seem to indicate that in some regions, in certain societies and in certain bygone ages,

1. Rām. VI.114. 27-28; VI.111.61.
2. Mbh. III. 224. 1-3; Rām. I. 32. 13 ff.
3. Kuntī—Mbh. I. 111. 9 ff. Satyavatī—I. 63. 71 ff. Ahalyā—Rām. I. 48. 19 ff; VII. 30. 30.

women exercised unrestricted freedom even to the point of general licence and as a consequence became depraved. All these are, however, utterances of carping critics and interested parties. It was due to ignorance of bygone ages or of far off countries and societies and also due to an uncharitable attitude that is often adopted towards women of other nations that such remarks are made. These are, however, not worth consideration.

Certain types of swayamvaras and Gāndharva form of marriage indicate the freedom of action granted to maidens by society. Among Non-Āryan ladies, freedom was exercised to such an extent that sometimes they offered themselves in marriage.

At the time the didactic portions were written women were uneducated. The traditional home education did not develop her individuality and personality. She could hardly be regarded as a rational being. In such a state of mind any question of freedom of thought could not arise, and it did not arise.

As far as freedom of movement was concerned it has been already shown that the Hindū ladies never observed purdah. Nevertheless, certain instructions about behaviour towards women prove that confinement within the four walls of the house was considered ideal. The rigid idea of chastity, the theory of perpetual tutelage for woman must have also helped in restricting the liberty of woman.

When child marriages began as a result of the various reasons already discussed, the freedom, which was exercised by maidens in selecting their future partner, was naturally lost. But this was in keeping with their calibre as they had lost all powers of discrimination and judgment and due to their ignorance were not capable of selecting their mate even if they were married after puberty, not to speak of when they were married as children.

Religious Status

As regards the religious status of women the nature of the data is contradictory again. According to Vedic sacrificial religion which is found in the Epics the wife was the religious partner of her husband and was known as Sahadharmiṇī and Ardhānginī. No sacrifice could be performed without her and therefore Rāma who followed the monogamous ideal had to place an image of Śītā while performing sacrifices after her exile and death. In the Aśwamedha of Daśaratha all the principal wives take part. From the data in the Epics the part played by women was not very important. Although a wife as wife had a role in sacrifice, women as women were considered objects of pity to be given charities along with the old and sick or as property to be given as gifts to the Brāhmaṇas. Sometimes when the co-operation of the husband was not available a wife used to perform sacrifices herself. Women had a knowledge of the Vedas and were "Mantravits." They also performed Śrāddha with their husbands. When there were no male members left in the family they performed funeral rites as well.

Women were well versed in speculative philosophy. They could hotly debate in august conferences about abstruse subjects. The Brahmavādinīs of the Great Epic like those of the Upanishads display wonderful knowledge and religious wisdom and were not lagging behind men in this respect.

It may have been in order to debar the non-Āryan favourite wife from performing Vedic sacrifices that the junior wife and low-caste wife lost the right of religious partnership with the husband. With the specialization of Vedic sacrificial religion, women were altogether denied Vedic religious education and thus could not take part in sacrifices. It was also due to impurity attached to them that they were excluded from performing sacrifices and Śrāddhas in the didactic portion. Asceticism degraded the religious status of women so much that religious pursuits could be taken only by abandoning women.[1] All this was in keeping with the character assigned to women. They were regarded as creatures meant for enjoyment, lascivious and having low tastes. Thus they were regarded as devoid of nobler sentiments and were thought incapable of religious and intellectual pursuits.[2] They could however, win a place in heaven through the services rendered to their husbands. They

1. Mbh. I. 2. 391

धर्मे मतिर्भवतु वः सततोत्थितानां ।
सह्येक एव परलोकगतस्य बन्धुः ॥
अर्थाः स्त्रियश्च निपुणैरपि सेव्यमानाः ।
नैवाप्तभावमुपयान्ति न च स्थिरत्वम् ॥

2. Mbh. XIII. 40. 11-12; 46. 13. Cp. M. IX. 14-18.

still possessed rights to listen to the Purāṇas and Ākhyānas. To satisfy their religious needs, women evolved a new religion of rituals, fasts, superstitions and devotional cults. These must have been much more interesting and appealing to them than sacrifices. The only harm done to women, which was of course a formidable one, was that after the denial of Vedic education women were generally classed with the Śūdras, a condition which is found in the Epics.

Political Status

As far as the political status in the modern sense of the term is concerned, it did not exist even for men during the various periods depicted in the Epics. The social pattern, however, was not so complex, and according to Varṇāśrama-dharma every one performed his duties according to his nature, occupation and age. Thus nobody thought of rights but they were naturally well secured. The greatest political right of that time i. e. succession to the kingdoms was, however, denied to women and even a strīrajya had a king.[1] Although an intellectual minority, men like Vasishṭha and Vyāsa, were in favour of conceding this right to women. It has been already shown that due to ignorance and to her characterization as Abalā women's sphere of influence was limited to the home. The onerous duties of administering kingdoms and conducting wars were not meant for them. They were considered light-hearted, whimsical, eccentric,[2] weak and unable to keep secrets.[3] No secret councils of the state were to be held in a woman's presence. It has been stated that success in all those matters which rests on the initiative and performance of woman will always be doubtful. But as has already been stated elsewhere, the home education had developed excellent qualities of sympathy and self-sacrifice in women, a fact which gave her considerable influence extending even to the political sphere. Thus although the influence she wielded in politics of the day was personal and indirect, it was always beneficial and was for the greater good. There are only

1. Mbh. XII. 4. 7. सृगालश्च महाराज : स्त्रीराज्याधिपतिश्च यः ।
2. Mbh. XIII. 46. 8-9; V. 35. 72; 36. 58.
3. Mbh. II. 5. 83; V. 37. 57. cp. M. VII. 149.

two exceptions, i.e. Kaikeyī and Śūrpaṇakhā who act in a contrary fashion. Even in these cases the former is not much to blame.

Being an Abalā, woman was conceded certain privilages in society. She was not to be killed. This rule was generally adhered to by great heroes to extreme limits but in very exceptional circumstances it was sometimes overlooked. Women were also to be treated kindly and talked to sweetly. They were never to be treated harshly.

Economic Status

It has been pointed out repeatedly that women were treated as chattel and as such could be sold or given away as gifts. Thus they were inherently incapable of holding any property. As perpetual minors they were to be under constant control of men. They were hardly considered persons having a separate legal entity. Other social factors were also in the way of woman's right to landed property. In those periods of warfare only powerful kings with large armies could hold to property for they alone could defend it. Thus, when property was either held by the great chiefs or in common by the family headed by the patriarch, there was no question of woman's independent right over it for she was utterly incapable of holding and protecting it.

An ordinary daughter could not claim any share in patrimony. In case her father was not living she was supported and married by her brother. The injustice of not allowing the daughter to inherit was, however, being realised. Some ingenious ways were devised to do away with it, for it has been said that she was like a son. In case she was a brotherless daughter, whether appointed or unappointed, she or her son inherited her father's property and wealth. The basis of her inheritance was that like a son she was the soul of her father; that of her son was that he performed the funeral rites of his maternal grand father. There was therefore no difference between a son and a grand son. According to Vyāsa, a brotherless daughter could even succeed to her father's kingdom.[1] In case a son is adopted by

1. Mbh. XII. 33. 45. कुमारो नास्ति येषां च कन्यास्तत्राभिषेचय ।

a father the appointed daughter was given the greater share, and if a son was born she was even then given a share. But if such a daughter was sold according to Asura form she and her son could not succeed to her father's property for the father lost all authority and right over her.

The mother's estate (Strīdhana) was equally divided among unmarried daughters. Although this is specially recommended for Brāhmaṇi it was meant for all. Thus, while the father's wealth was inherited by the son, daughters inherited the mother's wealth.

Women in those days possessed wealth through dowries and presents. All the relatives are enjoined by the composer of the Mahābhārata to give ornaments to women at the time of marriage and even otherwise.[1] The huge dowry given to princesses included every article that was needed in a royal household, which must have been used by both, that is, husband and wife. Dowries are known as "Haraṇam", "Gyātideyam", "Kanyādhanam" and they must have led to the idea of Strīdhana. Although the names of different kinds of Strīdhana are not specified in the Epics, examples of all kinds are found, and the idea of Strīdhana was doubtless in evolution. Over and above this Srīdhana, husbands could give three thousand coins at a time to the wife for her enjoyment.

The right of ownership of a wife was a limited one. Her right to maintenance arises out of jural relationship created between husband and wife by the sacramental character of the marriage. But woman's right over her husband's property was that of an usufruct and not of a proprietor. She appears as a good and trusted manager of her husband's property. Widows, specially those with infants, had to encounter economic difficulty. Only over her Strīdhana women had the right of disposal. From the perusal of the above mentioned evidence it appears that women enjoyed limited legal and economic rights. But in view of their general subordination and ignorance in every field it seems strange that the economic status was being exalted, at least in the fields of Strīdhana and recognition of Putrikā rights. The legal and economic status could not but be in conformity with women's social, religious and political

1. Mbh. XIII. 46. 2-3.

rights, and as compared to many other ancient nations it was not at all disappointing.

The women characters in the Epics are generally spirited wives and mothers, like Draupadī, Kuntī, Gāndhārī, Sumītrā and to some extent Sītā. Self-abnegation and self-sacrifice for righteousness is the dominant note of their character. Theirs was selfless love which requires no reciprocation but which is at the same time not blind to faults inherent even in those who are the objects of their affection. A true Sahadharmaṇī like Draupadī, was considered to be a pativratā first, but the connotation of pativratā gradually changed and she became a slave and blind follower of her master. Draupadī, Kuntī and Gāndhārī acted as guiding and correcting forces of their time. They worked for the cause of righteousness, justice and duty. There is another set composed of Sītā, Sāvitrī, Damayantī who were much concerned about their duties and faithfulness and needed no reciprocation for these but they are ideals that have guided Indian womanhood through centuries. The world has a mingling of the ideal and the common in every society. So if there were Spartan mothers like Sumitrā and Gāndhārī, there were also others who were just ordinary like Kausalyā, and even below ordinary as Kaikeyī. Simple women or women proud of their beauty like Ahalyā forgot their duty but Ahalyā is an example of failing humanity, and yet, realising her own sin she gets rid of those effects through penances and austerities.

Variety

The foregoing general survey points out the different types of characters, and indicates the variety of customs and different attitudes of society towards women. The reasons for all this diversity have becn already given in the beginning of this chapter. Thus, as a maiden woman was considered auspicious and an object of affection but she was a source of anxiety as well. In the sphere of marriage, the eight forms, freedoms and limitations in contracting it and the age of marriage all indicate the various customs prevalent among different races and ages. At home, although a Sahadharmiṇī wife was prized she was giving place to an ignorant and docile one. Pātivrata ideal was encouraged, yet bad wives were not very unusual. Widow marriage was practised among non-Āryans but the practice was abandoned by the Āryans although they still had the memory of such a custom. Niyoga took its place for sometime but as the idea of life-long chastity of woman and conjugal fidelity and constancy was required more from woman, Niyoga gave place to austerities and penances and finally to the custom of Satī. A mother was greatly honoured and respected and was classed first among the three "Atigurus" and was regarded as the foremost of the educators. Gradually due to her ignorance she was losing ability and consequently the right to guard the destiny of her progeny. Her position deteriorated to such an extent that fathers sometimes ordered sons to kill her. Although woman was to be honoured and respected in theory, she could be sold, pawned, dragged in court and treated roughly with the utmost disrespect. Privileges accorded to her were sometimes flouted, although it must be said that such cases were rare. Sometimes chivalrous attitude leads to honour and respect of woman. But for a warrior and ascetic, woman was also considered a source of weakness dragging man to worldly pursuits.

Survival

In these mingled ideas, many practices were the survival of the primitive and old times. The Rākshasa, Paiśācha and Gāndharva forms of marriage must have been older than civilization. Ārsha, Asura, Daiva, Rākshasa and Paiśācha forms of marriage, practices of polygamy and polyandry, Niyoga or even imperative chastity show her as property and possession of man.

Conflict and Final Adjustment

It was natural that in certain fields the old ideas developed while in others these came into conflict with new ones. The Great Epic mostly depicts an age known as Dwāpara (meaning Dwanda i. e. conflict) which deals with conflict. In every field, social, religious, intellectual and political, sages were trying to find out some synthesis by evolving a new culture by preserving the old and assimilating and tolerating the new. The same spirit permeates through the Gītā and the Mahābhārata. The same is the case with the status of women, but due to the biological make up of woman, every society is more conservative in its attitude towards her than towards man. Therefore, although the general belief is that the condition of women deteriorated on account of the foreign invasions the perusal of the history of culture suggests different reasons. It was in the attempt of society to keep up racial purity and continuity of family, to preserve old religion, to introduce certain improvements in eugenics as well as in its clinging to the fetish of women as perpetual minors, property and objects of enjoyment, that the deterioration of the position of women is to be traced. It is because of these that her freedom, intellectual and physical growth was arrested. The little progress that was achieved in certain fields was nothing compared to the loss of individuality and personality that did great harm not only to the women but to the nation as well.

It was in the reformed way of adopting the Rākshasa and Paiśācha form, in banning the Asura and the practice of Niyoga, in its treatment towards fallen and sinning woman, in conceding some economic rights to woman, in the form of Strīdhana and the succession of Putrikā and her son that woman's lot improved and she was being considered as an individual by some reformers. Still old ideas die hard. In fact when the ascetic attitude took hold of Indian society all the progress and honourable position gained by women in the Vedic period was lost for centuries again. She had no more the right of contracting marriage by her own free will but was married as a child having no understanding of the responsibility that would fall on her in Gṛhasthāśrama. An ignorant wife was to be a shadow and slave of her master. In her life as well as in death she was to be possessed by him. Not to speak of ordinary woman, even if she was a paragon of virtue, of whose chastity the god of Fire himself bore witness (as in the case of Sitā), she was to be exiled without hearing, at the slightest suspicion voiced about her character by vile persons. But after such treatment she was expected to spend her days cherishing and respecting the memory of such a husband. After her husband's death, as widow she was either to lead a life of austerities dedicated to his memory or to sacrifice herself on his funeral pyre. As a mother she was revered only because she gave birth to children, a natural duty which could be performed even by savages. But the position of a mother in civilized countries as an integrating and educative influence for which she was honoured in past ages, could never be sustained by ignorant mothers. Ignorance degraded her character while ascetics painted it black in a sweeping manner. In the religious field superstition took hold of her, in the family man dominated her. She lost her personality and individuality completely. Thus she became a quantity negligible, a vessel to produce progeny, and an article of enjoyment. Occasionally old ideas that woman should be respected and honoured are repeated, but with an ulterior motive for she was socially useful. This was merely lip homage.[1] It may be contended that women felt satisfied for there was no woman's problem in ancient India. But woman as an individual was hardly existing by the time the didactic portions were written. She was merely a piece of property. Thus the race of Brahmavādinīs, Sahadharmiṇīs and Spartan mothers was sacrificed at the altar of social convenience and was lost for centuries to come. With the downfall of woman, the downfall of the country and its people was inevitable, for in her disregard all action was futile as has been well said in the Mahābhārata. (XIII.46.6).

"स्त्रियो यत्र च पूज्यन्ते ।
रमन्ते तत्र देवताः ॥
अपूजिताश्च यत्रैताः ।
सर्वास्तत्राफलाः क्रियाः ॥"

1. Mbh. XIII. 46. 3-11.

APPENDIX—A

Eight forms of marriage in general

In the Great Epic, all the three lists[1] enumerating the forms of marriage, seem to be the later redactions and deal with the Dharmaśāstra material, as many identical ślokas are also found in the Manusmṛti. The first list does not define the forms presumably because the composer in his anxiety to drive the point home would not permit any break in the trend of the story with long digressions, which would otherwise have been unavoidable. In the second list the forms are defined briefly. In the third list only five forms are enumerated. The reason for this, may be, as Vaidya aptly states that although the eight were conventional forms only five forms were, well known or practised.[2] As already shown Ārsha was a condemned form in the Anuśāsana Parva, which mentions the third list of forms of marriage.[3] Prājāpatya and Daiva being similar to Brāhma may have been amalgamated in it. Brāhma naturally included first four forms with similar idea of the guardian's consent and Kanyādāna. Of these five forms, viz.—Brāhma, Gāndharva, Rākshasa, Asura and Paiśācha, only the first three are held to be the proper forms, the last two being regarded as improper.[4] Gāndharva and Rākshasa forms were naturally commended by the Great Epic, dealing with warrior traditions as the Kshatriyas practised both. But a similar śloka in the Ādi Parva presents difficulty.[5] Although the commentator of the Manusmṛti explains that out of the five (excluding Brāhma, Daiva, Ārsha) inferior forms i.e. Prājāpatya, Asura, Gāndharva, Rākshasa, Paiśācha only three are popular, Asura and Paiśācha being forbidden. These five forms, however, can be taken through the process of elimination also, for Ārsha, Asura and Paiśācha have been condemned in the Mahābhārata.[6] The remaining

1. Mbh. I. 73. 8-9; 102. 12-16; XIII. 44. 3-10.
2. Vaidya C. V. "महाभारत मीमांसा" page 230 ज्ञानमण्डल काशी।
3. Mbh. XIII. 45. 20-21.
4. Mbh. XIII. 44. 9 पञ्चानां तु त्रयो धर्म्या द्वावधर्म्यौ युधिष्ठिर।
पैशाचश्चासुरश्चैव न कर्त्तव्यौ कथञ्चन ॥
5. Mbh. I. 73. 11-12 has the same lines as note 4; M. III. 25 Com. (p. 82) of Kulluka (Nirṇaya Sagār ed. 1929).
6. Mbh. XIII. 44. 9, 46, 47; 45. 17-21. (notes 3, 4.)

five forms are Brāhma, Daiva, Prājāpatya, Gāndharva and Rākshasa. Of these the first three are commendable and proper. The last two forms were non-Āryan ones and although practised by the Kshatriyas, (according to all the lists) these were not assimilated by the Āryan society. Here "Adharmya" may be taken for "improper" and even "immoral" but not for "illegal" as G.M. Tripāthī thinks.[1] The lists of the various sons[2] and legal recognition of the marriages of Ulūpī and Hiḍimbā even without any religious ceremony, prove that the question of legality was not so vital. In a free society there was remedy for every evil and nobody was condemned downright for human failings.

It was maintained by the composer of the Ādi Parva as well as Manu that Rākshasa and Gāndharva forms were proper for the Kshatriyas and could be resorted to in the pure or mixed forms.[3] A somewhat similar statement in the Anuśāsana Parva, to this effect that Gāndharva, Brāhma, Kshātra can be performed together or separately, presents difficulty.[4] The Gāndharva form, defined and even practised when the Epic story was being enacted goes ill together with the Brāhma form,[5] which stands for the guardian's consent. It is, however, interesting to note that the definition of Gāndharva is completely changed

1. Tripāthī G.M. "Marriage forms under Ancient Hindū Law" pages 21-22. Explaining these lines from the Manusmṛti contends that there were no child marriages and consent of the girls was necessary element of marriage and as Rākshasa, Asura and Paiśācha forms had no consent, these were condemned and were considered illegal. His idea that Manu legalised only those forms where consent of the bride was taken is, however, erroneous as M. V-151 states यस्मै दद्यात्पिता त्वेनां भ्राता वानुमते पितुः । तं शुश्रूषेत् जीवन्तं संस्थितं च न लङ्घयेत् ।

2. Mbh. I. 120. 32-33; XIII. 49. 3 ff.

3. Mbh. I. 73. 13

गान्धर्वराक्षसौ क्षत्रे धर्म्यौ तौ मा विशङ्किथाः ।
पृथग्वा यदि वा मिश्रौ कर्त्तव्यौ नात्र संशयः ॥

Cp. M. III. 26 is nearly the same. The examples are already cited in page 71-75.

4. Mbh. XIII. 44. 10

ब्राह्मः क्षात्रोऽथ गान्धर्व एते धर्म्या नरर्षभ ।
पृथग्वा यदि वा मिश्राः कर्त्तव्या नात्र संशयः ॥

N.B. Here Brāhma is added to Kshātra and Gāndharva.

5. Mbh. I. 73. 27. सकामायाः सकामेन निर्मन्त्रो रहसि स्मृतः ।

Cp. Vi.Dh. S. XXIV. 20 द्वयोः सकामयोर्म्मातापितृरहितो योगो गान्धर्वः ।

by the redactors in this chapter.[1] Such Gāndharva could be performed with the Brāhma. Kshātra is Rākshasa of the legal lists.[2] Subhadrā'a marriage according to Kumbhakoṇam edition was a mixture of all these.[3] Even if Kshātra is suggested as swayamvara as this was also a practice among the Kshātriyas, Damayantī's marriage too was a mixed form combining all these three, and so would have been the case of Ambā, if Bhīshma had not intervened.

APPENDIX—B

Among the Āryans the Varṇa system based upon profession was flexible. In the beginning privileges of the first three Varṇas as well as their mode of living were similar. Due to these reasons inter-Varṇa marriages were quite common. The Epic composers also had memory of a period when there were no castes, which later developed from distinction of work and profession.[4] Gradually when the Āryan population increased the three Varṇas took to other professions.[5] There may have been a tendency not to leave their original privileges connected with their professions. This tendency may have been strong among the Brāhmaṇas, as they were more particular about keeping the old code of conduct and sticking to their highly specialized profession. They may not have liked to inter-marry with the the Kshatriyas and Vaiśyas who were not so particular about marriage and married even the Śūdrā and non-Aryans as already stated. Thus the Epic society was gradually crystallizing the Varṇas into the Jātis. In the didactic portions the

1. Mbh. XIII. 44. 5-6

शिष्टानां क्षत्रियाणां च धर्मएष सनातनः ।
आत्माभिप्रेतमुत्सृज्य कन्याभिप्रेत एव यः ।।
अभिप्रेता च या यस्य तस्मैदेया युधिष्ठिर ।
गान्धर्वमिति तं धर्मं प्राहुर्वेदविदो जनाः ।।

2. Vas. Dh. S. I. 28. 30-36.
3. Mbh. I. 243. 12 ff Kumbhakoṇam edition.
4. Mbh. XII. 188. 10 ff.

न विशेषोऽस्ति वर्णानां सर्वं ब्राह्ममिदं जगत् ।
ब्रह्मणा पूर्वसृष्टं हि कर्मभिर्वर्णतां गतम् ।

Rām. VII. 74. 9 ff. Mbh. III. 283. 31 ff.

5. Mbh. XIII. 90. 4 ff. List of the Brāhmaṇas following other professions.

examples of Viśwāmitra and Paraśurāma were cited as old stories and were remodelled just to prove that caste depended upon birth.[1] Thus the progeny of inter-caste Pratiloma marriages (which were prohibited by the society) formed lower castes.[2] When these Jātis (castes) formed water-tight compartments within the society, it would have been easier to adjust in one's own caste. The tendency was thus on the increase and inter-caste marriages were prohibited and discouraged through the discriminating legislation already mentioned before.

APPENDIX—C

Pravara and Gotra

Pravara

The question of Parvara is more ancient than that of Gotra. 'Pravara' means choosing or invoking. It is said that a sacrificer while invoking fire used to take the name of his illustrious ancestors, who formerly did the same. The word generally came to denote, illustrious ṛshis-ancestors of the sacrificer. Although the word Pravara is not found in the Ṛg-Veda there is mention of Ārsheya—its synonym. The Kaushītakī Brāhmaṇa[3] explains the purpose of taking the name of the ancestors, as gods do not take from him who has no list of the illustrious ancestors, therefore, the sacrificer or his priest pronounces the Ārsheya of the sacrificer.[4] When the sacrifice was done by each house-holder, in asking for the Ārsheya[5] the sacrificer chose such names of the ṛshis as he pleased, and further begged that the Ārsheya he sought, shall be on the model of that attained by those ṛshis. Upto Āpastamba it

1. Mbh. XIII. 4. 9-10; III. 180. 32, 37.
2. Mbh. XIII. 48. 5 ff.
3. Kau. Br. 3-2.
4. Karandikar in "Hindu Exogamy" chap. III. p. 51 has correctly shown that there is no such order. Also chap. V. page 96 Sometimes the remotest ancestor's and sometimes the nearest ancestor's name is pronounced first.
5. Karandikar "Hindu Exogamy" Chapt. III. p. 54-59 Ārsheya was a thing for which poets of Ṛg Vedic hymns aspired for while asking for 'Ārsheya they qualified it by connecting their desired Ārsheya with the name of a great sage. The termination "Vat" used for each Pravara name is very significant. It was a matter of selection first but later Śākhās were fixed.

was a matter of selection.[1] When fire worship was no more an individual duty but a communal duty gradually Śākhās of Pravaras were fixed up arbitrarily; excepting in case of Apri selection, nothing about descent could be said about the Pravaras[2]. When Pravara had practical meaning it was determined according to the schools of ritual and learning. Thus a group of Pravara ṛshis were attached to a Śākhā i.e. brotherhood of each division following the same ritual. Gotras as will be stated were at first surnames. By the time of Baudhāyana or even later all the forty-nine Pravaras were grouped under the names of eight great sages, who were thus supposed to be founders of the eight Gotras. This is the origin of Gotras in the present sense. This explains how different Gotras have the same Pravaras.[3] It is only after this arrangement that Gotra exogamy was introduced, in the modern sense of the term. It is therefore that Pravara exogamy based on Śākhās following the same rituals, is older than the present Gotra exogamy. As the Brāhmaṇas were exponents of rituals, Āpastamba was not sure of the Kshatriya Pravaras,[4] for Brāhmaṇas sacrificed for them.

Gotras

In the Ṛg-Veda Gotra is used for the cowpen and in some verses for assemblage also,[5] from which perhaps it came to denote a clan or family.

In the Upanishads sages addressed their pupils by the Gotra names i. e. Vaśishṭha, Viswāmitra. So Gotra relationship was by birth but is referred to in connection with sacrifice and education and not marriage. Marriage with Sagotra is forbidden only in Gṛhya and Dharma Sūtras but such conditions might have existed before that.[6] Gotras at first referred to surnames[7] of a family. In the time of Baudhāyana or even later

1. Karandikar "Hindu Exogamy" Chap. III. p. 58-59.
2. Ibid. Chap. III. 50-52 states that Pravara had nothing to do with ancestory when it was grouped with Gotras.
3. Ibid. Chap. IV.
4. Ibid. Chap. V. 58-59; 96-97 states that Āpastamba and Baudhāyana Srauta Sūtra recommend that the Kshatriyas can take Pravaras of their priests (आचार्य) or just Pūrarava, Manu, Ilāvat.
5. Ṛg V. II. 23. 18; VI. 65. 5.
6. Kaṇe "Hist. of Dh." Vol. II. part I. chap. IX. p. 480-81
7. Ibid. p. 489 (discussing Pravaras) five thousand and above Gotras

the Gotras were organized on a spiritual or Pravara basis. Pravara groups were brotherhoods of each division following the same ritual. Therefore Gotra exogamy was first based on surnames i.e. agnate blood relationship and later based on Pravara exogamy.[1] It is therefore that the list of the founders of Gotras is differently given by the different authors.[2]

In the Great Epic Gotra is mentioned in the sense of surname as well as that of spiritual brotherhood. When Yayāti wants to know Gotras of Śarmishṭhā and Devayānī, Devayānī utters her father's name.[3] The kings in Draupadī's swayamvara must have been introduced with surnames only,[4] for although it is said that they were introduced by the names and Gotras but in the relavent chapter no specification of Gotra is given.[5] Again in the Anuśāsana Parva a list of fifty sons of Viśwāmitra as the founder of Gotras is mentioned but none of these are accepted "Gotrakartās"[6] so surnames of their families may have been called after them. The śloka giving the popular opinion about the spread of progeny due to the eight sages including Agastya,[7] is different in the Mahābhārata which states that fifty ṛshis were responsible for spreading progeny.[8] Now these fifty most probably refer to Pravara sage group on the basis of which the spiritual Gotras were formed.[9] Perhaps this śloka

certainly refer to surnames Cp. Pāṇinī IV. 1. 162.

अपत्यं-पौत्र-प्रभृति गोत्रम् ।

1. Karandikar "Hindu Exogamy", chap. IV.
2. Kaṇe "Hist. of Dh." Vol. II. part I. p. 483-484.
3. Mbh. I. 81. 8-10 Cp. Panini IV. 1. 162. as quoted above.
4. Mbh. I. 185. 37 नाम्ना च गोत्रेण च कर्मणा च ।

nothing can be stated on this account as these have been considered interpolated portions by the Cr. ed. of Mbh. Pusālker "Epic and Purāṇas", p. 101.

5. Mbh. I. 186.
6. Mbh. XIII. 4. 49-50. It is interesting to note that Gālava, Viśwāmitra's son here, has been mentioned as his disciple in Mbh. V. 106. 19.
7. Kaṇe "Hist. of Dh." Vol. II. part I. p. 484. अष्टाशीतिः सहस्त्राणि ऊर्ध्वरेतसामृषीणां । बभूवुस्तत्रागस्त्याष्टमैऋषिभिः प्रजनो ऽभ्युपगतः ।
8. Mbh. II. 11. 54

अष्टाशीति सहस्त्राणि ऋषीणामूर्ध्वरेतसाम् ।
प्रजावतां च पञ्चाशदृषीणामपि पाण्डव ।।

9. Mbh. XII. 296. 17-18.

मूलगोत्राणि चत्वारि समुत्पन्नानि पार्थिव ।
आङ्गिराः कश्यपश्चैव वसिष्ठो भृगुरेव च ।

refers to the time when spiritual Gotras were being organized on the basis of Pravara which denoted different schools of ritual. The śloka "Mūla Gotrāṇi" refers to these first four schools which later developed into ten. The redacted portions i.e. the Śānti and Anuśāsana Parva sometimes refer to such Gotras based on spiritual brotherhood and gradually the sept exogamy which might have begun with surnames or on biological grounds i.e. excluding marriages between the progeny of the same ancestor was later transferred to spiritual brotherhood.

The redactors of the Great Epic use Gotra many times in the modern sense i.e. in the sense of spiritual brotherhood and not in the old sense i.e. surnames. But as the story part has been handled by the redactors it is difficult to assert that when Yudhishṭhira introduced himself as "Vaiyāgrapāda" in Virāṭa's court the Kshatriyas had Gotras of their own, as Kaṇe believes.[1] Vyāgrapāda is a ṛshi in the Mahābhārata whose son is said to be Dhaumya[2], who was priest of the Pāṇḍavas. Yudhishṭhira might have taken this Gotra from their priest and it was also convenient to use it under the guise of a Brāhmaṇa. Kshatriyas, however, were not particular about Gotra exogamy. It is absurd to think that when the Kshatriyas took Gotras of their priests, who might have officiated as priests for thirty Kshatriya families, these families would not have inter-married. Even in the 9th century A. D. the Kshatriyas were not particular about Gotra exogamy as Medhātithi states that exogamy operated for the Kshatriyas and Vaiśyas for seven generations.[3] Thus even the Brāhmaṇas who were not sure of their Pravaras and Gotras were enjoined to accept Pravaras of their gurus but were to marry with Samānapravaras and Sagotras with the only exception of excluding their teacher's daughter in marriage.[4]

Acc. to this śloka these four are the most ancient patriachs, while Agastya, Viśwāmitra and Atri came later. But according to tradition and even according to the Epics Vasishṭha and Agastya were brothers.

See also Pargitar "AIHT" p. 185-186 Atri being the latest of the lunar race out of eight mind —born sons of the Creator. The three others of the eight i.e. Pulastya, Pulaha and Kratu did not produce Brāhmaṇa families.

1. Mbh. IV. 7. 8-12. Kaṇe "Hist. of Dh." Vol. II. part I. Chapt. IX. p. 493-494.
2. Mbh. XIII. 14. 112.
3. Karandikar "Hindu Exogamy" Chap. V, p. 105 ff. and chap. VI.
4. Ibid. chap. V. p. 96-97.

APPENDIX—D

Polygamy

Among the Kshatriya specially of the royal family polygamy seems to have been very common. It was the old tradition coming down from the Ṛg Vedic and Brāhmaṇic[1] age. Although the monogamous ideal of Rāmachandra was respected, it was an exception,[2] mostly the Epic heroes were polygamous. Even Dharmarāja married twice.[3] Daśaratha had three queens and three hundred and fifty wives.[4] In the Māhābhārata the most revered person Srī Kṛshṇa had eight principal queens and sixteen thousand others, whom he married after he had released them from the prison of Narakāsura.[5] A person having hundred thousand wives could have the "Viruda" of high-souled[6]. These accounts are, of course, exaggerated and may be even fictitious but even fiction may reflect prevalent social conditions. Married princes came to swayamvara which means that the kings had no objection to bestow their daughters as second and third wife.[7] Still the first wife was thought to be sacred.[8] Two or several sisters were also married to the same person.[9]

Whatever Pargiter or other western savants may opine,[10]

1. Upādhyāya "Women in the Ṛg Veda" p. 109-111 Tait. Br. III. 8. 4. Śat. Br. XIII. 4. 19. Cp. Ram. I. 14. 35.

2. Vyāsa S. N. "Ramāyāṇakālīn Samāj" p. 132-133. There is no foundation for Rama's being polygamous.

3. Mbh. I. 95. 76. It may be a later passage for Davikā has not been mentioned any where not even in Mbh. XV. 25.

4. Rām. I. 13. 41; II. 20. 2-3.

5. Mbh. V. 158. 8.

6. Mbh. VII. 65. 1-2; III. 127. 13. XII. 29. 104; III 122. 6 (The four thousand wives of Śaryāti).

7. Mbh. I. 186. Salya, Śiśupāla, Jarāsandha and many kings with their sons came to swayamvara. They came to marry Draupadī and not see the show (24).

8. Rām II. 104. 4 वने प्राक्कलनं तीर्थं ये ते निर्विषयीकृता: । p. 466. of M.N. Dutta's translation, II. 64. 43.

9. Mbh. I. 66. 11 ff.

10. Pargiter "AIHT" chap. XXVII. page 328. Yet Jamadgni, Gautama, the Brāhmaṇa in Ādi Parva (I. 158 sec. Vaka Vadā), the Brāhmaṇa of Nakulopākhyāna (Mbh. XIV. 90), Droṇa, Kṛpa, Jaratkāru were all monogamous. The devotion of Atri and Anusūyā, Vasishṭha and Arundhatī, is famous. Mahābhārata also refers to Akshamālā and Vaśishṭha but he may have been another Vasishṭha.

monogamy was the general custom prevalent among the Brāhmaṇas. There are only one or two rare cases of polygamy among the Brāhmaṇas.[1] Monogomy may have been practised by them due to their penances or poverty. Polygamy, however, was not banned for them. It was considered Dharma[2] and was not even forbidden in the didactic portions.[3] It is easy to understand the Kshatriya polygamy. The male character is solicitous, mobile, craving for expansion, partial to novelty. The Kshatriyas were most free among the Āryans. In the course of their conquest and wanderings (e.g. Arjuna) they came in contact with the women of various races. Their centrifugal attributes coupled with adventureous life made them possess women where ever they went, for the social check in the adventurous life is less. Their riches also helped them to maintain as many wives as they wanted.

APPENDIX—E

Polyandry[4]

The various explanations put forward for Draupadī's unique case of polyandry e.g. her receiving a boon as a daughter of a ṛshi in previous birth or her being wife of five Indras,[5] must have been invented by the composer in order to do away with the repugnance generally felt for polyandry.[6] Kuntī's insistence and Yudhishṭhira's resolve in following her statement about Draupadī are nothing but poor justifications. Nevertheless, this custom among certain tribes as remnant of old usage, may have been prevalent when the Epic story was being enacted. This tradition in the mouth of people was too powerful and too strong to be changed. By the time the Great Epic was written it was not, however, widely prevalent. Certain examples cited in the Mahābhārata, that

1. Mbh. I. 229. 17-18 (The story sounds like a myth).
2. Mbh. I. 158. 35-36.
3. Mbh. XIII. 44. 11; 47. 7.
4. Vyāsa S. N. "Rāmāyaṇa Kālīn Samāj" p. 133-34—Discusses the baselessness of polyandry in the society depicted in the Rāmāyaṇa.
5. Mbh. I. 169. 6 ff. and Mbh. I. 197 (sec.).
6. J. R. A. S. Art XX. 1897 page 747-755. Kaṇe "Hist. of Dh. S." Vol. II. Part II. Chapt. XXII.page 847. Puts forward various pleas as polyandry was a headache for the Purāṇa writers and Kumārila later.

of Gautamī and Vārkshī[1], together with Sudeshṇā's not being surprised when Sairandhṛī told her that she possessed five husbands do prove certain familiarity of the Epic composers with polyandry.[2] In Sudeshaṇā's case the familiarity may have been due to the fact that she was a princess of Kaikeya, a country adjacent to the Punjab hills[3], where polyandry is still practised. This custom was certainly not respected by the Kurus.[4] The divergent views discussed about polyandry in the Kuru court also prove unfamiliarity with the custom.[5] It is also surprising that for Yudhishṭhira it was a path trodden by illustrious persons and therefore not sinful,[6] although it was against customs and the Vedas according to Drupada. In fact no satisfactory explanation could be given for this polyandry. The custom was unfamiliar even to the Vedic society so it cannot be said with certainty that it was practised quite frequently when the story part of the Great Epic was being enacted. It is, however, certain that the Pāṇḍavas were very familiar with polyandry but they were also a branch of the Kauravas who show utter unfamiliarity with this custom. It appears that Śataśṛinga, where Pāṇḍu lived for a long time may have been the same region of the Himālayas[7] where polyandry is still practised and sexual relations are rather free. Polyandry among brothers to keep family property and unity intact is still practised in Kinnaur and Jaunsār Bāwar areas.[8] Even in the

1. Mbh. I. 196. 13 ff.
2. Mbh. IV. 9. 30 ff.
3. Pargiter. F.F. "AIHT" Map facing page 294. From Spitī, Lāhaul (in Kulu Valley) upto Jaunsār Bāwar, in the Himālayas polyandry is still practised.
4. Mbh. II. 68. 35-36.
Draupadī is called 'Bandhakī".
5. Mbh. I. 201. 16; 202. 6-8.
6. Mbh. I. 195. 29-30; 196. 13-17.
7. From Lāhaul, Spitī to Jaunsār Bāwar. Cp. Saksenā R. N. "Social Economy of a Polyandrous People" 'Foreward' by Munshī in which he connects the cultural life of these people with the Pāṇḍavas, who are still worshiped by them. In Chap. II & III. after a long discussion Dr. Saksenā holds (page 30) that polyandry was an institution not unknown to the early Āryan settlers in the western Himālayas from where it gradually spread to Jaunsār Bāwar through the Kāngra valley. Still found in Hindūkush, Gilgit, Chitrāl polyandry is expressly stated to have been a social institution among the Medes (Āryans) of Persia.
8. J. R. A. S. 1897 An article XXV. 'Notes on Mahābhārata' page 758.

modern times it is seen that sometimes the young people visiting or living in the foreign countries imbibe their customs, which may appear strange to their countrymen. The Pāṇḍavas in their childhood must have grown familiar with the custom, and there may have been many illustrious ṛshis or persons following polyandry among brothers and so they had no hesitation in adopting it.

Cp. Vyāsa S. N. "Rāmāyaṇa Kālīn Samāj", p. 133-34, proves it baseless in Sītā's case.

Munśī calls this land of Jaunsār Bāwār as "a fossil of the age of the Mahābhārata" in forward to Saksenā's "Social Economy of a Polyandrous People" where the people still worship Bhīma and the Pāṇḍavas.

BIBLIOGRAPHY

Original texts of the Epics

Śriman Mahābhāratam	: Chitraśālā edition, Poonā in six Volumes with Nīlkanṭha's commentary. Vol. I, 1929; Vol. II, 1930; Vol. III & IV, 1931; Vol. V, 1932; Vol. VI, 1933.
Mahābhārata	: Southern Recension critically edited by P.P.S. Sastri, Madras, 1931.
Mahābhārata	: Critical edition, B. O. R. I., Poonā Ādi Parva 1927, 1933; Virāt Parva 1936. Udyoga Parva, 1940. Araṇyaka Parva 1943. Sabhā Parva 1944.
Mahābhārata	: Nirṇaya Sāgar Press. Edited by Mādhav Vilās Book Depot. Kumbhakoṇam, Madras, 1931.
Rāmāyaṇa	: Nirṇaya Sāgar Press Edition Bombay 1929.
Rāmāyaṇa	: North Indian recension by Bhagwad Dutt, Lahore, 1931.
Śrimad Vālmīki Rāmāyaṇa	: A critical edition with commentary of Sri Govindarāja edited by T.R. Krisṇacharya, Kumbhakoṇam.

English translations of the text and Index.

M.N. Dutta's translation of "The Rāmāyaṇa" in 3 volumes edited from 1891 to 1893, Published by G.C. Chakraverty, Calcutta.

Sorenson "Index to the Names in the Mahābhārata" in 3 volumes, London, 1904-1925.

Roy, P.C. translation of the Mahābhārata edited by Dutt Bose and Co., Calcutta.

Vol. I	: Ādi and Sabhā Parvas, 1919.
Vol. II	: Vana Parva.

Vol. III : Virāṭa and Udyoga Parvas.
Vol. IV : Bhīshma Parva, 1925.
Vol. V : Droṇa Parva, 1925.
Vol. VI : Karṇa and Śalya Parva, 1926.
Vol. VII : Sauptika, Strī and Śānti Parvas, 1927.
Vol. VIII : Śānti Parva, 1928.
Vol. IX & X : Śānti and Anuśāsana Parvas.
Vol. XI : Aśwamedha, Āśramavāsik, Mausala, Mahāprasthānika, Swargārohaṇa Parvas.

N.B. References in the Mahābhārata are mainly taken from Chritraśālā, Poona edition, wherever there is deviation other editions are named. References in the Rāmāyaṇa are taken from Nirṇaya Sāgar Press, Bombay. For translations sometimes P. C. Roy's Mahābhārata and M. N. Dutt's Rāmāyaṇa has been used.

Dharmaśāstras

N.B. S. B. E. stands for Sacred Books of the East edited by Max Muller, Oxford Clarendon Press.

Āpastamba, Hiraṇyakeshi and Gobhila Gṛhya Sūtra, S. B. E. Vol XXX Part II, 1892.

Āpastamba and Gautam Dharma Sūtras, S. B. E. Vol. II, Part I, 1879.

Institutes of Vishṇu, S. B. E. Vol. VII, 1900.

Vasishṭha and Baudhāyana Dharma Sūtras, S. B. E. Vol. XIV, Part II, 1882.

Śānkhayana, Āśwalāyana, Pāraskara, Khadira Gṛhya Sūtras, S. B. E. Vol. XXIX, Part I.

Smrtichandrikā—Devan Bhatt. Mysore, 1914.

Manusmṛti with Kullūka's commentary, Nirṇaya Sāgar Press.

Yagnyawalka Smṛti—With the Mitakshara commentary, Bombay, 1909.

Manusmṛti, Nārada Smṛti, Vishṇu Dharma Sūtra, Atri Samhita, Paraśara Smṛti from "Smṛti Sandarbha" Vol. I and II. Calcutta, 1952.

Dakshasmṛti, Devalsmṛti, Bṛhaspati Smṛti, Vaśishṭha Smṛti,

Baudhāyanasmṛti from "Smṛtinām—Samuchchayah" Ānandāśrama, Bombay, 1929.

Vīrmitrodaya Samskāra Prakāśa—Chowkhambha series, Banaras, 1913.

Udvahatattva—Chowkhambha series, Banaras, 1913.

"Maitrāyaṇī Samhita" Oundh. शक १८६४. वि० सं० १९९८.

Other Sanskrit works

Amarkosha with commentary of Bhanujee Dīkshit—Nirṇaya Sāgar, Bombay, 1929.

Harivamśa—Dutt and Bose Calcutta.

Upanishads—Natesan, Madras.

Upanishad Bhāshya—Astekar, Poona, 1927.

Mālatī Mādhava—Bombay, 1876.

Raghuvamśa—Bombay, 1910.

Śakuntalā—Nirṇaya Sāgar, Bombay, 1916.

Uttararāmcharita—Bombay, 1901.

Mrichchhakaṭika—Bombay, 1910.

Chhandogya Upanishad—S. B. E. Vol. I, Oxford Clarendon Press, 1900.

General works

Agrawal : "Pāṇini Kālin Bhārata", Banaras, 1955.

Altekar : "The Position of Women in Hindu Civilisation", Banaras, 1938.

Asoka Chatterjee : "Śanta's Parentage" Indian Historical Quarterly June 1957.

Altekar : Education in Ancient India", Banaras, 1934.

Allison : Disadvantages of Being a woman", London.

Badar clarisse : Women in Ancient India", Trubner, London, 1925.

Babel August : "Women in the Past, Present and Future" London.

"The Great Women of India"—Published by Mayawati, Almora, 1953.

Banerjee, G.D. : "Marriage and Stridhana", Calcutta 1923.

Davies, J.L. : "A Short History of Women", London, 1948.

Dās, A.C. : "Ṛg Vedic Culture", Culcutta, 1925.

Dharmā, P.C. : "Rāmāyaṇa Polity", Madras, 1941.

Dharmā, P.C. : "Social Life in Rāmāyaṇa" QJMS XXVIII, pp. 1-19; 73-80.

Dharmā, P.C. : "Women During Rāmāyaṇa Period", JIH. XVII, pp. 1-28.

Dutt, R.C. : "History of Civilization in Ancient India, " London, 1893.

Dwivedī, H.P. : "Prāchīna Bhārat Ke Kalātmaka Vinoda", Bombay, 1952.

Cousin, E. Margaret : "Indian Womanhood Today", Allahabad, 1941.

Griffith : "Ṛg Veda" English translation in 2 volumes, Banaras, 1897.

Hedwig Bachmann : "On the Soul of the Indian Woman" 2 volumes, Eng. Tr. by Shilavati Ketkar, Bostora Indian Portuguesa, 1942.

Hevelock Ellis : "Sex in society" Last and VI vol. of "Studies on Psychology of Sex", London, 1946.

Hopkins, E.W. : "The Great Epic of India", New Haven, 1920.

Hopkins, E.W. : "The Religions of India" Publisher India Office, London, 1896.

Hopkins, E.W. : "Epic Mythology", Trubner Strassburg and London, 1915.

Hopkins, E.W. : Journal of American Oriental Society. Vol. XIII. 1887. Art. III. "The Social and Military Position of the Ruling Caste in India."

Horner, I.B. "Women under Primitive Buddhism", London, 1930

Haridatta Vedālankāra "Hindu Parivāra Mīmānsā" Distributer Bharāti Bhandar, Allahabad Vi. Sam. 2011.

Indian Inheritance : Vol. I and II, Bharatīya Vidyā Bhawan, Bombay, 1956.

Indra : "The Status of Women in Ancient India", Lahore, 1940.

Jaiswāl : "Manu and Yajñavalkya", 1930 T. L. L. series, Calcutta.

Kaṇe, P.V. : "History of Dharmaśāstra," B. O. R. I, Poona, Vol. I—1930, Vol. II part I and II, 1941, Vol. III—1946.

Keith : "Religion and Philosophy of Vedas" Part I and II, London, 1925.

Keith : "Taittirīya Samhitā", Eng. Tr., Cambridge Massachusetts, 1914.

Karandīkar : "Hindū Exogamy" Bombay, 1929.

Krishnamācharī : "A History of classical Sanskrit Literature", Madras, 1937.

Keyserling : "The Book of Marriage", London, 1927.

Kauṭilya : "Arthaśāstra" Eng. Tr. by Shamasastry, Mysore, 1923.

Longlois and Seignobos : "Introduction to the Study of History", Eng. Tr. by G.G. Berry, London, 1898.

Law : "Women in Buddhist India" Ceylon, 1927.

Macdonell : "History of Sanskrit Literature" London, MDCCCV.

Mackenzie, D. : "Teutonic Myths and Legends".

Meyer, J.J. : "Sexual Life in Ancient India", in 2 Vol. London, 1930.

Mitter : "Position of women in Hindu law"

Mill, J.S. : "The Subjection of Women", London, Bombay, 1930.

Monier Williams : "Indian Wisdom", London, 1893.

Mukerjee : "Ancient Indian Education", Macmillan & Co., 1947.

Noble Margaret (Sister Nivedita) : "The Web of Indian Life", London, 1906.

Pāndey, R.B. : "Hindū Samskāras", Banaras, 1949.

Pāndey, R.B. : "Smybolism of Hindu Nuptials" Indian Culture, Vol. II. Jan-March, 1945.

Prabhu : "Hindū Social Organization" New Revised Edition, Bombay, 1954.

Pargiter, F.F. : "Ancient Indian Historical Tradition", London, 1922.

Pusālker, A.D. : "Studies in Epics and Purāṇas", Bombay, 1955.

Rapson : "The Cambridge History of India", Vol. I. London, 1935.

Sarkār, S.C. : "Some Aspects of Earliest Social History of India", London, 1928.

Saksenā, R.N. : "Social Economy of a Polyandrous People", Agra University, 1955.

Shāstrī, S.R. : "Women in the Vedic Age", Bombay, 1954.

Shāstrī, S.R. : "Women in the Sacred Laws", Bombay, 1954.

Shāstrī Srīnivāsa : "Lectures on Rāmāyaṇa"

Smith : "The Oxford History of India", London, 1928.

Sundarāchārier : "Studies in Rāmāyaṇa", Madras, 1945.

Siddhānta, N. K. : "Heroic Age of India", London, 1929

Thomas : "Women and Marriage in India", London, 1939.

Tripāṭhi, G.M. : "Marriage Forms under Ancient Law", Bombay, 1906.

Hussain, S.M. : The Uttar Pradesh Local Acts, 1836-1955, Vol. III, Lucknow, 1929. (for Naik Girl's Protection Act).

Thadanī : 'Mystry of Mahābhārata" Karāchi, 1935.

Upādhyāya : "Women in Ṛg Veda" Banaras, 1941.

Vaidya : "The Riddle of Rāmāyaṇa", London, 1906.

Vaidya : "Mahābhārata—a criticism", Bombay, 1905.

Vaidya : "Mahābhārata Mīmānsā", Kashi Vi. Era. 1977.

Vaidya : "Epic India", Bombay.

Vyāsa S.N. : "Rāmāyaṇa Kālīn Samāj" Delhi, 1958

Vātsyāyana : "Kāma Sūtra" Eng. Tr. with Sanskrit text by K. Rangāswāmi Aiyar, Lahore, 1921.

Vyāsa. S.N. : "Rāmāyaṇa Kālīn Sanskṛti" Delhi, 1958.

Westermarck : "A History of Human Marriage", London, 1903.

N. B. where other edition have been consulted the year is mentioned in the footnotes.

Winternitz : "A History of Indian Literatue :", London, 1903.

Winternitz : Journal of Royal Asiatic Society, 1897. Article on "Niyoga".

INDEX

A. Index of Names and Places.

(In the Index '°' mark represents Foot-notes Pages numbers.)

Abbāsaids 216°.
Abhimanyu 5, 65°, 138°.
Ādrika 209.
Agastya 21, 112, 209, 268, 311, 312°.
Agni 19, 66, 89, 208, 282 (—hotra), 233 (—shtoma), 64 (—pradakshiṇā)
Ahalyā 66, 112, 207, 207°, 208, 210, 217°, 296, 302.
Akshamālā 86, 313°.
Akrūra 210 (wife.).
Ambā 23, 51, 71, 73, 232°, 242, 242°, 308°.
Ambālikā 72, 136, 157, 157°, 159, 159°, 161, 161°, 169, 188, 189, 236.
Ambikā 71, 136, 157, 157°, 159, 159°, 161, 161°, 169, 188, 189, 236.
Andhakas 236, 237.
Anga 88° (King), 5 (people.).
Angada 188.
Āngirasī 179°.
Anūpa 3°.
Anusūyā 23, 31, 38, 43, 112, 165, 165°, 232°, 247, 268, 313°.
Arjā 242°.
Araṭṭas 36, 111.
Arjuna 20 (Yati), 42, 45, 50, 54°, 56°, 62, 62°, 74, 85, 89, 92, 93°, 94, 95°, 122, 128, 150, 185, 186, 187, 188, 194, (Car), 194, 206, 210, 255, 260, 261, 269°, 314.
Arshtisheṇa 167°.
Arundhatī 21, 22, 268, 313°.
Ashtāvakra 67, 230.
Aśoka 15, 239, 239°.
Assām 287°.
Aśwasena 185°.
Aśwatthāmā 258, 263.
Aśwamedha 233, 234, 298
Aświn 111.
Atri 95°, 312°, 313°.
Auśija 85°.
Ayodhyā 43, 175, 206, 237, 268, 272, 278, 284.

Babylon 220.
Bagdad 216°.
Balhika 287°.
Bhadrā 180, 190 (Kākshivatī), 208 (dr. of Soma.).
Bhangaswana 151°
Bhānumanta 248.
Bharadwaja 167, 209°, 280.
Bharata 141, 153, 163°, 166, 175, 269, 276, 277, 277°, 278, 279, 280, 282, 283, 283°, 284.
Bhārgava 204, 242°.
Bhattīya 239°.
Bhīma 85, 123, 123°, 130, 139, 141, 143, 150, 153, 190, 191, 192, 258, 259, 264, 316°.
Bhīshma 4, 30, 53, 60, 66, 67, 71, 72, 73, 76, 77, 81, 122°, 135, 137, 143, 158°, 161, 161°, 171°, 183, 185, 185°, 191, 206, 223, 228, 229, 242, 242°, 262, 308.
Bhṛgu 61, 207°, (wife) 223.
Bhūmanyu 167.
Bhūti 146.
Brahma or Brahman (the Creator) 76, 82, 97, 152, 268, 291.
Bṛhannatā 29.
Bṛhaspati 21, 160, 207°, 208.
Brynhild 182.
Buddha 9.

Chedi 109.
Chīna 287° (people and country).
Chirkārin 142, 149.
Chitrāl 315.°
Chitrāngadā 94, 95°, 125, 247°.
Ceylon 287°.

Damyantī 42, 51, 53, 74, 101, 109, 113, 123, 143°, 160°, 165 (—and her brothers) 224°, 228°, 268, 281, 302, 308 and 311.
Daṇda (King) 204, 244.
Daṇdaka 267.
Dāsarāja 56.
Daśaratha 3°, 12, 27, 120, 122, 129°, 150, 173 (wives), 175, 176, 178 (wives of—), 179, 189 (wives of—), 210° and 233 (queens), 236°, 267, 273, 275, 276, 277, 277°, 278, 279, 281, 282, 283, 284, 298, 313.
Devakī 121°, 180.
Devayānī 17, 19, 43, 51, 88, 125°, 165°, 311.
Devapī 167.

Devika 95°, 313°.
Dhaumya 312.
Dhṛstadyumna 54°.
Dhṛtarāstra 32, 105, 122, 122°, 130, 154, 161°, 193, 206, 211, 211°, 262, 263, 264.
Dīrghatamā or Dīrghatāmas 32, 162, 170, 185, 186, 206, 208.
Diśā 24, 229, 229°.
Divodāsa I and II 68°.
Draupadī 21 (Panditā and Brahmavādinī) 23, 27, 27°, 29, 30, 31, 32, 33, 43, 53, 54, 54°, 60, 61, 64°, 66, 73, 78, 89, 90°, 91, 91°, 95, 95°, 96, 96°, 101, 103, 104, 106, 107, 107°, 108, 111, 111°, 112, 115, 116, 118°, 121, 123, 129, 129°, 130, 151, 154, 162, 173, 182, 184, 193°, 195, 210, 212, 221, 221°, 225, 231, 233°, 236°, 238, 238°, 242, 244, 245, 247, 254, 255, 256, 257, 258, 260, 262, 263, 264, 266, 270, 280, 292, 293, 296, 302, 311, 313°, 314, 315°.
Droṇa 95°, 209, 258, 313°.
Drupada 38, 53, 54°, 60, 61, 63, 89°, 90°, 136, 163°, 166, 166°, 315.
Durgā 144°, 146.
Durvāsā 20, 164, 260.
Duryodhana 31, 32, 32°, 89, 130, 130°, 140, 141, 154, 165 (—and his brothers), 186, 191, 193, 194°, 256, 256°, 258, 263.
Dushyanta 20, 74, 75, 228°, 265.
Duśśāsana 193.
Dwārikā 176.
Dyumatsena 5, 62°.

Egypt 220.
Ekachakra 141.
England 224.

Gādhi 76, 152.
Gālava 81°, 311°.
Gāndhārī 31, 32, 42, 55, 110, 121, 151, 152, 154, 161°, 165, 193, 225, 231, 261, 262, 263, 264, 276, 280, 283, 302.
Gangā 43, 51, 58, 68, 151, 153.
Ganges 182, 192, 193°.
Gārgī 23.
Garhwāl 193.°
Garuḍa 88.
Gautama 45, 66, 95°, 185, 313°.
Gautamī 153, 155, 224, 265, 315.
Germany 50.°
Gharmya 234.°
Ghṛtāchī 209.°
Gilgit 315°.
Greece 216°.

Haihaya 136°.
Hamlet 188.
Hanumāna 109, 207, 224, 248, 267, 270, 271, 272, 273.
Haryāśwa 68°.
Hastināpur 179, 190, 236, 264.
Hemā 29.
Hidimbā 51, 85, 125, 143, 224°, 307.
Himālayas 36, 182°, 213, 315, 315°.
Hindukush 315°.

Ikshwāku 91°, 206.
Indra 38°, 124, 207, 207°, 208, 210, 213, 223, (Śakra), 226, 230, 314.
Indrāṇī 209.
Indraprastha 121, 169, 244.
Indus Valley 144, 220.
Irāvan 185.

Jacob 50°.
Jamdagni 95°, 313°.
Janaka 22, 38, 39, 53, 62°, 67, 83°, 266, 267, 276.
Janamejaya 60, 223.
Jānapadī 209°.
Jarāsandha 95°, 129°, 313°.
Jaratkāru (Sage and his wife) 21, 95°, 125, 136, 227, 266, 316.°
Jaunsār Bāwar 36°, 168, 168°, 315, 315°, 316°.
Jayadratha 27, 60, 73, 85, 255, 257, 262.
Justinian 76.

Kābul Valley 74°.
Kacha 17, 43, 88.
Kaikasī 38, 43, 51, 85°.
Kaikeya 195, 205°, 315.
Kaikeyī 12, 27, 56°, 67, 83, 107, 141°, 152, 232, 236°, 248, 275, 276, 277, 278, 279, 280, 281, 282, 283, 284, 300, 302.
Kālakā 152.
Kālāśoka 9.
Kālī (Goddess) 145, 146.
Kalmashapāda 163, 163°, (Mitrasaha)
Kangṛa Valley 315°.
Kaṇwa 151, 151°.
Kapila 213°.
Kapoti 113, 181.
Karaṇī 283.
Karṇa 19, 36, 53, 54°, 88, 89, 101, 113, 141, 162, 184, 203, 216.
Kareṇumatī 143°.
Kārusha 210.
Kāshmir 210.
Kāśirāja (dr. of—) 53.
Kaśyapa 165, 213° (dr. of—)
Kaurava 30, 31, 32 (princes and

ladies), 135, 141, 161°, 164, 181, 182, 187, 189, 193, 193° (ladies, wives and widows), 254, 256, 258, 263, 264, 315.
Kausala 248.
Kausalyā 12, 22, 23, 27, 104, 107 111, 121, 125°, 129°, 150, 152, 154, 173, 174, 175, 178, 238, 248, 268, 275, 276, 277, 278, 279, 280, 281, 282, 284, 302.
Kauśika 116.
Kauśiki 266.
Kavaśa 85°.
Kāyavya 73, 138, 140.
Keśinī 52, 268.
Ketus 179°.
Kīchaka (or—S. pl.) 182, 210, 255, 258, 268.
Kinnaur 315.
Kirāta 287°.
Kosala 9, 248.
Kosalendrarājaduhitā 248.
Kotika 238°, 255.
Kratu 312.
Kratu Ugrāyudha 185°.
Kripa 95°, 209, 313°.
Kripī 209,
Kṛshna or Śrī Kṛshna 11, 19, 65°, 72, 73, 93°, 95°, 110, 111, 153, 176, 181 (wives of—) 181 183 (widows of—), 186, 186°, 187°, 188, 193 (widows of—), 223, 236, 256, 258, 259, 260, 263, 269°, 313.
Kubera 123°, 213.
Kulinda 255.
Kulu 36°, 168, 315.°
Kumbhīnasī 55, 184.
Kunti 15, 18, 20, 21, 22, 27, 27°, 31, 32, 42, 65°, 71°, 94, 104, 121, 122, 123°, 129°, 137°, 139, 140, 141, 143, 143°, 150, 151, 152, 153, 154, 157, 158°, 159°, 160, 164, 164°, 165, 166°, 168, 170, 173, 179, 179° (children of—), 188, 190, 192 (—'s children), 192, 198, 203, 203°, 208, 211°, 216°, 223°, 224°, 230°, 236°, 247°, 255, 256, 258, 259, 260, 261, 262, 264, 276, 280, 296, 302, 314.
Kuntibhoja 259.
Kuru (army, court, dynasty, elders and ladies also), 9, 35, 36, 66, 86°, 104, 121, 129°, 130, 161°, 162, 168, 187, 191, 193, 194°, 195°, 225, 237, 238, 255, 256, 256°, 260, 263, 296, 315.
Kurukshetra 23.
Kuśa 274, 62° (—dhwaja).
Kuśanābha (drs of—) 29, 52, 54, 55, 75.

Laban 50°.
Lahul 36°, 168, 315.
Lakshamaṇa 101, 106, 140, 141°, 176, 188°, 196°, 224, 237, 267, 270, 271, 273, 274, 277, 281, 281°, 283,° 284, 285.
Lakshmī 146.
Lankā 109, 176, 224, (Rākshasī), 270, 272, 273, 285.
Lava 9, 274.
Leah 50°.
Lopāmudrā 21, 31, 43, 101, 112, 266, 268.

Madayantī 157, 160°, 162, 163, 180, 268.
Mādhavī 61, 68, 81°.
Madirā 180.
Madra 36, 76, (King of—), 216 (women of—).
Mādrī 62°, 76, 129°, 135, 135°, 157, 158°, 164, 165, 168, 179, (children of—), 180, 182, 236°, 260.
Magadha 3°, 49.
Mahādeva (God) 112, 112°, 145, 146, 146,° 155, 262.
Mahāvisha 167.
Māheswarī (Magna mater) 147.
Mahishasura 145.
Māhishmatī 36 (women of –), 145, 208.
Maitrāvaruṇa 209°.
Maitreyī 23.
Mamatā 160, 208.
Mānasputra 228°.
Mandapāla 86.
Manḍavi 62°.
Manḍodarī 32, 43, 111, 174, 194, 237, 285.
Mantharā 223 (w/o Bhṛgu), 248, 277, 278, 280.
Mārīcha 207.
Mārkanḍeya 184.
Mātali 55, 66.
Mātanga 24, 37°, 88.
Māyavī 232.
Mediterranean 144, 220.
Menakā 209, 209°.
Miśrakeśī 209.
Mithilā 232, 248, 276.
Muchukunda 153.

Nāgarāja 185.
Nahusha 209.
Nala 4° (story of—) 43, 51, 123, 128, 129, 169°, 228.
Nārada (sage) 5, 20, 38, 55, 121°, 165°, 228, 238.
Naraka Bhauma or Narakāsura 186,

187, 313.
Nārayaṇa 8.
Nīla 19.
Nivātakavachas 193

Oghāwatī 21, 266°.

Pampā 24.
Panchachūḍa (Apsarā) 213°, 228, 229°, 230.
Panchakanya 258°.
Pāṇḍavas 22, 30, 31, 54°, 65°, 98, 101, 102, 105, 121, 130, 139, 140, 141, 143, 143°, 150, 153, 164, 167, 168, 168°, 187, 193 (—ladies), 211°, 224°, 225, 236, 242, 248, 254, 257, 258, 259, 261, 262, 263, 264, 312, 315, 315°, 316, 316°.
Pāṇḍū 156, 156°, 159, 160, 160°, 161, 168, 179, 180, 2160, 269°, 315.
Pārāśara 198°, 208.
Pārśīka 287.°
Paraśurāma 142, 142°, 309.
Parīkshitā 42, 195.
Parvata (Sage) 20.
Pārvatī 107, 135.
Pātaliputra 9.
Patañjali 9.
Persia 287°, 315°.
Pingalā 232.
Poulama (Rākshasa) 61°.
Prabhāwatī 88°.
Pradhā 213°.
Pradweshī 125.
Pradyumna 106.
Prajāpati 46.
Pramadvarā 15, 15°, 16, 209.
Pramāti 209°.
Pratīpa 167.
Prathūdaka 182°.
Pravargya 233.
Prayāga 182.
Pṛthu 3°.
Pulaha 312.°
Pulika 239°.
Puloma 207°.
Pulomā 207°.
Punjab 36, 177°, 315°.
Pururavā 209, 310°.
Pushkara 129, 160°.
Pushkaradhāriṇī 112.
Pūtanā 223.

Rachel 50°.
Rajasūya 233°.
Raiva 208.
Raivataka 20, 237.
Rama 5, 6, 9, 12, 22, 32, 66°, 67, 83°, 91° 101, 101°, 106, 108, 114, 123, 128, 136, 140, 141, 142, 142°, 150, 154, 173, 174, 174°, 176, 178, 187, 187°, 188, 194 to 196, 207, 223, 230, 231, 234, 237, 242, 248, 248°, 266, to 275, 275°, 276 to 282, 282°, 283, 283°, 284, 285, 313 (--Chandra), 313°.
Raudrāśwa 209.
Rāvaṇa 27, 29, 32, (wives & palace of—) 52, 55, 60, 72, 73, 109, 116, 141, 174°, 178 (wives of—), 178, 192, 194, 223°, 231, 237, (—'s Antahpura), 238, 240, 268, 270, 271, 273, 285, (—s' mother).
Reṇukā 112, 130°, 208, 217°.
Richīka 150°.
Rohiṇī 180.
Romans 156°.
Ṛshtisheṇa 167, 167°.
Ṛshyaśṛnga 166, 166°, 209.
Ṛtuparṇa 53.
Ruchi 24, 88°, 112, 207, 230.
Rudra (God) 165, 165°, 223.
Rukmaṇī 73°, 116, 116°, 226.
Ruma 187, 188, 207, 285.
Ruru 55, 209.

Śabarī (Śramaṇi , Jaṭila-Tāpasī), 24, 37.
Sachī 58°, 207, 208, 268.
Sagara 135, 165.
Sahadeva 92, 150, 152, 154.
Sairandrī 212, 315.
Sāket 9.
Śakra 111, 134, 223.
Śakti 145, 220.
Śakuntalā 15, 15°, 16, 20, 43, 56, 64°, 74, 75, 76, 94, 209, 209°, 228°, 265.
Śālwa 242.
Śalya 36, 56, 76, 95°, 111°, 313°.
Salic law 231.
Sāma (Chant) 232.
Sāmbha 106.
Samvaraṇa 75
Śandilya 24.
Saṇḍilī 107, 108, 111°.
Sanjaya 165 (—'s son), 239.
Śantī 15°, 16, 112.
Śāntanu 58, 62°, 167, 167° (Aulāna), 185°.
Śaradwata 209°.
Saramā 270, 285.
Sarangī 86.
Saraswatī 146, 182 and 193 (river).
Śardaṇḍāyanī 157, 158, 160°, 162.
Śarmisthā 19, 20, 21, 43, 52, 88, 112, 119, 119°, 135, 165°, 211, 311.
Śaryāti 313°.
Śataśṛnga 168, 315.

Śatrughana 280, 283.
Satyabhāmā 106, 107°, 188, 259, 259°.
Satyavān 55, 62°, 104.
Satyavatī or Satyawatī 16, 20, 30, 42, 51, 58, 71, 76, 143, 151, 152 (Gādhi's wife) 159, 159°, 160, 161, 161°, 183, 185°, 188, 198°, 203, 203°, 208, 236, 296.
Saubhadreya 248.
Saugandika 259, 270.
Śaunaka 8, 150°.
Sauti 8, 11.
Sauvīra 210.
Sāvitrī 31, 38, 48, 51, (—'s father) 54, 55, 101, 104, 106°, 111, 113, 147, 180, 186, 268, 281, 286, 302.
Sāvitrīputrakas 147.
Schurtg 218°.
Siddhi 259.
Siddhartha 279.
Sigismund 214°.
Sigurd 182.
Śikhandī 223.
Simla 36.
Śiśupāla 73, 95°, 210, 223, 313°.
Sītā 15, 16, 26°, 27, 29, 31, 32, 38, 43, 44, 58, 58°, 60, 61°, 64°, 66°, 67, 72, 73, 91, 91°, 94, 101, 104, 106, 107, 108, 109, 110, 111, 111°, 113, 114, 116, 121, 121°, 122, 128, 143°, 151, 173, 176, 178, 188°, 192, 196°, 207, 209, 221°, 223°, 231, 231°, 232, 233°, 234, 236°, 237, 242, 247, 248, 248°, (—'s dowry), 259, 266 to 275, 277, 279, 281, 282, 284, 285, 286, 298, 302, 304, 316°.
Śiva (God), 11, 153, 252, 265.
Śivā 11, 22.
Śivī 68°.
Skandha 145.
Somā 47, 125°, 208.
Spiti 36°, 168, 315.
Sravaṇa 138, 140.
Śrāvasti 9.
Śri (Goddess of prosperity), 104, 109, 117, 139, 141°, 146, 204°, 254, 259.
Sṛnjaya 20.
Sṛngvat 38.
Śrutakīrti 62°.
Śrutāvatī 38, 38°.
Strīrājya 299.
Subhadrā 20, 27, 42, 65°, 73°, 92, 92°, 93°, 95°, 138°, 143°, 152, 173, 184, 231°, 237, 246, 247, 308.
Subhru 37, 42.
Sudarshanā 130°.
Sudeshṇā 157, 162, 210, 212, 255, 315.
Sugrīva 22, 187, 188, 207 (—'s wife), 207, 224, 232, 237, (—'s wives) 255, 285.
Śuka 209.
Sukanyā 21, 55, 101, 111, 112, 266, 268.
Śukrāchārya 17, 21, 51 and 88 (Śukra)
Sukumārī 20.
Sulabha 22, 32, 37, 40, 232, 266, 296.
Sumālī 51, 55.
Sumantra 3, 3°, 239, 279, 282.
Sumitrā 129°, 154, 275, 276, 277, 279, 280, 282, 283, 283°, 284, 302.
Śura 259.
Śurpanakhā 51, 187, 232, 300.
Surya 63°, 164°, 198°, 208, 216°, 224°.
Suśobhanā 56, 68, 68°.
Suyāja 271.
Swāhā 208.
Swāmī Rāmatīrtha 182°.
Swayamprabha 24, 37, 232.
Swetaketu 37, 164.

Tapatī 55, 75.
Tārā 22, 114, 174°, 177, 178, 187, 188, 188°, 190, 224, 231, 237, 284, 285.
Tāraka 207°.
Trījatā 270, 285.

Uddālaka 37, 164 and 208 (—'s wife).
Ujjaini 240°.
Ulm 214°.
Ulūpī 50, 51, 74, 85, 125, 185, 187, 307.
Umā 145, 146, 146°.
Upamanyu 155, 265, (—'s mother).
Upaplava 258.
Uparichara 16.
Upayāj 166.
Urvaśī 209, 209°.
Utathya 208.
Uttanka 45, 158, 164, 164°.
Uttarā 29, 31, 35, 42, 45, 55, 62°, 64°, 65°, 95°, 104°, 122, 136°, 137, 137°, 152, 173, 193, 210, 247, 264.
Uttar-kuru 35, 36°.

Vadānya 38.
Vāhīka 36 (—women), 161°, 167, 242.
Vaiśampāyana 8.
Vaiyagrapada 312.
Vāli 22, 114°, 178, (—'s wife), 187, 207, 232, 285.
Vālmīki 6, 8, 266, 268, 274, 275.
Vāmadeva a83.
Vapushṭamā 60.
Vārkshi 315.
Varuṇa 208, 209°.

Vasantasenā 171°.
Vaśishtha 9°, 86, 95°, 108°, 163, 163° (The Vaśishthas), 180, 209, 231, 267, 279, 310, 312,° 313°.
Vasu 126, 153 (Vasus), 209.
Vasudeva 65°, 92°, 93°, 180.
Vāsudeva 116, 263.
Vāsukī 136.
Vatsya 85.°
Vāyu 53.
Vedvatī 38, 232°.
Vibhīshaṇa 55, 174°, 177°, 206°, 207, 273.
Vichitravīrya 30, 156, 159, 161, 161°, 168 (—'s widows),
Vidulā 27, 32, 153, 154, 260, 265.
Vidura 36°, 57, 86°, 170, 211 (—'s mother), 211, 211°, 239, 256, 262.
Vijayā 92.
Vikarṇa 256.
Vipula 25, 207.
Virādha 271.
Virāta 45, 95°, 210, 310.
Vishṇu (God) 11, 38, 138, 223, 259, 281.
Viśrawā 85°.
Viśwāmitra 123, 209, 209°, 223, 309, 310, 311, 311°, 312°.
Viswāvasu 209°.
Vṛshṇī 176 (heroes and ladies), 222°, 236, 237.
Vyāgrapāda 312.
Vyasa 4, 7, 8, 19, 85,° 159°, 160, 161, 161°, 162, 163, 164, 165°, 182, 189, 208, 209, 209°, 211, 261, 262, 263, 299, 300.
Yaj 166.
Yama 139, 212
Yavakrīta 208.
Yayāti 16, 16°, 43, 51, 52, 68, 68°, 81°, 88, 119, 119°, 311.
Yudhisthira (Dharmarāja) 21, 30, 54°, 62°, 66, 67, 95, 96, 101, 102, 104 104°, 110, 118,° 122°, 137, 139, 140, 141, 143, 150, 152°, 153, 154, 161°, 169, 194, 195, 206, 211°, 214 and 225 (Son of Dharma), 228, 230, 231, 231°, 244, 255, 256, 257, 257°, (—'s brother), 258, 261, 262, 263, 264, 296, 312, 313 (Dharmarāja) 314, 315.
Yuyutsu 86°, 211, 211°.

B. General Index.

Abalā 174, 204, 217, 222, 222°, 290, 294, 299, 300.
Agamyāgamana 200, 201, 201°.
Ahimsa 15.
Ākhyāna 3, 4, 4°, 5, 6°, 7, 7°, 299.
Ambā 148.
Anuloma 86, 88, 89, 90, 283.
Anumaraṇa 180, 181, 181°.
Anyapūrvā 183, 183°, 242.
Apsarā 153, 209, 212, 213, 213°, 230, 295.
Āpaddharma 123, 166, 166°.
Ārsha (Form of marriage) 70, 78, 80, 80°, 81, 84, 293, 303, 306.
Ārsheya 309, 309°.
Artha 113, 115, 289, 303.
Arthavan Mantra 164, 166°, 291 (rites).
Āryan 12, 25, 36, 65, 73, 76, 84, 85, 86, 87, 87°, 90, 92°, (Indo—), 133, 135, 142, 146, 156, 182 (Indian and European—), 183 (—widows), 183, (Ṛg-Vedic—) 185, 186, 187, 188, 190 (—widows), 196, 206, 207, 207°, 235, 276, 287°, 292, 303, 307, 308, 314, 315,
Āśrama 7, 9, 24, 30, 59, 97, 98, 162, 265.
Assyrians 76.
Asura (race) 21, 76, 146, 152. (—women), 287°, 303.
Asura (Form of marriage) 17, 21, 62°, 70, 72, 75, 76, 77, 78, 79, 79°, 80°, 83, 83°, 84, 243, 251, 293, 301, 303, 304, 306, 307, 307.°
Atiguru 133, 303.
Ātreyī 136.
Aurasa 211°.

Bahuśrutā 27.
Bandhus 252.
Bhārata (The Book and the dynasty 7, 7°, 8, 10 (war).
Bhāryā 124, 161°.
Bhikshuṇis 24.
Bhīru 222, 222°.
Bhujishyā 211 (dāsī).
Brāhma (Form of marriage) 54, 55, 56, 60, 65, 68, 70, 72, 73, 79, 81, 82, 83, 83°, 84, 288, 306, 307, 307°, 308.
Brahmachari 110, 117.
Brahmacharya 24, 184.
Brahmachāriṇī 110, 110°.
Brahmahatyā 39, 136°.
Brahmaṇicide 136, 136°.
Brahmahan 87°, 205°, 226.
Brāhmaṇa (caste) 2, 2°, 3, 3°, 5, 15, 21, 22, 24, 26°, 29, 38, 43, 48, 48°, 54°, 60, 63°, 80°, 81, 81°, 82, 82°, 86, 87, 87°, 88, 89, 90, 95, 95°, 98, 100, 103, 105, 112, 116, 116°, 121,

123, 136, 136°, 138, 141, 153, 154, 158°, 158°, 159°, 160, 162, 162°, 163, 163°, 164, 165, 165°, 166 168, 169, 171, 180, (Ladies), 180°, 185, 185°, 199, (Gurutalpin) 200, 201, 203, 204 (—murder), 205°, 208, 210, 210°, 212, 215, 217, 219, 221, 221°, 222°, 223, 226, 233, 237, 238°, 239 (—Veda knowing), 239°, 245, 249°, 255, 256, 266, 267, 268, 270, 271, 298, 308, 308°, 310, 312, 312°, 313°, 314.
Brāhmaṇa (Books, time and literature) 9, 292, 313.
Brāhmaṇī 22, 24, 66, 86, 88°, 103, 105, 112, 113, 118, 120, 124, 151, 153, 154, 179, 180, 192, 201, 222°, 223, 223°, 249°, 265 (—mothers), 301.
Buddhism 8, 48, 97, 227, 227°.
Buddhistic 2°.
Buddhists 8, 9, 11, 37°.

Chāndrāyaṇa 92.
Charms (mantras) 165, 166.
Charus 136, 166.
Concubinage 170, 210, 211, 214, 218.
Concubines 206, 211, 214, 294.
Courtezens 48°, 213, 215, 215°.

Daiva (form of marriage) 63, 70, 81, 84, 303, 306, 307.
Daitya (Race) and Daityā 104, 146, 152 (dr), 194, 199 (women).
Dakshiṇā 65, 65°, 158.
Dakshiṇāgni 133, 133°.
Dānavas (race) 139, 141°.
Dāsī or Dāsīs 85, 87, 210, 211, 211°, 212, 225, 230, 240, 292, 85° and 86° (—putras).
Devara 159, 160, 184, 198°.
Devas 17, 135, 145, 164, 207, 213, 217.
Dharma 63, 66, 67, 77, 82, 86, 113, 119, 120, 122, 126, 127, 139, 189, 201, 225, (son of), 240, 251 (law), 289, 314, 240 (—lopa), 130 and 161° (—patnis, —Dārās).
Dharmaśāstras 7, 10, 11, 12, 23, 45, 57, 71, 82, 85, 87, 92, 98, 119°, 158, 162, 198, 206, 245, and 246 (—writers), 278, 306.
Dharmaśāstrakāras or Smṛtikāras 52, 87, 87°, 92, 211, 243, 249.
Dharmasūtras 23, 46, 47, 82, 158, 206.
Didhishu 49.
Dwija 183°, 186, 189°, (Dwijātis), 245.

Endogamy 90.
Exogamy 310, 311, 312.

Gāndharva (form of marriage) 17, 43, 47, 51, 56, 62°, 70, 73, 74, 74° 75, 83, 83°, 84, 297, 303, 306, 307, 307°, 308.
Gāndharva (race) 186°. 213, 225, 261, 262.
Gaṇa 215, 215°.
Gaṇikā 28, 214, 215, 216, 216°, 218, 295.
Gāthā 4, 4°.
Gītā 4.°
Gods 24, 67, 101, 186°, 254°.
Goddess of prosperity or wealth—see Lakshmī
Golaka 190, 192.
Gotra 91, 91°, 309, 310, 310°, 311, 312.
Greeks 8, 9, 76°, 156°.
Gṛhalakshmī 118.
Gṛhastha 115.
Gṛhasthāśrama 59, 97, 117°, 304.
Gṛhyasūtras 10, 23, 42, 61, 64, 64°, 117, 179.
Guru 33, 41, 133, 30 (—Kulas), 199, 199°, 201, 201° (—talpa.). 199 and 200 (—talpin).
Gyātideyam 65, 246, 301,

Haraṇam 65, 246, 301.
Hindū 1, 2, 13, 26, 45, 48, 61, 64, 79°, 80, 93, 94, 117, 145, 146, 148, 173, 183, 184, 243, 249, 254, 264, 266, 285, 288, 296, 297.
Hinduism 13 and 287 (neo—), 48.
Harmya 238, 239.
Hūṇa 287°, 306.°

Indian 1, 2, 15, 82, 116, 156°, 163, 191, 191°, 198, 217°, 218, 220, 226, 254, 292, 302.
Iranian 76.
Itihāsa 3, 3°, 4, 4°, 5, 6, 6°, 7, 7°, 26, 35, 37, 235°, 267,

Jananī 132, 141.
Jaina and Jainism 9, 97, 226.
Jalasamādhi 182, 182°.
Jāra 207°.
Jātaputra 134, 148.
Jātis 49, 308, 309.
Jaunsar Bawar 36, 168, 168°.
Jaya 7, 7°, (Itihāsa),
Jews 50, 188.
Jīvaputra 148, 148°.
Jīvasū 134, 148, 148°.

Kaliyuga 35, 184, 195, 215.
Kāma 113, 118, 119, 289, 7 (—śāstra)
Kānīna 19, 19°, 151, 202,

Kanyādāna 16, 55, 62°, 63, 63°, 65, 81, 288, 306.
Kanyādhanam 65, 246, 248, 301.
Kanyāputra 208.
Karma (Theory) 139, 173, 176, 257 (action).
Kathā 4°, 7.
Kāvya or Kāvyam 5, 6, 6°, 7.
Kāya (Prājapatya) 70°.
Kṛchha 50, 50°.
Krodhāgāra 276.
Kshātra (form of marriage) 307, 307°, 308.
Kshatriya 2, 2°, 22, 27, 32, 34, 53, 54, 72, 73, 74, 75, 80, 80°, 85, 86, 87, 87°, 89, 90, 95, 102, 118, 136, 153, 154, 157, 163, 177, 191, 223, 254, 256, 257, 265, 283, 306, 307, 308, 310, 310°, 312, 313, 314.
Kshatriyā, Khatriya ladies or Kshatriyāṇī 27, 32, 86, 89, 102, 118, 119, 154, 157, 157°, 169, 195, (queens), 257, 258, 260, 265, 306.
Kshetra 156, 156.°
Kshetraja 156, 161°, 211°.
Kshetrin 169.
Kula 57, 58, 63, 75°, 83 (Dharma), 84, 92, 152, 184 (—Strī).
Kuśa 180.

Lajāhoma 62°.
Lakshaṇa 58°.

Madhuparka 62°.
Māgadha 3 (Vamsa—Śamśaka), 3°.
Mahākula 57.
Mahāmātras 239.
Mahāvrata 199, 199.°
Mānasputras 228°.
Manes (see Ptṛs).
Mantra 22, 23, 26, 48°, 73, 166 (—oshadhī), 166, 166°, 203°, 208, 298 (—vits.).
Mātṛbandhu 162.
Matriarchal 147.
Matriarchy 99.
Matricide 139.
Mīmānsākāras 93°.
Moksha 22, 289.
Naga or Nagas (race) 21, 85, 100, 287°.

Nagaraśrī 216.
Nandi Śraddha 62°, 63.
Nārāśamsī 4.
Nishādas (race) 88.
Niyoga 30, 77, 104, 147, 156 to 171 (Chapter on Niyoga, therefore the word is repeated in every page), 185, 196, 197, 198, 207°, 211, 212, 240°, 245, 252, 260, 293, 303, 304.
Niyojana 67.
Non-Āryan 12, 25, 70, 85, 101, 112°, 135, 168, 185, 187, 196, 206, 207, 235°, 237, 245, 297, 298, 303, 307, 308.

Pahlavas (race) 11.
Paiśācha (form of marriage) 62°, 70, 70°, 71, 83°, 84, 241, 293, 303, 304, 306, 307.°
Pancha-kanyās 255.
Pāṇigrahaṇa 41, 62°, 63, 64.
Panktidūshya 50, 205.°
Pāradārika 203.
Parpūrvā 183, 183°, 242.
Pariṇaya 67.
Parivetta 50.
Parivitta 50.
Pati 122, 232.
Patighnī 108.
Patnī 83°, 86, 114.
Pātivrata 31, 103, 111, 113, 182, 186, 196, 197, 217, 241 (—Dharma), 265, 268, 281, 289, 294.
Pativratā 31, 52, 82, 96, 101, 102, 103, 106, 107, 108, 109, 110, 111, 112, 127, 129, 165°, 171, 172, 183, 186, 189, 207, 208, 228, 259, 268, 271, 275, 282, 294, 302.
Patriarchal 99, 132, 140, 142, 147, 151, 172, 295.
Patricide 139.
Paurāṇika—see Purāṇika.
Paunarbhava 183°, 186, 196.
Pitṛes 14°, 44, 58, 98, 117, 118, 126, 205.
Polygamy 79°, 80, 94, 95, 120, 129, 147, 169, 218, 293, 294, 303, 314.
Polygamons (Society) 30°, 34, 56, 170, 188, 230 (tendencies), 276, 289, 313, 313°.
Polyandry 35, 94, 95, 96, 96°, 129, 129°, 140, 147, 168, 225, 293, 303, 314, 314°, 315, 315°, 316.
Prajāpati (God) 46, 79, 79°.
Prajāptya (Form of marriage) 46, 54, 70, 70°, (Kāyā), 79, 79°, 80, 80°, 83, 84, 288, 306, 307.
Pratiloma 3°, 88, 90, 309.
Pravara 309, 310, 310°, 311, 312.
Pravargya 233.
Pravrajitā 24.
Prāyā 131,° 256.
Preceptor (Guru) 37°, 40, 41, 48, 133, 155, 199 (—'s bed), 200 (wife), 289.
Prītidatta 247.
Proshitpatikā 108, 189°, 272°.
Prostitutes 213, 213°, 214°, 215, 216,

218, 290, 294, 295.
Prostitution 218, 218°.
Punarbhū 183, 183°, 186°.
Purāṇa 2, 3 (—vids or—vits), 3, 3°, 4, 4°, 5, 6, 6°, 7, 7°, 10, 13, 26, 37, 144, 147 (writers), 163°, 173, 180, 189, 213°, 235, 257, 267, 287, 289, 299, 314°.
Purāṇika 3, 3°, 25 (—devotional cult).
Purdh 237, 240, 296, 297.
Purushārtha 97, 118, 289.
Putrikā 20, 83, 84, 93°, 94, 248, 249, 250, 250°, 251, 252, 294.
Putrikādharmiṇī 16, 93, 125, 250 (—Status.).

Rākshasa (form of marriage) 54, 62°, 70, 71, 72, 73, 83, 83°, 84, 207°, 241, 243, 293, 303, 304, 306, 307, 307°, 308.
Rākshasa (race) 83, 83°, 84, 187, 217
Rākshasī (or s. pl.), 85, 224, 267, 268, 270, 271.
Ṛshis 2, 8, 19, 21, 22, 23, 81, 91, 98, 101, 121, 162, 165, 165°, 166°, 193, 207, 208 (wives of the six Ṛshis), 208 (wives of), 209, 210°, 213, 214, 217, 228, 229, 236, 266, 272, 275, 296, 309, 312, 314.
Ṛtu 46, 46°, 119°, 126.
Rūpyovana Sampanna 42.

Sagotra or Samāngotra 85, 91, 91°, 93, 163, 312.
Sahadharmiṇī 26, 31, 32, 67, 101, 102, 127, 267, 268, 274, 275, 297, 302, 305.
Sahoda 202.
Sairandhrī 212, 213.
Śakas 9,10,11,287°, 180° (--Sythians)
Śākhās 309°, 310.
Samānpravara 85, 91, 93, 312.
Samāvartana 23.
Samhitā 6, 7, 9, 15, 215, 228.
Sanyāsa 80°, 97, 98.
Saptapadī 64, 64°, 66.
Sapiṇḍa 85, 92, 92°, 93, 159, 160, 160°, 162, 163, 252.
Śāstra 7, 12, 16, 64, 158.
Satī or Suttee 111, 171, 178, 178°, 179, 179°, 180, 180,° 181, 182, 183, 188, 191, 196, 197, 292, 294, 295, 303.
Saudāyika 245, 247, 248.
Smṛti (or —s pl.) 39, 48, 54, 59, 70, 71, 78, 80°, 92 (Kāras), 93°, 164, 173, 180, 183, 196, 245 (writers), 267.
Śrāddha 16, 49, 63, 87°, 114, 138, 183°, 186, 190, 210, 210°, 232, 251, 252, 264, 281, 298.
Śramaṇī 24, 37.
Śruti 27, 67, 268.
Śtridhayakshas 238, 239.
Strīdhana 245, 245°, 246, 248, 249, 249°, 253, 301, 304,
Strīdharma 126.
Strīrājya 299.
Strīvada 222°.
Śūdra 26°, 54, 79, 89, 90°, 201, 223, 235, 299, 308.
Śūdrā (or—s. pl.) 54°, 70°, 75°, 82, 85, 86, 87, 87°, 88, 138, 185, 185°, 212, 217.
Śulka 56, 76, 247, 278.
Sūta 3, 3°, 4, 53, 54°, 80°, 43 (—putra.).
Sūtras 10, 23 (—period), 29, 39, 42 (gṛhya), 47, 62°, 69, 69°, 70, 71, 78, 82, 85°, 91°, 114°, 158, 164, 169, 179 (—period), 196, 228, 310 (Gṛhya and Dharma—).
Svadharma or Swadharma 126, 127.
Swātyāyana 22, 22°.
Swayambara or Svayambara 38, 43, 51, 52, 53, 54, 57, 68, 72, 72°, 80, 80°, 95°, 237, 260, 293, 297, 308, 311, 313, 313°.

Trivarga 113, 115, 118.

Udgātṛ 233.
Upanayana 41, 48°.
Upanishads 5, 9 (—ic), 23 —period), 37, 119 (ic), 133, 257, 298, 310.
Upayāma 41, 42.
Uttarīya 238°, 271.

Vaiśya or Vaisya 70°, 75°, 79, 80°, 86, 87, 87, 90, 118, 211, 283, 308.
Vaiśyā 86°, 283°.
Vāṇaprastha 79°, 105, 189, 189°, 264, 277.
Vānaras (race) 101°, 187, 207, 217, 271°, 285, 287°.
Varṇa 49, 84, 85, 87, 88, 90, 91, 308, 90 (—Śankara), 201° and 299 (—Śrama dharma).
Veda or Vedas 2, 2°, 4, 5, 6, 6°, 7, 22, 23, 54°, 63, 92, 98, 156, 201, 225, 228, 235°, 290, 292, 298, 315, 5 (Atharva—).
Vidhawā 174, 173, and 289 (—dharma).
Vedic 4°, 9, 13, 22, 23, 25, 26, 29, 34, 37, 40, 97 and 135 (anti—), 99, 103, 133, 135, 160, (pre—), 177,

225, 232, 233°, 235, 267, 287, 287 (Pre—), 292, 297, 298, 299, 304, 309°, 315.
Virasū 132, 134, 148, 148°.
Vīrśulkā 53, 54, 225, 293.
Vṛshalīpati 87°.
Vṛtā and Mantravat—61°.
Yautaka or Yautuka (from you or yuta) 65, 249.
Yavana 11, 287°.
Yoga 22, 235.
Yogin 259.

C. Index of Some of the Authors.

Agrawala, V. S. 23°, 117°, 133°.
Altekar 15°, 21°, 25, 25°, 27°, 44, 44°, 62°, 74°, 84, 163°, 171, 171°, 233°, 234°, 242°.
August Babel 116°.
Bader, C. 283, 283°.
Banerjee 246, 246°.
Bühler 11.
Chatterjee, A. 15°.
Das, A. C. 13, 13°.
Davies, J. L. 220°. 226°, 228°, 229°, 241°.
Dharma, P. C. 8°, 9°, 12°, 45, 46, 63.
Dikshit 8.
Donald Mackenzie 182°.
Dutt, R. C. 1, 2°, 9, 9°, 16°, 23°, 36°, 37°, 43, 66, 73, 146, 266, 266°.
Dwivedī, H. P. 216°.
Griffith 275, 275°.
Haridatta Vedālankāra 36°.
Havelock, Ellis 45°, 214°, 215°, 218°.
Holtzmann 160, 161°.
Hopkins 9, 9°, 10, 10°, 11, 11°, 54, 54°, 80, 80°, 162°, 178, 178°, 208°, 218°, 257, 257°.
Horner 48°.
Indra 147°, 156°, 235°.
Jacobi 6, 8, 162°, 227°.
Jaiswal 9, 147°, 249°, 251, 251°.
Jolly—Julius 4, 4°, 133°, 167.
Kālidāsa 55°, 100°, 109°, 151°, 245, 259, 259°, 265.
Kāṇe 9°, 10, 10°, 11, 11°, 22°, 29°, 44, 44°, 46°, 47, 69°, 70°, 76°, 89°, 92°, 97°, 114°, 115°, 136°, 147°, 149°, 164°, 173°, 180°, 181°, 182°, 191°, 202°, 205°, 207°, 213°, 216°, 221°, 222°, 228°, 229, 229°, 230°, 231, 233°, 234, 234°, 239°, 245°, 247°, 249°, 251°, 310°, 311°, 312°.
Karandīkar 309°, 310°, 311°, 312, 312°, 314°.
Kautilya 3°, 5, 5°, 30, 30°, 163°, 196°, 206°, 211°, 214°, 216, 216°, 245, 246, 251, 252°.
Keith 8, 234°.
Keyserling 35°, 220°.
Krishnamachari 4°, 7°, 9°, 10°.

Longlois and Seignobos 14, 14°.

Macdonell 1°, 3°, 6°, 7°, 8, 8°, 9, 9°, 10, 10°, 11, 11°, 12, 180, 182°, 227.
Manu 17, 41°, 44, 44°, 46, 46°, 47°, 48°, 49°, 50°, 52°, 58°, 59°, 63, 63°, 71°, 72°, 74, 74°, 75°, 77°, 78, 78°, 79°, 81, 81°, 82, 82°, 84°, 86, 86°, 87°, 90°, 91, 91°, 92, 92°, 93°, 98°, 109, 110°, 119°, 120, 120°, 123°, 124°, 126, 131°, 133°, 136°, 143°, 158°, 159°, 163°, 169°, 170, 170°, 171°, 186°, 196, 196°, 200°, 201°, 202°, 203°, 204°, 205°, 211°, 212, 212°, 215°, 220°, 221°, 222°, 223°, 227°, 228°, 229°, 230°, 245°, 247°, 249, 249°, 250, 250°, 251, 251°, 252°, 298°, 299°, 306, 306°, 307, 307°.
Meyer 27°, 60°, 80°, 82°, 132°, 142°, 153°, 156°, 159, 159°, 160, 160°, 161, 161°, 162°, 165, 165°, 166°, 205°, 214°, 216°.
Mill, J. S. 244°.
Mukerjee, R. K. 21°, 23°.

Pandey, R. B. 39°, 42°, 45°, 47°, 58°, 61°, 62°, 64°, 74°, 79°, 92, 92°.
Pargiter 2°, 3, 3°, 4°, 6, 6°, 10, 10°, 11°, 27°, 35°, 68°, 95,° 162°, 163°, 167°, 312°, 313, 313°, 315°.
Prabhū 45.
Pusalker 2°, 311°.

Radhakrishanan 45.°
Raichaudharī 239°.

Saksena 36°, 96°, 168°, 315°, 316°.
Sarkar S. C. 147°, 161°, 163°, 164, 164°, 165, 165°, 166, 167, 187, 187°.
Shastri, Srinivas 218°.
Shastri, S. Rao 16°, 147°, 170°.
Shaw, Bernard 228.°
Smith 180°.

Thomas, P. 180°, 183°.
Tripathi, G. M. 70, 74, 203, 307, 307.°

Upadhyaya, B. S. 42°, 69°, 103°. 156°, 183°, 211°, 225°, 313.°

Vaidya, C. V. 10, 10°, 32°, 74, 74°. 76°, 144°, 146, 189, 189°, 306, 306°,

Vyāsa, S. N. 15°, 83°, 92°, 198°, 313°, 314°, 316°.
Westermarck 35°, 160°.
Whiteney 8.
Williams, M. 9, 9°, 283, 283°.
Winternitz 4°, 5°, 8, 9°, 10, 10°, 162, 167. 218°,

D. Index of Important Books

Āp. Dh. S or Āpastambha 23°, 29°, 42°, 47°, 50°, 69°, 70°, 78°. 84°, 92°, 101°, 114°, 129°, 133°. 139°, 143°, 157, 157°, 170, 170°, 196°, 199°, 235°, 244, 244°, 281°, 309, 310, 310°.
Āp. G. S. 4°, 26°, 42, 47°, 58°, 61°, 101.
Arthaśāstra—see Kautilya-Author's index.
Ashtādhyāyī 23, 91°, 114°, 147°, 311°.
Āsv. Dh. S. 69, 79°.
Āsv. G. S. 4°, 7°, 10, 23, 23°, 24°, 42°, 61°, 62°, 84°, 69, 233°.
Atrī Samhitā (Sam.) 78°, 133°, 151°, 155°.
Baud, Dh. S., B. D. S. or Baudhāyana 45°, 50°, 57°, 64°, 69°, 70°, 73°, 75°, 78°, 84°, 85°, 86°, 87, 88°, 92, 92°, 159, 159°, 169°, 170, 170°, 196, 196°, 199, 201°, 202°, 228°, 310, 310°.
Bible (Holy) 50, 50°, 156°, 160°, 188.°
Bṛhdāraṇyaka Upanishad 16°, 23, 23.°
Chhāndogya Upanishad or Up 5°, 42°.
Daksha Smṛti 133, 180°.
Epic India—See Vaidya C. V.
Gaut. Dh. S. or Gaut. or Gautama 26, 29°, 47°, 49°, 50°, 69°, 70°, 79°, 86°, 91°, 92, 92°, 93°, 133°, 136°, 157, 157°, 158°, 159°, 162°, 169°, 170, 170°, 196, 196°, 199, 201°.
Gobhiia G. Su. or G.G.S. 23, 23°, 61°, 133, 133°.
Great Women of India 146°, 148°. 281°, 283°.
Gītā or G. 269°, 304.
Hindu Samskāra—See Pandey, R.B.
History of Dharma-śāstra see Kāṇe, P. V.
Kathak G. S. 42°.
Khadira G. S. 42°, 61°.
Mahābhārata a Criticism and Mahābhārata Mīmānsa—see Vaidya C. V.
Maitrāyaṇī Samhitā or Mait. Sam. 29°, 74°, 228.°
Manusmṛti or M.—see Manu.
Mārkaṇḍeya Purāṇa 115°, 139°.
Nārada Smṛti or Nārada 53°, 71, 71°, 75°,87°,174°,183°, 186°, 194°, 199°, 201°, 202°, 205°, 250°, 251°, 252°.
Nirukta 76°, 93°, 160, 160°, 198.°
Padma P. (Purāṇa) 5.
Parāskara G. S. (Gṛhya Sūtra) or P. G. S. 4°, 23, 23°, 27°, 29°, 61°, 86°.
Ṛg Veda 35, 42°, 62°, 63, 63°, 69, 76°, 85°, 87, 92, 92°, 94°, 99, 103, 103°, 104, 104°, 114°, 144, 144°, 146, 146°, 148°, 160°, 167°, 182°, 198°, 207°, 208, 233°, 309, 310, 310°.
Religions of India—See Hopkins.
Śatapatha Brāhmaṇa or Śat. Br. 4°, 29°, 92, 92°, 222°, 233°, 235°, 313°.
Taittarīya Brāhmaṇa or Tait. Br. 233°, 313.
Taittarīya Samhitā (or Sam.) 29°, 74°, 100°, 226°, 228°, 235°,
Taittarīya upanishad 119°, 133°, 137°.
'The Great Epic'—See Hopkins.
Udvhatattava 44, 44°, 92°.
Vas. Dh. S. or Vaśistha 39°, 45°, 47°, 50°, 53°, 57°, 58°, 64°, 69°, 70°, 73°, 78°, 79°, 86°, 93°, 108°, 133°, 136°, 157°, 158, 158°, 159, 159°, 168°, 170°, 183°, 186°, 202°, 243°, 308.°
Vātsyāyaṇa or Vat. Kāma Sūtra or K. S. 24°, 28, 28°, 46, 46°, 58°, 75°, 103°, 104°, 108°, 110°, 115°, 117°, 118°, 170°, 216, 216°.
Vishṇu, Dh. S. or Vi. Dh. S. or Vi. S. 4°, 8°, 18°, 41°, 47°, 49°, 50°, 59°, 63°, 69°, 71°, 74°, 79°, 84°, 86°, 88°, 90°, 91°, 93°, 109°, 133, 139°, 160°, 183°, 186°, 196°, 200°, 201°, 202°, 206°, 222°, 247°, 250°, 251°, 307°, 310°.
Vishṇu Purāṇa 46, 46°.
Vyāsa Smṛti or Veda Vyāsa Smṛti 109°, 245, 245°.
Yāgjyawalka or Y. S. 46°, 50, 55°, 57°, 58, 58°, 59°, 64°, 70°, 79°, 84°, 86°, 89°, 90°, 91°, 92°, 93°, 94°, 108°, 133°, 158°, 199°, 200°, 201°, 202°, 205°, 211°, 213°, 245, 245°, 250°, 251°, Mitāksharā's Com. (on Y. S.) 58, 58°, 213.
Yāska 245 and 245° (Nirukta).

ERRATA

Page	Line	Footnote	Incorrect	Correct
3.	15		Purāṇika	Paurāṇika
,,		6	Māgadha	Magadha
5.		3	Padama	Padma
15.	20		Prmadvarā	Pramadvarā
,,		3	Kalīna	Kālīna
,,		6	Lomapida	Lomapāda
,,		,,	India	Indian
19.	5		Śarmishtha	Śarmishṭhā
20.		2	I. 219, 18 ff.	I. 219. 18 ff.
21.		3	Mbh. III. 97 5-6.	Mbh. III. 97. 5-6.
27.		8	Rām. II. 60. 9-10, 67	Rām.III.60.9-10;67.
28.		1	"Prabandha-Kosha"	"Prabhandha-Kosha."
30.	25		Satayawatī	Satyawatī
36.		1	Kulhu	Kulu
,,		,,	Sipiti	Spiti
37.		2	vanaras	Vanāras
,,		5	Saintly	saintly
44.	10		'Vīrmitrodaya	Vīrmitrodaya
48.		2	Upnayana	Upanayana
49.	Third sub-heading		Seniority	seniority
50.	14		'parivettā'	Parivetta
51.		1	Mbh. I, 152. 27 ff;	Mbh. I. 152. 27 ff
54.		1	(G. S. III. 24).	(G. III. 24.).
62.	First sub-heading		Patriarchical	Patriarchal
,,	15		patriarchical	patriarchal
61-62.		5 of page 61 (continued in 62	(Mbh. I. 198.5	Mbh. I. 198.5
64.		5	agnia	again
66.	27		Ahalya	Ahalyā
75.		1	Śūdrā	Śūdras
77.	5		surviving. from	surviving from

Page	*Line*	*Footnote*	*Incorrect*	*Correct*
79.		6	No. 4	No. 4)
88.		4	सदा	सदा ।
95.	10		hus	hus-
96.		1	Polyandry	polyandry
100.		1	सव	सर्वे ।
108.	16		pātivratā	pātivrata
,,	18		pativāta	pātivrata
109.	9		a loud	aloud
110.	2		Here	here
,,		1	reality	reality (Brahman)
111.		8	Epics.	Epics."
117.		1	gṛhasthasram	gṛhasthāsram
119.	15		Com and	Command
,,	18		Kshatriya	Kshatriyā
,,		5	Śarmishtha	Śarmishṭhā
,,		8	its	it
,,		,,	Connot	Connots
122.		6	पति:	पति: ।
125.		4	No. 1. p—of	No. 2. p. 185 of
130.		4	Sudharśana	Sudarśana—
133.		1	गुरु:	गुरु: ।
,,		6	states that,	states,
,,		7	curse	curse.
136.		2	Brahmahatya	Brahmahatyā
,,		2	Brahman	Brāhmaṇa.
,,		3	sentence	death-sentence
137	14		Yudhishihira	Yudhishṭhira
201.	1		Dharma[1]-	Dharma[1].
,,		1	Gurutalpa	Gurutalpa.
202.	18		kān-na	kanīna.
,,		4	Upāpātaka	Upapātaka
207.		5	Tantravratika	Tantravartika
208.		6	17 ff 307;	17 ff; 307
209.		8	Gṛtāchī	Gṛatāchī
211.		3 and 4	V. S.	B. S.
213.	6		he	the
,,	7		the	he
216.		2	Kautilyas	Kautilya's

Page	*Line*	*Footnote*	*Incorrect*	*Correc*
219.	1		women	the woman
221.	16		women	the woman
227.		*line* 2	प्रभदासु	प्रमदासु
,,		,, 4	ascetiasm	asceticism.
228.	10		Samhitā	the Samhitās
,,		2	Turtil	Turtil-
,,		4	(quoted	Quoted
229.	1		creator	Creator
230.		10	commen.	commentary.
232.		4	......	delete.
233.		1	II 33 ff	II. 33 ff
,,		3	mantra	mantras
,,		5	31-32	31-32.
234.		1	4	4.
,,		1	was	was;
238.	25		Harmya	Harmya.
,,		4	(sections)	(sections.)
239.	First-Sub-heading		ādhyakshas	adhayakshas
241.	2		'harems"	harems
242.		6	[8] परपूर्त्रा° ।	8. परपूर्वा° ।
246.	28		by the	by their
246.	19		own"[3]	own."[3]
247.		1	Hist of Dh.	"Hist of Dh."
250.		1	135	135.
,,		,,	wealth	wealth.
251.	18		it	them
,,		7	Nārada	Nārada.
253.	23		woman	a women
254.	29		have	was of
255.		6	35-36	35-36.
257.		6	11-12. 13 ff.	11-12, 13 ff.
272.	27		failed	fails
275.		3	forsaken	forsaken.
278.		1	II,	II.
285.	30		hcld	held
287.		2	5213	52.13
,,		2	areall	are all

Page	*Line*	*Footnote*	*Incorrect*	*Correct*
290.	10		applied with	applied to them with
,,	14		involved. She	involved. A woman
293.	20		any. was	any, was
303.	4		of	for
307.		1	state s	states
312.	19		their	his
313.		1	111	111.
319.	23		clarisse	Clarisse
322.	Last line		Mystry	Mystery

Index

325.			Bṛhannata	Bṛhannala
327.			Kosalendrarājaduhitā	Kosalendraduhitā
328.			Jaṭila	Jaṭilā
329.			(Śukra)	(Śukra).
,,			Swayamprabha	Swayamprabhā
332.			Polygamons	Polygamous
333.			Purdh	Purdah
334.			you	yu

Preface

vii	33		work	work.
ix	11		Dates	Date.
xvi	6		252	253.